A BOOK O

A study in h

"WHO HATH BELIEVED OUR REPORT?"

J. D Tatham.

A BOOK OF JEREMIAH

Published by KIT Publishing

Printed by
Leiston Press
Unit 1b
Masterlord Ind Est
Station Road
Leiston
Suffolk
IP16 4XS

ISBN: 0-9545281-0-7

When he was hungry, she fed him. Thirsty, she brought him drink. When sorrowful, she hugged and comforted him and made him laugh, when he was unsure she reassured him. She asked for no return, but said that she would be there for him tomorrow if ever he needed her. He filled her mouth with laughter and her tongue with joy when he gave her to understand that she should be his companion for life.

Of such is the Kingdom of Heaven.

Wiser counsels prevailed. She was cast aside as being no more than a 'nice kid' ,or little child, in less patronising terms and, being only a country girl from Newfoundland, was replaced by a highly educated rich lady from England who was neither. With this wisdom concurred his mother and his sister and his brother and the ministers of the gospel who fawned upon them, for it is always better to be truthful.

To establish their truth, they assembled together, as was their custom, and declared belief in one who said; "except ye receive the kingdom of heaven as this little child, ye shall in no wise enter therein", who said, "I thank thee, O father, Lord of heaven and earth that thou hast hid these things from the wise and prudent and revealed them to babes.... ", "their holy angels are ever before the face of their Father in heaven". Him they declared to be:

God of God, Light of Light, Very God of Very God, begotten not made, being of one substance with the Father, by whom all things were made, who for us men and our salvation came down from heaven and was incarnate by the Holy Ghost of the Virgin Mary and was made man, and was crucified, also for us under Pontius Pilate, he suffered and was buried, and the third day he rose again, according to the the scriptures, and ascended into heaven and sitteth at the right hand of the Father, and he shall come again with glory to judge both the living and the dead, whose kingdom shall have no end......"

Of such is the Church of England.

Introduction and Acknowledgements.

The theme of the book is hypocrisy. It tells of a life which could have been designed to shew it. Of itself, an individual life can only indicate hypocrisy in itself and other individuals. The hypocrisy of the Christian religion is essential to its existence as a religion. It is forced on it, most directly, by the work of four men, those who wrote of Jesus in the Gospels; but almost certainly, assuming their reports to be dependable, by one man, Jesus himself. Whether an individual is seen as more so than another is of little significance. Rather, they are as single spots on a patient with a rash; symptoms of a general infection. If, as found in the gospels, Jesus speaks truly of God, and 'fulfils the law and the prophets', then, less clearly, the same hypocrisy is essential to all religion, if there is, indeed, God. Whether such a being exists in reality is, in this context, insignificant, since all religions claim that He, She or It does.

In countries where the institutions of government, from the Crown to the Infant school, invoke both the authority of God and of Jesus, as, explicitly, in the Coronation of the Monarch, who undertakes that all law and governance in her realm shall be subject to that of the Gospel, the hypocrisy infects them all. Presidents of the USA seem ever prone to say, "God bless America".

An upbringing at the heart of the established Church and his education perfectly fitted the man, I have chosen, to illustrate this. By chance, he was an evacuee in the war, so attended about ten different schools by the age of thirteen, and had as many 'homes' as years in his life. He 'studied' and taught theology. His marriage was almost perfectly designed (not by him), to make him see how this hypocrisy extended into government, and the law. From early childhood he had an inarticulate fear that this would be the case. He sensed that, if anyone were to cross the designated upholders of the religion, they would invoke the power of the entire established order. What would provoke the most hostile reaction would not be a denial of the being of God, and thus the truth of the sayings attributed to Jesus, but the opposite. What would provoke the greatest anger would be to take them at their word, and, "Believe their report".

Prominent members of the Christian religion, in high civic positions, were prepared to manipulate the legal processes of which they were sworn upholders, and even make use of perjured evidence, in one of the highest courts of the land, concealing this fact by failure to issue a summons. A major political party's spokesmen on home affairs in the upper house was prepared to connive in this, while making eloquent speeches, complaining of the failure of courts to ensure the protection of unrepresented defendants.

A doctor could be led to parting with information gained in a consultation, provided the patient was seen as of no consequence, whereas those to whom the information was given were wealthy and influential. An Archbishop of Canterbury and Bishops were ready to give solemn undertakings, go back upon them, even when given in writing; then refuse to reply to letters asking why this had been done. A governing Body, consisting of four bishops, sundry archdeacons and canons of the Church, were ready to endorse, as a condition of the continued employment of the head of the department of 'Divinity', that he abandon what they called Nicene orthodoxy, as the basis of his teaching, while solemnly asserting it, when conducting services. The word which perfectly describes such behaviour is the lovely word 'shifty'.

If any citizen of this land thinks that human rights legislation offers any protection against such things, he lives in cloud cuckoo land. Laws designed to protect the citizen from such things have been enacted almost since Magna Carta. If anyone is led to believe that the invocation of the gospel by those in authority serves to moderate such shiftiness, they delude themselves. It makes it necessary; its concealment more cunningly contrived. Jesus was clear that 'for every idle word they utter, shall the children of men be called to account'. Those who direct and guide the lives of others are wholly unimpressed by that warning, as if he added an exempting clause. If he did, it did not reach the evangelists.

In this case, these incidents became almost comic, in retrospect, because he escaped 'by the skin of his teeth' and, in many cases the shifty dealings of his adversaries tended to rebound on them. He came to see what might be called, the 'Goliath syndrome'. If an adversary can be led to disdain one, he or she may overlook the fact that, in addition to sticks and stones, David carried also a sling, which, given the circumstances of the contest, would be the most effective weapon. Incidents which were not funny at all, can be seen as if scenes in a farce. They were not, however, performed on stage, but in courts such as that of Chancery, in the offices of Notaries Public, by "true and trusty friends of the Supreme Court." Had they been performed on the stage of the London Palladium, the extent to which disbelief would have to be suspended would have defied credibility.

The book is an account of the muddles he got into by believing the report of those of the Christian religion, taking them at their word in their declarations of belief. It would be mistaken to imagine that he was acting as a little child, if that implies trusting innocence. Those of the Christian religion like to distinguish being childish and childlike, though Jesus made no such distinction. Being childlike implies all the qualities we like to feel that little children have, but which they seldom shew. Being childish implies qualities we do not like, but which most little children shew in abundance. He was the latter. He did not in any positive way, at least initially, "believe their report", rather he acted as if he did, as if to say, "See you."

He had enough knowledge to do this, but not much more. Like David, finding Saul's armour too heavy, he relied on a sling and stones to stun his adversary. A more apt description would be found in the sayings, "The stone that was rejected by the builders has become the keystone of the arch. To those that believe, it is elect and precious, to those without, it is a stone of stumbling and rock of offence, and on whomsoever it falls, it crushes in pieces". While he could find nobody in the Christian religion to say, unequivocally, that the sayings of Jesus were "elect and precious", by using them as stones of stumbling and rocks of offence, he assured himself of their power and truth. It was through their negative and destructive capacity, that he came, unwillingly, to see their positive worth.

He was driven to see that the Christian religion's credal declarations about Jesus were undoubtedly the truth, if they referred to the one whose sayings are reported in the gospels and no other. Only one possibility gave it truth, however the gospels were produced, that there was indeed God, as all who attend any service of the Christian religion declare.

The later Isaiah asked a double question. "Who hath believed our report?" is followed by, "to whom hath the arm of the Lord been revealed?" Perceiving this did not require mystical or visionary revelations, but the opposite. He was driven to this conclusion, by his mind alone. It had nothing whatever to do with what we know as supernatural phenomena, only the ever present possibility that there is the Infinite, a possibility that, in the nature of the case, can never be established as non existent.

The book begins by describing the puzzlement of a child, surrounded by knowing adults, who made what are, by any standards, amazing declarations about a singular man, while obliging him to listen to them doing so. Having done so, they seemed to be sure that almost all that this man was reported to have said was in need of radical revision. He therefore found himself asking if the opposite could be the truth, and was driven unwillingly to believe that it was.

Those who assisted in this are mentioned in the narrative. Three of them must be acknowledged for their part in the actual production. First is John Carey, of Merton College Oxford, who suggested it in the first place. Second are Joy and Jimmy Harvey of Woodland Rise, Sheringham, who count as one, it being impossible to think otherwise of them (this their children will acknowledge!). John Carey said, quite rightly, when reading a synopsis, that there were two books, and that the exegetical arguments to sustain the case, should be treated separately from the episodic biography. He was also insistent that any biography should be as strictly chronological as possible. His own mastery of written English provided a constant reference point, as did his amazing ability to choose the telling word and phrase, not least in his recall of the word 'shifty', which seems to have lapsed from common use over the last fifty years.

Reading some chapters, Joy found that, for one unaccustomed to reading such matter, detailed discussion of passages from the Gospels, proved a block to reading further. On the other hand she found the relating of the episodes of the story to familiar passages from them and even the Old Testament enlightening. She had no need of argument to sustain the view, whereas others might. She and Jimmy also had a sharp eyed awareness for any over complicated argument, and scribbled in the margin such comments as, "bloody confusing". In all cases they were right..

The third, who must be mentioned in this context, is Neville Mallett of Cremer's Drift, Sheringham and, with him, his long suffering, self effacing, wife, Linda. They like Joy and Jimmy count as one. Neville had to put up with hearing the entire book many times over when he wanted a peaceful pint! Linda had to put up with his returning late, and on some occasions made her feelings more clear than any passage in this book.

I would like to record my gratitude to Glenn and Louise Barnes of Leiston Press for their patience with incompetent typing. The constant cheerfulness and welcome they gave, whether meeting them face to face, or communicating with them by telephone, made it a pleasure to deal with them. I would unreservedly commend their services to anyone else.

"Who hath believed our report.....?"

Chapter One

"Jeremiah" -A tale of hypocrisy.

This is the story of a man of no significance. I will call him Jeremiah.

He achieved little. He lost 'even that which he had', largely through his own stupidity, which was considerable, fecklessness and ineptitude. He was and always had been 'inadequate', but longed to be otherwise. He longed to be part of the assured and knowing 'conversation' and spent most of his life seeking to do so. When he did, in various roles, always something happened which made him unable to believe in the role, or in the entire play. He would do something silly and be cast out.

For a while, he played his part with conviction, but lost it. Others did not. Why could he not be like them? He would say that acting was a silly thing to do, deceiving people and the actors themselves. The more sincere and compelling the performance, the more it deceived. The better a play was written and produced, the more it deceived. The better a story was written the more it did so.

Plays and stories led children to believe nonsense. Rabbits did not wear tweed jackets or smoke pipes. Rats and moles did not go boating. Toads were not vain, wealthy, puffed up fools. Stoats and weasels were not vandals. There was no such a thing as a Hobbit. Whatever did it matter, if people enjoyed these things and they were the stuff of education? There is no Santa Claus: he has no sleigh or reindeer. He brings a present to nobody; nor did John the Baptist announce the birth of Jesus; but it was best for everyone to think that he did. Tidings that an axe is being laid to its root, unless one is sure that one is not nesting in the tree, are not glad; but they have to be made so, to provide for hymns, carols and the rest of it.

What might happen to a child at infant or junior school, who pointed out that these stories were nonsense, not just those that underlay nativity plays, but the multitude of children's stories, which involve animals being endowed with speech, human thought and feeling? How might it be, if, as was the custom in infant schools, the teacher ended the day with a story, asked the children what they thought about it and one small boy said, "It's rubbish, Miss"? This is not as fanciful as one might imagine. Jeremiah supervised a student teacher on school practice, where a small boy, a local farmer and TV personality's son, did so. If such a child were to persist into the junior and even into secondary school, he might be seen as disruptive or educationally sub-normal. His parents might be summoned. He might be taken to a psychologist. Is it a mark of lack of intelligence to point out what everyone knows to be nonsense?

The pantomime, in which Jeremiah played, was that of the Christian religion. It had no dame, but had demon kings, like Herod. If the news, brought by the Magi, were the truth, it would be the end of his dynasty and much else as well. Even if people did not like Herod, they would agree that all possible steps should be taken to eradicate such a child. Herod 'built' them a Temple, as kings and rulers do. If they thought, rationally, that this child was the chosen one of God, they would realise that such steps would achieve nothing. Rulers of people cannot think rationally of the possibility of there being God. If they did they would not be Kings, Presidents or anything like that. Rulers and directors of other people's lives cannot be 'meek', or 'servants' of all, however much they say these things. Those in authority do nasty things, or pay others to do so for them, in order to safeguard, not just themselves, but a way of life and its cherished institutions. If they and their servants do not do such things, they are the beneficiaries of their predecessors having done them, and as beneficiaries of those acts, might as well have hired them to do them. "My people love to have it so".

Every minister of the Christian religion knows that it is a pantomime. It is part of the pantomime that three kings, who had names and were wise, came to the stable. It is part of the pantomime that shepherds brought a lamb and that there were an ox and ass in the stable, even that it was a stable. It continues beyond that. This child is 'our childhood's pattern'. Little is known of his childhood. What is known would make most parents think him precocious, ill mannered and 'spoiled'. Does it matter? People enjoy singing, "For he is our childhood's pattern", and everyone has a surge of goodwill to all men, or some. It hardly lasts beyond Christmas lunch. What harm does it do? It had been going on for years, and would continue. It provides a lot of fun for children, light and excitement in the drab days of winter. It's good for business. It brings families and friends together; but is hell for those excluded.

The myth that provides the pantomime does far more 'good' than the story in the gospels ever would or could. Who can be sure that the gospels are dependable? They are a lot more likely to be than a Victorian poetess, who wrote hymns about it; but she had the inestimable advantage of being inspired by the Holy Spirit. The story, told by the evangelists, is dark. Most mothers would not be overjoyed, if astrologers arrived bearing gifts, one of which was embalming spice for a corpse; yet they be could certain that it would be needed. Ironically, in this case it appears not to have been.

There was a Mayor of London, called Whittington, but he did not arrive in the city as a poor vagrant, nor did he have a cat. He was probably grasping and devious, doing deals in smoke filled rooms with aldermen. The Pantomime provides much good moral teaching. Mayors and those in authority are honest, genial men, who get rid of corrupt and devious people around them. They would certainly lock up anyone who walked into a cathedral and overturned the tables of those who bought and sold therein. It taught that good triumphs over evil. Christmas is the family festival. They were the "Holy Family". The fact that

Mary was an unmarried mother and the child fathered, out of wedlock, by God, is best not mentioned. The Archbishop said that such could never be the basis of a good society. It hardly upheld 'family' values. Nor did most of what that child came to say or do, when grown up.

If Jeremiah objected to what his own sons and daughter were taught about Christmas and Jesus at school, it did not help them. If he told them that it was misleading nonsense, it would not help them or anyone else. If they came to see that they were being fed misleading nonsense in that aspect of their education, might they not mistrust all that teachers told them? Worse would it be, if he applied the same to the rest of what the evangelists told of this man and what he taught. Thinking that it would be different, he sent his sons to a school run by monks of the order of Benedict. The pantomime was better performed.

Saying these things annoyed the rest of the cast and the producers. It implied that the play was not worth producing, or worse, was a fraud. They were either such fools that they could not see this, or seeing it, were yet prepared to persist with it, because it kept the tills ringing in the box office. He was, himself, in two minds. If the play was a fraud, did it matter? People enjoyed it. Many, who did not come to see it, enjoyed the theatre building itself, which offered other facilities. Just because he did not like the pantomime, or had grown sick of it, why spoil it for everyone? He did not have to act in it. He had been glad enough of his pay, when he did.

Everyone knew that the real Mayor Whittington bore no relation to the pantomime figure. There could be a note in the programme. It might provide diverting chat in the interval. The show would go on. Jeremiah and his family before him had gained much by taking part in it, and must have known that it was bogus. While playing the role, however, he found it credible, believing in it with heart and soul and voice. Like 'good Christian men', he could rejoice. Nobody seemed to be any too clear what souls were, but everyone had one. The trouble was the mind. 'Good Christian men', unlike Jesus, leave this behind. It would not scan if included. Scansion and rhyme are vital. People can sing along. They, also, have the happy result of making nonsense seem profound sense.

There were other reasons for remaining in the pantomime. He had a house and mortgage, a wife and three children. He sprang from a theatrical dynasty. Both sides of his family had been actors in it for centuries. If, suddenly, he decided that it was a fraud and a deceit, he alleged fraud against all of them. His wife's family, though not coming of a dynasty of players, were prominent in the theatre. Her father was a producer and part time performer. They were respected, 'decent people', pillars of society. If some of his forebears had been given to eccentric behaviour, it was a matter for laughter, not allegations of fraudulence.

His mother's family made a fortune in the seventeenth century, dying wool in Norwich. They 'gentrified' themselves by acquiring the patronage of a small parish in the Waveney Marshes, establishing an unbroken succession of Rectors, extending over almost 200 years. Given to eccentricity, one of them replaced the fallen church tower with a ziggurat, apparently to please his wayward and extravagant son, who was wasting the family fortune, studying the archaeology of Mesopotamia.

One bought an estate on Achill Island, off County Mayo, later leasing land from Lord Erne on the mainland. He became his agent and fell foul of the Land League. What remained of the fortune was lost, but he endowed the language with a widely used eponym. Their name was Boycott. Captain Boycott was Jeremiah's step great grandfather, but actually his great, great uncle, his great grandfather having died, when his son was four. He was never a Captain. The son duly became a clergyman and the last in the family to hold the Rectorship; but had to abandon it, largely for financial reasons. He died before Jeremiah was born.

His father's family achieved prosperity in the Wine business. They owned and ran a Wine Merchants in Pall Mall, and had done so since the Fire of London. They held the Royal Warrant, supplied almost all the Clubs, Colleges of Oxford and Cambridge and many noble houses. Like the Boycotts they had been clergymen for generations. At one time they could have not just fielded a cricket team of clergymen, but two, with umpires and scorers as well.

As a family, they were still well to do, apart from Jeremiah's own father, who had the misfortune to find himself fighting in two world wars. He did not actually fight in the second. He was on his way to Malaya, when it fell into the hands of the Japanese, so spent the war in India. The first world-war cost him his chosen profession. He had won a scholarship to Cambridge to read law. The College agreed that it was his duty to fight for King and Country.

When he volunteered, he was assured that he would be home by Christmas. One was not permitted to put one's hand up, and say, "May I be excused. I only agreed to come and fight for a year". They shot you, if you did that. Such events gave Jeremiah a sense of the part that chance played in one's life. Had his dad not volunteered to fight for king and country, but become a lawyer, no doubt joining the family firm, he would never have met his mother. Had it not been for the Fire of London, the wine merchants business would not have existed as a legitimate one. Prior to the fire, they had been smugglers of gin from Holland. This, they stored in the crypt of Finsbury Parish Church. Their stocks, or rather, those of their friends, who founded the legitimate business, were undamaged in the Fire.

His paternal grandfather was also a Norfolk rector. They had not one, but three livings, of which they were patrons. As they were now combined, the stipend was considered 'good'. Life was made easier by a steady private income from investments and the wine business. They had a large Rectory, a handsome regency house, built onto an older farmhouse-like building. It had eight bedrooms, and four rooms for the servants, a gardener's cottage and full time gardener. The garden extended over 4 acres. There was a tennis court, putting green, some woodland, and an immaculately tended kitchen garden with fruit cages, asparagus beds, a wide variety of apples, pears and plums. There were chickens and pigs, a large barn, four good loose boxes and a garage with two cars in it, a large greenhouse and vinery.

The ordained members of the family numbered headmasters of public schools. Some had been dons at either Oxford or Cambridge. One had been public orator of the latter; another had been the Master of an Oxford College many years ago. There was a short article about him in the Sunday Times, which described him as the most unregenerate figure in unreformed Oxford. His triumph had been the means he used to acquire the mastership, which would allow him to 'lead about a wife'. Lacking the funds to offer the necessary bribes, he solved 'the problem of survival' by seeking a bride with a substantial dowry. He concluded negotiations with a wealthy industrialist, saying, "Make it guineas and I'm your man". His other claim to fame, so it was said, was that he hired ducal gamekeepers to make sure that no undergraduate escaped his sermons. One of them won him a place in the Dictionary of National Biography, as it lasted three and a half hours. Its conclusion was that all "Jarmans" be thrown into the "Jarman" ocean".

Whether the pronunciation of the word Jarman indicated origins in Norfolk, or was just an affectation, was not known. It can be seen that such stories, which seemed very funny, would make Jeremiah less able to see that the hypocrisy of the pantomime was in any way serious. It led him to see something else. A degenerate "Pharisee" made it less convincing.

When the Pope visited England, he was shewn praying with the Archbishop at the shrine of S. Thomas. His Holiness was deep in prayer. His host, after shutting his eyes and bowing his head, began to look around. He seemed to have other things on his mind, and appeared to be thinking, "Hurry up, you old fool. There's an anthem to hear, a hymn to sing, and we are due for lunch with the Mayor in half an hour". The Pope's sincerity would convince one that Jesus was wrong, when he insisted that prayer be in total secrecy. The unease of the Archbishop might lead one to think that he may have been right.

The non-clerical members of the family were in good positions in the 'establishment'. One had been Master of College at Eton. Many attended that academy themselves. This cousin also won an Olympic gold medal, and commanded a battalion of the Coldstream guards, later becoming head of the British council in Athens. Another was the player manager of the Cowdray Park Polo Team, after rising to the rank of Brigadier in the Indian Army. Another was on the Board of Cadbury's. One had the wine merchants, another a merchant bank, another had the law firm, also in Pall Mall. An uncle was known as 'father' of the Stock Exchange; an aunt trained and ran the Bach choir, another was an RA. They seemed to be everywhere where it was handy to have someone. His father's younger sister had the current Queen's mother as her godmother. A cousin achieved fame on the screen, walking about the battlefield at Arnhem with his umbrella up. 'Captain' Boycott was also 'immortalised' on screen. His maternal grandmother's half brother was a distinguished professor of Hebrew at Oxford. His Hebrew Lexicon remains the standard work in English.

All were devotees of the established Church, most at the 'high' end of the spectrum, his grandfather at the very high end. He dressed up in coloured clothes to take the Sunday service and wore a biretta, doffing it at every mention of the Lord's name. He burned incense, rang bells, and it all seemed much more important, as a form of service, than matins. As a child, Jeremiah thought that rectors were high church: vicars were lesser beings who only had matins. Rectors had tennis courts and gardeners, and servants in their houses, cars in their garages and petrol during the war.

This was because they had officers of the RAF billeted in the rectory; one became an author and wrote of his time there in a book called "Georgian Interlude". Writing to rectors as vicars was one of the deadliest of sins and was likely to cause an explosive outburst.

Even as a child of eight or nine, Jeremiah felt uneasy. He sensed that, if one fell out with the rectors, one would be up against the whole tribe. He sensed, without realising why, that the one thing that would bring the wrath of the entire clan on one's head would be to mention anything said by Jesus, in whom they all declared belief. One saying of Jesus told him that this would be so, "Except ye turn again and be as little children....".

He was always being told off for behaving like a child. If he had said, "But I thought you believed in Jesus and what he said", he would get a 'thick ear' and be sent to bed. Even vicars, headmistresses, non-conformists and others would fall in with that opinion. He never thought of it in articulate terms. It was an uneasy feeling.

This uneasy feeling, later in his life, makes the analogy of the signpost appropriate. It was as if everyone told him that he was pointing in the wrong direction, and he himself thought so; yet, for about an hour each week, the same people appeared to say the opposite, when they went to Church.

Even the hour in Church, in which creeds, extolling the man who spoke of being as little children as 'God of God', were recited, seemed equivocal. 'Ministers of the Gospel' would preach about many ways to the kingdom of heaven and eternal life, seldom that prescribed by Jesus in the Gospels. Jesus seemed to take the opposite view, being emphatic that there was only one way, which was entered by a narrow gate and was itself narrow. That his way was seen as less desirable than most is not surprising. It involved such things as rich young men being told to sell all that they had and, having done so, to come and follow him.

The words attributed to Jesus, they said, were deeply mysterious. They did not seem to be so. It did not seem difficult to understand, "Swear an oath by nothing at all". How would they react, if anyone among them sought to take the way prescribed by Jesus? How might, not only the ministers who preached, but those in their congregations react? Comments of his mother in his youth tended to highlight this. Whereas others seemed to speak eloquently of the lines of some hymn or prayer, she had the uncomfortable habit of relating all to sayings of

Jesus.

His grandfather had a 'short fuse'. He would explode and roar down the table at whoever offended him. Often the target was his diminutive wife. At tea she sat at the opposite end of a huge dining table, hidden behind an array of apparatus for pouring cups of tea. There were two teapots and a silver kettle on a stand, housing a methylated spirit burner. There were milk jugs, and bowls with sugar and tongs. When subjected to a roar from her husband, which usually ended "Don't be such a bloody fool, woman"; she would mutter in a quietly acid voice, "I cannot think what makes educated men so stupid". She habitually shortened the 'u' in both educated and stupid, giving her acidity even more bite. She was the only one of his grandparents not to have been born in a rectory. Her family were well to do, many of them lawyers. One was tutor to the Crown Prince of Siam. Jeremiah did not know which he feared most, his grandfather's bombast, or granny's quiet and acid scorn. On the whole, he thought the former less dangerous.

Other High Church clergymen came for tea. There would be animated discussions about how far they had got in achieving 'full catholicity'. Had they introduced incense, or worn a biretta yet? Did they ring a bell? If one achieved all these, the kingdom of heaven was at hand. Those who only went 'half-way' were scorned. They called each other 'father'. Those who made do with matins did not count. Non-conformists were beneath contempt, especially those who had chapels in the parish. Names like Wesley were unmentionable.

Jeremiah noticed that a much-favoured hymn, "Hark the Herald angels sing", was by the infamous Wesley. If he was so scorned, how were they happy to use the hymn? Later in his youth, he asked that question. His grandfather was dead. Granny was not, nor was her energetic and forthright elder daughter. He faced the united power of bombast and scorn

What worried him, in an inarticulate way, was that the entire 'conversation' of school and Church and everyone connected with either, seemed to express a wholly different understanding from Jesus' words. Of this, the matter of turning back to being as little children was evidence. Obviously there must be an explanation. All were certain that Jesus was the Son of God and equally sure that the last thing anyone should do was be as a little child. It was a disease to get over as quickly as possible. Those who did were made monitors and prefects.

Teachers seemed to think everything in the gospels deeply mysterious and meant doing all sorts of things that everyone else could do, but he could only pretend to do. He could not sing in tune. This seemed important. He wanted to believe what they said, when they declared belief, but without the complications. He was what would now be called 'dysfunctional'. He could manage in a world, where there was no need to have any anxiety for the morrow about what to eat or drink or what clothes to wear. He could manage happily in a world where nobody resisted evil. He did not like resisting evil, because it usually meant getting hurt. He found the assured moral rightness of people, especially those who went to church, frightening. Worse was what people of assured moral rectitude did to others. They would do it to him. It was frightening because it seemed not coherent with anything Jesus said.

The kind of world, where his heavenly father knew what good things he had need of before he asked, would suit him well. It did not seem to work like that. You had to pray for things; then hardly ever got them. There was a prayer, which, to his childish mind, promised that, where two or three were gathered in 'thy name', thou wilt grant their requests. Knowing grown-ups would point out the wisdom of what followed, 'as may be most expedient for them'. He could not see anything inexpedient in getting what he asked.

Most frightening was the assured rectitude of grown-ups. What about the story of the woman caught in the act of adultery, (he had no idea what adultery was) and what Jesus said? "Whoever is faultless among you........?" There were a lot of faultless people about. Almost everyone seemed to be. Those that were not, quickly learned to become so. Twelve could be found to sit on a jury, another on the bench, two or three in a magistrates' court, not to mention many others, ever ready to climb onto the moral high ground. Faultless people were terrifying.

People spoke of religion relieving burdens. It said so in the service, "Come unto me all ye that travail and are heavy laden....". It added a burden. As well as having to go to work, you had to go to church say prayers and do all sorts of other things. The only people, for whom this seemed not to be the case, were Rectors. So far from delivering anyone from evil, people in the Christian religion found lots more things to be evil than anyone else. He hated Lent and the 'hosts of Midian prowling around'. 'Steep and rugged pathways' were not to his liking, nor was 'fighting the good fight'. Everyone else seemed keen on these things, singing about doing so with enthusiasm. Considering the lilies of the field and the birds of the air was much better.

He not only wanted to believe their 'report' of belief in Jesus, he wanted to believe that they believed it. They must do. They all knew more than he and dragged him to Church to hear them say so. His contemporaries had the same school prayers. They went to Church, on Sundays. Many of them went to Sunday school, which he never did. His mother had enough trouble getting him to church. Because he wanted to believe that everyone believed in the Jesus, whose words they read out, he disregarded evidence that it might not be the case.

What he was unwilling to see, for most of his life, was what Jesus saw, in his woes to the scribes and Pharisees. His allegations do not seize upon 'bad apples', or individual failings of some scribes or Pharisees, who fail to maintain the high standards they demand of others; but on activities, which were the essential duties of any scribe, Pharisee, Sadducee or doctor of the law, in any religion.

This same hypocrisy, if the evangelists be right in their report of Jesus, he forces on the Christian religion. The Christian religion must cast aside Jesus, as the gospels report him, and only find acceptable anything in the gospels, when it has been subtly altered. It needs a parable of the *good* Samaritan, with, by implication, a *bad* priest and Levite. That is not the parable of Jesus. As dutiful representatives of their sacred offices, the priest and Levite were bound to pass by on the other side. To approach what might be a dead body defiled them, just as it would defile a scrubbed up surgeon to go to the aid of anyone in the theatre who was sick. A Samaritan, being the off-scouring of the earth anyway, had no such inhibitions. He was free to have compassion.

Why was Jeremiah unwilling to see this? In the first place he was indebted to the Christian religion for his upbringing and education and the fact that, for twelve years, as a Bishop pointed out, it enabled him to earn a good salary. He enjoyed the fruits it bore. He liked going into great cathedrals, hearing choirs singing evensong. He loved the great works of liturgical music. He could not bring himself to apply the ruthless logic of Jesus, 'if you make the tree corrupt; make the fruit also'.

The Christian religion did not make them hypocritical. It is the four evangelists' report of Jesus, whom it proclaims in its creeds and hymns, which does so. The 'god' of the Christian religion, one could allow, not the "God and father of our Lord Jesus Christ", as found in his teaching. In relation to the religion, of which he is a prominent upholder, the Grand Inquisitor, in the 'poem' of Ivan Karamazov, is no hypocrite. Only when confronted with Jesus and the gospels is he made one. Exponents of the Christian religion would speak with great fervour of the wisdom of such as S. Paul and many others. They would extol the wisdom and deep spiritual insight of many men and the prayers they wrote. It is not S Paul, nor S Peter, Augustine, Luther or Calvin, who are declared to be God of God and Light of Light.

The God, of whom Jesus spoke in the Gospels, really is God. He is what the word God means, as any little child understands it, one who could do anything and needed nothing. The two are inseparable. Jesus, as reported in the Gospels could only be the Son of God, if that being is what the word implies, regardless of any image or concept anyone might have. Only such a being would have Jesus as his only begotten Son. He did not need to be miraculously conceived for this to be, only speak and act as he did. No religion on earth could accept what he said, nor could any other belief. He is said to have redeemed mankind. One thing, as found in the gospels, from which he would redeem mankind, would be religion. This was the problem for Jeremiah, as a product of an educated, upper middle class family. While he found redemption from the Christian, or any religion, welcome; almost all that he enjoyed in our cultural heritage was a fruit thereof. Jesus says, "all things highly praised by men, are abominations to God".

This seemed, oddly, to be fulfilled. As soon as anything was exalted, it either fell into disrepair, or became obsolete. When people began to sing the praises of the Prayer Book as a monument of language and spiritual insight, it fell into disuse, likewise the Authorised version of the Bible. When people sung the praises of our architectural heritage, the great cathedrals began crumbling. The same might be said of the National Health Service, the Monarchy, Parliamentary

Democracy and much else. He came, unwillingly, to see that much of what passed for deep spirituality, in the old Prayer Book, depended on the sonorous obscurity of its language. Creeds seemed more credible in Latin. At school he had to learn Latin, and spent much time trying to sort out the 'main' from the subordinate verbs. As with all else, he was no good at it, and preferred to daydream about sailing boats. It would take a grammarian to find the 'main verb' the opening of the Prayer of Consecration.

English, as a literary language, whatever 'myth' the devisers and teachers of the national curriculum may prefer to foist on children, was a product of the Christian religion. Its matrix was not authors like Shakespeare, but the Tyndale-Coverdale translation of the Bible. Tyndale took the oral vernacular of 'him that follows the plow', and made of it a powerful literary medium. But for his work there could have been no Shakespeare, as now we know it. If the Tyndale-Coverdale Bible was the first and great 'commandment' of the English language, the second was like unto it, the Book of Common Prayer. It could be said that on these two books hang our language and literary heritage. Their influence does not end with language. The translation of the Bible introduced, into our culture, a tradition of violent polemic and ridicule, much of it directed at the posturing of rulers of people, and their religious acolytes. It seems to find expression in many of Shakespeare's plays.

In today's multicultural society we cannot have Jesus saying, "No man comes to the Father except through me". We cannot even admit the undeniable fact that the Christian religion and, with it, the books of the Bible, has had a vastly greater influence on our 'cultural heritage' than anything else.

Everyone sought to tell Jeremiah of many ways 'to the Father', all beyond his ability. He did not much like the way of Jesus, as found in the gospels, but anyone, with no ability, could follow it. It took no great wisdom to understand his sayings, especially those incorporated into his direct, general, public teaching, found in such collections as the Sermon on the Mount. Jesus expressed himself in clear, simple, unequivocal, direct sentences.

Those, who sought and maintained 'alternative routes', frightened him. He found them frightening rather than fearful. He was frightened of those whom he could not trust and were inconsistent. How could one trust anyone who declared belief in one who said clearly and unequivocally, "swear by nothing at all", for example, yet argued that it was the duty of all 'good men and true' to do so? How could you trust those who declared belief in one who said, "Do not Judge, lest you are also judged......", yet argued that it was a divine calling that men and women should do exactly that? How could one trust those who declared belief in one who said, "Except ye turn again and be as little children"; yet made it almost a crime to be childish? One could never know where one was with people who spoke and acted thus. Even in his sixties, he found many, in their twenties frighteningly adult.

A mother shewed him the school-report of her ten year old daughter. The teacher wrote of her progress in 'Religious Education'. "She has achieved a sound understanding of Sikhism, Islam and Judaism and of their differences with Christianity". Obviously the teacher thought this true, and must have believed that he had, himself, such understanding. It had the approval of the headmaster. Jeremiah had not a sound understanding of the Church of England, let alone of other Christian denominations. He had a little knowledge of Judaism, having read and 'studied' parts of the Old Testament, and some of the Rabbinic writings. He had read the Koran. Of Sikhism, he knew only that they wore turbans and had a Golden Temple, to which uninvited visitors were none too welcome. He envied the assurance of the young teacher in his knowledge and ability to pass it on. Unless educational standards had soared, and this teacher was monumentally erudite, it had to be nonsense; dangerously misleading nonsense.

The difficulty, presented by the four gospels, is pressing. The teacher may be massively erudite and would need to be. On the other hand he may, mindlessly, be following a prescribed book. If the parent tells the child that the teacher has written piffle, it is hardly likely to enhance the child's respect for authority. That children passed through school with a detached attitude, for this reason, might assist their ability to learn. It would not encourage the values that schools seek to promote.

At secondary school, the teacher of 'R.E' assured a class, probably more than one, "If you believe in God, that is all right. If you do not believe in God, that is all right as well". No doubt, he was saying what he was taught and trained to say. Speaking thus, he assured all before him that anything said by Jesus of Nazareth should be disregarded. For Jesus, as reported by the evangelists, whether anyone believes in God or not, is of paramount importance. One needs, also, to be sure that the 'god' in whom one believes is truly God, not some imaginary 'supernatural being', a product of man's fervid religious imagination. Jesus spoke of his Father as 'the only true God', and said to his disciples, "Ye believe in God, believe also in me".

There was irony and hypocrisy in the teacher's position. Having spoken thus to children, it is almost certain that that he would be seen at services of the Christian religion, whether in school assemblies and 'acts of worship', or in Church, if only on such occasions as weddings, funerals, Carol services and Remembrance Day. There he would give public assent to the very man, whose words he had advised all to set aside, as being raised from the dead, presumably by God. It is hard to see how any other being could do so.

Jesus left the world with an insurmountable problem, by speaking words, which were intractably impossible of incorporation into any religious, political, or other system of belief. Ultimately, the problem did not derive from Jesus, but God, and the possibility that there exists a being which is what, logically, the word implies, for that is the single reality to which the sayings of Jesus give exclusive expression. While sayings such as "I thank thee O father Lord of heaven and earth, that thou hast hid these things from, the wise and prudent, and revealed them to babes", are coherent with that reality, they have no place in the assured and knowing 'conversation' of religious, or any other belief.

To this Jeremiah wanted to belong. He felt safer within it and spent most of his life trying to convince himself that the Christian religion did, when it declared belief in "One Lord Jesus", refer to the one of the four gospels, who had become a higher being, who was 'Christ'. Any evidence that seemed to support this, he grasped. The story of his life might be seen as the progressive undermining of such evidence, leaving two possibilities. Either Jesus in the Gospels was the most deceitful man who ever lived, or he was all that he said he was, and, "no man comes to the Father but by me".

His friend Neville told him of an airline pilot, about to take off, when he heard an explosion. He believed that it was a burst tyre, as, some years before, this had occurred. It was not. The rear 'can', on one of his engines, had fractured, punctured a fuel tank, and it was on fire. The pilot took account of all information, which appeared to confirm his diagnosis, but discarded the vital bits of information that would have told him that he had a serious fire. This well illustrates what Jeremiah spent his life doing. His life was like a dipstick in the sump of the Christian religion. 'Dipstick' is a suitable word in its colloquial use. He was one

What he took much longer to see was that, aside from being hurtful to him, it mattered to anyone else. If people enjoyed the pantomime and the fruits it bore, what harm did it do? Many, spoke of the sense of peace, assurance, and of the 'wholly other', they found in great cathedrals. It helped them function better in their work. If this was a delusion, did it matter? One could not have such places without religion. One would not arrive at a great cathedral from the sayings attributed to Jesus. He would not see that the hypocrisy of the religion was significant, beyond the fact that it led people to be nasty to him. It was as if the aeroplane was a single seat aircraft. It was not. 50 passengers had died.

If such buildings and their music give people a sense of assurance, which enabled them to 'perform' better, they make the pantomime more credible. What, then, if Jesus spoke the truth, and there is indeed God? If one substituted the pantomime figure for the Jesus of the Gospels, one did the same for God. What made the matter truly serious was the possibility that there is indeed God, and that God is what, rationally, the word implies, a being who is, by definition, beyond all means of influence or control, and therefore, alone, dependably good. That this must be is obvious, childishly so. Anything subject to influence, and so control by man, could be influenced and controlled by very nasty men and women. Of that, our age should have no doubt.

He found this perfectly expressed in sayings attributed to Jesus in the gospels, "God alone is good". Having seen that, he thought that the only phrase that fittingly described such clarity of thought was that it was 'childishly simple'. Why was God, by definition, beyond all means of control? Such a being, alone, must be eternal and create all things. He, She, or It, is, therefore, perfect, in the sense of being complete and needing nothing. He had arrived at yet another saying of Jesus. If, as must be, God creates everything, or is not God, such a being has a perfect right to do as he wills with all things, as they are his; yet another saying attributed to Jesus. As any child, unless taught otherwise, knows; if God cannot do 'all things', he is not God; another saying of Jesus.

He began to see the sayings attributed to Jesus in a wholly new light. Whoever may have uttered them, and however the evangelists may have collected them, they derived from and gave single and exclusive expression to one 'word' or logic, that of there being God in reality and truth. He, thus, arrived at a collection of sayings attributed to Jesus, especially by the IVth evangelist, "Ye believe in God, believe also in me " and "Believe me that I am in the Father and the Father in me, or else believe me for the works' sake".

The raison d'etre of religious belief is that it provides the means to a seemingly controllable 'environment'. It is, then, at one with scientific beliefs. It implies that there are ways by which God, as the creator and sustainer of the world and all that therein is, can be influenced, and so 'encouraged' to act favourably. Both seek to keep the uncontrollable as remote from day to day life as possible. That is what every sensible and 'responsible' citizen wants. The last things anyone wants are "Acts of God". You lose everything and not a penny from the Insurers. There might be some who prefer to base their lives on that which is beyond all means of control; but no society would encourage them, though it might 'gild their tombs', when they are dead.

Religions, at their most basic, promise a deity, which is open to influence by those who know how. They provide ways of securing rain or sunshine when needed, by the offering of sacrifices, fasts, pilgrimages, prayers, performing dances and so on. They provide many more things, in this way, also. They sustain a social and moral order. More important still, beliefs give the semblance of sense to language, which is otherwise nonsense. However much any religion avoids saying it, it assumes that God acts through prescribed channels. The existence of sacred buildings, whatever they may be called, implies no less. If a Shrine, Temple, Mosque or Cathedral is set apart as especially holy, God has no option but abide by the rules laid down for him, or, as some would claim, laid down by him. He had a duty to be 'more omnipresent' there than elsewhere.

It is ridiculous to say that a being, which is omnipresent, is more so in some dedicated building; but the possibility of there being, in truth, God makes all religious language self-contradictory and ever open to ridicule. This contradiction lies at the heart of religions, which inevitably imply that a being which is, by definition, beyond all control, and so, alone, dependably good, is open to influence by men.

What determines that which may be called 'good'? If, in truth, there is God, the answer is simple. Whatever erudite men and women may decide is 'good' (or contrariwise bad) counts for little, if there is an eternal being who creates all things. Such a being must have the 'last word', and the first. "Only God is good".

It is futile to deny that dedicated buildings, like temples, cathedrals, shrines and mosques, are seen as being places where God dwells, more than elsewhere. If it were not so, people would not take off their hats, shoes, wash their hands, or even moderate their conversation on entering them. The same applies to sites seen as 'holy', to which people make pilgrimages. Most religions insist that God needs endlessly telling that he is almighty, ever living, most merciful, all wise, and many other things. By now, he should have got the message. The expositors of religion will claim that, while these things are explicitly addressed to God, they are said for the sake of men, especially children. Why, then, address them to God? An audience of men and women would think it an insult to their intelligence to be told, fifty times a day, that God is Almighty. In this alone, we move into a 'conversation' of idle words and confused language. Any little child knows that if God is not almighty and ever living, he is not God. They are taught by grown ups, to think 'God' too silly to know it himself.

Such derision of religious language and observances is dismissed as childish and sacrilegious. It is what such as Isaiah said of them. Religions imply that God needs men to act as his appointed agents, in order to impose his laws. Whether they are Kings or Presidents, Emperors or "committees", Judges or Inquisitors, makes no difference. If God needs anything, he is not God. Any child knows that, until taught otherwise. It is ironic that those who expound these fundamental religious assumptions are called 'theologians'.

If one took, as an example, the marriage service of the Prayer book, it is explicit. If all is done in due order, in the right place, by a duly designated person, God has no choice but to join this man and this woman. The same applies to the service of Holy Communion, the Mass, Lord's Supper or Holy Eucharist. This is no new idea in the Christian religion. Any thought that a return to 'primitive Christianity' might suffice to rid the religion of such superstition is ruled out by the fact that, in one of the earliest writings after the New Testament, stands a paragraph beginning; "Let that be a valid Eucharist.....". It then lays down the conditions, which make it so. God, then, has no choice but to abide by the rules and play the game.

Having spent much of his life, like the pilot whose plane was on fire, disregarding evidence that pointed to it, Jeremiah was driven to see that the most radical critique of all religion derived, not from the possibility that there is no God, but that there is. This found final expression in the sayings attributed to Jesus. It was also the basis of the prophetic polemic. The single indictment of Jesus against the accredited upholders of the religion was one of hypocrisy. This, as I have said, he sustained with allegations, which did not seize on individual failings, but upon actions essential to their duties. The more sincerely they carry out those duties, the greater the hypocrisy.

This hypocrisy, essential to the being of Christianity as a religion, is nothing new. One thing makes it different today. Everyone, who upholds that religion today, has accessible means to know everything that Jesus is reported to have said. It is no small thing to make public declarations of belief in a singular man as being "God from God". Adding the declaration that he was born of a virgin and raised from the dead serves to underline it. Unless extremely unusual things occur in cemeteries all over England, it makes this man somewhat unusual, if not unique.

Though regular attendance on the services of the Christian religion has declined, many, if not most, do so at one time or another in the course of a year. People are seen doing so on Television. Among them are pillars of the community, teachers, doctors, magistrates and the like. Any 'idiot', watching people of such standing 'report' belief in God and Jesus, might think that, before doing so, they would have taken care to find out what this man said, and would not make, or assent to, such public declarations lightly. They, especially teachers of children, magistrates and the like, expect that of others. Companies who make misleading claims for their products are liable to prosecution. A pet food producer was banned from claiming that its dog food "prolonged active life". Jesus promised a lot more than the prolonging of active life. Some 'idiot' might think that those attending services of the Christian religion mean what they say, and "believe their report".

What makes this truly serious is not that there may be no God, but the possibility that there is, which is what all who attend acts of worship declare, or have declared for them. If people do not themselves believe what is said in public services, and refrain from participation in hymns and the recitation of creeds, or saying 'Amen', nobody watching can know. They are, 'spoken for' by the act of attendance. It is seen by many, as a duty of office, to appear at such gatherings and be seen to do so, as if conferring a favour on God.

The later Isaiah asked a double question. He not only asked, "Who has believed our report?"; but added, "to whom has the arm (power) of God been revealed?"

It was only much later in his life that Jeremiah came, or was led, to see how abominable this hypocrisy was. There would be the 'good and the great', those who made and enforced laws and taught others to respect them, giving public assent to belief in God and his only begotten son, whom God raised from the dead; yet, by their public acts, assuring all that the words of the only begotten son should be disregarded. Most obviously is this the case, in the services of the established Church. The judiciary, for example, go in solemn procession to a Cathedral and assent to belief in one who said, "Do not Judge....", and said nothing to suggest that those who did so, as a full time professional occupation, were, in any way, exempt. At the Coronation, her Majesty solemnly undertook that all law and governance in her realm should be subject to the law of the Gospel. She'd have a job on her hands if she sought to do so.

At great public weddings, which conclude with the prohibition, "let no man put asunder", it is not unusual to see the principal guests boldly advertising the benefit of men doing exactly that. Many would not only have called on men to put asunder, but, having done so, married others, whom they would take with them, making it clear to all that the tasteless epithet, which Jesus used of those in such a state, did not apply to them. One needed to be sure that, either God did not raise this man from the dead to do so, or that there is no God. If not, one is taking the name of the Lord 'lightly' and encouraging others to do so. This is done with the approval and blessing of the accredited ministers of the Gospel. If one has such assurance, it makes the entire performance a lie. If one had not that assurance, it was tantamount to declaring that Jesus was himself a deceiver and misled the people. That is what his contemporaries said of him.

Such public performances, then, embody a lie, a lie if there is no God, a yet more dangerous one if there is. It would be unfortunate, for any who 'believed their report', if there were no God. It took most of his life for Jeremiah to be driven to see this. The events, none of which he sought, (though may well have provoked), which led him to this conclusion will be described in what follows. It is easy to see that one, brought up, as I have indicated, should be unwilling to see this. A further source of unwillingness was that, as I have said, from his early childhood, he had an uneasy feeling that, if any were to take those who declared belief in One Lord Jesus Christ at their word, they would react with great hostility, much as the later Isaiah described in his famous answer to the double question.

That it should have become famous owes more, in all likelihood, to the fact that Handel set parts of the answer to a hauntingly beautiful melody in his Oratorio, 'Messiah', than to anything else. Handel, or rather Mr Jennens, however, omitted the opening question.

Chapter Two

"He grew up before him as a tender plant, as a root in dry ground."

In his thirties, Jeremiah attended a meeting of experts on religious education, who spoke knowingly about concepts of God. Research had shewn that children, who did not know and respect their 'dads' in childhood, could never attain a proper concept of the fatherhood of God. What was a 'proper concept' was less clear. The vital time was primary school age.

"That leaves me out. I hardly saw my dad until I was eleven. Had he not been with my mother at the bus stop, I would not have known who he was". "Of course you won't"; agreed the expert. "With so careless a parent, no child could get a concept of a loving father".

"It was not like that at all," said Jeremiah. "If you recall there was a war on, and able bodied men were asked to go and fight. Is it your contention that no child whose dad was away at the war for five or more years, can ever have a concept of God as Father?"

Many years later Jeremiah met Bobby. She lived in Sheringham in Norfolk. Bobby was German, from Berlin. Despite having lived in England, since the war, she had a distinctly German accent, and was fun. Bobby was just Bobby, and might as well have been born in the town.

The expert on concepts of God would write her off completely. Her parents were not married. Unmarried mothers were not allowed to keep their children, who were put into children's homes. The nuns who ran the home were cruel, as if it was the children's fault that they were born out of wedlock, as was Jesus. Then came Hitler, who closed the homes. The children were exported to the east. They were dumped on trains and, when they reached their destination, were herded into halls; where farmers' wives looked them over as potential workers. Bobby had never seen people like these farmers' wives before in her life. They looked terrifying, as they walked round inspecting the children. Bobby was about seven. She described how she tried to shrink into nothingness, as one particularly formidable matron stood over her, "O God don't let her pick me."

The woman did. Back home, she and her husband were not unkind, but she started work, first in the house, then on the farm. She told the tale with many chuckles, saying repeatedly that her Father in heaven had looked after her. She spoke without affectation, almost taking it for granted.

At the end of the war, with the Russians advancing into Silesia, she bundled her belongings into a sack and hid on a train to Berlin. She should not have been on it. She had last been in Berlin when about five and was now a teenager. All she had was her grandparents' address. The journey, thanks to allied bombing, took a fortnight. When she arrived and was lost, a friendly woman in strange clothes took care of her and walked her to the address. Bobby asked her what she could ever do for her. "All I ask is that, if you pass me on the street, you say, Hullo". She went to the factory where the woman worked every day, for over a week and sat on a bench, to say, "Hullo"; but never saw her again. Her grandparents said that she should not sit there, lest she be thought to be spying.

The woman's strange clothes indicated that she was a foreign worker. The train that Bobby hid herself on was the last train to leave Silesia.

Bobby could have told the expert more about understanding the concept of God as a loving Father than all his research. Striking was the laughter, with which Bobby told the tale. The lack of a 'dad' might serve to provide such a 'concept', more than having one. If one has a human dad, one can forget about a Heavenly Father. Human dads, kind and 'loving' though they may be, cannot do 'all things'. Experiences like Bobby's might incline one to think that one's heavenly Father could.

If the use of the word 'dad' irritates, Jesus was unequivocal, "Call no man on earth thy father; for all have but one father, even in heaven".

Jeremiah's childhood was boring by comparison. His parents had been in Malaya. The price of rubber slumped in 1934, so they came home. Jeremiah was born after their return. His sister was nearly ten years older. What seemed a misfortune, at the time, proved to be no such thing. Their friends were imprisoned by the Japanese.

His dad tried to find employment in several fields on his return. In the end, he decided to learn hotel-keeping. They were sent to a pub/hotel at Bodiam. Hop pickers came and camped in the grounds. The Rectory family did not think it a suitable environment for a six month old child, so he was taken into their care for the first two years, with a nanny and a nursery. It nearly broke his doting mother's heart. They found work managing the domestic side of a sanatorium on the Norfolk Coast. First, they rented a bungalow; then had rooms in one of the doctors' houses. The family was reunited, for about a year. This was Jeremiah's fourth home.

It was l939, Jeremiah was four, and, once again, his dad went to fight for King and Country. The sanatorium was evacuated to Cheshire. It moved to a huge house, where the staff lived in the building. Small children were not allowed in a TB sanatorium, so Jeremiah became an evacuee. First, he went with one of the doctors' children to a village in Leicestershire. They had an uncle there. Jeremiah was lodged in a cottage. It was not a happy time. The cottage had no sanitation, but a 'thunder box' up the yard. The people in the cottage were very fussy, so the outside lavatory became his haven, even though it did not smell very nice, where he was allowed to play with plasticine. The village school used slates. When an Inspector came they were given pots of water to wipe them clean, otherwise they used spit. The lavatories were vile. About all he remembered of it was a dentist coming to check teeth, and the letters of the alphabet round the wall.

Another memory was that the other children's Uncle Jim, with whom they stayed in a comfortable house, contracted pneumonia and was thought likely to die. It was felt right that a child of five should stand by the bedside of a man, assumed to be dying, to say his last farewell. He hardly knew Uncle Jim, and found the whole business horrible. He could not recall whether Uncle Jim died; but thought that he did not. How long he was there he could not recall. For some reason he was moved, this time to lodge with a formidable woman called Miss Hubner, of German origin. She had a flat in a YMCA, which she organised. She and Jeremiah did not get on. He thought that she was one of the enemy. One day, without knowing what it meant, he told her that she was a 'German Joo'. He thought this was the full and proper designation for Germans. Miss Hubner thought otherwise. How long he was there he could not remember, nor whether this was the occasion of his next change of address.

He not only did not know if he had a dad; he hardly knew if he still had a mother, though she sent him parcels, and letters. He did pay a visit to the sanatorium. He met his dad once, when he was on embarkation leave. It was something of an adventure. He was put on a train with a luggage label tied to a lapel, Identity Card in pocket, Gas Mask round neck, to Derby.

He was found on the bridge over the railway, crying plaintively, 'Mum and Dad', by some kindly railway police. They took him to a small waiting room, where he was given a 'bed' on a brown, leather covered, seat, with a comic to read. Who collected him he could not recall. It seems to have been his dad. Train times were chaotic. When, many years later, he went to Derby for an interview, he had a sense of 'deja vu' on the station. He told a group of people, investigating such phenomena, of the strange feeling of having been there before, assuring them that he had never set foot on Derby Midland Station in his life. Some time later, his dad came to stay. He asked, "Do you remember Derby Station?" "No", said Jeremiah. "Why on earth should I?" "It was on that bridge that they found you crying Mum and Dad". As soon as this was recalled, he could go straight to the room where they had looked after him.

After Miss Hubner, he was transferred to a Miss Butcher; where it was he did not know. She had been a ward sister and was a large, formidable lady, but he got on all right with her. All he remembered of her home was a linoleum covered staircase, that his bedroom had pale blue curtains and a rose wash stand. He knew the bedroom well, as he had measles in it. He was about seven. As far as he knew he never went to school. He could read pretty well. He could read before war broke out. Having been a matron, Miss Butcher was strict about the room being darkened, so the curtains were drawn and anything he might read was taken away. That did not matter for the first few days. As he began to get better, it was boring.

She had left one book behind. It was a small India paper edition of the New Testament. It had gilt edged pages and smelt wonderful. In those days it was standard practice to leave Bibles by bedsides. While Jeremiah had doubtless been taken to Church, unwillingly, once or twice, he had never had a scripture lesson nor been to Sunday school. He knew that Bibles were considered holy books, but that was all. Miss Butcher was no sylph and had a heavy tread. There was no carpet on the stairs. The risk of being caught was negligible. It was something to read, and smelt lovely. Why not?

He decided that "St John" would be the most entertaining, so he read it. No doubt, the fact that it was furtive made it more compelling. He did not understand the opening, but it was mighty impressive. The story this man had to tell was going to be very important: even a young six or seven year old could tell that. "In the beginning was the word and the word was with God and the word was God....", was something more than, "Once upon a time". So he read on and on.

The impression it made was extraordinary and never left him. The first abiding impact was its immediacy and vividness. It was a visual, aural and almost tactile immediacy, involving a sense of smell and warmth. He had, no knowledge of any 'background', nor of the time in which it was set. He did not feel that it was very recent. The visual impression was wholly uninformed. Houses were made of soft red brick, and it was warm with sunshine. One story, above all, left an in-eradicable impression, that of the occasion when Jesus met Nathaniel, and spoke of seeing Philip under a fig tree. The tree was standing by a wall, which was soft pinkish buff in colour. It was warm. What the men under it were wearing did not matter. It was visual, without being pictorial. He heard people speaking, saw and smelt.

That this impression never left him had nothing to do with it being a holy book. It was much the same with stories he was later read at school, such as "Tales from Homer". When teachers shewed pictures, they spoiled the stories. Almost the only books, which pictures did not spoil, were those by Arthur Ransome, which he had not yet met. A picture of Mole in a boat wearing glasses destroyed Wind in the Willows forever. He had never seen a fig, let alone a fig tree. No doubt the smell he associated with it was a concoction of woody smells. When he did see a fig tree, years later, it seemed to smell about right.

Many years later, he read the lessons at Matins in a country Church. At Easter, it was the story of Mary at the tomb in that Gospel. He was transfixed by the way in which Jesus said the word, 'Mary'. For weeks beforehand, he would say the two syllables over and over to himself, trying to achieve the right inflexion. When it came to reading it, the same immediacy, he had experienced as a child, overwhelmed him. He could smell the stale miasma of the open tomb, hear and see. His endless rehearsals proved a waste of time. By the time he reached the word, Mary, his voice was so choked with emotion that he could hardly make a sound, and walked back to his seat looking and feeling a complete idiot.

What seemed obvious was that Jesus was right. Anyone could see that. Whatever might happen to him, he was right. He did not need the evangelist to tell him that, "in him was light, and the light was the light of men". There was a cleanness and clarity about everything he said. It made everyone else seem deceitful and stupid. He spoke with authority and directness. Nobody else did. His words, "Let whoever among you is faultless, cast the first stone....", were the equivalent of the U S Cavalry arriving at the crucial moment in a Cowboy Film. Why could nobody else speak like that? "No man ever spake like this". Reading that book seemed to spoil all others.

He read of the crucifixion without horror, not knowing what it was. It seemed inevitable, almost from the start, that it would end thus. You did not need the resurrection to know that, even if the man was put to death, he was 'right'. If he was right, then somehow, he would be all right. He had reached the conclusion that Job was driven to, in the famous words set to music by Handel.

It would not be true to say that he remembered this story throughout his childhood. He certainly did not, apart from odd snatches; though, when ill with flu, he read it again. Aside from a few attendances on services of the Church, which meant nothing, his first introduction to anything connected with the Christian religion was at the 'opposite end' from that of almost anyone else. He had begun with the most violently exclusive and divisive representation of Jesus, which did not trouble with his childhood at all. He seems to have assumed, without ever thinking about it, that everyone else had too. He had read it, just as a book, not as a religious text. He had not looked for hidden meanings or moral instruction, just to while away the time. He assumed that all the grown ups, who made him go to Church, must have read all and more than he had read, especially rectors and vicars. It was not until thirty years later that he realised that they had not.

He had no detailed recall of what was said. It was the indelible impression of the obvious truth of this man that was impossible to eradicate. No doubt such as rectors had read it all, but in bits and pieces, as a quarry for significant words. They came to it from the Christian religion, and sought, in it, what was useful to that religion. He had, by chance, come on it the other way round. They, as he later understood, took the Christian religion as the established truth, and read the gospel in order to establish that truth. He had seen or felt that Jesus, in that Gospel, was clearly the truth and sought to make the religion establish it. He strove to make it do so, but could never succeed. It might well have been so for those who heard Jesus in Galilee, for some of his disciples, and even for the Rich Young Man.

The evacuation, as far as lodging with strangers was concerned, lasted about two years. It seemed like ten. He could recall vivid incidents, but the connecting narrative became confused. When he learned of the limiting dates, it seemed impossible to fit everything in. This, he was to experience many times.

The sanatorium buildings on the Norfolk Coast remained undamaged throughout the war. The house, to which it moved, had a land mine dropped in the garden, which blew the windows out. Whether this caused his mother to leave, he did not know. She obtained employment, as cook, at a little school, owned and run by his formidable Aunt Edith, who looked like the late Queen

Mary. As a mother she may well have been quite pleasant. As a headmistress she was awesome and, often, 'not amused'. She had daughters, who were in their 'teens' and were highly cultivated. One played the cello, which proved it. He and his mother shared a bed sitting room at the school, so he received some schooling. About all he learned was that one had to sit up straight at meals. Aunt Edith must have had a husband, what he was Jeremiah never knew.

His only other memory of the place was that there was wild garlic in the grounds and a lake of sorts with a crumbling culvert bridge, and the smell of rubber. It was at Chapel en le Frith and was often down wind of the Ferodo works. His mother was friendly with the Vicar and his wife, whose name was Green. He learned that they were a very "nice couple". Nice hay may have been and, doubtless, very good and kind, but his services were boring and tea with them was about as dreary as could be imagined.

The Midlands interlude was not to last long. It was possible to return to Norfolk.

Chapter Three.

"A root in Dry Ground"

His mother found rooms in a large, opulent, house, belonging to a family who had once lived in her father's parish. It had extensive grounds, a small farm with cows, a lake with rowing boats and luxurious bathrooms, whose baths had sliding glass panels and showers. There were lavatories with low level cisterns, rather than chains. The kitchen had a huge Aga like cooker that was called an "Esse". Once again, she was in the kitchen. His sister was at boarding school and soon to leave. The owner of the house had an engineering works in Norwich. He was said to be a very clever engineer, and not a man to be taken lightly. His factory was involved in 'war work'. This made both him and the factory very important. It produced electric motors for submarines.

There was another family lodging there, a mother and three daughters, the father being away at the war. They, too, had known Jeremiah's mother for many years. They had lots of money, and a beautiful house, which had been requisitioned by the Air Force. When not fighting wars, the husband was a leading Norwich lawyer. Jeremiah loved rowing about the lake in one of the boats, which had always to be bailed out. He was about seven and could not swim, but nobody seemed to bother about such things then. Today he would be called a 'disturbed' child: then he was a thorough nuisance. He wanted his own way, and if he did not get it would throw a tantrum, but only when at home. Elsewhere he was a creep. Being an evacuee had taught him how to be what people wanted him to be, and say what they expected him to say. He could switch roles with bewildering rapidity.

For the first time he went to school seriously. The school to which he was sent was not far away, a short bus journey. It was a pleasant country house with well tended grounds. It was apparently his sixth school, and he was in his ninth home. It was run on the basis of the PNEU system, and had moved to the hall from its original buildings, because of the war. His sister and two cousins had attended it. Girls seemed to fare better than boys. They thought the world of the place. Jeremiah and his older male cousin had different views. His cousin was very, very, clever. Jeremiah was not. This cousin, for the rest of his life, Jeremiah thought the most brilliant and clear minded man he had ever known. He could apply his clarity of mind to anything, and could explain anything clearly, as nobody else ever could.

The headmistress was known as Auntie Gladys; her husband, who had nothing to do with the place, was Uncle Percy. Some of the pupils boarded there. Most went home only for weekends, transport being difficult. Jeremiah had a spell as a 'weekly boarder'. The boys' dormitory held about six of them. They were, in Norfolk, names to conjure with. One was the son of a large Norwich shop, which also had a printing business, and had been in the family for 200 years. Another was the son of a family famed for its mustard. Others, too, were of well to do stock. How he envied them: even at eight, they had assurance.

The day began with prayers, taken by Auntie Gladys. Even at the tender age of eight, it seemed to Jeremiah that the sons and daughters of the well to do were, in some way, more 'God's dear children', than was he. He found it strange that this thin faced woman with gold rimmed spectacles, should talk of all being "God's dear children", then deal out humiliating punishments. She had a habit of tagging boys with nasty names. His cousin had been given the name "Cheetah". He had, been invited, with one or two others to spend some time in the private quarters of Auntie Gladys, to play cards. The game selected was, "Strip the jacks naked", though, in such genteel company, it had a less vulgar name. His cousin had been seen riffling through his cards before playing. Auntie Gladys said, "There is a horrid animal called the Cheetah". He was tagged as such from then on. He regarded her with utter contempt, as any fool could see that knowing what cards were in one's pile in that game made not a shred of difference.

The owner of the engineering works died suddenly, while reading the paper on the terrace. Jeremiah had walked past him, sitting there, on his way back from the boat, not realising that he was dead. The house was suddenly solemn. Something had happened, but nobody would tell him what it was. It meant another move.

His mother rented a small gardener's cottage, tied to a large Manor on the other side of the road. It had three small bedrooms, a kitchen with a Norfolk oven in the wall, a small sitting room and a scullery. The scullery had a 'copper', in a corner, and an earthenware sink. The sink in the kitchen had a hand pump, but it did not work. There was no sanitation, but an 'earth closet' up the yard. The contents had to be buried in the garden. Water for washing was obtained from rain butts, or, when they were empty, in buckets from the pond. Drinking water was ferried from the manor house tap, in one of those large oval tanks on wheels that were used in gardens. The head gardener next door would bring the water over, as he kindly took care of the contents of the earth closet.

Jeremiah's mother could make a home anywhere. She turned the kitchen into a sort of dining/living room and made the scullery into the kitchen. The cooking apparatus was a two burner, 'Florence', paraffin stove. You could have an oven by placing a tin box with a door on one of the burners. With this equipment his mother produced a hot breakfast every day, a hot lunch and high tea, with cakes and puddings and even bread, when the Norfolk Oven was used.

He continued at the same school. As the daughter of the Manor attended it, they cycled to the forge at the bottom of the road, left their bikes with the blacksmith and got the bus in the morning. The forge was on the nearside of the road for the journey to school. Out of school, Jeremiah's friends were the sons of the farm workers. At that time, social strata were clearly defined. His friends at home called the daughter of the Manor "Miss Rosemary". She had an elder brother whom all feared. He had things like shotguns and air rifles. He went away to school.

At school 'Miss Rosemary' was known simply as 'Rosebud'. When he was invited to play with her at the Manor, his friends called her Miss Rosemary, but stopped short of calling him "Master....". It was altogether different when they stayed at the Rectory. Then everyone called him "Master....", with great deference. They had a curious habit of calling grown-ups by their first name, with the title Miss or Mister. Wives of members of the family were Mrs, followed by their husband's first name. When daughters of the family married, they were known by their husband's surname. He found nothing strange in moving between these two worlds, but belonged in neither.

The farm friends were wholly attuned to their way of life and school, just as 'Miss Rosemary' and those, with whom he shared the dormitory, were wholly attuned to theirs. He was attuned to neither. He kept quiet about having no inside lavatory or bathroom. The fact that baths were taken in a galvanised iron tub, in front of the fire under the copper, he kept secret, and hoped that Rosebud did not tell. He knew what proper baths were from the house they had lodged in, and from the rectory. Baths in front of the fire were much more fun.

While at the cottage, where they lived for the rest of the war, a wealthy family was very kind. They owned the brewery in Norwich. They would have him to stay in their luxurious house and passed on cast-off clothes, as their son was the same age. They had a butler, thick carpets, rode horses and shot guns. They had a large car, and the food they ate was such as he had never seen. After the war, they would take one of the Brewery's pubs at the seaside for a month. Jeremiah was invited for a week. It was fun, but he did not much like the seaside.

His extraordinary double life continued for many years. It might be said to symptomise his life from then on. At no school, nor in the army or at university, indeed, for the rest of his days, did he ever he feel that he belonged, but only appeared to, by performing a part.

His stay at Auntie Gladys's academy ended abruptly. When arriving at school, the boys had to change into indoor shoes with elastic sides. Outdoor shoes were left in a conservatory. He noticed that the assured sons of well to do folk did not bend down to remove their houseshoes, but flicked them up and caught them. As with everything, when he tried to look clever, it ended in disaster. He flicked, but his shoe would not come off. He flicked harder with the same result. He gave a huge flick. The shoe came off like a sling shot, flew into the air and; "Oh my God!" It cracked a pane of glass.

Auntie Gladys castigated malefactors at Morning Prayers. Always she said that she was punishing them for failing to 'own up'. Had they owned up, all would have been forgiven and forgotten. Own up he would, but not to the old harridan herself. He chose, instead, the youngest, newly appointed assistant matron, who was probably no more than sixteen. She assured him that it was nothing to worry about He had owned up, and Auntie Gladys would not mind. There was plenty of glass behind the potting shed. Thus reassured he went home with Rosebud.

Next day after Prayers, Auntie Gladys did mind. Not only was he harangued before the school; he was summoned to her sanctum. He was told that what he had done was revealing of grave moral turpitude. It shewed lack of respect for the property of others. The pane of glass was valued at one shilling. He was to bring one penny, every Monday morning, and present it to her at Prayers, duly confessing his sins. What about owning up? Whether Auntie Gladys forgave and forgot, he could not tell. Almost certainly she forgot all about it. He did not.

The incident laid a deep mistrust for all grown-up conversation for the rest of his life. It was not just that she seemed to have forgotten all about not punishing offenders who owned up; it was that grown-ups seemed to see things in a different light. He had not shewn disrespect for property at all. He had just tried to do what the older children did, and had an accident. Grown-ups were always like that. If he found a fascinating bit of garden equipment in a potting shed and tried to play about with it, 'you should know that children should not mess about with things like that. You had no business in the potting shed anyway'. It was the same when they had marvellous looking radio-grams with an array of buttons. He would find it irresistible to press one. This would set in motion an apparently unstoppable sequence of events, like the operation of an 'auto-changer', which deposited one record on another. How on earth did you stop the thing, before the whole house rang with the Ride of the Valkyries? He was always having to make up stories to cover such eventualities.

Auntie Gladys' telling off raised a deeper anxiety. Her excuses for his misbehaviour became veiled accusations. She realised that, having been an evacuee, he could not be expected to behave like 'proper little boys', especially as he played with the 'village boys' at home. Living in a cottage not a proper house, no better could be expected of him. It was almost like blaming a bastard for being one. His sister had been a model pupil.

His sister had been a model everything. She had been head girl at every school. She came top in every exam she ever took. She paid attention in lessons. She did her work properly and kept it tidily. She was now trying to pass her 'First MB', to get a place in medical school, as she had not done the right subjects in 'Higher', whatever that was. She biked four miles into Norwich every day, to go to the 'Tech'. It mattered not how many bombs fell, off she went. When his sister set her hand to anything, she did it. She did not give up half way through, as her feckless little brother, who never finished anything. He hated this, and made his unfortunate sister's life as near hell as he could. It was about the only thing he was any good at. It is a testimony to her, that despite this and embarrassing her, whenever he could, in front of her posh medical student friends, she remained a steadfast and loyal friend to him.

Having been publicly humiliated by 'dear Auntie Gladys', he felt that everyone was looking at him, realised that he played with the village boys and had not a proper bathroom. The village boys would realise that he could not flick his shoes off without breaking windows. He could not wait to get on the bus and go home. As the bus stopped, he called, "Race you to the bikes", and made for the door, to jump down and rush over the road. He forgot that there was an apparatus that buses towed which produced something instead of petrol. He ran round that and made for the forge.

He never got there.

His rush was interrupted by a USAF lorry. The driver did his best to avoid him, stopped and put the unconscious eight year old into the truck and took him to the base hospital. What the unfortunate Rosebud made of it all, he never knew. The first his hapless mother heard was when the roadman knocked at her door and said; "Your boy; he lie dead on the road, Missus".

His mother leapt on her bike and rode to the spot, to find nothing. Having discovered what had occurred, she got a taxi to the Air Base. There they told her that her beloved child was not dead. They had patched up his cuts and abrasions, which were not serious. He had no broken bones. They had sent him on the Norfolk and Norwich Hospital for X rays to his skull. By the time she got there, he had been X-rayed. His skull was not fractured, but he had been transferred to the children's hospital, where she found him, still unconscious, except for short spells of incoherent speech which consisted mostly of "oh dear". There she had to leave him. Her husband was inaccessible. That night Norwich suffered its biggest air raid of the war.

Norwich was, incidentally, the most severely bomb damaged city in Britain during the war, with 85% of its buildings destroyed or damaged. Unlike Plymouth and Coventry, it was not done in one or two heavy raids, but more or less continuously, as returning bombers dropped unused bombs on their way home. These seem chiefly to have been incendiaries. The area round the cathedral was spared. Hitler was a great admirer of the building.

Jeremiah had a fleeting memory of consciousness when his mother was there, and of being surrounded by screens with floral patterns. He also remembered coming round briefly in the shelters, and being given rice pudding and stewed apple. He finally recovered consciousness on the Sunday afternoon after the accident, when the Band of the Salvation Army was playing on the ward. He thought he had reached the pearly gates. The Airmen came to visit him and turned his bed into a sweet shop. They also produced the summit of luxury, bananas. This gave him further evidence of the gulf between the conversation of a child and that of grown-ups.

The sister came to his bedside, as soon as they had gone, and collected up most of his bounty, saying that she felt sure that he would wish to share it with all the other dear children. He did not have any such sureness. He would keep every last morsel for himself, while distributing largesse to such as he felt inclined to. This served to make him even more wary of grown-ups and their words, especially as the sister took all the nicest candies away. His stay in the Jenny Lind was short.

His aunt, who was unmarried and lived at the Rectory, 'ran' the St John's ambulance (she was very energetic and bossy, so she ran anything she had anything to do with.). Her ambulance was a sandy colour, but so were they all. The window behind his bed gave onto the parking area, where the ambulances came and went. One afternoon, gazing out of the window, he saw a sand coloured ambulance draw up. "That's Aunt", he felt certain. Minutes later his aunt appeared at the entrance to the ward. He was put on a stretcher, carried to the ambulance and driven to the Rectory. After serious concussion it was decreed that he spend a month lying flat on his back.

His aunt had been a ward sister. The Rectory was no longer required as billets for fighter pilots. It was here that he would convalesce, his mother staying from time to time. Auntie Gladys never got her money. If this was an example of being cared for by one's heavenly Father, it seemed a bit like taking a sledge-hammer to crack a nut!

If the early life of Jesus was as described by S Luke, the same applied. Arranging a miraculous conception to produce a precocious ill-mannered son, who ended-up as a sort of lay reader in a provincial synagogue might have seemed a bit excessive.

Chapter Four

He had no form nor comeliness.

Jeremiah was an undersized weakling. He had no friends outside school, save the farm lads, who were much more assured and growingly so. After the accident, it was decided that he should go to a proper boys' boarding school. Again he found himself among the children of the well to do. Their parents had cars, lived in houses that had gardens like the rectory, but were internally better appointed. They had gardeners and maids, and gravel drives that sounded wonderful, when cars scrunched over them. Worst of all they seemed to think that schoolboys wanted to play football in the holidays.

The school had grounds of over 100 acres. The house seemed huge. It had been built for His Highness Duleep Singh, and had a wonderful cricket ground with a large thatched pavilion. Here he spent much time daydreaming of what it would be like to be the son of well to do parents, and be good at things like cricket, or even able to sing. Whenever he sought to join in, he was aware of a tuneless noise, so opened and shut his mouth, but made no sound, Little things may be significant. Because he did not sing, he may have been more conscious of the 'lyric', than those who could.

His dreams of being the son of well to do parents knew no bounds. He imagined himself the son of a Duke, with everyone calling him "My Lord", driving cricket balls to the boundary with ease and a straight bat. There was an odd factor in these dreams. While he might be taller and have different coloured hair and so on, the 'I' remained constant. Had he glimpsed something of the existence of man as a "living soul"?

This time was the beginning of his first continuous experience of the Christian religion. He had scripture lessons. There was Morning Assembly, at which senior boys would read the lessons. Through these, he became acquainted with what seemed an easy way to live, considering the birds of the air, who did not have to toil or gather into barns, where one's heavenly Father knew what one needed without having to be told. If he was God, of course he did; but he had to be told, nonetheless, as he 'liked it'. How old did you have to be before you could say what God liked? God did not seem to understand, even though told a million times, that it would be much easier to learn Latin by sleeping on the book. On Sundays they walked in crocodile to the local church. Before going, there was an assembly. Each boy was issued with a penny for the collection. On Sunday evenings there were prayers again. There appeared to be contradiction. So far from producing an easy way of living, it seemed to make it more irksome. All you could do on Sundays was write letters home, then sit about doing very little.

It was 1944. He was nine.

At home, his mother would take him to church on his bicycle. It was very boring, except when mountains skipped like rams and the little hills like young sheep; or the valleys stood so thick with corn that they shall laugh and sing. His friends from the farm did not have all this tiresome church going on Sundays. His mother did not even try and make him go to Sunday school. It was then that he had his first clear evidence that there was something very strange about the Christian religion, in relation to the gospel that he had read.

The Vicar and his wife came to tea. It was always a problem when posh people came, because of the outside lavatory. This was a triumph of his mother's sanitary sense. Mostly these things stank. Hers did not. What she did was simple. She put the ash from the fires through a sieve. Into this she sprinkled powdered disinfectant.

When the reverend pair came, it was 'best behaviour'; no giggling when one should not. This was hard as the Vicar's wife tended to fart loudly whenever she got up or sat down. Here was further evidence of the superiority of rectors and their wives. All sat down to tea. The conversation was boring. The reverend pair spoke of how clear the stream was this year, and what lovely watercress they had gathered. His mother seemed to think it marvellous, too. Jeremiah thought that there were much more exciting things to do and talk about than watercress in the stream.

When there was a pause, he said, "Streams of living water flowing to eternal life". If he had downloaded hard porn from the internet, there could not have been a more shocked silence. After much 'Ahemming', a desultory conversation resumed. After they departed, the lady producing a veritable obligato, as she mounted her bicycle; his mother spoke to him. He must not quote words from that source in front of clergymen and their wives. Children of his age should not know such things, and they were not proper things to say at tea. She did not seem to mind, but people like clergymen and their wives would. She was even more emphatic about saying anything like that at the rectory, "Grandpa will have a fit, so would Granny", so would his energetic and forthright aunt.

This grown-up Christian world was very strange. Church was full of words that it was not proper even to mention outside, especially virgins and their wombs. So impressed was he at the impropriety of these words that he dared not ask what the word abhor meant either. It was full of things that "you will not understand till you're grown up", like those dreadful commandments, which everyone had to keep; but nobody would explain; so how could one keep them? Sometimes the service began with the Vicar reciting them. After each one, you had to pray, "Lord have mercy upon us and incline our hearts to keep this law". If they were God's laws they must be right, so one had little option but to pray as directed, even if one did not know what many of them meant. He dared not ask, in case he did so in the wrong way, implying that he did not want his heart inclined to keep some law.

His mother seemed to fear that he would say something that would cause upsets, especially among short-tempered high Church clergymen and their families. The fearful ten commandments were displayed on gilt panels either side of the chancel arch, at the church where his grandfather was rector. Everyone said that Sunday was the first day of the week. Diaries and calendars confirmed this. When it came round, it became the seventh day, when nobody was allowed to do anything, although there was breakfast on the table and a hot lunch. Unless there was a weekly miracle, someone must have been doing something. It was not only confusing mathematically. It meant that you were only allowed to do anything that was not fun on a Sunday. What was or was not a "graven image" was also a problem. His High Church grandfather's church was full of what anyone might think were graven images, they were not only bowed to, they were smoked with incense. Obviously they were not graven images, so what *was* a graven image? It must be something spectacular.

It is hard to say whether what he had read or what he had not read was more significant. He had not heard the usual children's stories. Before the evacuation his mother and sister had read him one or two by Beatrix Potter. He hated Alice in Wonderland, thinking it frightening and cruel. This was about the first time in his life that he consciously experienced Christmas, or birthdays. His mother arranged a sort of party, but he hated it. He felt silly.

His mother never made any pretence that there was Santa Claus, reindeer or sleighs, while everyone else seemed to believe all that nonsense. He must have started at school quite well, as he won his form prize. It was a book by Arthur Ransome, "We did not mean to go to Sea". He became an avid reader of these books. They were about the only children's stories that he read. Hardly ever do those tales go beyond that which is possible, even if they stretch the bounds of the probable, and the children involved are those of well to do families. It meant, that his childhood was largely free of an imaginary world of supernatural beings, ghosts, magic, or anything of that kind, even Santa Claus, sleighs or reindeer.

There was the excitement of D-Day, Arnhem and V E Day. In the midst of all that there were the Liberators and Flying Fortresses droning overhead every evening, and the doodle bugs coming the other way. One landed near the cottage. The explosion shook the place. Everyone had to get out of bed and rush outside. Though they had a home dug shelter, his mother thought it safer to bury themselves in the straw at the bottom of a stack in the rickyard nearby. There were no more explosions that night; not close anyway. Next day everyone was on bicycles to investigate the crater, and scour it for treasured bits of the doodle bug. They used to stand outside in the evenings and watch them going over. It was dangerous when the motor stopped.

The kind of occupations, then thought proper by knowing grown-ups, were different from those of today. Egg collecting was one. The rarer the bird, the more treasured its egg. One could earn a bit of cash by collecting magpies' eggs and destroying their nests. At harvest time boys were stationed round the patch of uncut corn to kill rabbits as they ran out. There were no such things as combined harvesters. 'Binders' were the high tech means of cutting corn, which was stacked in the rickyard near the cottage. The sheaves were carried up to the top of the stack with an 'elevator', powered by a horse, walking round in circles. It was a great event when the thrashing machine arrived. It was a coal-fired steam engine, which drove a 'drum', which thrashed the corn, and an elevator, which carried the loose straw to another stack. Then everyone stood around with sticks to club the rats to death as they ran from the bottom of the stack.

After VE day, the men of the family began to reappear. With uncles and cousins, there were eight in the family who had been away, nine, if one included the uncle who had been killed. The last to return was his dad.

With the end of bombing, travel became easier, so they went to the Rectory more often. It was a tedious train journey, taking almost as long as getting to London. The very High Church Services were more attractive than matins. It all seemed much more important. His grandfather decided to restore the rood beam as a memorial to his lost son. Jeremiah was there when it was installed. The lady who carved it was making some final adjustments to the face of Jesus on the cross, scraping some bits of wood off one nostril and dabbing on a bit of paint. This made his ears wide open, many years later, when he first came on the later Isaiah's ridicule of images.

As a child of eleven, whose 'mental age' would, in today's language, be considered much less, it was not the ridiculous nature of the matter which struck him, but the opposite. What did one do with the trimmings from Jesus' nose? Were they very holy?

When the three figures were fixed in position, Jeremiah was sent up the ladder to hold in place the shields that were under them. The left hand end of the beam ran into the arch at exactly the point, where the prohibition of graven images stood. The Church was full of statues in niches. The important ones had lights, where the wicks, floating in oil, burned under them. The glass bowls, in which they floated, were in deep reds and blues. The one over the altar was very important. Everyone fell to one knee when in its line of sight. That was because behind two gold curtains was a locked box, in which was the 'reserved sacrament', so God was in the box. In a way, this seemed a good idea. God was in every Church, and was even more in the locked box. It was good to know where he was; even more important, perhaps, to know where he was not. Then, they said that God was everywhere. Though other ministers of the gospel did not agree with locked boxes on altars, they all agreed that God was more 'there' in Churches than anywhere else. The system seemed to stop when the carpets were cleaned.

While it was handy to know where God was more present than elsewhere, it had its drawbacks. Only very specially qualified people had access to God, and seemed to pass this to their friends. If God made the rules, which said that he belonged especially in certain places, there it was. Little children were not allowed. You had to get past all these other people. It seemed different from that

Gospel. People said that he would never go to heaven if he lied, or did all kinds of things, like pushing buttons on radiograms. Heaven must be full of ministers of religion and their friends. They were fine if you were in the family and behaved yourself, and especially if you did not mention anything said by Jesus.

Friends of Rectors and Ministers of religion, seemed to be the same old gang, and that included such as Auntie Gladys, not to mention all the formidable brothers and sisters of his Rector grandfather. Just as he was the poor relation at school, so was he at the Rectory, though he spent more time there than any others. They all had big houses, cars and running water. They mowed their lawns with motor mowers, just like the well to do families, with whose sons he was at school.

That such people 'knew', in some mysterious way, how to deal with God, almost as Aladdin and the genie, did not strike him as inappropriate, but the reverse. The important thing was to know exactly how to manipulate the genie. The fact that everything seemed very mysterious, as illustrated by such things as Sundays being both the first day of the week and the seventh and what exactly constituted a graven image, enhanced the importance of it all, rather than make it seem ridiculous; as long as it was all going on. It seemed to require continued performance, and dressing up.

The village where his paternal grandfather was rector, itself, seemed more important than most. It had a railway station. Adjacent to the station was a maltings, beyond that a foundry. This was a wonderland of heat and power, at the heart of which was a furnace. Scrap iron was thrown into the top. At the bottom was a plug made of clay. It was very exciting when the plug was pierced and molten iron flooded out, to be carried away by men with specially lined buckets on long handles, and poured into moulds. The maltings were bombed, leaving a railway siding of unused coal. The fact of there being a maltings and a foundry seemed to make being a Rector even more important. Vicars did not have such things.

He was at the Rectory when the verdicts were announced at the Nuremburg trials. His grandfather listened to the sentences being pronounced after lunch, sitting at the head of the table from which everything but the cloth had been removed with a copy of the Daily Mail in front of him. It had a picture of the accused standing in the dock on the front page. He noticed that his grandfather encircled the heads of those condemned to death with a noose, and seemed greatly to enjoy so doing. For some reason this horrified him.

He was there for "V-J Day", when his dad's younger brother was home, though yet in uniform. They had a huge bonfire. He got the impression that his mother distanced herself from the exuberance. She seemed to think that, while we should all be glad that we had not been invaded and had emerged victorious, such festivities were inappropriate. She would tend to say things quietly like, "I am sure that there are a lot of German mothers who are feeling very sad".

Soon after this, his dad returned from the war. Jeremiah was eleven. He was given a week off school. It was the first time he had seen him for more than a couple of days, since he was four. They hired a sailing cruiser on the Broads. One breezy afternoon a white enamelled half decked racing boat, with a black number on her sail, swept past them. Her name was Red Admiral. His mother said in a tone of reverential awe; "That is a lovely boat. It is a One Design". In that vision, one feature of his adult life was determined. Whatever he might do, he would own one of those 'lovely boats'.

His dad remained in the army for some years after the war, but was posted to the west of England. It meant leaving the cottage, and another change of school. They moved down to Taunton, first renting rooms in a country house a few miles out of the town, later finding a flat some five miles away from the District Headquarters where he worked. Jeremiah was sent to a prep school in Wiltshire, whose headmaster was a cousin. It was a very happy school.

At this time he was to see another side of both Rectory life and that of the well to do. His grandfather became ill. He had been infected with a virulent form of tuberculosis when visiting one of his parishoners. It was seen as his mother's duty to leave her home and children and go and help out, by being, in effect, the cook, housekeeper and sick room attendant. Neither the younger daughter, nor the well to do daughter in law could thus be troubled, yet both had more leisured lives, with servants and helpers, and even a nanny on hand. They had more important things to do with their time. It also seemed to be the case that their children needed mothers at home. His mother was away for about four months.

Though he did not know much about it at the time, he later learned that which he was himself to experience later on. Those of the Christian religion appear to have an awareness of those who are likely to regard the sayings of Jesus as having final authority, and who will thus find it very hard to say, "NO". They, also, seemed to endow people with a character and degree of intelligence that is fitting to their current occupation.

The rectory, though large, was not an easy house to run. His grandfather, long ago, had sought to be at the forefront of domestic technology, and had installed acetylene gas making plants, one in the Rectory Yard, the other alongside the Church. This enabled him to do away with oil lamps. They consisted of gasholders with the same kind of expansion system as those familiar to cricket lovers at the Oval. At the bottom is the producer unit, which is simple. It consists of two drawers, each filled with 'carbide'. A lever is switched to one or the other which sprays the carbide with water, producing gas. Gas lighting meant that, while the rooms in the house, which were occupied, were fairly well lit and warmed, it was quite a performance when entering a room. There was a single light in the hall. All passageways, stairs and corridors were in darkness. If one moved about after dark one took a candle.

This, combined with high ceilings, and walls festooned with trophies such as tiger's heads, the skins of pythons, and a mass of German armaments, trophies of two world wars, meant that going to bed, having heard a frightening story, could be a terrifying ordeal. There was a long passage leading through a butler's pantry to the kitchen, a huge flagstoned room with an old style range at one end. This had to be cleaned and relit every morning, not only to produce kettles of water for early morning tea, but also kettles of soft water for the men of the household to shave; though there was a boiler which remained alight night and day. The water from the well was hard. Every morning it had to be pumped with a huge cast iron hand pump into the tank in the loft.

Jeremiah's mother found herself sharing the 'between-maid's' duties with the only resident maid. This entailed rising at 6 a.m, to clean and fire the range. It was ironic that on Sundays she found herself performing this duty so that the Rector, when well enough, and any other males could shave in soft water, and then go off to Church; to have breakfast on the table on their return. It crossed nobody's mind that the daughter in law herself might wish to join them. She did not, but liked to have a lie in. It was as if those, who attended the "Holy Communion", conferred a privilege on those who did not by allowing them to be 'facilitators'.

Soon after this, Jeremiah moved on to secondary schooling. His dad hated his public school days. When in his nineties, there was some archive film of the First War shewn on TV. Jeremiah asked: "How on earth did you leave school and go through all that?" His dad replied; "If you had been at Haileybury, boy, you would have found it a holiday camp!" He had never had a moment's terror during the entire world war, in trenches and gun pits, that compared with being at that school.

His mother had a hatred of schools amounting to an allergy. Her elder brother had been thrown out of school altogether by the age of ten as unteachable. He had passed through the whole of the first world-war as a Private Soldier in the Norfolks. Considered too old and stupid to fight with them in the second, he managed to be taken on by the RASC. By 1943, he had risen to the rank of Colonel. He was present at the Teheran Conference, where he met Churchill, Roosevelt and Stalin.

Long after she died, a retired doctor, who had been a lifelong friend of the family, said to Jeremiah, "Of all people, I think I miss your mother more than anyone, for her conversation, her intelligence, her sharp critical faculty, her wit and her humility". It seemed to Jeremiah that her critical faculty was apparent in what she would not say, almost more than what she would. By saying nothing, she made it perfectly clear, that she thought Santa Claus, Guy Fawkes night, tooth fairies, and even birthdays were nonsense. She made it equally obvious that she thought the same of stories like those of Beatrix Potter, even Wind in the Willows, Alice in Wonderland, and others that involved animals being endowed with human faculties, fairies, or other mythical beings. "A lot of old foolery" was her account of it. She felt much the same about 'High Church' activities. If a "lot of old foolery" was well performed, it made it no less so. It made the performers more silly.

Being delivered to secondary school was a fearful experience, for an undersized, inept boy of thirteen. The scale of the buildings was awe inspiring. There was a huge Gothic Chapel, and the school was built on a spur of the South Downs. The buildings were dressed with knapped flint and had lancet windows. The senior boys, or 'men', as they were called, looked like adults and swaggered about with an assurance that he could never have, but longed for all his life. By comparison with most schools it was fairly humane.

It was a new world. The masters walked about and taught in gowns. The Chapel was very impressive, with the masters standing in canopied stalls about 3 feet above the boys. On Sundays they wore hoods as well as gowns. Two, who taught science, had doctorates from London University and wore scarlet robes. There was Evensong every evening, a Sung Eucharist, and Evensong, with a sermon, on Sunday evenings. Every morning, there was an Assembly in the 'Great School', taken by the very impressive looking Head. He was a man who said little, but Jeremiah honoured and respected him for the rest of his days. Thereafter, all dispersed for their lessons. It was more complicated than prep school, as there were different sets in different subjects. The other complicating factor was a subject listed as "Options". Boys could choose one area of study in which to specialise, Classics, Modern Languages or Science. Jeremiah opted for science. It was new, and seemed more exciting. Thus it was that he found himself in the science labs, being issued with what was the standard chemistry text-book for school certificate, as it was then called.

The issue of "Matriculation Chemistry for Schools", proved not only a disappointment, but raised a question that was never to go away. He could not wait to open this new treasury of knowledge. On the first page was the fundamental rule of all chemistry. It was that the atom is the smallest *indivisible* unit of matter. He knew, as did everyone, that the thing had been split long ago. The Chemistry teacher, a woman, who was a doctor of London University, acknowledged this. Science was ever progressing.

There was a less optimistic view, which was that all scientific laws were likely to be 'wrong'. It would be silly to imagine a small thirteen year old, whose chief quality was his inadequacy, thinking thus. A world of certainty had vanished. It was apiece with the whole grown up-conversation, which he found frightening for its assured rightness. He was far from thinking anything like 'knowledge is power'. Having power over others was something that did not interest him, what did, was preventing others having power over him. It was as if he sought a certainty that would enable him to clear a room of accusers with a single sentence. When would he begin to acquire their certainty about what God liked? It seemed the most essential knowledge to acquire. If one knew what God liked, one could have him in one's pocket. It did not, then, occur to Jeremiah that, if one achieved that, the roles of God and oneself would be reversed.

They were taught of the discovery of oxygen and burning. For centuries it was thought that, when materials were burned, it purified them. The ash represented the pure form of the material. What was given off was phlogiston. The teacher shewed that, when magnesium was burned in a closed container, it became heavier, so something was taken in, not given off. She told them how the phlogistonists maintained their theory, by arguing that it had a negative weight. They were then taken to a laboratory, given little china containers with lids, in which they burned magnesium. The container and its contents had to be weighed, and a calculation made. What was the point of proving what one already knew, and knew what answer you had to get, before getting it?

Someone discovered oxygen, and the phlogiston theory went up in smoke. The theory being maintained on the basis of a negative weight, lodged in Jeremiah's mind for the rest of his days, as typifying theories based on observation. The early theory that substances lost something, on being burnt, seemed the obvious explanation of the observable phenomena. What struck him was the way that, when the observable phenomena contradicted this, the theorists could cling to it by propounding crackpot ideas.

The wish for certainty was childish, but adult 'conversation' assumed certainties, when it came to dealing with people and especially their misdeeds. Most seemed to assume that this certainty, especially when it came to moral matters, derived from the Christian religion. Here, everyone knew what God did not like. One thing, alone, made it questionable: the reported sayings and acts of Jesus. Jeremiah could act as if deeply religious, but that was all. It was like being an evacuee again. 'While on stage', it seemed credible, but as soon as the performance was over, it dissolved into emptiness. This did not seem to afflict the rest of the school. They seemed to pray fervently when it was the time to do so. He could only try and look as if he was. He persuaded himself that, if he gave the appearance carefully enough, the reality would follow. Many aspects of religious observance suggest this.

Every year there was a confirmation. For a year or so, those who were to be confirmed had classes in the evenings. Jeremiah was assigned, with sundry others, to the elegant Assistant Chaplain, a youngish man of aristocratic family. The classes were pleasant, informal, diversions, once a week, in the evening. When it came to the service, usually conducted by one of two local Bishops, there was almost a book made, on which event would be the basis of the Bishop's address. It would either be the boat race, or the annual Oxford and Cambridge athletics match. The assistant Chaplain was the champion of the non-games-playing fraternity in the school. He dismissed the episcopal address, saying that he was tired of having his life planned between Putney and Mortlake. Jeremiah did not have his life laid out, either backwards down the Tideway or running in circles. He was in University College Hospital having an appendix removed.

He was taken to the confirmation at the school's mission in Camberwell, and was driven to the ceremony by his housemaster, a weird and frightening man, along with the assistant chaplain. His parents were there. After the service there was a gathering for cups of tea, cakes and biscuits. As a he was a product of the school, which financed the mission, the Bishop came to speak with them. He enquired, as Bishops are prone; "And what do you hope to become, my boy, when you grow up?"

Jeremiah mumbled something that he felt suitable. His world of imagination centred on sailing boats and, in particular, the beautiful Yare and Bure One Design. He would like to design sailing boats. The Bishop thought this a very worthwhile occupation. It was not what Jeremiah had the urge to say. He had an urge to "believe the Bishop's report". The words used, when laying hands on the young were less prosaic than today. They said; "Defend, O Lord, this thy child with thy heavenly grace........"

"I want to be what you said, My Lord, a son of God!" Had he considered what became of the "only begotten Son", he would have dropped the idea, just as later, when he pondered the story of the rich young man, he thought eternal life less desirable. That he felt this was not, in the circumstances, strange. The journey to London had been one of muted conversation. Both the driver and the chaplain felt it fitting. They had, insofar as they said anything, sought to remind him of the solemnity of the event. Thus he had high expectations, and was attentive to what the Bishop said. Tongues of fire would come down from heaven and he would achieve an instant mastery of many languages.

Such a response would have everybody spluttering into their teacups. It later occurred to him, that, had he made such a reply and known the four gospels almost by heart, he could easily have tied the Bishop, his housemaster and the assistant chaplain in knots, for the rest of the day, if not a week. He did not relate this to the story of Jesus being presented in the Temple at the age of twelve, by which time he would have a large measure of the Old Testament by heart.

The conversation on the return journey was free and easy. They included him as they spoke of how many miles the car did to the gallon, what was its cruising speed, and other such things. It was as if, having been confirmed, he was now a full member of this wondrous adult conversation, which knew about cars, gear-changes and all the rest of it. He felt this highly satisfactory.

Having completed his school certificate, Jeremiah decided to abandon science, which he found tedious, and chose history. Having his heart set on some way of life that would enable him to own a one design, and having seen that, while the Christian religion seemed to impose a greater burden than it relieved; this did not apply to rectors, he would be one. They had to conduct services on Sundays, but for the rest of the week, there seemed little that they had to do. He also felt that the service itself and all the praying would be more convincing, if he were the one to say the prayers, rather than add, "Amen". It was a bit like being on stage. No doubt the most ham-fisted performance of a role like King Lear seemed convincing to the man who performed it, who probably believed that he was an aged king.

His mother's father had been Vicar of a Broadland Parish, with a boat dyke reaching almost to the Vicarage Garden. Her uncle had a Broadland parish at Ludham, not far away, and he had Yare and Bure One Design, number 3, built for him. His mind was made up. He would become a clergyman in a riverside parish, not a very big one, such as would provide him with plenty of leisure time during the spring and summer, during which he would enjoy sailing his One Design. The first choice of village had to be Horning, whose vicarage lawns ran down to the river, but Upton or Ludham would be fine. The rectory at Acle was a mile from the river. Irstead would be a good spot too. At a pinch there was the family living, where his mother's family had established its unbroken succession of rectors, but that was on the other side of Yarmouth.

There was a difficulty, that wretched Gospel he had read as an infant. He sensed that the two were not easily reconciled. Chaplains and teachers at school reconciled them, so did the bishops, archbishops, and ministers of religion. There was no commandment saying, "Thou shalt not own and sail a One Design", even if one should not covet one's neighbours' boat. He could never shake off the certainty that the Jesus, of whom he read in the gospel, was true; that he spoke truth and, himself, embodied all that he said. There had to be some equally assured truth somewhere, which enabled one to pass from that to a Broadland vicarage with a One Design moored nearby. Obviously, teachers and clergymen knew about it, but none seemed very convincing when explaining it. It seemed more believable because it was mysterious.

It is hard to know whether a pupil is unintelligent, or finds whatever it may be that he or she has to learn unconvincing, so hardly worth the effort. If science was beyond him, so was history. Everyone else was congratulated on his work. He was told that his understanding was not mature. Teachers would say that nobody knew, for certain, what was the answer. They were sure that whatever he wrote was not it. He was not concerned with the truth of anything, but what would be acceptable. He tended to scan books, hoping to fall on the acceptable answer, not to gain understanding. He never read thoroughly, but thought of other things.

There seemed a certain futility in it all. Each term they were issued with a little blue book, which listed everyone in the school. At the front were the teachers. All had been scholars of some College, yet here they were, going through the same routine year by year. It seemed much the same with the things they taught. The study of history enabled people to understand the past and why things happened as they did. A problem lay in the soup tureen at the rectory. The handle on the lid was a scale model of the tureen. The problem was; 'was the handle on the model also a scale model of the tureen and, if so, how many miniature soup tureens would there be?'

All study was like that. They were asked to write about the causes of some event; let us say the English reformation. Each discerned cause became the effect of an anterior cause. Unless, on the analogy of the tureen, one could trace these back to one uncaused case, was there any point in doing it? If one did, all would end with either, "Adam and Eve", or God. If the former, answers would be interminably long, if the latter, brief. That could be elaborated. One might say of the English reformation, that it would not have happened as it did, had Katharine produced a son not a daughter. What might have happened, if it had been otherwise, none could know. Had he read the Old Testament, he would have seen that this was how they wrote of history. The Hebrew verb has only two tenses, but has a vast array of 'moods'. They could have said that Henry's wife was caused to bear a daughter and no son. All would know who caused this. They could be direct and say that the Lord caused her to bear only a daughter. Such a view saved much wearisome study, but would get few marks. That it would get no marks did not mean that it was not the truth.

It was obvious that one needed to find it all convincing, to obtain entry into the grown up 'conversation', and get marks. When it came to the English Reformation, it seemed that the answer was, in truth, 'chance'. Jeremiah wanted a world where things simply dropped into his lap. It was not just that the effort, needed to obtain things, made having them hardly worth it. In order to acquire the means thereto, one had to belong, in heart and soul and mind and strength, to the accepted 'conversation'. He had no objection to doing so, just lacked the ability to maintain it.. Then, it was worse than never having done so, as one was liable to lose everything. It was almost better not to have, than to have and lose. This might apply to life itself. If one were not born, did it mean that one was 'eternally' non-existent? The more comfortable and well appointed one's life, the less one would find the prospect of losing it welcome. Death was the only certainty.

The assured knowing of why things happened and why people did what they did was the key to being grown up and mature. On the one hand he wanted, above all, to belong in this knowing 'conversation', or appear to. On the other, he feared and suspected it. The episode with his shoe symptomised all. Auntie Gladys *knew* why he had done what he did. What she knew to have caused him to do so, bore no relation whatever to the thoughts he had when he did it. His housemaster and many other masters seemed like Auntie Gladys.

The attitudes of boys changed when they became prefects. Things that, a week before, seemed silly and matters of laughter became serious. Being a school prefect enabled one to wear a very smart tie. In his last term he was made a prefect. He lost no time in buying one of the coveted ties. The 'captain' of the school took him aside and explained, with great solemnity, that responsible attitudes must now be maintained. He nodded agreement. It was all very odd. It was obvious that one could not have 400 boys wandering into breakfast at any time they chose. On the other hand he found it hard to see why some boy, being 30 seconds late entering the dining room, mattered much.

There was a wide gulf between pretending to believe in things and believing in them. If one did not believe in things with heart and soul, it was hard to keep up the appearances. This became the story of his life. Just when he thought that he had all the appearances of the true believer, some silly thing would have to happen, which unmasked him. He was very sensitive to accusations of hypocrisy, on this basis, and would get angry. The gospel he read as a child was the one thing he could believe with heart and soul and mind.

A few days after acquiring the coveted tie, there was a general inspection of the Army Cadet Force. He stood in the front rank, behind one of the masters who was an officer. It began to rain. He said to his neighbour, "Oh shit, we are going to get soaked". He was overheard, "talking on parade". A notice went up to this effect. The headmaster took him aside and said how he had let everyone down.

He was no good at anything, though he was beginning to learn how to get away with it, by making himself the court jester. A contemporary in his house was a keen athlete and forever reading books about who had won this or that. One afternoon he shouted, "Was it a relation of yours who won a gold medal in the Olympics with Harold Abrahams?" Jeremiah had never heard of any relation having done anything of the kind, but replied, "Oh yes, it was my Uncle!"

He thought that would be the end of the matter. It was not. The other, when practising jumping over something, next day, told his housemaster, who coached athletics, that Jeremiah's uncle had an Olympic gold medal. The man in question had taught at Eton and coached the athletes. Their housemaster knew him. He said to Jeremiah, "I understand that Wilfrid was your Uncle....a very sardonic man....". Two teachers, having been scholars of that school, had been taught by him. The whole thing had got out of hand. Here he was, in his last year, basking in the reflected glory of a man who, as far as he knew, was no relation whatever. When he returned home he thought it wiser not to ask. It was better not to risk exploding a useful myth. Whether true or false it served a useful purpose for many years, and even enabled him to obtain credit in shops. If he knew it to be true, it would not improve its usefulness. If he learned that it was false, it would be hard to maintain it convincingly.

Chapter Five

Good Order and Military Discipline.

Despite his ineptitude at polishing things and keeping himself, or anything, tidy, Jeremiah enjoyed National Service. As with exams, he got through by the skin of his teeth. He even enjoyed the early days of basic training, after the shock of the first morning. It was enjoyable, when all in authority were 'them', and we were 'we'. It was easier to live, when 'they' gave the orders and 'we' are not paid to think, but do as you are told, which is more or less what the great believers in 'discipline' trot out. Even in the army, those who say this tend to retract it immediately. Even Lance Corporals and Corporals would find it hard to deal with those who only did as they were told.

One could use the demand for 'discipline' to mess 'them' about, within limits. The great thing was that there was no moral 'ought' or 'should' involved. If you could get away with anything, you did; no matter what problems it caused for those higher up. 'We' were there to cause 'them' as many problems as possible. The wonderful thing about obeying orders to the letter is that it passes responsibility ever upwards. Those at the top must be as gods.

The rule was, "Obey the last order given, then it cannot be *your fault"*. Of course it could, and everyone knew that, so it was unwise to push it too far, especially if one wanted a commission, or a stripe. Even better, in a world of 'discipline', is to "go two miles when told to go one". Believers in 'discipline' forget that those, who only do what they are told, have all day to think up ways of circumventing the rules, or, better, turning them back on the rule makers.

Two years national service taught Jeremiah what anyone, who learned of Jesus in the gospels, would understand about 'discipline'. Like it or not, it is a way of teaching. One learns *from* it. It is obvious if one thinks of Jesus' disciples. They submit to the master's instructions, in order to learn from him and gain understanding. Nobody could be more clear; "Take my yoke upon you and learn of me". Crucial, then, becomes, 'Who is the master and what does one learn by submission to his instructions?' Jesus is equally clear, when he sends the disciples out and calls them apostles, which, being interpreted, means representatives. As such, they do not teach their own 'ideas' or word but, as ambassadors, represent the word and words of their master. The odd thing is that while many, even if occasionally, go to public services and declare themselves to be his disciples, he is the last man on earth they learn from. Many would learn more from tales about rats and moles taking picnics, ridiculous legends like Oedipus, or even Mein Kampf or the Prince, than anything said by Jesus.

That this should be is hardly surprising, since Ministers of religion from the Pope and the Archbishops, Moderators of Assemblies, the General of the

Salvation Army to the newest ordained curate, seem to know better, both how and what to pray, than did Jesus. When the Pope went to Gdansk, he knelt in prayer, at the spot where the priest had been killed. A vast crowd looked on, a yet bigger one on television. There was this holy man in his white cassock kneeling in prayer, unashamedly, before all. What a fine example! His sincerity was there for all to see. He was sincerely of the opinion that Jesus was wrong to have said, "When you pray do not stand on street corners or in meeting houses to be seen by men, as the hypocrites". With this, members of the Salvation Army and, less obviously, those of other denominations are in accord. It is hard to argue, in this case, that the evangelists are reporting words of Jesus, modified to suit the needs of the early community. If the Pauline epistles be a guide, they were urged to meet together for prayer.

If the commanding officer gave a standing order that, whenever anyone might pray, they should go into their inner room and pray in secret, it would be seen as conduct contrary to "good order and military discipline" to do otherwise. That there might seem to be good reasons for standing and praying on a street corner, or in a meeting house, would count for nothing.

Without national service he would probably not have seen the simple, clear, logic of the Centurion's belief and perception. In theory, the chain of command is essential to the military. An 'acting unpaid' lance corporal, under the authority of his superior, passes on orders with his authority and power. Since the sequence extends to the Commander in Chief, it is with his power that such orders are given. The centurion applies this to Jesus. If he speaks *under* the authority of God, he commands with the power of God.

Some conscripts were allowed to go to university before doing conscription. Among the recruits, were a few sharp-witted young graduates. They seemed especially to resent being obliged to perform military service. The forum where such resentment could find expression was "Padres hour". It took place in the Camp Cinema once a week. He saw, for the first time, how a clergyman could be run round the houses on the basis of the sayings of Jesus in the Gospels. Since the Chaplain was given the rank of major, care had to be exercised. The deferential, innocent-seeming question, seeking information, could be devastating. The answer may have satisfied the questioner, who said, "Thank you very much". It may not have satisfied others who were present.

Military discipline taught more invaluable lessons. It taught one how to shew respect without having any. It taught one to recognise a 'good scive', when one saw one. That was an utterly fatuous, but amenable, occupation, which enabled one to avoid doing anything purposeful. It taught one how to prolong pleasant tasks for a whole day, and, if possible, involve ten people in doing them, when a single able-bodied man could have completed them in an hour. It taught one the inestimable value of always looking purposefully busy when one was not, and keeping out of sight, if doing nothing.

One learned the benefits of the 'rule of law', for those who did not enter the 'spirit of the law'. It taught wonderful ways of playing the system back on itself and so clogging the administration with as much useless paper as possible. The more such as adjutants could be stuck in their offices reading fatuous letters, memos and the like, the less time would they have to inspect things.

Above all, it taught a glorious amoral vocabulary, especially when it came to theft. Never was anything stolen. It was "won", "acquired", "obtained", or "borrowed". Best of all, one spoke of "relieving" a rightful owner of his property. After completing full time military service, Jeremiah was in the TA. They paraded weekly in a drill-hall, a brick walled building with an iron girder roof. There was a bar, armoury and various offices. The floor was made of wood blocks. The troop sergeant and the corporals decided to have a dance.

"Wherever will you have it?" "In here, Sir". "You cannot have a dance in this place". "That will be fine, It will knock your eyes out, time we've finished. If you and your wife could roast a large turkey, and cook a ham, we'll take care of the rest". "How many do you expect? "We'll have to allow for a couple of hundred, all told".

The drill hall was to be turned into a grotto. "However will you do that?" "Leave it to us".

On the night it knocked your eyes out. Caves lead off the main grotto over the dance floor. There was a cave for the bar, a cave for the band and a tunnel, leading to the cloakrooms. The rough rocky wall hung with creepers, mosses and ferns. There were witches flying on broomsticks and the lighting would have done credit to the Royal Shakespeare Company. They had built an entire building within a building with chicken wire and papier mache. It had all been painted in greys and ochres. There must have been 500 large sized Christmas tree lights. "Whatever did it all cost?" "Not a penny, Sir" "Wherever did you get all the newspaper? " "That wern't newspaper, it was best quality printers' paper, Corporal.... works for ...... the printers. He had a lorry load delivered".

Everything had not only been 'won'; they had it delivered by firms, who had been, 'relieved' of the materials, and even paid them while doing it.

For reasons, too obvious to mention, a similar amoral or neutral vocabulary was used with regard to killing people. It was as if the enemy were not people with families. One destroyed targets, or eliminated obstacles. Even with 25 pounders, targets were well out of sight.

A more serious aspect of 'learning to do what one is told' was made horrifically clear in some interviews on the wireless. The interviewees were former guards in Hitler's camps. They had learned much by obeying orders. They learned, as they said, that if one caricatured men and women as subhuman rats; then disfigured them appropriately, by dressing them in hideously shabby clothes, shaved their heads and starved them, while making them perform grotesquely demeaning tasks, it became relatively easy to herd them into 'showers', knowing that lethal gas would come from the shower heads. They learned that, once one had done this, there was no way of turning back. If one did, one had to admit to oneself the horror of the original action; while, risking the same fate, not just for oneself, but one's family. It might be better if children were to learn of the one whose story brought the word disciple to the English language.

This led Jeremiah, later, to ponder Jesus' words, when he restates the commandment, "Thou shalt not kill". Having said that anyone who is angry with his fellow man (without cause), or anyone who calls his fellow an 'empty head' is liable to judgement, he says that anyone calling his fellow man a MORON, a sub human idiot, will be cast into Gehenna (the vile dump outside Jerusalem). This is more or less what Hitler did in his anti-Jewish propaganda. By caricaturing Jews and other despised people as sewer rats, he and his henchmen could lead men to turn, venomously, on people, with whom they had lived as neighbours. Men, who would not ordinarily have harmed anyone, could be led to demean, injure and kill their fellows.

It was said that, in his anti-Jewish propaganda. Hitler and his supporters drew on some of Luther's more violent words and phrases. The utterance of words of this kind, in this way, can lead to more injury and killing than any serial killer would contemplate. They can be used to arouse passionate hatreds, long after they were uttered and, often, when used, as in the case of Luther, in a context wholly alien from the original one. The Nazis were certainly not the first, nor will they be the last, to use language in this way. To an extent, all who urge others to fight their wars do so. To caricature the enemy as the 'Bosch', 'Huns', or 'Nazis', makes it easier, for otherwise peaceable men, to aim at and shoot them. It makes it easy to forget that they too have wives and families, and probably have little more desire to be fighting than their opponents.

Having been conscripted into the Royal Artillery, Jeremiah scrambled through the selection boards and was sent for Officer Training to the Cadet school at Aldershot, where RSM Ronald Brittan reigned supreme. The first six weeks of training were in infantry warfare. The officers and NCO's were of infantry regiments. They were derisive of gunners. In a moment of impulsive folly, Jeremiah applied to be transferred to the Infantry, and his dad's old Regiment, the 'Norfolks'. The commanding officer of his company was of that regiment. He was pleased that a cadet should want to move to his own regiment.

At this time, Jeremiah received, from his old housemaster, news that shattered him. In his house at school, there had been a lad, whose name was Peter. He was ebullient and without malice. His parents were rich and aristocratic, his mother the daughter of a belted earl. Thy had estates in northern Scotland, owned race-horses, shot grouse, and fished for salmon. His father had commanded a regiment of the Scots Guards, and was a director of nationally famous companies. His elder brother had been to Eton; but Peter had failed the entrance exam. He was no scholar, but was no less intelligent for all that.

Peter had shot himself with his 12 Bore at the Infantry Officer Cadet school, a day or two before the passing out parade. Jeremiah was packing his kit to move up there as the letter came. However could this be? Here was this lad, so full of life; it was beyond imagining that he could be dead. Peter could stand a lot more rough and tumble than he could. That was not the thought that stayed with him for the rest of his days. It was the feeling of certainty that, if he had been with Peter on the fatal evening, he could have said, "Come and have a drink, mate", or some such thing, and Peter might yet be alive.

When he reached Eaton Hall, he learned that, in the weeks after Peter's suicide, two others had done the same. This had led to enquiries into the regime and many had been removed. It seemed that, early in his time there, Peter had been out for the evening in Chester. He had driven back in his sports car, and committed a cardinal sin. He had driven over the 'square'. For this he had been put on 'orders'. Knowing Peter he would not have paraded as a defaulter with remorse, but with cheerful insouciance. If one is involved in such things as exercises, defaulters' parades are tiresome. Defaulters paraded early in the morning in full service and marching order with the guard, and again in the evening when the new guard was posted. Having spent the day crawling about in mud, while everyone else slumped about on their beds, the defaulters had to get their kit cleaned for inspection.

It was bearable for a week or two, but it seemed that Peter was on 'for life'. This could be easily arranged. A defaulter's kit was liable to inspection down to the last needle in his 'housewife'. A fault could result in another week. This had happened to Peter. Before passing out, the cadets were told into which regiment they were being commissioned. Apparently, Peter was told that he was going to the Middlesex regiment, not the Scots Guards. Jeremiah could not make out whether this was done for joke or was truly the case. The last straw, so it was said, was when his girl friend stood him up for the passing out ball. That was the story that circulated.

How could sane men get so worked up about a square of tarmac? When he came on the later Isaiah's mockery of the image-maker, Jeremiah thought of Peter. Isaiah ridiculed the man who cut down a tree and hired a cunning workman, to make him an image. With part thereof he makes himself a god, he fixes it so that it will not blow over in a wind. He says, "Aha, I have god". With the rest, he makes a fire and says, "Aha I am warm"; the latter being the more useful. Exactly the same would apply to flags, ensigns, regimental colours, and the crucifix from which the lady had chipped bits of wood, to improve the Lord's nose. What of the rest of the material from which a sacred ensign, which men salute, is made? "With the rest of it he makes a dwile and says, Aha my floor is clean". What of the rest of the tarmac from which the sacred square was made?

How ridiculous this kind of thing was, the later Isaiah saw. On the other hand, could any society or culture do without these totems and symbols? *One* could and did. Ministers of the Gospel blessed this bric a brac. In Sheringham they held a service to 'dedicate' some iron railings round a war memorial. That would not stop the dogs cocking their legs against them. Stray dogs had better understanding of the words of the prophets, than those who stood and declared that they believed in the Holy Ghost, 'who spake by the prophets'. "The ox knows its master's manger, the ass its owner's crib, but my people doth not.........". The Christian religion would be better without crosses, crucifixes and fishy symbols, if it sought truth. Those driving around with fishy symbols on their cars seem to forget that Jesus said, "Let your light shine before men in such a way as they may see your good works and glorify your Father in heaven". Putting a fishy symbol on a car is hardly a good work. Even such famed examples of the image-maker's art as the Pieta are deceits. The grieving mother looks younger than her dead son. It may shew tenderness and sorrow, but in a romanticised way. If crucifixion by nailing were shewn, as truly it was, few could bring themselves to look on it.

A story came back about a lad, a month ahead of him, also in the Norfolks, with whom he had been at school when nine years old. He had been commissioned, gone to the Depot at Norwich, whence he was flown to Tokyo. Thence he was flown out to join the battalion in Korea. He arrived when they were resting in the rear. Later they moved up into the line. The lad was sent out on patrol at night. Unable to disentangle himself from a mosquito net, when the patrol was surprised, he was killed with a bayonet. The awful reality of infantry warfare dawned on Jeremiah. He would lie awake imagining himself in that position.

He got through the training at Eaton Hall, passing out as a newly commissioned officer in the Royal Norfolk regiment. The parade was taken by HRH the Princess Margaret. It involved a lot of bull. It was on the Polo Ground. It poured with rain, but all passed off without incident. On one of the final practices RSM Leonard Lord had said, "If you lot don't improve, her Royal Highness will say to me, 'Regimental Sergeant Major Lord, you ain't doing your job', and I'll hang my head in shame....". His rich Aunt came to see her nephew passed out by her Royal Highness.

It did not take long to replace the blue and red Artillery flashes with the more distinctive yellow and black ROYAL NORFOLK. The Norfolks also wore brass pips, not cloth ones like any 'ordinary' regiment. He had a week's leave, so went home to his parents, who now kept a pub, half way down the high street at Burford.

He was not good enough to join the battalion. On his cousin's advice he had applied to be seconded to the Mauritian Guard. He did not join that, but was sent out to what was then the Gold Coast. That had the advantage of trebling one's pay and more. One was paid 'local overseas allowance' and 'inducement pay', otherwise known as 'danger money'. What danger there was, was hard to know; but if the War Office felt inclined to double one's pay, there were few complaints. The greatest danger was cheap whisky. Some of the field officers were ex Indian Army, and they could get rid of a distillery in an evening. Once again, Jeremiah put on an act, and scraped through without disaster. He had learned what was a good scive, so was appointed cinema officer and sailing officer, the regiment being on the coast at Takoradi.

He was befriended by a regular soldier and his wife, an officer in the Engineers, called Arnett. His wife was Elisabeth. They had a son and a daughter. Later they had another daughter called Penelope. Jeremiah became her godfather. They were to be loyal friends to him through thick and thin, especially when he needed friends. Another friend he made was not in the army. He was secretary to the newly formed independent cabinet headed by Kwame Nkrumah. On arrival at Accra, it was customary for those in the services to sign the Governor's book, putting the name of their parent regiment. George Levack came from Norwich and knew his mother long ago. Seeing the Royal Norfolk regiment, he wrote to Jeremiah, and asked him if he would like to come and stay in Accra, if he could get any leave.

His other friend was a West Indian lawyer with a radiant smile, called Probyn Marsh. When Probyn learned that he was going to Cambridge to read theology, he said, "You will meet the greatest Englishman alive, his name is Henry Hart". When Jeremiah returned to England, Probyn was attached to the West Indian High commission, and was very kind to him when he was in London, but then went back to his beloved Jamaica.

There was a general Inspection. All had to wear their medals. At the time, owing to a mutiny, Jeremiah was commanding his company. He should have checked all medals. It would have been a waste of time if he did. The Company Sergeant Major was called Amadu Wongara. He came from Togoland, and had many medals. Unfortunately the Brigadier did recognise medals and noticed that, in proud position at the end of the row of medals, was an Iron Cross second-class. When he taxed Amadu with this, he smiled broadly and said, "I fight for them before I fight for you, Sir!"

Chapter Six

Bewilderment.

Jeremiah got into Cambridge to read theology. There were some ten others in his College reading the subject. He had high hopes that the problem of finding a seamless union between the Christian religion, particularly as found in the C of E, and the awful impression of truth, left on his infantile brain, would now be solved. It had to be 'God proof'. A great university like this must know everything. There were 'Regius Professors'. It won the boat race. Even God must recognise its authority. If enjoying life in a riverside parish was not an extension of the Gospel of S John, it would not be his fault. It must be in such places, that people acquired their certainty about what God liked and disliked.

For all that his family had been in the pantomime business for generations, he had played little part in it. He had read one gospel. He had looked at the others in bits. Aside from tales like that of David and Goliath he had not opened the Old Testament; but had been to chapel every evening and had been a server at school. He had never been to Sunday school, nor taken part in any church activity. The others had. Most had been Sunday school teachers. He had not a word of Greek or Hebrew. The epistles he had never opened. He had heard them read as lessons, but found them complicated, beyond his understanding and unconvincing. People spoke enthusiastically of being justified by faith. It seemed a somewhat dubious bridge between what Jesus was reported as saying, and the kind of life he sought.

It did not make any sense to him, any more than did being saved by the blood of Christ. Like many things, it seemed to carry conviction if people were singing about it. He also felt unsure about all that people made of the resurrection. It was not that he doubted that the tomb was empty. It seemed a crazy story to make up. It finally vindicated Jesus. Rather, it shewed that God vindicated him. It seemed obvious at that level, so why complicate it? One needed it to be complicated, if one did not one came up against rich young men being told to sell all, narrow gates and ways, and fearful, exclusive, words, like those in the gospel he had read as a child. Appearances of someone, after death, do not demonstrate 'eternal life'; they demonstrate an appearance.

There was another difficulty, his dysfunctional ineptitude. People would speak of having faith, prescribing all manner of means, by which one might increase it. They were like gymnastic training, involving 'spiritual exercises', not physical ones. Both were beyond him. It was not 'a yoke that was easy or a burden that was light'. He was not sure what a soul was, but they did not seem to provide rest for anything. Jesus did not prescribe such exercises, but said, "If you have faith as a grain of mustard seed, it will grow".

There was problem with the entire vocabulary of words like 'faith'. People spoke of having faith, even having great faith, almost as if it were the psychological equivalent of having strong arms. Would 'great faith' in anything count? It seemed like saying that, if one believed anything strongly enough, it would work out all right. That would apply to such as Hitler, Stalin or Alexander the Great. Faith had to be distinguished from belief. If one used the word 'belief', it begged a question that the word 'faith' did not. One could have 'faith', without specifying in what. Those, who propounded the Christian 'faith', seemed to speak in this way. Jesus did not. It was like distinguishing between being childish and childlike, which, again, he did not.

In studying 'theology', one exchanged ritualistic complexity and mystery for that of a more 'intellectual' kind. Both were satisfactory in keeping stories like that of the Rich Young man at arm's length. More accurately, perhaps, one was enabled to keep the one, who spoke to the Rich young man, at a distance. It was as if one wandered about Galilee, when he was alive, looking for Jesus, but never finding the place where he was teaching. 'We have looked for him in all sorts of places but never found him, so we've done our best'. Many rabbis seemed to say things very close to what Jesus is reported to have said, so 'we might as well continue with them'. Jeremiah had an uneasy awareness that this failure was not altogether accidental. He was expert in not finding people, who involved him in doing things he did not want to do.

This was probably the first time in the history of England, when anyone could have ready access to all that Jesus is known to have said. The Gospels were available in a form that made them available to almost all. Penguin Books had issued a new translation of the Four Gospels by the General Editor of their 'Classics'. It was probable that, for anyone living in England today, who could afford five shillings and could read, there was more ready recall of all that Jesus taught, than would be available to the disciples after his death.

The trouble with Cambridge was that one could not only sit behind books and daydream about what one might do; one could take steps to do it. One could have girls up for weekends and go to dances. One could go to cinemas, and prop up bars. One could sit around, drinking coffee; one need not go to lectures. One could spend afternoons going backwards down the river. Once you started that, it was hard to stop.

'The Director of studies' was a craggily handsome man with iron-grey hair, black eyebrows and a limp. He was a clergyman, but had fought at Galipoli, where he had been badly wounded in one leg and won the MC. His first remark about the degree course in Theology was; "The Theology Tripos is specifically designed that men may row". He spoke with frequent sighs of exasperation. He was clearly a man not to be trifled with. He did not supervise those reading the 'honours degree', in their first year. They went to a younger and much less fierce man, who was chaplain.

Fortunately, it was the other way round, when it came to learning Hebrew. Some fifty students assembled in a lecture room. They were evenly divided on either side of a central aisle. Jeremiah sat on the back row on the left. Two men walked in. The first was a mild faced, youngish man with spectacles. The second was a smaller man, wearing a square, which he doffed to all, revealing cropped dark hair. He took charge, saying that it would be simplest to split the students down the middle. He would take those on the right. Jeremiah was relieved. The younger man looked a soft touch. His relief was short lived. The older of the two came prowling down the aisle and stood over him. He pretended not to be there, and wondered what he had done to attract this unwanted attention.

The man who stood over him said; "move across to my side young man, if you would be so kind." He said to his colleague, "We have a son of Belial among us, I fear. I would not wish him on you". It seemed that Jeremiah had laughed somewhat derisively at something that had been said, "You Sir, are a Mocker".

That chance led to his obtaining a degree. Henry Hart did not belong to the school of thought, in which languages could be learned by sleeping with grammars under the pillow, or in cinemas and pubs. He was a wonderful teacher, a man of vast learning; reading, in addition to Latin, Greek and Hebrew, Sanskrit, Arabic, Aramaic and Coptic, as well as being fluent in German and French. He was also one of England's foremost experts on ancient coins. He was prepared to devote vast amounts of time and energy to teaching bears of very little brain elementary Hebrew. He promised that, if any continued with Hebrew after the first year, he would give them a tutorial every week. The fee was the hire of a punt for an afternoon at the end of the summer term. As he then bought all occupants of the punt tea at Grantchester, it was a nett loss. .

His teaching was methodical. Every word in a Hebrew book was to be written on the left of the page, behind a ruled margin one and a half inches wide. On the other side of the margin it had to be parsed in detail. After a year, more common words could be omitted. These books, he went through every week. Any mistake was surrounded by red ink. In beautiful Hebrew script, it was written at the end of the page, with the instruction to copy it out correctly 20 times. There were threats of rope's ends, floggings, and much else. It was the one thing Jeremiah learned to any degree of competence in his three years. Mr Hart gave him the confidence that, given a lexicon, grammar and syntax, even if it took a long time, he could translate any bit of Hebrew in the Old Testament. Whenever he set about doing so, he found himself looking for a ruler, and drawing a margin.

The man who taught Greek was of a different kind. He was younger, very clever, and had an acute sense of the ridiculous. He was not as remorseless as Mr Hart, so Jeremiah's Greek was enough to read the gospels, but not much else. He was, however, to have a profound influence. His name was Roland Walls. He was Dean of Corpus.

In his final year the chaplain left. Jeremiah found himself being supervised by the craggy faced man of beetling brow. Mr Blyth did not suffer fools at all gladly.

Still less did he suffer portentous, overblown, nonsense. Jeremiah was the embodiment of both. Mr. Blyth set them an essay on something to do with the prophet Isaiah. Jeremiah went off and read, or tried to read, immensely learned books on Isaiah. These he read, as at school, skimming the pages, while thinking of other things, hoping that his eye might fall on something that would provide 'the answer'. He put an impressive bibliography at the end. It did not impress Mr Blyth, who sighed and groaned as he produced the sheaf of paper. "If I set you an essay on the prophet Isaiah, I expect you to read the book of Isaiah, not a lot of books that you don't understand about the book of Isaiah. Nobody could understand them without first reading the book". He did not stop there. "I would have thought that it might have dawned on you, by now, that people have read and pondered the book of Isaiah for over 2,000 years, and will do so for the next thousand years. If the books you read are even opened in fifty years their authors may think themselves lucky".

He was not sure what happened to the offending essay. He had a memory that the irascible Vice Master ripped it up and flushed it down his lavatory, but that may have happened to someone else. He came to wish that he had met Mr Blyth in his first term.

Mr Blyth had a wonderful gift. He spoke of such as Amos as if he had met him on Trumpington Street only an hour before. The way he spoke of these men and their words thrilled Jeremiah. Their terse violence of expression made him tingle with excitement. This was a new world. What must it be to use words like that? The throb of vitality and power in such words, uttered centuries ago, excited him, as nothing else he had ever read. They were even more thrilling in Hebrew, which, as a language, lent itself to such terse, unequivocal expression. He wrote one essay that received Mr Blyth's approval. In it he was asked to set the perspective of the prophet and that of the priest alongside each other. He contrasted 'religion', as embodied in the priesthood, with belief in God, as being the 'logic' of the prophets. The two he argued were irreconcilable. On this occasion he read the words of those he was writing about.

Mr Blyth said that it owed its clarity to being a 'one eyed vision'. It therefore lacked the perspective of stereoscopic vision, so was like that of the prophets. He was too stupid to see it, but Jeremiah had achieved the opposite of what he sought. So far from finding a covered way from the Gospels to the Christian religion, as he knew it, he had opened a leak in the roof. He came to resent the way in which many spoke of the Old Testament, and, indeed, wrote of it. Some would speak of it as 'the word of God', as if it presented a single coherent view. It seemed, rather, to represent the, often violent, conflict of two irreconcilable views. Books which were entitled 'the Old Testament, or biblical, Doctrine of ......', seemed to imply the same.

A committee decided what books were included in the Old Testament. Was God allowed to say only that which the committee approved? It must be something to be a member of that committee.

Another man, whose help, beyond the call of duty, enabled him to end up with a degree, was Charlie Moule, the Lady Margaret Professor. Jeremiah found his lectures, like most others, wholly beyond him. He might have fared better, had he learned Greek properly. Charlie would always quote from the New Testament in Greek. Had he translated it, Jeremiah would still have been bewildered. He could not fathom the business of devising doctrines of this and that from scattered texts. It was like solving crosswords. When it came to the classic doctrines of redemption, salvation and so on, they seemed convincing as long as one was listening, (and liked or respected whoever was talking), had one's nose in a book, or was involved in argument. As soon as one was not, "What on earth is it all about"? It was wholly otherwise with the sayings attributed to Jesus, or, for that matter, the words of such as Elijah. They seemed to endure forever. One did not need endlessly to repeat, "If a man strike thee on one cheek, turn to him the other also", for it to have meaning. It was all too obvious what it meant.

He knew that one had to make a pretence of understanding these things to get marks, and avoid the awful clarity of the sayings of Jesus. He could not even make a convincing pretence. Professors were available for questions on two evenings each week. Charlie would be in his rooms on Tuesday and Thursday evenings. Professors were such as one passed with eyes cast down. To knock at their door needed courage. Things were desperate, so he made his way to Clare College and knocked. A friendly voice said, "Come in". There was Professor Moule, sitting in front of his fire with a very learned student on the sofa. His name was Hugo and he talked like a Professor. He was talking enthusiastically about the use of the 'optative'. Jeremiah wished he had never come.

Charlie said, "I hope this does not bore you" "Oh no, its fascinating", lied Jeremiah, who would not have known an optative if he fell over one. "Would you like to ask your question?" "It can wait, please don't let me disturb you....". He did not mind making a fool of himself in front of real professor; that could be taken for granted. He was not going to do so, in front of a fellow student who talked like a professor.

In the end Hugo and his optatives left. "I am sorry you have had to wait so long. What did you want to ask?" When Jeremiah confessed to being completely baffled, Professor Moule did not disdain him for his stupidity, but felt guilty, for not making himself clear in his lectures. "Do you think that there are many who find themselves baffled? If there are and if you would like to gather some together; nobody ever comes on Tuesdays, we could have a seminar".

Jeremiah found three or four, and they assembled at the appointed time. Charlie was as good as his word and better. There were cups of tea and coffee, biscuits, even a packet of Senior Service cigarettes. It was decided that, each week, one of the group would prepare a paper and talk about some topic for ten or fifteen minutes, when it would be discussed and analysed. Had Charlie not done this, it may well have been that more than Jeremiah might have left with no degree. Many years later, Charlie told him that 'his seminar' had continued, and that it had become a post-graduate group. Books had been published as a result.

Before returning to Roland Walls, there was another who greatly helped him get enough marks. He did so by the limpid clarity of his lectures and the amazing coherence of their structure. One needed no notes to recall them, everything followed from what went before with such cohesion. His name was Owen Chadwick.

Jeremiah became friendly with Roland. He was effervescent. Roland had said that Mr Bezzant, the Dean of Trinity, was giving a public lecture on the following Sunday. "It should be worth going to". It would be worth going to, not for the lecture, but the likely fireworks it would provoke. Mr Bezzant lectured on the textual criticism of the New Testament. He took very radical views, such as shocked the more fundamentalist students. They would be hunting him like a pack of hounds. Jeremiah said that he thought he would go. He set out to do so; but turned aside to quench a raging thirst. Emerging from the pub he met Roland on his way back from the lecture. He was full of it.

An indignant student had asked, "Tell us, once and for all Mr Bezzant, do you or do you not believe that the tomb was empty as the gospels relate?" Roland described the silence, as the question was asked in a very hostile tone. Mr B, standing on a podium with a reading desk and light in front of him, was taken aback at the hostility of the questioner. He had the habit of blinking and pushing his spectacles up his nose. He said; "All I can tell you is that I would sooner be found on the side of Jesus of Nazareth, crucified, dead and buried, than on that of any man who has ever lived or ever will. Does that satisfy you?"

Roland said, "Nobody durst ask him any more questions". Everyone turned for the door.

Often, Roland would relate this story. If Jeremiah happened to be there, he would say, "Jeremiah *was there* ". He was not. He was in the pub. He would vary the ending from time to time. Sometimes he would say, “crucified dead and buried, full stop". On other occasions he would add, "and not raised from the dead", or "with no resurrection", and so on. Sometimes he would add nothing. It would depend upon whether he felt that his audience had got the point. Jeremiah asked him what was the original version. Roland said once that he could not be sure. Jeremiah felt that *he* could be sure, that the version that Roland had given him, ten minutes after the talk, was the accurate one.

Because Roland, so often, called on him for confirmation, he came to believe that he really was there. He lived in this delusion for twenty years. He could picture the scene, himself standing by the exit. The exit did not give directly onto the street, but had a vestibule, entered by a heavy oak door with a glass panel. The glass was in small, leaded panes, with a purple, yellow and green border. The door had large brass handles, on one of which his hand rested, as he wanted to be away. For some reason, the scene returned to him as he lay awake one night. What puzzled him was, 'where in Cambridge was this hall?' He 'ran round the streets', in his imagination, trying to think of every lecture room, Church hall or, even Church which he had entered. He could not place it. "Of course I cannot place it. I never went to the lecture!"

The incident led him to understand much of the ways of oral transmission, and the value of second hand witness. It told him something else about the gospel tradition. There are only two collections of Jesus' public, direct, general teaching. The most famous is 'Matthew's' Sermon on the Mount. Jesus is described as teaching the crowd many times, and, no doubt, did so more often than they report. If one considers the 'Matthean' Sermon, it is complete. One needs nothing more. It is wholly coherent as the expression of a single underlying word. Perceive that word and you could elicit a hundred variations of sayings like, "if a man would make you go one mile..." or, "If a man sues you for your coat give to him your cloak as well". It appears that Jesus did this. The 'Lucan' form envisages a thief snatching a cloak, and being given a coat as well. Moreover, Jesus implies that this teaching constitutes a complete 'package'. "If a man hears these sayings of mine and does them, he is like a man who builds his house on rock...."

It is likely that Jesus would use much the same examples whenever he taught, varying them slightly. He would, no doubt, do as Roland, adding to sayings to clarify. Given the repetition of substance, there would be little difficulty, for those continually with him, to recall his sayings, if in somewhat varied form. Particularly would this be the case, if, having spoken to the crowd, he further illustrated what he had said when with his disciples.

Jeremiah also learned, from this and other incidents, that, if one knows anyone over a period, and perceives their 'word' or 'conversation', one knows what they would say. As significantly, perhaps, one knows what they would not. This applied to Mr Bezzant. He tended to leave much to inference. He would not have added to the words that Roland first reported. He said, "We cannot know that the Rich Young Man did not go and sell all, and return to follow Jesus. If you were a millionaire and had kept the commandments from your youth up, you would go away sorrowful, if you had to sell everything and were determined to do so". He did not go on to say that the young man did go and sell all that he had. Mr Bezzant may not have believed that the tomb was empty, but he seemed prepared to learn a great deal more from Jesus, as reported in the gospels, than most that do, or say that they do.

Chapter Seven

"Eton, Magdelene, Brigade of Guards...R. C. Walls ....Ruin"

Roland had been educated at Kelham, when Herbert Kelly was alive. Brilliantly clever, he had gone to Cambridge, and was elected to a fellowship at Corpus. Why did he spell ruin? He would refer people back, not to the doctrines of the Christian religion, but the four gospels; "The Lord did not go around ordaining priests, he called disciples. Anyone might think that, when the Lord said, On this rock I will build my Church, he had the C of E in mind".

As a bachelor, the life of a fellow was perfect. He had a pleasant suite of rooms, and three excellent meals every day; but had an inability to say, 'No', to proposals for improving the work of the Church; so was easily drawn into grandiose schemes, hatched by others, who would remain secure in elegant comfort, while it would mean a savage cut in salary and benefits for Roland. If the scheme failed to deliver what was hoped for, Roland could be left to sink. Such is the language of the Christian religion, though it would be expressed in other words. It is not the language of the gospel. Jesus said, "Take me and let these go their way".

Certain ambitious clergymen decided that it was time to set up a more 'relevant' means of training for the 'Sacred Ministry'. It should be relevant to the latter part of the twentieth century, recognise that England was an industrial nation and that most lived in towns. Before going to their theological colleges, particularly one in Cambridge, they would spend a year in industry, studying, under the guidance of a suitably qualified tutor. Who better could there be than the Dean of Corpus? Being a bachelor and half monk, he could be expected to forsake full board and lodging, the congenial companionship of fellow academics, and his prospects. He could drop his income by more than half, accept a Canonry in Sheffield, feed himself and pay a housekeeper.

'*We*' realise that the gospel demands sacrifices, especially when another has to make them. One of those who set up the scheme sent a note to Roland, referring him to a line from Ps 93; "The waves of the Sea are mighty and rage horribly, but thou Lord that dwelleth on High art mightier". No doubt it was sincere. Such sincerity comes easily, when one is on dry land, a hundred miles from the nearest wave, while the other at sea in a coracle. No doubt, many said, "of course, I would have been happy to undertake such position, but I have a wife, children and higher responsibilities". As far as is known, none said that he had bought five yoke of oxen. Doubtless, much was said of 'talents', forgetting that they are sums of money in the *parable*.

So it was that R C Walls departed from his green pastures and became the Residentiary Canon of Sheffield Cathedral. He had a Canonry, a housekeeper, and some students. He suggested that Jeremiah should come. For some time he had had a regular girl friend, she wanted to come as well, but this was turned down. It was as well, as a few months later she had had enough of his ways. He was due to go to a College near Oxford, which had no part in setting up the scheme. They agreed to delay his entry.

Participants had to find work and lodgings for six months, saving enough to provide for six months in the canonry, where they would study. Work was found through the 'Industrial Mission'. Jeremiah chose private enterprise. A friend of a friend was managing director of a famous stainless steel company; but the job he had arranged was vetoed by the man in charge of the mission. Steel was entering a recession. Jeremiah was unemployed; but found work as a ward orderly in a paraplegic hospital outside the city. This provided board and lodging, but, as the pay was £2 per week, his contribution to party funds was negligible.

After six months all gathered at the Canonry. It was like being at university. Roland set essays each week. Each afternoon there was a seminar. It was based on the text of the gospels. This was to be the core of the course. Roland said; "We will see where the shoe pinches. If there is to be a 'sacred ministry', this must be its foundation". For Jeremiah the shoe was not even the shape of a foot. Almost everything, he came later to think, derived from those seminars. He noticed a sudden change in his ability to produce essays. Instead of the usual D's and C's he began to get A's. One was so highly thought of, that it was put in the common room with a note saying that all should read it. Why this should be he did not know. As there were no exams to pass or marks needed, he did not have to try and produce the 'acceptable answer'. He did not need to rush off to books that, he thought, would guide him to it.

Most important, he simply read the books he was asked to write about. He found, on the shelves of the City Library, almost every translated work of Soren Kierkegaard. These he read in totality. He also read several books by Dostoevsky, but not Karamazov. They had some extraordinary visiting lecturers. One was a man of great academic gifts, who had buried himself in a down-town Sheffield parish, called Alan Ecclestone, who was also the chairman of the local communist party. Jeremiah thought the world of him. The central core of the course, being the study of the gospels, was the crux. It may have been this that enabled him to write clearly for the first time in his life. He had a single vantage point from which to see everything.

The year ended, they spent a week on Iona, went home, and thence to their several theological Colleges. There was much meditating to be done in chapel. It was beyond him. He could only look as if he was doing so. Here, he caught up with many he had known as undergraduates. It shocked him. What had become of the searing words of Elijah, the earth shattering words of Jesus himself? It was as if these transcendent words were a youthful frolic. The real business was what setting to use for the psalms, whether the Eucharist should be the main service on Sunday. Should one sing Kyrie eleison or Lord have Mercy? It struck him as bathos. He went to see the Principal.

The Principal was a remarkable man, quiet and reserved. He said that, if, after his experience in Sheffeld, Jeremiah had continued and become a country clergyman, it would have been deceitful. He still felt that there had to be a sure way from the gospel to the Christian religion; just that he could not find it. His very clever cousin lived nearby. They used to go sailing together.

He had written to the girl friend that had cast him aside. She wrote back immediately. Perhaps they could resume their friendship. He would write back and suggest that they met. His cousin said that he was going up to London on the following Saturday to watch Fulham play football. They drove to London to find that they were playing away. Instead they went to an exhibition of racing dinghies. As they drove in, there were two young women. They asked directions to the car park and toured the show together. The smaller of the two was quiet. Jeremiah thought, "That is whom I want to marry". They were invited back to her flat for coffee. He did not even know her name. In the van, he found a pair of gloves, a name-tag was inside. All thought of his former girl friend vanished. He wrote, explaining that he had her gloves.

He now had to find employment. First he went up to Sheffield to see Roland. "Oh my God, Jeremiah, what have you gone and been and done!" Others had had some trouble on returning to their colleges, but none had left. The Colleges expected a magical solution to all problems, involving a few painless adjustments to the accepted ways; perhaps a slightly modified translation of a psalm or two, and some new tunes. If a different position were adopted by the priest, when celebrating the Lord's Supper, the kingdom of God would be at hand. It did not turn out that way. They received from Sheffield argumentative, truculent students, who, before, had not been so. The scheme was allowed to die. Roland was left to get on with his canonry, until a new Bishop was 'elected'. 'When a Pharaoh arose that knew not Joseph', he found himself out of work. Meanwhile, those who had devised the scheme went from strength to strength. Two ascended to the 'purple', one a very deep shade of purple. While he took his seat in the Upper House, Roland found shelter in a run down community Library, made of corrugated iron..

Chapter Eight

Go get thee a wife beloved of her friend..................."

Jeremiah found work as a supply teacher and fell on his feet. He was sent for a term to a boarding school run by the L.C.C near Ipswich, as an assistant housemaster. On his day off he went up to London to spend the evening with the girl he had met at the boat exhibition. Sometimes she came up for the weekend. Sometime before, he had been invited to go to her home for a weekend. She lived near Plymouth. I will call her Hannah. They were collected at Exeter.

They were met, not by her father or mother, but a young man of his own age. When they reached her parents' home, her father took him to the pub. There was some hard talking between Hannah and the young man. The following day, they went to the wedding of one of his fellow students at Sheffield. The next day they returned to London. He had bought tickets to see the Nutcracker, never having seen a ballet before in his life. On the way back he said, "I expect you would prefer that I dropped out, and won't want to go to the ballet next week". She said. "No". She did not want that and wanted to go to the Festival Hall. This was what he hoped she would say. He liked making generous offers, which were refused. One got the credit, with none of the cost.

He was coming to see a different basis for trust. Unless there was a shared 'conversation' or language, how could there be any basis for trust? For this, there had to be recognised points of reference. The only final ones seemed to be the sayings of Jesus. If someone either clearly rejected them, or saw them as unequivocally final, one knew where one was. What seemed impossible, as a basis of trust, was a conversation, which said, "Yes", but then equivocated. Nobody, in Jesus own words, seemed to let their 'conversation' be either "Yes, Yes" or "No, No". Even those who said "No", often veered away from it.

Those who rejected belief in Jesus, had many, often unspecified, 'reference points', which were needed to endow their language with dependability or truth. Without these it tended to fragment, as, usually, did the points of reference. Was it possible to prevent others directing one's life, without directing others? It was obvious that, when it came to the exercise of physical force, one could not prevent its use. What he hated was 'moral' authority, which told him what he ought or should do, without its basis and points of reference being clearly declared.

He had little ambition. The ideal life would be something like that of A C Blyth; but he had not the brains. He would love to hand back essays as he did, with his painstaking reading and analysis. A colleague later said of him, "in truth you have overweening ambition. Nothing that would ordinarily satisfy most men is enough for you. You would not think it worth being a composer if you could not excel Mozart!"

George Levack had visited him, while he was at Cambridge. Walking down Queen's Lane, George noticed a poster, advertising a lecture by R W Southern, about Anselm. Southern had been his tutor at Balliol. "He won't set the Thames on fire", he said, "but he is a fine scholar and knows Anselm like a friend". Jeremiah had heard of Anselm. One remark of Southern's he never forgot. To the end of his days, Anselm suffered a feeling of unfulfilled ambition. How could this be? He had been Abbot of Bec and Archbishop of Canterbury. He had confronted the king himself and been exiled. The king had been forced to abase himself and beg him to return.

After his spell at the boarding school, he found himself in vastly different surroundings, in a secondary modern school behind Kings Cross Station. He found lodgings near the Archway, not far from Pentonville Prison. His landladies were two salvationists. The one who opened the door weighed eighteen stone. Seeing his surprise, she said merrily, "Dont worry lad, there is an even bigger one indoors". These happy ladies had an aggregate weight of 40 stone. He had a bicycle, as it was the easiest way to get about London. They advised him to bring it inside. He asked for a key, as most evenings he was out with Hannah. "Key", exclaimed the couple, "whatever do you want a key for?" Did you not see what was hanging over the door?" Over the door was a seaside bucket. On it was an old 'economy label' with WELCOME written on it. "That door is never locked", they said. "Welcome means welcome. It is not much of a place, but anyone is welcome to come through that door". One of them said, "Can you imagine the Lord Jesus locking his door to anybody?" He could not, but the Lord Jesus did not live a hundred yards from a notorious prison. The other chipped in, "whoever comes to me I will in no wise cast out."

Extraordinary folk came in at that door, many were given beds for a night or two. All had enormous breakfasts. Many a time, senior police officers with braid on their caps would arrive, begging them to lock their door and not allow such people in. Their words fell on deaf ears.

Jeremiah's attempts to teach in a secondary modern school were futile. He was useless, worse than useless. He and Hannah became engaged. The effect was curious, a presentiment of things to come. Attitudes changed. Up to that moment nobody seemed to care what they were doing. Once engaged, it became like a company flotation. All seemed to know what they and he 'ought' or 'should' do and wanted to give him the benefit of their long experience. The premiss, upon which all did so, but never admitted, was that he and Hannah would wish to be as they were.

As far as anything in the gospels went, all bets were now off. It is now time to think carefully about the future. Did the words of the one, all declared to be God from God, cease with marriage? Did he not say something about not being anxious for the morrow? It was seen as silly to argue for such a view. It ended up with, "is it wrong for anyone to take out insurance?" It was not any part of his case to say what was 'wrong'. He feared that, if he spoke as he often felt, he might end up without a wife, so settled on being a licensed court jester, and making interesting 'academic points'.

As the wedding drew near, the sense of being a public flotation became more intense. Wedding presents seemed a means by which others sought to impose a life style. What struck him as bizarre was the wedding itself, not only the service, but all that went with it. It was as if, unless a bride wore something borrowed, the marriage might be less of a marriage. God would not join this man and this woman. If the correct things were done, in the correct place, by a designated person, God had no option but do so. It seemed to go down to the choice of hymns and flowers in the bouquet.

The Vicar called, when two naval officers were sitting with drinks in their hands. He spoke of an ancient tradition, whereby the priest met the bride at the door of the Church, dressed in a white cope. Alas, he had no white cope. One of the officers laughed, "Have you tried Moss Bros? They'll be clothing most people!" The Vicar did not find this funny. Hannah's father bought him one. ."Bloody old scrounger", laughed everyone, but clearly white copes seemed to matter. It was an ancient tradition, or so he said; but so was smallpox.

Jeremiah could imagine himself being impressed with such ancient traditions, if people had talked of them; even more, if he was the one to talk. It looked nice, but, when it was his own wedding, it seemed ridiculous. It would be fine for other people. Was one any more married for a white cope? The Vicar seemed to think so. 'If one did things one should do them properly'. What made it ludicrous was, "those whom God hath joined together.....". Would God be impressed with all this? In the eyes of the Vicar, presumably, 'Yes'. What, then, of those he had married without his white cope? What of those who were married elsewhere, without priests in white copes? Her Majesty was, doubtless, met by an Archbishop wearing a white cope. It would not do to have the Vicar greet the bride in torn jeans. That would be an insult to God.

"You would not appear before the Queen in torn jeans". That was the argument. When it was happening to him, it seemed ludicrous. The argument was incontrovertible, *if the analogy held.* If one was going to assemble in a consecrated building to worship GOD, almost parade before him, it followed that, just as preparing to troop the colour, one had to dress properly. If all that was fitting for the presence of the Queen, how much more, when it was God who was present. In actuality that was not true. No Vicar took anything like the trouble to dress as carefully as a guardsman on the trooping of the colour. On that analogy God was less to be feared than Her Britannic Majesty.

Jeremiah had experienced parading before Her Majesty's younger sister. She hardly looked at anyone, as she wandered down the ranks chatting to the Commandant and the Lord Lieutenant. It was not she who was to be feared, but the entourage that trailed behind her. She seemed to have more 'holy angels' than God. They *were* to be feared. They could put great millstones about one's neck.

That God was going to be present for this parade was sure. The service opened with that declaration, "Dearly beloved, we are gathered together in the sight of God.....". It was more or less what RSM Lord had said before the great parade; though he did not call them "dearly beloved". He did not, of course, mention the sight of God. He was more concerned with the sight of the Princess Margaret. Nonetheless the 'religious' argument, by analogy, could hardly be questioned. (Except on theological grounds!) If people were going to parade before God, they had to dress properly. In one way or another, all religions agreed on that. Was one not in the sight of God all the time? If one were not, God would not be God. If in the 'sight of God' all the time, it makes every religious performance, in dedicated buildings or anywhere else, nonsense; deceitful nonsense. It implies that God is like a human ruler, but less to be feared when it comes to proper dress on parade. Jeremiah had seen surplices flung on by Vicars about to take a service. That would not do for one's first parade as a raw recruit. If all this be true of God, and he is ever present, one would need to go to bed in full dress uniform. It was lucky he had been converted into the genie in the lamp. He could then be kept safely in the lamp, when necessary, which was most of the time.

He could not believe that everyone took it all so seriously, including Hannah. He alone seemed to find it bizarre. What did the marriage service permit that was not permitted before? It only permitted one activity that was hitherto not allowed. They could freely do anything but sleep together, as it was euphemistically known. It took on the appearance of a virgin being made ready for sacrifice. The white cope and white dress went with that. If all this was needed to marry Hannah, so be it. A 'small' wedding would seem more convincing than one with lots of guests and a cope.

Jeremiah had been at school with the Vicar's son. He hardly knew him, but having been at such a school, having studied theology, if it could be called studying, he could be expected to see the importance of these things. That was a trifling matter. What was serious was that he dared not share his sense that all was ridiculous with Hannah. If she shared it, it would mean a rift in understanding with her parents, and everyone else. The same would apply to his family, who seemed equally to be caught up in it all. It was a very solemn occasion. It was Hannah's 'great day'. Such talk struck him as piffle. He said "Yes" unconvincingly, and had a drink. He could see that being married was important, but wedding days were not. It was like Santa coming down chimney, when you had not even got one.

The pantomime reached its nadir when they had a talk from the Vicar. He began, "Now this is not the occasion for theological argument!" He went through the service, stressing the importance of many aspects thereof, and what they signified. He would greet the bride as she entered. No mention was made of the white cope. He seemed to overlook one matter. The service opened "dearly beloved, *we* are gathered together..........to join this man and this woman..........". It ended, "Those whom *God* hath joined together, let no man put asunder". Have not 'we' got ideas above our station, white copes or no white copes, morning suits and ladies finery? Did it mean that, if everyone dressed properly, said and did the right things, and all was in order, God had to 'do his bit' and join this man and this woman? That was polishing the lamp with a vengeance. Whether made explicit or not, as in the Book of Common Prayer; it is implied in every service of that kind, the Holy Communion, Lord's supper, Holy Eucharist, and, especially, the "Mass". What, then, if the right words were not used? Couples could choose which form they wanted. Were Catholics not "coupled by God"? What of Methodists and Baptists? Theological argument had been forbidden. Being forced to keep silence, the thoughts stayed in the mind.

They were riveted into it by the ludicrous fact that, half way through the service the Vicar started reading the wrong bit. Jeremiah hissed at him, "You have got the wrong bit". The Vicar went blithely on. Nobody noticed. If he had turned two pages by mistake and not noticed, he might have started burying them. If it was, as the Vicar said, that all details were greatly significant; had 'God done his bit', if the Vicar lost his place? If he had turned two pages and meandered into the burial service, would he, or any in the congregation, have noticed? It would have been a handy, 'all-inclusive', package deal.

What also struck him was how credible it could all be, if one were the Vicar. One would have to find it so. Because one could say that some article of clothing had been worn for a thousand years, it seemed to make it right and good; just as when commentators point out such things on Royal occasions. Teachers do much the same, when they divert attention from the nonsense of maidens allowing princes to climb up their hair, and moles boating with water rats, by talking about how well the story is written, or some aspect described. Without knowing it, he reached another conclusion. The most radical critique of all things religious derived, not from the assumption that there was no God, but from the assumption that there is. This applied to the reported sayings of Jesus. They were all too credible, if there is truly God.

None of this greatly troubled him at the time. He was marrying the woman he loved and felt sure he would marry, the first time he saw her. One thing, had he been more studious at University, might have disturbed him. Repeatedly, there had dropped into his mind the name Hosea. He dismissed it as nonsense. He had dipped into that book. Mr Blyth would talk of the prophet Hosea, and one word connected with him, the word translated 'lovingkindness'. Lovingkindness suitably translated the Hebrew word 'HeSeDh'. Kindness implied kinship. When Gomer left Hosea he did not behave in a very 'gentlemanly' way. Hosea may have been a thoughtless and difficult husband. Nevertheless, he hedged her way with thorns, fenced her in and stripped her as naked as the day she was born before her lovers...." in order to shew mercy and lovingkindness".

The word implied something other than what we mean by 'love'. It was a dutiful love. Jeremiah could see that Mr Blyth embodied that in his refusal to suffer fools like himself and the nonsense they wrote. In being so searingly contemptuous of it all, he exhibited that of which he spoke. Jeremiah never felt, in any way, hurt by his supervisor's rudeness. He felt a fool in front of his fellow students, but doubtless Mr Blyth had intended that.

Many years later, a friend called Jimmy, whose wife was Joy, whom we will meet later, put his finger on the matter of weddings. It came to pass in those days that their elder daughter was engaged to a young man of deeply religious family. They were not of the Church of England, Rome, Greece or Russia, but of that of God, no less. (It is odd how all carefully avoid being that simply 'of Jesus', who did, after all, speak of founding "my Church"). Speaking to Joy and Jimmy of a forthcoming wedding, which both were attending, the father in law to be, in pious solemnity, of which he was the master, assured them, "God will be present". Jimmy asked, "Has he been invited?" He then asked, less audibly, "More to the point, has he RSVP'd?" Jesus said nothing so silly as the member of the Church of God about weddings. He seemed more concerned that there was plenty to drink at the reception. When their daughter married, it was Jimmy who took a leaf out of Jesus' book.

Chapter Nine.

Keeping warm by the fire.

Jeremiah and Hannah lived in a flat overlooking Hadley Wood. He continued to make a hopeless mess of trying to teach, otherwise all seemed as good as could be. After about a year came the first sign of a cloud in the sky, no bigger than a man's hand. They decided that they could afford to buy a car. They decided to buy a new van, which, in those days, was cheaper. Many did this. They ordered a new minivan. Having done so Hannah wrote to her father and told him of the plan.

His response was swift and decisive. "You are not tradesmen so should not travel in a tradesman's vehicle". Vans commanded low part exchange prices. He would arrange with a friend, a main dealer, to supply, at cost, a mini de luxe saloon. He would make up the difference. They could collect it, when they came for Christmas. Jeremiah did not want this, Hannah said, "Dad is only being helpful, please do not turn down his offer. He will be hurt". Jeremiah still did not want it, but gave in and cancelled the order.

They went down for Christmas. The car was no longer new. Being a novelty everyone had had a go in it. That did not matter very much, but little kids like new toys. He soon got over that, but the long-term effect he could not. It took him to Claudius in Hamlet, who possessed the "effects for which he did the murder", but wanted forgiveness. Jeremiah possessed the effects of having a car with four seats. He would enjoy the benefits of the higher part exchange price it would command. He would feel, and be, indebted to his father in law for every car he possessed. If one is indebted to anybody, one is indebted to his or her 'conversation'. One could not cast aside the 'conversation', while benefiting from its fruits; "If you make the fruits good, make also the tree." Jesus was ruthless in his rationality. His father in law seemed to rub this in, always referring to 'our car'.

It was incidents like this that taught him how central were the clauses, "Forgive us our debts, as we also have forgiven those indebted to us". The only means, by which anyone could know that their debts had been forgiven, was by repaying them in full, or more. How on earth could he free himself from indebtedness to his father in law? He could see why Israel was told to lend to others but to borrow from none. If they were indebted to a 'heathen' power for anything, how could they know that the gods and beliefs of that power had not provided what the 'Lord God' seemed unable to provide? If they repaid the debt in full and more, the indebtedness was transferred, as when they did hard bondage as slaves in Egypt.

He wondered whether it would have been different, had it been his dad who had provided the car? Parents could hardly put their own children into their debt, as children do not volunteer for birth. One was also indebted to those who taught one at school, university and elsewhere. Insofar as one benefited from that teaching, one was indebted to the 'conversation' that it represented, and thus to its gods. Could Jesus have rebutted testing questions, by referring the questioner to 'his own' scriptures, without the teaching of the rabbis in the synagogues and schools? Yet he said "Call no man on earth thy teacher....."; but those, who taught Jesus, rejected him, for 'believing their report'.

His mother was diagnosed as having a terminal cancer. It was a very rare form of the disease. Diagnosed earlier, it would have been curable. His sister was living in what was then North Borneo. She was married and had two children. When her mother was diagnosed by the Norwich heart consultant, as having congenital heart defect, she was beside herself at his stupidity. If she had a serious congenital defect, it would have shewn before she was sixty-five. She took the next plane back to England.

Such air journeys were long and tiring. When she walked into the room where her mother was with the consultant and the local doctor, she was in no mood to suffer fools. Had they taken a history? When she had spent six weeks in a local hospital what tests had they done? When one of them said that they had done all that anyone could, her patience was exhausted. She rounded on them and said, "You are no better than licensed murderers".

When, as a result of his sister's flight home, 'Momma' was taken into hospital again and given the proper tests, they diagnosed argentifiloma; but it had spread to her liver. Jeremiah and Hannah had driven up to visit her in hospital. Nobody knew that there was anything very seriously wrong. It was Sunday. Being a doctor, his sister could ask questions and root around. She returned to her mother's room. "Have they discovered what it is?" "Yes, Ma, they have. You have a very rare cancer. There is nothing that can now be done." "How long have I got?" "Six weeks to six months".

She spoke, as to a patient, in a cool, clinical, voice. Up to that point there had been happy chatter about Newmarket heath in summer. Whatever could anyone say now? In words that he would never forget, his mother resolved the matter. She said simply; "We have received good at the hand of the Lord; shall we not also receive evil? The Lord giveth; the Lord taketh away..........."

It was doubtful if she had ever read the book of Job, but had heard that passage and laid it to heart. Jeremiah suddenly saw a value in such words. They enabled people to articulate thoughts that would otherwise be amorphous. They enabled one to reach an understanding of situations that made other words seem trite banalities. He recalled a footnote in Karl Barth's "Dogmatic", referring to a man named Kohlbrugger. Barth had asked, what he could ever know, however perfectly, which would give more understanding, than the simplest acquaintance with the treachery of Judas, the denials of Peter, or the woman with her cruse of ointment? Was England casting away something of priceless worth, as, led by the Churches, it turned its back on such works as Coverdale's Psalter and the gospels?

Was it denying to its children, for evermore, the possibility of having the kind of disaster, that had unexpectedly overtaken his mother, resolved in a single sentence? For all that, it put the delight of Newmarket Heath in late spring into a different light. His mother would never enjoy it again.

The staff at the school were assembled for important information. It was to be closed. All were assured of their employment. There was a baby on the way, which meant finding different accommodation. He applied for jobs everywhere. One puzzled him. They wanted a lecturer in Divinity at a 'Training College' at Derby. The only time he had seen the term, 'Training College', was on the title page of his mother's cookery book. He could not understand why those learning domestic science, needed a lecturer in Divinity, but if they did, who was he to complain? He wrote off and applied. He then learned that it was a College for training teachers. He was called for interview. The College was expanding rapidly. There were two staff in the department, one was the Deputy Principal, the other, the chaplain. The chaplain was a shortish, rotund, man with greying hair, and pale blue eyes. He spoke with a trace of Gloucestersire. The deputy Principal was more flamboyant. He interviewed Jeremiah.

The other candidates were clergymen. After they left their interviews, two of them said, "I was offered the job". They said the same when interviewed by the governors. Jeremiah thought it hardly worth staying and went to get his coat. One of the others said, "I would stay, if I were you. They have paid for you to come up from London. We have only come about ten miles". He was called back. The Governors wanted to ask him some more questions. The then Chairman said, "There is one important question we feel bound to ask. If we offer you the job, will you take it?"

He felt like saying, "too right I will", but said' "Yes of course", and muttered some inanities. He was quite good at this, but always felt how silly they were, afterwards. He was now on a four-figure income. It was only just four figures, by £6, but who cares? £1006 seems a lot more than £996.

Their first son was born soon afterwards. When Hannah came home, Jeremiah exhibited a trait, which did him no credit. He came home from school and rushed home to see his wife and child. He walked into the room to be confronted by her Aunt. She said, "Get out of this room. Go and have a bath and change your clothes. You have been on a train". It was as if she owned the place. Maternity hospitals had never bothered about anything like that. Jeremiah turned on his heel and walked out, to the pub. He did not drink much, but was furious and upset. Not half as upset as his poor wife.

The College was expanding and taking in many more students, mostly men. It had new buildings on the outskirts of the town, but there had been delays with them, so term would not begin until mid October. That gave time to buy a house, and move in.

On his father in law's advice, he obtained a bank loan rather than a mortgage. Years later, his father in law said, "Why do I not make you an interest free loan?"

It was helpful, but, as with the car, once accepted, Jeremiah was 'possessed of' the effects'. This time it seemed worse. Though many would think him silly, he felt caught all ways, especially when the loan became a gift. If he spent money, he felt that those round his father in law would think, "But for the loan, you would not be able to spend money like that". It was always there. He was fond of his father in law, and enjoyed his company; but if one is indebted to anyone, they inevitably expect their advice to be heeded. It served to enhance his sense of inadequacy.

The car and the subsidised house, with the indebtedness incurred, became crucial. He saw that if one enjoyed the fruits of a tree, one could not but make the tree that bore them good, without living a lie and making all one's words empty. You would not be in a position to act and speak as you do, but for the 'conversation', which provides the means by which you do so. Such indebtedness extends beyond the matter of cash, but is more obviously quantifiable in that form. It would apply to an inheritance. If one inherited a large estate, one inherited the means by which it was acquired. His father in law had become a man of considerable wealth, and influence. Jeremiah must have been insane. He sought ways to free himself from this indebtedness.

He was given a schedule of teaching. One task was to 'go through' the set Gospel with the first year students. It was St Matthew. He set about preparing it. Had he given the same care and attention to studying anything at Cambridge, his whole life might have been different. All was fine, until they reached the Sermon on the Mount and such instructions as, "I say unto you swear by nothing at all....", "Do not resist (him that is) evil", etc. There seemed few acute literary problems with regard to these sayings, so he sought to promote discussion. In order to do so, he put forward the suggestion that they could be taken, even if one allowed for a degree of hyperbole, to mean what they said.

When Jesus said, "......Swear by nothing at all", it was simple, he meant 'Do not swear any kind of oath'. He pointed out that in this case, Jesus explained his prohibition of the use of oaths. It implied control over that, by which the oath was sworn. "Do not swear, even by the hairs of your head, because you cannot make one of them grey or black". If one swore by Almighty God, one implied that God was in one's control.

It provoked a lively discussion. What amazed him was that not one found any reason to think that these sayings should be understood in this simple way. Those in the group, who had 'fundamentalist' views on almost every verse of the Old Testament, the Book of Revelation and all else, did not maintain them with regard to the simple, clear instructions of Jesus himself. One could find devoted 'Christians' who took fundamentalist views about any verse in the Bible. None seemed ever to do so with regard to anything said by Jesus. Nobody seemed to want to stop arguing against his suggestion.

When it ended and he got on his bike and rode home, it was as if a cold hand gripped him. Whatever had he done? What might happen, if a student was persuaded of that view? He had overlooked the fact that every clergyman had to swear an oath, in order to take up an appointment. Witnesses in court did the same, laying their hand on the very book, which contained the prohibition. What about another saying that had arisen: "Whoever divorces his wife, save for the cause of fornication, and marries another, makes her an adulteress"? Suppose that one of those in the lecture adopted that view in a school, or at home?

He would walk happily down the corridor to find a note in his pigeon-hole, summoning him to the Principal. Alongside her would be an outraged parent, an even more outraged Vicar, headmaster and others. He knew what would be said; "Was this not a highly irresponsible suggestion to have made to impressionable young people? Did you not consider the consequences for them, if they took it up and passed it on to children? We took a risk in appointing one so young, when we gave you the job, but thought that you would respond in an adult way. We had high hopes....., but I am afraid we shall have seriously to review your future, unless you make determined efforts to give more thought to what you say".

Saying such things would be seen as immature. He would not have dared to ask the obvious question, "Responsible to whom?" Still less would he have dared to point out that Jesus had said, "Except ye turn again and be as little children.......".

For the first time in his life he found how to pray and mean every word of it, "O Lord, please make everyone forget what I said....". He thought, "What the hell am I praying for?" It was tantamount to praying that the tomb was not empty, wanting Barabbas released, that there was no virgin birth, that every reported miracle was mistaken. He might as well pray "let thy kingdom never come". How on earth could 'even God' erase all that? His whole way of life depended on those words not being taken as the simple truth. His newly acquired four-figure income depended on none of the students 'hearing these sayings and doing them', thanks to him. It was not just his employment, as a lecturer, but his wife and child, home and all else, that was threatened by the words the evangelist attributed to the very man, whom all declared to be "God from God".

How might it be, if a student, thanks to his suggestion, adopted that attitude and got into trouble; meanwhile Jeremiah would be dwelling at ease. He could say, "You misunderstood me. I did not mean you to take me literally. It was only designed to provoke debate. If you had listened to what I said a week or two later, I made it clear that that view could not be maintained". It could hardly have been more hypocritical. This, alone, shews how far such as he were from the teaching of Jesus. The one sustained indictment he made against the accredited upholders of the religion of Judaism was 'hypocrisy'.

Jesus spoke casual to, audiences. The Sermon on the Mount was given as a complete package, "if anyone hears these words of mine and does them, he is like a man that builds his house on rock". Given those closing words, anyone might go home and act on the basis of what he had heard. He said the same half way through, "then shall you be children of your Father which is in heaven....". What more could anyone want? Anyone listening did not need to go back and hear any more. They did not need Jesus, 'in the flesh', only his words.

They would soon be in trouble with their wives and families and the synagogue. Having heard an instruction to 'give ones cloak as well', from one who spoke with authority and had a reputation as a miracle worker on a prodigious scale, one might receive a summons. If someone were to act on that basis, it would not endear him to his wife, her family, or his own. If one ceased attending a synagogue, saying, "the Rabbi from Nazareth said that, whenever I prayed, it should be in total secrecy", it would not endear one to those of the synagogue. All would seek to persuade him that this Rabbi was wrong. "If he is wrong, how it is that he opens the eyes of the blind and cleanses lepers? You don't". That was more or less the argument of the man born blind in the IVth gospel. All that those of synagogue and temple could then say would be, "he casts out demons by Beelzebub...."

Above all, would this apply to the Rich Young Man. He had been given a clear and unequivocal instruction, "Go and sell all that thou hast -- come and follow me". What if he went and did so? Some weeks later, he returned to Jesus, saying, "I have done as you said......."; and Jesus said, "That was a silly thing to have done, I did not mean it literally"; or, "Had you heard me teaching last week, you would have known that I had reason to modify that view. I now realise that we should all be stewards of our wealth.....", as any minister of religion would say. If the rich young man had wanted contrary advice, where would he have gone? Jeremiah knew the answer to that question. To the nearest synagogue!

Immediately he thought of the possibility of Jesus retracting such a saying, the idea became ludicrous. He did the reverse, and hardened them. He said, "Take me and let these go their way".

What must be like to sit and give such instructions to a crowd, none of whom one might ever see again? One had no chance to retract or modify anything. Must not Jesus have felt, as had Jeremiah? Unless he realised what a muddle his words could land anyone in, he must have been obtuse. The evidence did not suggest that. It would be worse, if one was followed by "mighty works such as no man could do, save God be with him".

He went back to the story of the Rich Young Man. He was not sure that it made a lot of difference, if one had riches or trusted in them. If one did not trust in them, one probably would not have them. If one had them, one would, almost inevitably, come to rely on them. He liked the idea of eternal life. All would be well, for all things are possible for God. Eyes of needles could expand to allow one or two camels to pass through. To *one* possibility he was, happily, blind; but if camels could pass through the eyes of needles, all things being possible for God, why give those instructions to the young man?

He would never make any such a suggestion, directly, again. It was fine, if he did so in an academic way, "Of course we might have to leave open the possibility that such saying could be understood in this way, but only such as Kierkegaard and Tolstoy thought so". One could then hide behind others. He was determined that, as soon as the set gospel was changed, he would drop it like a hot potato. Three years later it was. They decided to replace the first gospel with the fourth. That was worse. The department had now two more staff. One was a clergyman. Jeremiah argued that, so deeply spiritual and sacramental was the IVth gospel, a more religious understanding than his was needed. He did not believe a word of it, but the clergyman was keen to deal with it. He had not read it as a child.

Chapter Ten

The Reverend T V Hurdle and the law and the prophets.

Speaking quietly and slowly, Tom did not make an instant impression. Rather than give direct answers, he would refer to places, in which he thought they lay. If, there was chat over the ways of those who rule, Tom would say, "They should read I Samuel VIII". He would seize on words like 'reality', saying, "I would love them to tell me what reality is". When people spoke of myth, he would ask; "Because something is not historical, does it mean that it is not truthful?" When people derided language as mythological, Tom would point out that much language was of that order. If what was 'mythological' was that which was not actual; "Do we not speak of 'sunrise'?"

Tom was a physicist by training, and a respected one. He got a 'first' at Cambridge and specialised in crystallography. He had then taken up theology and was taught by Sir Edwyn Hoskyns, whom he greatly admired.

Spending much of his life in the Ely Diocese, Tom taught science and maths at King's school, Ely. He loved horse racing and cricket. There had been a discussion about a boy, who was seen as backward. Tom questioned this. The boy could calculate probabilities in his head with greater speed and accuracy than any in the maths department. "Whatever makes you think that?" "I have watched him doing it. You come with me to Newmarket races and you will see for yourselves. His father is an on course bookie. The lad works out the odds. You try maintaining a book for a race with fifteen runners and see how you get on, trying to make sure that whichever one wins, you will not be broke. He is going to be a bookie when he leaves school. Why should he have any interest in proving Pythagoras theorem?"

The Christian religion became more convincing if one removed the gospels. Religious beliefs and activities became more convincing, if one left out the objective possibility of there being God. Otherwise, irreverent thoughts entered one's head, like, "Why did God need informing a billion times every day that he was almighty, everliving, most merciful, and all the other things that people told him?" That Kings, Princes and Governors liked being told that they were 'their Majesties', 'Highnesses', and so on, was another matter. They needed this flattery to convince them that they were essentially other than ordinary folk, because they were not. God is essentially different, or is not God.

The Deputy Principal was a pleasant man, greatly interested in sociology and psychology. Seen in subjective terms, religious beliefs and activities fulfilled fundamental human needs. Whether there was indeed God, mattered less than how mankind perceived such a being. Believing in something seemed more important than whether that, in which anyone believed, was truly God. It was 'natural' that mankind should project such a notion and seek ways of appeasing, or otherwise pleasing, the being who was felt to order everything, if only to obtain a secure environment, physically and socially. Religion provided a useful service. There was much talk of the 'religious needs' of children and adults.

The Diocesan Education Officer and others decided to hold a day of enquiry into the religious attitudes of students. Jeremiah hated this kind of enquiry. Crucial was not what people thought of God, but, objectively, what the word God meant and whether such a being existed. If everyone conceived God as a garden gnome in the sky, and God was not, but was what the word implied, they would have made a bad mistake. Those who knew about concepts of God, argued that we were achieving ever higher and more mature ones. It was not much use being God if nobody believed it. It was as if God needed a democratic mandate to be God.

After chapel on Sunday, Jeremiah told Tom of his misgivings. Tom agreed. Jeremiah said that he was going to refuse to take part. On Monday there was a meeting of the department to make arrangements for the day of enquiry. Jeremiah said that he would not take part. The Deputy Principal, an understanding man, said that, if he had conscientious scruples, he respected them. Tom said that he thought that the enquiry might be useful.

As he went through the corridor to lunch he saw a note in his pigeon-hole. It said, "See Ps.41:9. Sorry, Tom". He went back to his room, pulled down the Old Testament and read: "Even mine own familiar friend whom I trusted, with whom I ate bread, hath lifted up his heel against me".

His opinion of his friend soared. He knew that he would have been incapable of such complete contrition. Here was a man, vastly his superior, prepared to make no excuse. By referring to that verse, Tom had provided a reference point for conversation and understanding, setting both under the same judgement. Incidents such as this were the means by which Jeremiah learned, returning to them afterwards. Without such shared points of reference, one could discuss anything for a century and reach no understanding. Apologies became meaningless.

There is an essential difference between warning of the judgement of another, and judging. If one stood next to someone in a shop, saw him shoplifting, and pointed out that there was a camera pointing at him, it was not to 'judge/condemn'. One could say, "I got caught myself a month ago". One needed to be sure that the other was shoplifting. He felt honoured that Tom thought that he shared such a reference, and that nothing more needed saying. It did not. Trust and friendship were strengthened.

Tom became his mentor for the next three years. The part of the Old Testament, in which Tom was interested, was the beginning of the book of Genesis. 'One could derive the entire gospel from the story of the Fall'. Jeremiah asked, "What is original sin?" Tom talked about his garden, "If you keep your garden weed free for five years and grow beans and peas, then let it all go, what comes up? Not beans and peas".

The other area of teaching in which Jeremiah was becoming increasingly interested was the development of early Christian doctrine. He was reading books that he should have read as a student. He found the arguments of such as Athanasius fascinating, for their subtlety and use of words, even more, those of Augustine. He asked the same sort of questions as Tom. Jeremiah found himself doing so. Another feature of the arguments deployed by Athanasius and his supporters at Nicea, he found significant in contemporary application. If one persuaded people to agree to a proposal by argument and pressure; when the pressure was removed, they began to have second thoughts, and undermined it.

Misunderstandings, even those involving abstract words in languages like Latin and Greek, could give rise to bitter quarrels. These came to involve men who had no interest in the arguments, but could be worked up to fight each other by slogans and chants. He saw how easily such disputes became 'ethnic', when linked with old cultural traditions, as in the case of Augustine and the Donatists; where the Catholics, led by Augustine, consisted largely of Roman settlers, the Donatists mostly of native Numidians. He began to see the awful truth of Jesus' own words. He and his teaching would set husband against wife, children against parents, ethnic group against ethnic group and nation against nation.

Religions became dangerous, when established and could dominate the civil power. Augustine had seized on the command in the parable, "compel them to come in", to justify the use of the civil power to compel people into the Catholic Church. He had done as Jesus said of those "without", taking what was explicitly a metaphor as the truth. The King who compelled all to come in was God, not Caesar. That was at one with praying "Thy kingdom come". If God was truly God, he need not ask any human power for help.

Disputes could 'grumble' on for centuries, becoming ossified in religious and cultural heritages, over which wars were fought; when few, if any, of the participants had any interest in, or knowledge of, the recondite theological matter which originated them, as in Yugoslavia, Sudan, and other such places.

There would be visiting lecturers, who spoke of new methods in education with enthusiasm. One shewed what concepts could be learned by using very expensive mathematical equipment, consisting of blocks and flat squares of wood. It taught "number concepts". Children learned 'the twoness of two, and the fiveness of five'. Any questions? "Yes" said Jeremiah, "How does one get a concept of the noughtness of nought?" The speaker did not provide a very convincing answer. On Sunday after chapel the head of maths asked; "Wherever did you learn to ask questions like that?" "It was not my question" said Jeremiah, "It was asked by Augustine, when the Romans sought to teach mathematics by sense perception".

An expert in religious education had displays, designed to shew the difference between good and bad people and things. He had charts with 'nasty things' on one side and 'good things' on the other. The 'nasties' were things like the smallpox virus. The countervailing 'good' was vaccination. God made the good things and inspired good men. If that were so, "who provided the viruses and the bacteria?". They were punishment for human wickedness and arrogance.

That was not convincing. If such were the penalties for wickedness and arrogance, those who had access to vaccines could avoid them. It did not say much for the eyes of God. Jesus rejected any such half-baked solution. When a man born blind was seen, he was asked; "Who sinned, this man or his parents?" "Neither. It was that the works of God might be seen in him".

His mentor's questions about the meaning of myth led Jeremiah to think that many modern theories were of that order. 'Evolution' was applied to matters outside the description of how species differentiated. Had it not become a mythology? Did it not have a doctrine of salvation in the, 'survival of the fittest'? Like many religious doctrines, it seemed to mean much but, analytically, meant nothing. Since the only means of knowing who were the fittest, was from the fact that they happened to survive, it amounted to, 'The survival of survivors'. Those, who expounded it, implied cognition on the part of members of species. They spoke of monkeys "solving the problem of survival". He started to mock this language, "Whatever are we to imagine? Did the leading monkeys call an assembly and say, 'Look here chaps, it is evident that the trees and forests are declining and, if this process continues, they will not bear our weight. That means we will all become meals on legs for predators, so we must all go on a diet. Meanwhile our expert monkeys have taken in hand a programme of gene modification so that, as a breed, we become smaller'. It is the logic of Beatrix Potter.

He read, "Origin of Species". Darwin did not invent the cliché, 'Survival of the fittest', but used it as the title of the central chapter of his book, and needed it to give apparent relevance. It hardly matters to anyone, now, how species came to be as they are. Given that famous slogan, it trails the possibility that those, who rightly read the signs of times, can ensure survival, for themselves and their progeny, so have their names 'in the book of life'. Jesus must, above all, be excluded. It is hardly a recipe for survival to say, "whoever seeks to save his life shall lose it".

Darwin rejected the notion that he had deified nature. He avoided this by his preference for the adjective 'natural', so avoiding the question "what is nature?" Was it substantially any different to speak of "natural selection", from saying "nature selects"? The scriptures of evolution were more vulnerable, in the analogy, whence the thesis sets out. It stands, in relation to the rest of the book, in much the same way as the early narratives in Genesis stand to the rest of the Old Testament. Breeders of animals, in particular pigeon fanciers, selected specimens with characteristics desirable for their purpose, as breeding stock. They had a clear, cognitive, aim. This was transferred to 'nature' or that which is 'natural'. That implies cognition and purpose in 'nature', whatever that may be. The alternative was to suggest that there was cognition on the part of the members of a species. What did it matter to the members of any species that the species survived? Most were concerned that an individual specimen did so. Manifestly it did not.

The word 'god' exists, whether or not there is such a being. Mythologies like evolution would not prevent such beliefs. That there appeared evidence to support them did not mean that they were not mythologies. Those who upheld the old mythologies saw evidence to support them. All such theories invoked some kind of 'original', which laid down the laws that govern these processes. This 'original' could be called 'god'. If so it was a madcap world we lived in. It was as if the 'original', that laid down the laws, was an experimenter in a laboratory, setting ever more hazardous obstacle courses, to see which could survive and which could not. One might even imagine two such opposed beings, one of which provided the obstacle courses: the other developed beings to overcome them. That came close to many old mythologies of 'creation'. Could mankind 'survive' in such a world? It seemed that 'God' had set great problems for man, first by leaving the word 'god' in the dictionary, second by endowing man with a sense of his transcendent significance, a soul; even if it was a delusion.

Reading writers like Athanasius, Augustine, and the words of such as Elijah, Jeremiah began to wonder whether such beliefs might not be recipes for extinction. Those who believe in some sort of life 'after death' are likely, even if the belief be bogus, to act with less inhibition than those who do not. Those, who believe that this life is all that anyone has, are likely to seek to preserve and prolong both it and the institutions that make it comfortable. The former are likely to contemplate the destruction of lives and institutions with greater equanimity, which makes them dangerous. If 'this life' is all, what of those who gain little from it? They would become an underclass with no interest in the preservation of the way of life of the society they live in. They would have not the smallest inclination to preserve the environment. What has it ever done for them?

It would apply to youngsters at school. Whatever teachers and others might say about the opportunities that education afforded, it would be apparent to many, by the age of twelve, that it would not do so for them. One or two in any class could disrupt it for all. If one is obliged to undergo schooling or anything else, which does not seem to benefit oneself, there is an urge to prevent others benefiting from it either. It is those in that underclass, often very intelligent, who are a menace. He came to see why it might be, even if there be no God, that 'Israel' (as a dispersed people, not the state) seemed to be the only ethnic group which had the capacity to survive for millennia, despite the efforts of many powers to extirpate them. It had the earthy realism of the well-known stories of the Old Testament, in contrast to the ludicrous tales on which the young of other cultures were fed.

Jeremiah had a friend who taught German. Talking of these things in the pub one evening, his friend, who was in no way religious, said, "I could not deal with the Old Testament. It's far too realistic".

Israel had the book of psalms, which were unlike other poetry. Most verse is written by the literati, for the literati. The Psalter sees life from the underclass viewpoint in two ways, from the point of view of Israel as the 'underclass' nation, and from that of the 'underclass' within Israel. These it exalts as the chosen of God, just as Jesus exalted the Poor in Spirit, the Meek and those who sorrow. Few Jewish children took to things like drugs, or become delinquent, as they were then described.

The Psalter is unlike most other verse in another way. Most poetry depends on regular metre and rhyme. Lines need a set number of syllables to scan. This, with the search for rhyme, often means using strange words, or upsetting the sense order. If something rhymes or has a rhythmic structure, especially if set to music, many tend to endow it with profound sense, when, analytically, it is nonsense. Hebrew verse never needs to do these things. By making the middle of each line the crux, lines can be as long or short as needed. There is no need to disturb the natural sense order of words, or use strange words to achieve rhyme. Anyone can see that, by taking Coverdale's translation of Psalm 23, and setting it alongside the attempts to render it metrically. What we call culture is, for them, a delusion to be mocked and derided. They mock such things to prevent anyone believing in them. Some mock the pretensions of rulers of people, warning against putting trust in them. 'The psalmist' would find democracy tragi-comic. If democracy involves endless consultation, he does, as in Ps 2.

Some Psalms deride the pursuit of riches and power, as did the prophet Jeremiah. It is the other side of the coin from exalting the poor and the meek. It gives the underclass something to live for, just as do the sayings of Jesus; but the book of Psalms is a 'mixed bag'. It is useful to those, who seek wealth and power, to have a labouring class taught that the kingdom of Heaven belongs to the poor. It is also handy for collectors to have people taught the danger of 'laying up for themselves treasure on earth'. Can any society and economy endure without such words? If they are taken away, and those at the bottom have nothing to 'go for', either in this world or that which is to come, they are likely to seek other means of acquiring such things, or spoil it for everyone else. Crime and violence are almost bound to increase.

Darwin and his followers played a major part in undermining the credibility of the established religion. That is not to blame them. The rulers of England made use of the words of Jesus and thus of God; recently, for example, in introducing compulsory religious education. Now they were being taken away. Though his grandparents and forebears had been 'kindly enough', they were the upholders of the established order of power and wealth. There was something grotesque in spokesmen for the rich and powerful encouraging everyone else to seek the kingdom of God, so be content in their poverty and 'meek' status. We taught a 'conversation' of delusion, exalting such as Brunel for their achievements. But for an army of meek and poor, they would have achieved naught but dreams, like Leonardo with his designs.

While Darwin had done much to destroy the Christian religion's credibility, nothing in his book had the smallest impact on anything said by Jesus. He had undermined a pantomime loosely based on that life. He had destroyed the credibility of one mythology and replaced it with another, which was, potentially, very much nastier. Nowhere in his writings would one find anything that exalted the poor and meek, nor even the peacemakers. One could not find words that would silence accusers, such as "let whoever is faultless among you...". If anything it would lead to the opposite.

The new, scientifically based, theories seemed little different from ancient mytholgies. They all sustained forms of belief. All implied a transcendent guarantor of their perceived laws. They too had their priesthoods and prophets. All, for obvious reasons, needed to make converts. Their modes of divination were different. All shared a common purpose, which was to push the ultimate, uncontrollable, origin of all things into ever greater remoteness, providing an environment, as secure as possible from the dreaded "acts of God". Nobody, except insurers, wanted them. It was a choice between beliefs, rather than the abandonment of belief.

There are those who find it preferable to rely on that which is uncontrollable. They would tend either to be those who, for one reason or another, found the 'controlled environment' beyond their abilities, or mistrusted those who established it, preferring to live by 'chance'. They might see that, which was beyond all means of control, as being good, even if it manifested itself in what others might see as calamities. That which is beyond all means of control must ultimately overcome that which is controllable. Only that which is, by definition, beyond all means of control by men, can be relied upon as good.

The quietly spoken Chaplain had opened a can of worms. He led Jeremiah to see the significance of beliefs based on observation, when they became 'mythologies' and were transferred to areas of life, distinct from that to which the theory applied. The word 'evolve' became a sacred mantra. If a new proposal was put before the staff, the proponents of the new scheme need only say, "It will evolve", for debate to end and a consensus be reached. It may have had more to do with everyone wanting to go home.

Atheists, agnostics and religious people believe in more things, often with greater fervour, than those who believed in God. Believers in the true God were nuisances. They withheld belief from anything else, including religious observances. When pressed, the language of fervent believers in education, democracy or democratic values, discipline, evolution, family values, and all manner of things, dissolved into confusion, as did that of religious beliefs. They reacted with as much hostility to its being derided or questioned.

Jeremiah had an irritating habit of asking questions in silly ways. He was taken to a lecture, given by a Professor of Astronomy. The only thing he grasped was when the Professor explained that we were seeing a certain star, as it was when Caesar landed. He asked, "How could we be sure that light travelled at the same speed then? Did Caesar check the speed of light?" It annoyed the Professor. Having rebuked Jeremiah for his lack of seriousness, he felt that he had over reacted, and mused that, if it were possible to contemplate alteration of the speed of light, all assumptions of astro-physics would need revising.

Tom was a genuinely 'good', intelligent and kind man. Jeremiah was not. He enjoyed mocking. He would behave like this at home, when visitors would come for an evening. It might be that some man or woman had an absorbing interest in the tombs of the Pharaohs and the Pyramids. They were happy to expound this, closely questioned by Jeremiah. After an hour, he tended to make a flippant comment like, "All thy ended up with was the world's largest coffin!"

The guest would assume that he had been laughing at it all from the start. That was not true. When submitting them to endless questions he was genuinely interested. It was as if a demon possessed him. This used to upset his unfortunate wife. "Why is it, when you have spent the evening submitting a friend to questions like an inquisitor, as if you are interested, you have always to make a flippant comment ? They take these things seriously". She said that he was seditious.

He was frightened of those who had these great interests and beliefs, and did not wish to see them dominating others, in particular himself and his children. They were those who advised people in authority. He may also have felt a lurking need to protect that which he had seen as being true, when he read the IVth gospel in his childhood.

The orthodox branches of the Christian religion, which had formal written services, seemed safer. They recited the Creed, which set Jesus apart from all others. The creeds did not declare belief in St Paul, or anyone else, as being God from God and Light from Light. Having made such declarations about this singular man, he felt and thought that those who made them would be bound to put stones from their hands, if recalled to his words, "Let whoever among you is faultless....". If not, such declarations were empty noises.

These questions began to affect other aspects of his life, particularly in relation to education. They, now, had two sons. The elder was starting school. There seemed to be an obvious difference between man and any other species. Mankind needed children. If any species ceased to breed, it would die out. That was obvious. In no other species did the adult population need the young, in order to continue living themselves. Man needed the young to 'keep the show on the road'. Humans needed a future assurance, to live as they do, presently. If not, they would be stranded like beached whales. It did not lessen an adult dog's capacity to live, if its puppies, once full grown, vanished forever, any more than it did for swallows. It might improve their ability to live. There would be more flies to catch. Not only did the established human population need young to keep the show on the road economically, they also needed an amenable culture and way of life maintaining.

It was the 'sixties'. A significant minority of youngsters adopted an attitude, something like that of the 'Prodigal', "We see no point in spending our lives toiling away in boring jobs, in the hope that we can earn enough to provide for our retirement, so that, we can say to ourselves, 'we have enough, let us take our ease'. We would prefer to enjoy life now, and let tomorrow care about itself". Neither society nor its economy could survive, if the younger generation adopted such attitudes. They were almost those, which Jesus fostered. The youngsters, who cut loose, had a case. "Look where your ways have led. They led to two world wars, the folly of the slaughter on the River Somme, and now to the ever present threat of nuclear catastrophe or worse".

The constant theme of the politicians was that security depended on being ready and armed, so that aggressors would be deterred. In 1939 we had been caught unprepared. As years went by, they could say, "Thanks to the fact that we are now ready and armed we have had peace". Despite being unprepared in 1939, we had been given deliverance, whereas nations like Poland and France had not, nor had Germany. There was a wholly different possibility, "Those that live by the sword, by the sword shall perish".

There was much talk of 'self fulfilment'. It was the function of educators to facilitate this. Women who had been very successful in some chosen career would speak of 'giving five years of their lives to raising a family'. It would 'fulfil them'. They said such things on the wireless and television. What did that say of the children, but that they were living sacrifices on the altars of their parents' desire for 'fulfilment'? Teachers were prone to speak of children, as if born to provide them with opportunities. What of God, for all are his children? Would he appreciate his little ones being made living sacrifices on the altars of human self-fulfilment, or anything else? All seemed to depend on children not being allowed to think of themselves as living souls, save in affectation.

What if a child, brought into the world with no choice, did not like being sent to school, to be taught many things it did not wish to learn, but little that it did? It would be taught these things in order to fit it for a job that it did not want to perform, as a duty to a society and economy, of which it did not seek to be a member. Might it not prefer never to have been born? If no radically different alternative was available, it was likely that such youngsters would grow up to be resentful.

The College became more pretentious as it got larger. It was decided that each department should present itself and its relevance to the students when they arrived. The theme was to be self-fulfilment. Jeremiah found himself doing this. He produced a duplicated handout, filled with seemingly optimistic sayings about it. He spent ten minutes talking as if he believed in it. Helped by the technician, he had made slides from some Sunday Colour supplements. Some shewed burial chambers and mummies with jars of grain, left to sustain them; but with jars containing the digestive organs, which had been removed. He then shewed a sequence of slides depicting the mode of disposal of bodies in a crematorium, ending with small urn of ashes, which, the article suggested, might actually be anybody's. There was 'human self fulfilment!' The paths of glory lead but to the grave...("and so does every other bleedin' path", a friend had later said, "Your f.....ing Gray missed that one!")

Societies, economies and nations needed the young to have a sense of duty to them. On that basis, his old dad had been led to give up twelve years of his life to fighting for king and country. Such a view, necessary though it was, broke down on one ineluctable fact. No child volunteered for birth. It did not choose its parents, still less the society or nation into which it came. From this all else sprang. It should not be the young who have a duty to the society into which they are borne, but the opposite. Since none chose to be born, and if, as needs be, a society, through education and other means, feels free to force its 'conversation' upon them, it would seem appropriate that each should, at the age of eighteen, be given a painless means of exit from life. "This is what we have forced upon you, if you don't like it.......". That would give all parents and teachers, or any who made laws that directed the lives of others and their children, cause for much pondering.

Jesus said, "Call no man on earth thy father, for all have but one father, even in heaven." In that light, we, as a society, might be seen as committing collective 'child abuse'. Many years later a Minister of Education said, "Children are our greatest asset". It sounds fine, until one thinks of what is actually said and implied. If it be true that all are children of their Father in heaven, anyone would tremble at such an utterance. Are we setting out to use 'his children' as other assets; coal, iron ore, oil and so on, or money in the bank? Towards the end of the book, Deuteronomy, is a fearful catalogue of curses, which will fall on a faithless people. One implies that they will, be afflicted with domestic infidelity, "You will marry a wife and another will lie with her".

Given the prospectus of life that he had set out, how many would choose to be born? If parents, who could now choose whether or not to reproduce, felt the future uncertain or bleak, should they not refrain from doing so? Whatever might happen, if all of breeding age decided not to do so?

It would be unliveable. Everything would close down, beginning with the maternity hospitals and child care industry, then the nursery schools, and so on, until all that remained were a few aging undertakers. The way, in which the youth of that decade cut loose from the shackles of tradition, threw this possibility into bold relief. It was a pity that they did not see that the reported teaching of Jesus almost perfectly articulated their case in words, which the upholders of the traditional ways would have found hard to answer. There is also the possibility of the 'Israel in Egypt syndrome', in which an underclass, or immigrant group, out-breeds its hosts.

Public education seemed akin to a confidence trick, designed to persuade the young that all was done for their sake, when it could, as truly, be seen in the opposite light. In recent years, the compulsory teaching of religious and moral education played a part in this. Jeremiah read the parliamentary debates, which preceded the act of 1944. Most saw the Christian religion, as providing the most useful basis for re-establishing traditional moral values and respect for lawful authority, after the war. That may be so for religion. What of the Kingdom of God? Did Jesus expound that to uphold the moral values of the kingdom of England? If education was concerned with truth, there were only two possibilities, that there was God, or there was not. The first was inseparable from the teaching of Jesus in the gospels.

Neither the evolutionary hypothesis, nor other scientific theories prove that the world is not created. They make it more difficult to believe that it is. That makes it unfortunate for mankind if there is God, unless man expects God and his word to change to accommodate his changing views. If that were so, whatever such a being may be, it cannot be God.

Thanks to Tom, he came to see that all beliefs were vulnerable when it came to language. What was space? How could anyone say of a child that it was 'spoiled', without knowing what, ideally, it should be, or become? It was one thing to speak of space as an interval between two objects, another to endow it with existence as a 'thing in itself'. How could anyone know whether the universe was infinite? Physicists had problems in finding words. When asked what was matter, they started talking about energy. If none could say what is matter, what the hell is anti matter? However valid a thesis, it is vulnerable, if its words are confused.

Tom decided to return to parish work near Cambridge. Jeremiah begged him to stay longer. "You'll be all right," said Tom, his eyes twinkling, "I've brainwashed you". Then he dropped a bombshell. "I've told the boss that you are just the chap to take over the course on Genesis I-XI, because you can read Hebrew. The boss agreed!" "I don't understand all that myth stuff". "Yes you do", said Tom, I have never heard a better exposition of the Tower of Babel than you gave the other evening when you reported on that conference".

"I never mentioned it. I said that it was like the prophets of Baal on Mount Carmel, leaping and cutting themselves, when Elijah mocked them by their gods." "Well", said Tom, "did not that produce confusion of language?"

He smiled again. "If I move on, there should be a senior lectureship going!"

Chapter Eleven

"Old wives tales myths and legends".

Jeremiah was in safer waters in the early chapters of Genesis, than the gospels, in particular, the Fourth. There could be nothing dangerous in these ancient tales, which most regarded as little more than a collection of old myths. He took care in preparing his lectures, and set about translating the chapters, making a very literal translation for the students. Then he turned to commentaries. It seemed clear that the well known opening chapter with its seven day scheme, had borrowed from the ancient Babylonian 'myth', where the triumph of Marduk over Tiamat was, apparently, the basis of a seven day festival. From this, words used in the Hebrew story had also been derived, like that translated 'the great deep'. The problem lay in the word 'create', even more, as he came to see, in the word God.

By reserving the word, 'create', for acts of God alone, the Hebrews implied that creating is that which God alone could do. Man might make things, produce, order and even harmonize them, what he could not do was to create them.

'Creative activity' was much in vogue in education. 'Creativity' was a great word in the world of art as well. People were described as creative thinkers. He enjoyed contrasting this with God, creating the heavens and the earth at a word. Children used existing materials to make models of existing things. Painters and others did not create. They might rearrange, or achieve pleasing and harmonious patterns with coloured fluids on paper and canvas. People would nod sagely and say that what he said was important to remember, a point of view that should not be overlooked.

With the vast vocabulary of words available in English, which described ways of making and producing things, why was it necessary to use the word 'create'? Was it seized upon to suggest that, when people did things described as being 'creative', they were in some way participating in the work of the Creator? If so that took one back to the ancient myths and the religions of old, in which it appears that the worshippers cultically participated in the work of the deity.

It was better still, if he could hide behind others. 'It is worth remembering what Augustine, Aquinas or Calvin said about the matter of Creation, unwise to dismiss their views'. It contributed to the debate, in a manner not unlike the story of the rich young man in the gospels; as if Jesus had spoken to him, in order to stimulate discussion. He would need to be certain that the young man would not do as he said. If not, it would have been a costly way to stimulate discussion, for the young man.

Such a view was one among many. 'We' would, then, find it wholly in order to stand up and say that we believe in One Lord Jesus Christ, God of God, Light of

Light, Very God of Very God, just as 'we' find it wholly in order to declare that we believe in God as the "Creator of heaven and earth and of all things visible and invisible".

As long as Jeremiah could distance himself in this way, all seemed fine. It could hardly be better. A year or two after Tom departed, the Deputy Principal went on to higher things and Jeremiah became a principal lecturer and head of department. Being a large department, he received a responsibility allowance. In the space of four or five years his salary had trebled. He and his wife bought a larger house in the country. They had three children. Life was good, but he was finding it more and more difficult to distance himself from the opinions he threw out. 'At heart', he meant what he said. God alone created. For man to claim to do so was not only to delude himself; it deluded others. It was tantamount to claiming to be as gods, or, which amounts to the same, considering God to be as man, if on an enlarged scale; but, in truth, a somewhat reduced one.

Without realising it, he was being forced to think about what it means to believe truly in God, the Creator of all things, as the *present* reality. This was something he had not considered since being a little child, when it seemed obvious. "I thank thee O Father, Lord of heaven and earth that thou hast hid these things from the wise and prudent, and revealed them to babes". It was, if what the fourth evangelist reported of Jesus be true, the essential pre-requisite for belief in him. "Ye believe in God, believe also in me..."

The opening narrative seemed no great problem. It was based on older Babylonian 'mythology', but was emphatic that God saw all that he had created, "and behold it was very good". The narrative that followed, said to be more primitive and naive, presented a growing difficulty, particularly in its conclusion, the story of 'Adam and Eve' and the 'fall of man'. The story was clear as to the nature of the one forbidden tree. It is the tree of the knowing of good and evil/bad. The 'fall' of man is caused by his demanding that knowledge, as the basis for life, and so "be as God(s), knowing good and evil". That this should be, defied all sense. It also defied all Christian exegesis of the matter and the cardinal doctrines of the redemption of mankind. It defied the very raison d'être of most religions in society. It is to their representatives that rulers go, to seek 'ethical' guidance. Religions were the prime repositories of such knowing. Rulers of people must be seen as being those who are, most certainly, possessed of such knowledge. They make laws, direct and govern the lives of lesser folk.

Jeremiah consulted commentaries ancient and modern. All seemed sure, as he later learned was St Augustine, that the explicit nature of the tree was insignificant. A recent commentator wrote that, for the oriental mind, knowing good and evil was to know anything. The more he pondered this, the less convincing he found it. All knowledge led to a discernment of what might be seen as good or bad. It was the duty of parents and teachers to lead children to understand right from wrong, good from evil. Nonetheless, the old story, much as the story of Creation, provided a basis for 'debate', provided he distanced himself from what it said, implying that it was a preposterous idea. In the 'conversation' of this world, it is; though language became confused when people sought to say what words like 'evil' meant.

Many reputable writers distinguished the word 'create', as that which God alone could do. None took the view that the one thing, forbidden by the creator, was the knowing of good and evil. He could not hide behind anyone, apart from Jesus himself, who said, "Do not resist (him that is) evil". You could hardly do that without knowing what it is.

In the fourth gospel, the Baptist points to Jesus, saying, "Behold the lamb of God that takes away the sin of the world". 'According to the scriptures', this could be one thing only, the demand to know good and evil. Jeremiah began, dimly, to see that, if any heard the words of Jesus as final and complete, they would be hard pressed to know what was good and what was evil. Such notions were 'unthinkable' and, certainly, unsayable, except in apparent jest. What he said, as if only joking, he meant, what he said 'seriously' he did not. He was a man, not at unity in himself.

His conversation was like casting flies, throwing out comments about the forbidden tree, to see who would rise to them. It was easier to do so in relation to 'ancient myths' than sayings of Jesus. What he would have done if anyone had 'taken the fly', he did not consider; but came to see a fearful consequence in making 'disciples'. What if, having done so, one changed one's mind? He began to see the finality of Jesus' own teaching as crucial. One might lead anyone to become a disciple of Jesus, but not of oneself. His teaching was 'finished'.

Jeremiah's way of life depended on upholding the 'serious conversation'. If, in truth, God prohibits, for man's good, the knowing of good and evil, all is turned upside down. This story, like many in the Old Testament, was like the edge of a vortex which swept one down, through the 'law and the prophets', to the sayings of Jesus in the gospels, as complete. If what the composers of that old tale saw was the truth, the entire language of religion and all that invoked it needed radical reconsideration.

It is not hard to see why it was that he should be so transfixed by the designation of the one forbidden tree. It took him back to his childhood, when grown-up certainties of what was right and wrong terrified him. It took him 'forward' to Jesus himself, who said clearly, "I say to you, do not resist (him that is) evil". Did anyone know what was 'evil'? Did anyone know, for sure, what was good? Jesus said, 'God alone is good'. All debate about what was good and bad, right and wrong, if there is truly God, is a delusion. It's like chessmen in their box, discussing, 'on first principles', how they should move about the board. They were all cut from the same wood, turned on the same lathe by the same hands. Pawns, then, should be entitled to rush about like Queens. Once taken out of the box and put on the board, their discussion and conclusions count for nothing.

The evidence of history seemed to bear out the truth of the prohibition, and Jesus' words, apparently, gathering it up. Hitler and the fascists sought to extirpate what they felt to be an assured 'evil' and achieve that which they saw as undoubtedly good. Stalin, likewise, seemed to have been actuated by similar certainty. So were those who tried and burned heretics, sent children on crusades, or hijacked aircraft and flew them into skyscrapers. Judas, Caiaphas and the Council, doubtless, thought the same. There was a fearful consequence. Once set upon a course based on such certainty, there is no turning back, especially if any, who did so, persuaded others to follow and support them.

The builders of empires, today and in the past, were fired by a similar certainty; yet their fruits were acts of grotesque cruelty. Many a noble Roman believed that the civilising power of Rome was good. It imposed slavery and forced labour. Those who upheld its virtues diverted themselves with hideous gladiatorial combat; then sat at home reading Catullus. It was the stuff of education that the achievements of past and present civilisations were exalted. It was a wonderful achievement that Pharaoh built his pyramid, that the Romans built their stadia and aqueducts. It is a language of deceit. Pharaoh did not build the pyramid, he robbed and enslaved thousands to enable him to have it erected, just as Solomon, when 'he built his' temple.

Any society, devised by man, needs an assumed knowledge of good and evil, right and wrong. Without it, all hope of enforcing law-abiding behaviour is futile. There had to be a 'moral consensus' to regulate behaviour, especially in those areas of life where the imposition of law, by penalty, was not only difficult, but often, if not always, counter productive. One needed a similar consensus to endow language with sense. The more technologically advanced any economy became, the more necessary it became to know good and bad.

Every saying attributed to Jesus provoked the serpent's question, "Did God really say.....?" Did God really say, 'Do not combat evil', 'Do not stand like hypocrites praying on street corners or in meeting houses to be seen by men', 'Do not even let your left hand know what the right has done when giving alms?' Did God really say that that which came out of a man made him 'ordinary'?

These opening chapters end with the terse but witty tale of the 'Tower of Babel'. Was not confusion of language the key fact in the decline and fall of civilisations, empires and economies? Confused language has the capacity to make the technological advances, which enable an economy to thrive and become supreme, instruments of its own destruction. The single prohibition of God to man, in the story of the 'fall', would have that effect, as would the sayings of Jesus, as he himself warned.

Jeremiah read a book, written long ago by Anselm of Canterbury, called 'Proslogion'. He read and reread it, becoming more and more irritated at his own stupidity. He saw the general drift of the argument in the second chapter, the famous 'ontological argument' for belief in God; but was aware that he was not following the 'proof'. It was as if he were presented with the theorem, shewing that the angles of a triangle amounted to two right angles. He could see that they did; but was not following the step-by-step demonstration. Poverty of Latin proved his saviour. He obtained a copy in that language with notes. It took him a long time to read. He found himself taking the key phrase, translated as, 'that than which no greater can be thought', as an algebraic expression in brackets. It is less cumbersome in Latin.

The penny dropped at last. He was struck by the beauty of the argument. He came to understand how mathematicians spoke of the beauty of an equation.

Anselm lighted on a real difficulty, to which few gave much attention. Jeremiah tended to understand things through parables. He used to take his children to a place near Derby, where there was a canal and a main railway line. Both ran straight, for as far as one could see. When two trains approached in opposite directions, it seemed certain, when distant from one another, that they would collide. So was it when anyone discussed belief in God, except as little children. Unless there was clear agreement about what the word meant, as a 'postulate', argument was futile. The trains passed harmlessly by each other. There might be a sudden explosion of rattling and noise, but that was all. Each, then, went on to its allotted destination.

Anselm imagined how he might debate the existence of God with the "fool who has said in his heart there is no God". For the argument to have any sense, there had to be a shared definition of the word 'god'. If there were not, the 'fool' would deny the existence of a 'supernatural' being, whose existence Anselm would think preposterous. By defining such a term, one endowed it with a form of existence. It existed in one's mind.

It is here that Anselm's definition is so ingenious, since, as he makes clear, the denial of its existence in 'reality and truth' involves a contradiction. Manifestly, 'that than which no greater can be thought' exists in the mind, as a concept. It is immediately possible to think of that which is greater than that which exists only in the mind. That which exists both in the mind, and in 'reality and truth', must be greater than that which exists in the mind alone. Anselm goes on to distinguish that which may be said to have 'necessary existence' from that which exists contingently upon it. He can conceive the non-existence of anything, except that which has 'necessary' existence.

He did not believe or think that his proof would make anyone believe, who was not prone to do so. As the rest of Proslogion makes clear, his argument is the fruit of belief, not its foundation. One might ask whether his definition has any conceivable meaning. Nonetheless the argument is devastating in its brilliance, and served to establish two things in Jeremiah's mind. It is far more difficult to assert an atheist position, by argument, than most would imagine and impossible to 'prove', since it means proving a negative. Whether or not there is God in reality, the word 'god' exists. As a postulate alone it provides a clear and credible 'theory' as to the origin and truth of all things, even if an unwelcome one.

Reading Proslogion raised the childish matter of belief in God, and the question of what it was that one believed in. To a child it was obvious that God could do 'all things'. If he cannot, he is not God. If God is really God, and gave ten laws to his people, those laws can be left entirely to God for enforcement. If God cannot, as the Creator of all things, enforce his own laws, unaided by any man, he is not God. Little children also understand jealously (as distinct from envy). If any man set about enforcing God's laws 'for him', God would not assist him in doing so, but the opposite, to shew that 'I am what I am'. If you claim to enforce the laws of God, you imply that God cannot. Speaking as Isaiah, one would say, "Thus saith the Lord; do you think that you are gods and that I am unable to uphold and impose my own laws?"

The same would apply to the created Universe. "It is mine, and I have the right to do as I will with it", is not only an argument familiar to a little child; it is what Jesus implies in the conclusion of one of his parables. One might extend this, "I designed it, and it will only provide a good habitat for man according to my design. It is perfectly designed for those who do not seek to know good and evil. To realise this you need only look at every plant and animal, all of which live contentedly without such knowledge". One might add that it is perfectly designed as a habitat for the Poor in Spirit, the Meek, the sorrowful and those who hunger and thirst after righteousness; ill designed to sustain a human population hell bent on everlasting economic growth. This raised questions about the meaning of words like love and mercy. Is it an act of mercy or love for the Creator to pretend that the world is otherwise than he has made it? Is it an act of love or mercy for the Creator to change the design of the universe to accommodate the changed opinion of mankind? What, then, of those who trust his original word?

Reading Proslogion opened Jeremiah's eyes to another crucial fact. Whether God exists in reality and truth or not, we are left with the word 'god'. As long as that word exists, people will be ever prone to believe in some form of supernatural being. That they may be led to believe in some crackpot product of the fervid imagination, which could not possibly be God, is another matter. The word 'god' is unlike others. It carries a clear, if childish, logic. If it does not imply a being, which is eternal, and 'perfect', in the sense of needing nothing, which creates all things, it does not befit the term 'God'. It might befit a 'supernatural' being.

Unless the term 'god' implied what any child understood by it, it could not represent God, in truth. In religious language, or theology, if God is not what the term logically implies, all dissolves into confusion, ever open to mockery and derision, by those with the minds of little children.

This resurrected his childhood fears of grown-up certainties. If the language of religious and other beliefs was vulnerable, but much depended on their being maintained, those, who upheld them, would feel it necessary to do nasty things to any who derided it, in order to maintain its apparent validity. They might burn heretics, behead or stone 'blasphemers', even crucify them. It was a frightening world for any who did not belong in the accepted 'conversation'. He was coming to see that the most devastating critique of all such language derived from taking people at their word, 'believing their report'. This applied to any proclaimed belief. Believers in democracy would say that all should be decided by vote. Take that to its logical conclusion, nobody would have any time to do anything but vote on things. Presumably, if something was decided by a popular vote, there should be another referendum weekly, if not daily, in case the 'will of the people' had changed. If that were not done, it would imply a crazy belief, that a certain group of people, at a particular moment, were endowed with ultimate wisdom.

There was a corollary. Only those, who had such assurance of there being truly God, could 'risk' pointing out the nonsense in the language of beliefs, upon which many institutions and societies depended. Believing in one for whom all things must be possible, allowed them to contemplate the destruction of anything with relative equanimity. They might even see it as beneficial, if a social order and the beliefs, which sustained it, be they never so religious, impeded belief in the true God. If they felt assured of eternal life, they could contemplate, the loss of everything in 'this world'. It not only allowed them to contemplate the 'unthinkable', it allowed them to use language with abandon, and force all to an extreme either/or, regardless of the consequences, as did Elijah, as, above all, did Jesus.

While in a moment of assured belief, someone might speak in this way; nobody could rely on it being so 'in a week's time'. 'The cares and riches of this life', might rob them of that certainty, leading them to retract their extreme words. Where would that leave those who had believed them? The words heard by the beloved disciple, as Jesus dies, are, "It is finished".

Uniting the 'logic' of the word 'God' with the being it indicated was crucial. If the being of God is not as the word, logically, implied, all speech about God is necessarily self-contradictory and vulnerable. Jeremiah, if dimly, began to see why the words of Jesus, following those of the prophets, had such power. They united the, childishly understood, 'logic' of the word 'god' with the being. God is what the word logically implies, the only uncreate, eternal being, by whom all is created, who needs nothing and so is perfect. God is, thus, beyond all means of influence and so, ultimately, control by anyone. Such a being alone can be seen as dependably good. This, the twentieth century should understand. Controllable institutions can fall into the hands of very nasty men. It matters not how much good they may appear to do, whether schools or hospitals, organs of governments, means of mass communication, or anything else.

Religious beliefs must avoid a clear identification of the being of God with the meaning of the word. The reason is simple. Religious observances, whether fasts, pilgrimages to this or that place, specified times for collective praying, weeks or days of prayer, sacrifices, or even the designation of certain buildings as sacred, imply a degree of control over God, by those who know. Their language, ironically called 'theology', carefully avoids saying this, hence its need for interminable elaboration, (all else besides either "yes, yes or no, no"). Jeremiah was an organ grinder's monkey, handsomely paid by those, whose entire way of life depended on 'interminable elaboration'. A few tricks and jumps after the music stopped were permissible, and might even gain him extra peanuts. 'Look what a clever little monkey'.

He persuaded himself, that, if it came to an 'either/or', those, who declared belief in One Lord Jesus Christ, would stand by their declarations of belief. Many spoke of seeking that great ideal, and of progressing ever closer to the Kingdom of God. The Christian religion was coming ever closer to the sayings of its Lord and Master, under the guidance of the 'Holy Spirit'. Such words were fine, as long as they 'buttered no parsnips' and all could be sure that they never got there. The story of the 'fall' seemed to force this question upon him more sharply than any other, probably because it was an old 'myth'. One need not believe in 'Adam and Eve'.

Who would want to inhabit a wholly good earth or world? Many would say, "If only it were a perfect world, free of wars and rumours of wars, quarrels within families and between ethnic groups, free of famines and disasters, sickness and disease. We have to live in the 'real' world, but we are striving to make it better". If people were not persuaded to feel so, would any have children? Jeremiah had already come to see that any society and economy depends on people having children, to sustain itself. All must, then, be persuaded that evils are steadily being overcome. The Christian religion must join the chorus. Yet, as all who uphold it must know, Jesus promised nothing of the kind; "Think not that I have come to bring peace on earth, not peace but the sword. I will set husband against wife, children against parents.....ethnic group against ethic group and nation against nation".

At the end of the story, man is promised "cursed be the ground for thy sake", but to the woman he saith, "In sorrow shalt thou bring forth children....." . If it were a 'perfect world', free of all sickness, wars and rumours of wars, there could be no human achievement. The only conceivable result of human 'achievement' would its corruption. Those who would find themselves least needed would be those in 'high places'. We do not need a perfect world, without nasty things, what we need is what we have got, a cursed earth, and need it for our children and children's children, if they are to achieve 'success'.

Are we to believe that, thanks to democracy, we are coming ever nearer to the truly good world? Hitler rose to power through democratic processes. Austria welcomed him by an overwhelming majority in a referendum. Can anyone believe that the Kingdom of God is a democracy? Who among us would want a wholly good earth or world? The answer, if we paused to think, would be, 'bloody few'. Almost all that we depend upon, in our economy, relies on the dependable existence of some form of 'evil'. The more people know of things considered 'evil', the better way of life they can achieve.

Those in the medical profession and pharmaceutical industry, for example, need two things above all, diseases and money. The higher the status of anyone within the profession, the more he or she benefits from the existence of disease, the more money he or she earns. The more anyone in that industry labours for little reward, the less he or she needs these things. Whereas the medical industry and service might survive on the basis of the latter, it almost certainly cannot do so on the former, whereby, whether we like it or not, the most highly paid do 'very nicely' out of the pains and sicknesses of other folk. Any who devote themselves to alleviating sickness, pain and disease, 'going two miles when bidden to go one', might point beyond their work as 'professionals', to the one who healed all manner of sickness and disease freely. They might point to the command of Jesus, when he answered the lawyer's question with the parable of the Samaritan, "Go and do likewise". Aside from that, we have to face the fact that, in direct proportion to their status and salary, those of that profession, trade or vocation are the chief beneficiaries of sickness disease and injury. For both patient and physician, it upholds the certainty that it is neither blessed to be poor, nor 'meek'.

In the same way, judges and many lawyers are the chief beneficiaries of crime and disputes, together with senior police officers, journalists and crime writers, and those who produce films about them. The chief and only beneficiaries of famines and disasters are Directors of Famine Relief Charities. Such events are worth a good salary, many fringe benefits, and almost surely a knighthood to the Director of a large organisation, if not a peerage. Where would the teaching profession be without ignorance, or an economy that needed ever greater knowledge of many kinds of good and bad? The chief beneficiaries of all these things are, inevitably, those who direct and govern the lives of everyone else, with their religious acolytes around them, like the prophets in Ahab's court.

Would anyone know what to do in a world at peace? Would all armies be disbanded? What, then, of the arms industry? Where would all the institutions, we think 'good', be without its profits and the 'spin off' from its research? Where would any government be without all these things? What would a government do if there were no crime? Would it disband its law enforcement agencies? Their claim to be benefactors rests on promising to provide health care, education, protection from crime and external enemies. A very good earth or universe would leave all with nothing to do or talk about, apart from considering the lilies of the field and birds of the air.

Jeremiah began to see that knowing good and 'evil', leads to a loss of 'integrity' of being. The mind became alienated from 'feelings'. It was with his mind alone that he could perceive the possibility of these things being true, as with the sayings of Jesus. With his mind alone he could see that the epithet that Jesus applied to those who divorced wives or husbands and married others, had to be the truth. With every other faculty, he found it impossible to believe. He had many friends who lived thus, they were pleasant, law abiding, upright, 'caring' people. If one was persuaded that a habit, like smoking, was injurious and sought to persuade all that it was, one needed all smokers to suffer as much injury as possible. When it came to friends who smoked, one wanted the opposite.

He was being driven back to the very books he had sought to avoid. A childish and simple question would shew why. What manner of man or woman might yearn for a wholly good earth? It would be such as found themselves unable to cope in what we call the 'real world'. In Darwinian terms, they would not be 'of the 'fittest'. The opposite of the 'fittest' would be 'poor in spirit', 'meek' and, almost surely, 'sorrowful'. They might have no other course but to 'seek first the kingdom of heaven and its righteousness'.

In whatever parables and metaphors it may be seen, 'heaven' or eternal life must be 'wherever' and 'whenever' there is nothing evil or nasty to know or be known. The alternative, a world in which there is an unlimited supply of evils to know, would better be described as hell. That was what man asks for and is given, passing it on to his children and children's children. "In sorrow shalt thou bring forth children...".

Jeremiah heard a short story by Dostoevsky in which he imagined his death. He was conscious of being buried in his coffin. There was a drip of water, which irritated him. He said, "Take me out of here". Instantly he was transported through space in his coffin until he came near a beautiful planet, which he recognised as being the earth. He alighted on an earth that was as the garden of Eden. It was filled with happy people, ready to care for him and make him welcome. Nothing was too much trouble. Thus, his idyllic existence continued, for ages. It concluded, "but I corrupted them all....". With this he awoke, saying, "I must warn everyone", but realised that they would think him mad.

In whatever terms we may conceive eternal life or heaven, it must be 'wher*ever* 'or 'when*ever*' there is nothing bad, nasty or evil, nor any desire to know these things. Those who enter therein must have unlearned all that they know of them. Jeremiah imagined someone arriving in such a paradise, having devoted his or her life to learning more and more about good and bad, right and wrong, and teaching men so. He was shocked at what was happening. There would be young men and women, living as companions, neither marrying nor being given in marriage. There would be people smoking cigars, eating butter and, worst of all, nobody going to Church to worship God.

Nobody seemed to be old. As far as could be seen, nobody got ill, or did any work. All they needed was to hand. Everything 'grew on trees'. This would never do. Did these people not realise that unless they gave God humble and hearty thanks for the wonderful world they lived in, he might take it all away? Nobody seemed worried about it. They were impossibly childish. "We don't bother to do anything like that", they said. "Of course, God made this perfect world and we are happy in it, but God hardly needs telling. He knows we are happy". What some said shocked him, "Why should we be grateful to God? We did not ask him to create this world, nor ourselves in it. God is not like man. His thoughts are not as yours. It would be silly to say, 'Thank you'. If you did, you would be saying it all the time. That would be ridiculous. Happy folk don't say that they are. We don't need to tell anyone, least of all God".

The newcomer, having devoted a lifetime to these matters, has many arguments.

He stressed the 'positive'. "You should see some of the inspiring buildings where we worship God. We have wonderful music and great choirs who sing the praise of God. To hear and participate is uplifting". Some might say that, if the newcomer found it all so wonderful, he should return whence he came, and end up on the dung hill to provide manure for another crop.

The newcomer managed to gather a few who listened. What he would need, to establish his case, would be for some, hitherto unheard of, misfortune to strike someone, not among his group of 'disciples'. The last thing anyone would think would be that this had happened as a consequence of his arrival. Before long, there would be times for prayer, then great Cathedrals and all the rest of it. There would be disputes about which way they should face, whether this or that form of architecture or some other was truly pleasing to God, or this or that form of service, when to fast, pray or go on a pilgrimage. There would be quarrels over these things. Meanwhile all manner of misfortunes would occur. The more they did so, the more people would hang on the words of the newcomer and his disciples. He would have 'corrupted them all'.

There could be a defence against this. "No thank you. We know what it is like where you have come from. It is untrue to extol your wonderful heritage, as built to the glory of God or to his greater glory. How can anything add to the glory of the One who creates all things? Many harmless men fell to their deaths building those places. We know all about your world and its conversation of knowing good and bad. We decided that we did not want it. The one, who got us out of it, said that if ever we should feel a need to pray, we should go into our private room and pray in secret. That is what we do. His prayer ends 'but deliver us from evil', so we leave that to God. It makes life less burdensome and we don't need to know what is bad and good. We took his yoke upon us and learned of him, and we found rest unto our souls. Your way leads only to the rubbish dump".

That is the world, which, as he himself said, was manifested about Jesus; "If I by the finger of God cast out demons, then is the rule of God come among you". Would anyone want that? The only ones, who might, would be such as found the established 'conversation' of knowing good and evil beyond their ability, those not among the 'fittest'. For most, it would be a last resort, when all else failed. Jeremiah knew this, all too well, in himself. If it provided whatever nobody else could or would, as when someone, who had been to all kinds of physicians, was healed by Jesus, it would be wanted no more. In that case, one needed an endless sequence of 'disasters', to reduce one to 'poverty of spirit'.

It is a fearful comment on the nature of mankind. When nothing 'better' avails and we are 'down on our luck', our imagined friends abandon us; but we are picked off the floor by one who embodies meekness and poverty of spirit, offering comfort when we are sorrowful, and speaking of these things, we are glad of them. Once on our feet, they become a nuisance. Thanks to them, we can aspire to better things. They must be cast aside. When one, who speaks the words of the rule of God, and himself embodies them, might heal us, all others having failed, we rejoice. Having been given health, we might find that we had every reason to be rid of such a man, just as in the story told by the evangelists. The fourth evangelist, or his source, comments that Jesus needed no one to 'tell him what was in man'.

If the world is created wholly good, how is it that it does not seem so? Whence came evil and all manner of nasty things, and why? The answer provided by the old story is bleak and unequivocal. 'You are given a world full of evil things by the Creator, because you ask for it and need it'.

How can God afflict mankind, even 'innocent' children, with all these horrors. How long is any child allowed to remain 'innocent'? If Jesus' teaching be any guide, it is for as short a time as possible. Jesus gave all the instruction that any man or woman needs about how and how not to pray in less than fifty words. How many billions of words have the religions of the world, including Christianity, churned out since, all, in one way or another, demonstrating the inadequacy of his words? Yet, what he says about prayer is self evident to any child; so much so, that it needs not to hear those words. If any little child might feel a need to pray, it would not think of doing so except as Jesus said, in secret. It feels silly when seen doing so.

When, consciously, did childhood begin? Cognitively, it seems to do so, almost gradually. It does not begin with the process of birth. One does not 'see birth'. What, then, of Jesus' words about not 'seeing death'? It is as if one emerges onto a 'stage' prepared for one's entrance, with everyone else as 'background players'. No words, attributed to Jesus, need saying. All are self evidently true. Do we, then, arrive in this world, from one whose reality is that to which his words, alone, give expression? Eternal life cannot be 'after death', unless, in such terms, it is equally 'before birth'. It is necessary, for those who bring up and educate children, to make them children of 'this world' as soon as possible, and forget their citizenship of the eternal, whence they came.

In addition to the early chapters of the book of Genesis, Jeremiah found himself going through the early chapters of the book of the prophet Jeremiah and part of Deuteronomy in Hebrew.

These books are related. The prophet lived and spoke in the last days of the kingdom of Judah. He is led to see that if, the Lord 'watches over his word to perform it', the kingship, the kingdom, the Temple and all that went with them must be destroyed. In religious and political terms it was a time of high optimism, somewhat reminiscent of England in 1953. They were ruled by an upright young king, called Josiah. The Temple had been the subject of a sweeping reform, based on the discovery of an apparently ancient lawbook, unearthed during repairs. All heathen cult objects were removed, the Temple purified and the cult reconstructed to accord with the demands of the newly discovered book, containing long forgotten laws of God, delivered to Moses in the wilderness. This book is thought to be the core of the present Deuteronomy.

The rapacious power of Assyria, which destroyed the northern kingdom of

Israel, had declined, as had that of Babylon. To the south, Egypt was not the power it had once been. Josiah was enabled to extend the borders of the kingdom to those of his forefather David. In these heady times, and while still young, he was 'inspired' to take an army to the pass of Megiddo, to waylay an Egyptian army led by Necho, on its way to finish off the waning power of Assyria. (In Hebrew the 'hill of Megiddo' is 'Har Megiddo', hence Armageddon.) There he was killed in 609 BC. 20 years later the Babylonian army laid siege to Jerusalem, took the king and many of the nobility captive, installing their own nominee king in his stead. Eleven years later the city was besieged yet again and, this time, destroyed, leaving the Temple in ruins. Many were taken away captive. "A voice was heard in Ramah, lamentation and the weeping of bitterness.........". What then of the reforms of the temple, 'according to the laws of the Lord?' How did all this shew that the Lord watched over his word to perform it?

'I Samuel VIII', describes the occasion on which the tribal elders decide that it would be sensible to have a king/ruler, like the nations round about. They were faced with an organised enemy, who had settled on the coast, the Philistines, whence the name Palestine. They were technologically more advanced than the Israelites, having steel weapons, while there was 'no smith in Israel'. They were also more cultured than the Israelites, making the term 'Philistine', applied to uncultivated people, inappropriate. It was the Israelites who were the jerry builders, 'if a dog leaned against a wall built by a Jew, it would fall down'. Whereas temporary alliances between tribes had been enough to ward off invading tribes in the past, the Philistines presented a long-term threat. It was sensible, therefore, to have a centralised form of rule with a king to lead them in battle. Hitherto the leader had been, Samuel, who was the 'man of God', but he only appeared, when occasion arose. Having taken their decision, the elders consult him. Samuel consults God on the matter.

He is told, "It is not you they have rejected from ruling over them but me"; but to give them a king/ruler as they demand, having, first, warned them of the consequences. Samuel's warning shews that he has, on the basis of praying to God, a more earthily 'realistic' grasp of the nature of all forms of rule by men, than any political analyst. Any human ruler will be dependent on those who empower him. He will have to reward them, and will not obtain the means by digging into his own pockets, but those of others. Once set up, such a form of rule must inevitably grow. It becomes impossible to get rid of it, only replace it with another, as occurred when the kingdom split and the northern tribes, broke away and formed a separate kingdom.

Jeremiah was struck, not only by the truth of the warning and its baleful conclusion, "You will cry unto me in that day for the king you have chosen, but I will not answer", but the clear logic of the original words to Samuel, "It is not you that they have rejected from ruling them, but me". If God is the eternal creator of the universe, such a being must be more than able to govern, safeguard and provide for his people, defending them against all their enemies, without assistance. If not, he is not God. It is the same 'logic' as underlies the tale of the garden. Their own history supported it. They needed no ruler or king to safeguard them from the Egyptian cavalry. God led them through the wilderness, 'great and sore', without the help of any ruler. When Moses got 'ideas above his station', he was rebuked.

This simple and childish logic cannot change. If there is God in truth, such a being must be able to rule and safeguard 'the people of his own possession' and all people on earth and impose his laws, without the help of any men or women. If such a being needs the help of men, not only is 'he' indebted to them, 'he' cannot be considered God, for God must be able to do 'anything'. If it is assumed that God is unable to impose his own laws unaided, no matter what grandiose titles be given him, it implies that he is, in truth, a very feeble being, who needs men and women to impose his ways and laws, by stoning those guilty of adultery, and so on. He cannot, effectively, be God without their help.

The great king David, whose heirs were to rule the kingdom of Judah, was hardly in a position to impose and enforce 'the laws of God'. In one act he stole Uriah's wife, committed adultery, then had Uriah murdered in an attempted cover up. His punishment was left to God. Why is not that of any other malefactor? Does God deal only with kings, princes and governors, while they deal with lesser beings? There is ruthless rationality in the words to Samuel. He needed no mystical vision, dream or trance to reach that conclusion, only the clarity of mind of the little child. Nothing could change that 'word', if God were truly God. No amount of coronations, solemn anointings by priests, or the sacrifice of every sheep and ox on the face of the earth could change it. Months of fasting and weeks of prayer make no difference, nor yet did an upright king who reformed the worship of God. What they do is to obscure it.

This ruthless and childishly clear logic led 'back' to the story of 'Adam and Eve'. If the world is created, it must be created wholly good, why then should it be filled with nasty, evil and bad things? The answer the story gives is simple, 'You need them, ask for them, and have got all that you demand and more: all that the demand implies'. "Cursed be the ground for thy sake...". It is futile to have the knowledge of good and evil, unless there is what seems 'good' or 'evil' to know. The demand for it assumes that it is there to be known. The 'response' of God is just as when the tribal elders demanded a king. Having pointed out implicit logic of the demand and told Samuel to warn of the consequences, they are given what they demand and more. They are given all that the demand implies.

The prohibition derives from the 'logic' of there being God, who creates all things wholly good. It cannot be otherwise if, in truth, there be God, for 'he' determines that which is good. All the praying, fasting, vigils and pilgrimages in the world, cannot change it. It is futile to pray for a better discernment of good and evil. All one might hope for, if one sought assurance of the truth of there being God, would be ever greater confusion, as to which was which. If such confusion made life impossible, someone might say, 'God alone is Good'.

Any human enterprise is, then, bound to collapse, 'as a victim of its own success'. Unless there be discovered a pill for eternal life, which is logically impossible, men are bound to die. They will die of something. Once discerned, someone will seek to find a way of preventing or alleviating it. There is, then, no end to the amount of sickness and diseases to be found, analysed and treated. The only way to sustain such an enterprise is by endless economic growth. That, itself, bodes fair to render the earth nigh uninhabitable for many, if not most. If, at the same time, mankind loses belief in God and, so, of the possibility of eternal life, the need to take all possible steps to extend life on earth becomes more pressing.

The 'responses,' attributed to God, in both stories, giving both what is demanded and all that the demand implies, are possible only for a being of infinite power. This set the demands of Jesus in the Sermon on the Mount, such as "If a man sues you for a coat, give to him your cloak as well", in a new light. They are demands to act, in enacted parable, as God alone can act. The chapters of the book of Genesis, bequeathed to Jeremiah by his mentor, forced his return to what was clear to any child, that God is all and nothing less than the word implies. Belief in the one true God means, not religious observances and beliefs, but the end of them. There was no altar nor temple, nor a list of laws in the garden, nor any marriage ceremony.

Crucial to the story of Creation, is not so much the meaning attributed to the word create, but the word God. If there is God now, there ever must have been and ever will be. If there is God, the world, whatever its perceived extent, is created and governed by a being beyond all means of influence and control, as the *present* reality. Whatever intervening processes may be discerned do not change this. They obscure it. It is therefore good for man ever to be recalled to the power of the infinite, unless we can be sure that no such being exists. Better, if such a being does exist, to learn to live in direct dependence upon it.

Jeremiah could see this, but with his mind alone. Every other sense rebelled against it; even more, against the consequences of such a perception.

However much it may have borrowed, the opening account of Creation describes the world as any untutored and unaided eye sees it, and as, instinctively, almost all perceive it today. In his oratorio, 'Creation', after a period in his life of much doubt, Haydn reverts to a very naive depiction, with lambs appearing full grown, tigers prowling, created as they now are. Naive it may be, but it is a world that is joyous, fun to live in and bursting with vitality..."In it was life and the life was the light of men". If there is God, the universe, as we now see it, is created. Any attempt to see it otherwise will lead people to misconstrue the evidence, with potentially disastrous consequences for themselves and their children.

If all is created by God, who is, by definition, eternal, we have to allow the possibility that, in linear time, the process of creation can act 'backwards' as well as ‘forwards’; 'beginning' and 'end' are reversible. History can, as it were, be created backwards. Jesus himself speaks in this way, saying that Abraham rejoiced to see my day. He gathers the 'ends' of time into the midst. He speaks of himself as having come 'from above' and of returning thither, nor confines this to himself. "To them gave he the power to be the children of God".

In 'reality', then, every child enters life on earth from the eternal, from a world, in which the sayings of Jesus alone stand; for they alone articulate that word. There is much about early childhood that would tend to sustain such a view. As I have pointed out, the sayings of Jesus are self evidently the truth for little children. If they are ever allowed to think of there being truly God, they need no saying.

If all is created, we have no means of knowing whether some newly discovered object is newly created or has been there all along, but unnoticed. We cannot know whether anyone had genes years ago, or even has them now, save when they are removed for examination. In one of Augustine's dialogues, the questioner asks whether his knowledge God was like that of his knowledge of the course of the sun. Augustine says that it is not. He could not know whether some hitherto unknown cause, or the 'hand of God', might mean that the sun would not rise tomorrow. "You do not believe that will happen"? "No". Said Augustine, "you did not ask what I believe, but what I know". Is it possible that we are given the appearance of the world that our knowledge needs, and are delivered into the hands of those expert in that knowledge, taking our children and children's children with us; just as the man and the woman are given the world that their demand to know good and evil needs?

The same 'logic' can be seen in the story of the kingship. It seems a sensible decision, almost democratic. It must have seemed even more so and pleasing to God, when Solomon built the Temple. But, of course, Solomon did not build the temple, or even pay for it, any more than William built Westminster Abbey. To sustain such a world as good, language has to become amenable lies. We are, then, led further and further into this world of lies and nonsense, which must be sustained. It becomes ever more incredible and unthinkable that God made it clear that to demand a king was to reject him from ruling over them. "You will cry unto me and I will not answer".

Oh, but God is ever merciful, full of understanding, a God of love and forgiveness. This entire vocabulary, beloved of those of religion, comes into question. Did not God love the world *so much,* that he gave his only begotten son? No he did not. He "loved the world in *this way*, that he gave his only begotten son, to the end that all that believe in him should not perish, but have everlasting life". It is no act of love or mercy to pretend that God is not what the word, logically, implies. If God is not what, logically, the word implies, all religious and 'theological' language is confused and self-contradictory, pretending that God is not what he is.

The designation of the one forbidden tree and the original words spoken to Samuel derive from the logic of the word God. They go without saying. The Ten Commandments, given to Israel are, without anything being added, such as no man or woman could impose and enforce. As the word 'god' and the being indicated are at one, so is the purpose and expression of those ten 'words'. Israel is and claims to be the people of God's own possession. The ten laws given to her, for her life as a nation or people, are such as God alone could impose.

Given the words spoken to Samuel concerning the kingship, what would be merciful for God? If God were, by our criteria, merciful and forgiving, he would, overlook their 'mistake' in demanding a king. (Samuel comes to say almost as much). That would be tantamount to saying, "Sorry chaps; you were right and I was wrong".

At this time, Jeremiah could hardly see that phrases like, the 'response of God' were misleading. Although, in the stories of the Garden and the demand for a king, it appears that God 'reacts' to the demand of the man and the woman and of the people; it is, in truth, the word of God that remains unchanging. The destruction Israel, as a nation, derives from the way they have chosen. It is 'built into' kingship, or any form of rule by man, that it leads to this, just as does a way of life based on the knowing of good and evil.

Of this we can find innumerable parables. We take it for granted that any product will work, if the makers' instructions are followed. If we choose to disregard the servicing instructions for a car, we have no grounds for complaint if it breaks down. If we disregard the makers' instructions about the use of brake fluid, we endanger others. If one were to extend the parable, and imagine the appointed agents of the maker recommending owners to disregard his instructions, one comes close to parables of Jesus and his 'woes' to the scribes and Pharisees.

If, as we have it, it is forgiveness to overlook mistakes, it is to delude everyone. If, mistakenly, someone turns right, not left onto a motorway and so heads north instead of south, it is no help to say, "It does not matter, keep going as you are". That would suggest that Edinburgh and London might obligingly change places. Apart from all else, it would be inconvenient for those living in either city. With every mile, one compounds the error. With the establishing of the kingship and its inevitable development, they go farther in the 'wrong direction'. Temples and all that goes with them serve only to delude them that this is not so. That there may be an excellent cafe on the way to Edinburgh does not make it the way to London.

There was a horrific parallel to this kind of argument. It was the height of the cold war. The major powers argued endlessly that security lay in being armed and prepared with ever more destructive arsenals of nuclear and other weapons. If the possession of such weaponry provides peace and security, every nation should have them. That, either by accident or design, could lead only to catastrophe. The attempt to make nuclear power seem 'good' by turning it to peaceful ends, in power stations and the like, could, as well, lead to catastrophe. Such installations could make the breakdown of an economy, or, even more, an outbreak of civil war, or 'terrorist' attacks, have terrible consequences.

Samuel's warning, that they will cry unto the Lord in that day but he will not answer, is of the same order. They are in no position to hear. Temples and solemn anointings serve to re-enforce the deafness. The building of the Temple 'proved' that the Kingship was 'good' and approved by God. It was a long while before Jeremiah was led to see this on the analogy of taking a wrong turning, longer yet to see that the prohibitions given to mankind and then to Israel might be seen as notices, warning of uncleared minefields, or even as instructions to put, not soapy water, but oil in an engine. It is not an act of mercy or love to remove danger signs and allow people to wander in minefields, taking their children and grandchildren for a picnic. It is not helpful to them to say, "I forgive you for doing so", unless one urgently tells them to change their minds, turn round and exit by the way they came.

He came to see a group of seemingly oft-repeated sayings of Jesus as summing this up, those in which he categorises various permutations of divorce followed by marriage to others as 'adultery'. In the famous passage, which appears to have been appended to the beginning of 'John VIII', he tells the woman, "Neither do I condemn thee. Go in peace, sin no more". It is no use telling those who have divorced partners and married others, 'sin no more'. It is almost inevitable that they will return home and continue living as before. If the second marriage is established, they have a home and children thereby, gathered friends as a 'couple' and especially if it is seen as blessed, 'in the temple of God', the possibility of Jesus' words having truth becomes unthinkable.

The word translated 'sin' means, at root, to aim at a target and miss. The word 'evil' derives, in Greek, from a word that means that which is burdensome for little reward, and the pain that derives from it. Jesus said that 'all the sins and wickednesses of the children of men would be forgiven, only the 'blasphemy' against the Holy Spirit of God would never be forgiven'.

Chapter Twelve.

"The old order changeth."

The Principal, who had appointed Jeremiah, was soon to retire. There was much speculation as to the likely successor.

When he took over the department, while numbers were maintained, they did not recruit many 'first choice' students. There had been a display of the Church Colleges and their prospectuses, when Prince Philip opened the new buildings. For certain subjects, there might be reasons for spending three years in Derby; if one were studying Theology, there were few. The entries under 'Divinity', or, as most preferred, 'Religious Studies', were more or less the same. He decided to change the entry. Out went all mention of sociology, psychology, and the comparative study of religion. The latter, he thought, could only be based on superficiality.

The B.Ed degree was instated as a four-year course. The Chairman of the University Academic Board, the Professor of Christian Theology, said that his department would, under no circumstances, award degrees, of which theology was an element, unless students offered Greek or Hebrew. He also insisted on their having an acquaintance with the development of Christian doctrine. Many argued that such things were a waste of time for those teaching in junior and infant schools. Jeremiah was 'the only one in step'. The subtleties of argument involved in the debate of the Nicene definition were valuable for their own sake. Having to learn a language like Hebrew, where one faced the problem of turning a series of unfamiliar symbols into a noise, would give those teaching infants, an idea of the problems encountered by young children. Whether the arguments had validity he cared not.

If these were to be part of the B.Ed, they could not be learned in the last year alone. He lost no time in establishing them as part of the syllabus, included in the prospectus. The purpose of the course in Christian theology was to give students as sound an understanding of the great tradition of Christian doctrine as possible, within the limits of the course. To this end there would be courses in the biblical languages, early doctrine, the history of the Church in England etc. At the next meeting, the Professor did a 'cat in pan', on the matter of languages. Jeremiah already had his entry printed. He said that, on the basis of the Professor's earlier insistence, he had advertised courses in Greek and Hebrew and early doctrine. He was allowed to be the odd man out.

Many, including the new chairman of his governing body, a Bishop, told him that no student at the level of Colleges of Education could possibly tackle a language like Hebrew. All he could do was to await the results of the new entry.

There were enough first choice applications to fill the department twice over. Though not permitted to take only first choice applicants, it transformed the teaching. They had students, who had applied because they wanted to study what that College alone offered. The results, in the certificate, reflected this. The chief external examiner, the Professor of Theology at Durham, was so impressed with the scripts he received on the matter of early Christian doctrine, that he wrote to the Principal. He would have been pleased to read such well informed and competent answers from full time honours theology students in their third year. Better was to come with the B.Ed. The only students to be awarded First Class honours in the College had offered Hebrew.

Learning such things seemed to give them a confidence among their fellow students. Divinity did not seem a soft option. Having to follow the arguments of such as Athanasius, Augustine and the like seemed to sharpen minds. All seemed set fair.

He wanted the syllabus to be established, before there was a new Principal. The fashion, at the time, was for all embracing departments. Subjects like History and English were being grouped as 'humanities'. Religious studies would fall under such a head. Divinity would not. There was also the matter of assessment. The traditional method, by examination, was being replaced by various forms of continuous assessment.

It was the custom to send a sample of examination scripts to the Chief external examiner. Jeremiah sent them all. He insisted that the scripts should have not a mark left on them by the internal examiners. The entire responsibility for the grades awarded would be left with the external examiner. If there was any dispute, his umbrella was up. Other Colleges had moved to forms of continuous assessment. In order to moderate them, there was a scheme whereby lecturers from different Colleges looked through the work, as external moderators, before the chief examiner did so. He had been to other Colleges to perform this task. One had about six hours to look through the work of about 20 students, accumulated over three years, and interview those selected as 'borderline', or to be given high grades. All one could do was confirm the assessments already made, alter a plus or minus here and there, to shew that one had been.

The Chief external examiner proposed that a student, who had been awarded very good grades, should be failed. He had, himself, been of the opinion that the student should be awarded a high grade, for an excellent study of some aspect of the Dead Sea Scrolls. All would have been well, had the external examiner dropped to sleep quickly. Instead he thought about one or two phrases in the study. They seemed familiar. They were familiar. He had written them. He went downstairs and got a brief Introduction to the scrolls that he had himself written. The entire study had been lifted from his own book. He felt that an outright failure was deserved because the student had not the wit to choose a book written by someone else. The board overruled this decision. Jeremiah argued that this was unfair to the students from his College, whose grades were based on written examinations.

His motives were base. The new appointment would be a moderniser, keen on both continuous assessment, and combining studies. The longer the syllabus and system of assessment were established, the more secure they would be. Examinations were not the only element. Course work was taken into account and all did a special study. Many seemed to obtain higher grades in examinations than their course work would lead one to expect. There was an argument against even that. "Of course they do, they have to work in the months before exams. It allows them to mess about in the earlier part of their time". When he suggested that this was a good thing, he was made to wish he had shut up.

Chapter Thirteen

An Ice Cream

Hannah decided to learn German. They enrolled at the College of Technology. The teacher was called Baker. As a teacher of German, as a spoken language, he was without equal. All had to be "Auf Deutsch bitte." He conducted his classes 'con brio'. His qualities as a teacher were exceeded only by his qualities as a loyal and generous friend. Derbyshire born and Derbyshire bred, he may have been "strong i' th' arm". He was not "weak i' th' 'ead".

One Sunday afternoon he and his wife and two daughters went to the park for the afternoon with Jeremiah, his wife and two sons. As they walked ahead, talking of things that seemed to be of great moment, Hannah called out that their son would like an Ice cream. "Tell him, I will buy him one on the way back". Jeremiah was too lazy to walk back to buy one there and then, and unwilling to interrupt the conversation. They walked round the park, threw sticks into a lake for the dog to swim after, went to a pitch and putt, and returned to the car park, by a different route from that by which they had come. As Jeremiah got into his car, the Baker said; "You never bought the Ice Cream. How can a child ever trust you if you do not keep your word?"

The Baker tended to be like that. He would seize on such things and be inflexible...inflexibly right! He did not do so often, but when he did, he was unanswerable. In that way he was reminiscent of Jesus in the Gospels. There was nothing that could be done about it now, so they drove home. It would have been forgotten, but for the fact that at 9 o'clock on the Monday morning, Jeremiah's Hebrew class arrived to begin the second set book.

The book of the prophet Jeremiah opens with an account of the prophet's call. He comes on a twig of almond. Because it flowers before it puts forth leaves, it is known as the wakeful tree in Hebrew. It looks dead, but suddenly bursts into flower. The prophet sees it as the Lord shewing him. "Jeremiah what seest thou?" "I see an almond twig", is the not very profound or spiritual reply. "Even so I watch over my word to perform it". (There is a play on the word for an almond, and the verb to watch over).

"Different story from me and the Ice Cream", thought Jeremiah.

In the narrative of books like Samuel and Judges or the prophets, trivial incidents, in the context of world history, prove greatly significant. The son of some country priests near Jerusalem sees a twig of almond, and 'his' world is turned upside down. A hedge trimmer from Tekoa sees a plumbline and it is the same. Some man, of no account, has a wife, who is unfaithful and leaves him with their three children. The result is a furious indictment of the infidelity of

Israel.

The third evangelist lists the good and the great of the time. Beginning with Caesar, he works his way down through the Governors, to the Procurator and the High Priest. They serve to establish the date, when the "word of the Lord came to John the son of Zechariah in the wilderness of Judea". Who the hell might he be, and where in the great empire, ruled by Augustus, is the wilderness of Judea? It's one up from Galilee. What business had God to send his word to some nobody in a place like that? He should work through the established channels. There were plenty of priests and seers in Rome. Augustus was semi divine.

It would be easy to translate the incident into the kind of narrative to which Hebrew lends itself. It could say that Jeremiah was caused to forget, or 'the Lord caused him to forget'. It could say of the Baker, 'Then the word of the Lord came to the Baker, Go tell that Jeremiah that he forgot to buy his son an ice cream. I watch over my word to perform it".

What struck Jeremiah on Monday morning was: "What if the word that the Lord 'watched over to perform' was that of Jesus in the Gospels?" This, he was beginning to see, was not essentially different from that of the law and the prophets. If what God said is what God is, the only way, by which God could not watch of over his word to perform it, was by ceasing be God. If God is eternal there is no such option. He was coming close to the opening of the gospel he had read as a child.

If the earth is created, it will manifest that underlying 'word'. It would have the equivalent of an auto-immune system, so reject mankind if it lived on any other basis. One would then expect what is now called the 'environment' to become degraded. Harvests would fail, the rains would come when not wanted, not when they were, and so on. Plants would become diseased, animals would produce maimed offspring, the moral law which upheld society and its laws would break down and, with it, family life, just as in the curses that conclude Deuteronomy. This was, at the time, a novel thought. Few, then, worried about the 'environment'. Jeremiah did not derive this anxiety from any empirical evidences, but from an ancient book. That he was prompted to do so was the result of forgetting to buy an ice cream.

This trifling incident was not forgotten, either by himself or the Baker. Some fifteen years later, he and the Baker having moved to different parts of the country and lost touch, the Baker phoned him. Within a couple of minutes he asked Jeremiah, "Have you forgotten the Ice Cream?" He had not. The Baker asked whether he had genuinely forgotten or was too 'mean' to do so. Jeremiah could recall his feelings at the time. That this should be was not surprising, as all one can remember of any event is the impression left on one. A mass of feelings was present. One was that it was a nuisance for him, and he did not want to turn back. Another was that he had been told that Ice Creams and, especially frozen lollies, were agents of tooth decay.

How uninformative words like 'mean' were. Many, being 'mean' over certain things and unwilling to spend money on them, were not so about others. Jeremiah was one. It, therefore, indicated 'priority'. That made the matter worse. The wishes of a little child had a low priority for him, yet he stood and declared belief in one who said, "Except ye receive the kingdom of Heaven as this little child....". He had forgotten. Would he have forgotten if it had been someone important to him like a bank manager, from whom he sought a loan?

Chapter Fourteen

A Pharaoh arose that knew not Joseph

The New Principal was appointed about a year before taking office. He was greatly interested in religious studies and the religious life of Colleges. Although he spoke reassuringly of how honoured and humbled he felt at his appointment, always ready to listen and the last thing he had in mind was to impose his own ways, Jeremiah was uneasy.

In order to leave the newly appointed Principal in no doubt as to his position, he wrote an article in the professional journal. It seized on flatulent use of language in articles therein, many of which were contributed by the Principal elect and those who shared his views. He called it "Faith in Education", typed it on his father in law's typewriter, and posted it, after the closing date. He was taken aback, when he received a letter from the Editor, saying that, even though it was late, he had decided to make space for it because it was such an original point of view. The old Principal was still in charge. She, on the verge of retirement, could enjoy the ridicule of such language.

The new Principal was keen on continuous assessment. Jeremiah's retention of examinations had been achieved by observing the letter, not the spirit of the rule. There was a footnote to the system of assessment by 'formal assignment', saying that there was no reason why examinations should not constitute a 'formal assignment'. The new Principal, ahead of his time, thought 'self-assessment' better still. Students should be led to assess themselves as having failed.

He was keen to have a department of religious studies, not one of 'Divinity' or 'Christian Theology', though he never mentioned this directly to Jeremiah. "What is in a name?" Jeremiah knew that much would be in a name. Here was a curious 'syndrome', which Tom had mentioned. Innovators will demand changes of names and titles, but accuse objectors of being obsessed with them. Given the continuing high level of recruitment of first-choice students, and the fact that their students had, alone, achieved first class honours in the B Ed, he felt that he was in a strong defensive position.

The lecturer, who taught the history of early English Christianity, was chaplain. He decided to resign; so Jeremiah put an advertisement in the Times for a replacement, specifying the work in the department, which was what the chaplain was paid for, as a senior lecturer. Normally, when posts carrying senior lectureships were advertised, there were many applications. He was surprised, when the Principal's secretary handed him only four. Even more surprised was he to be told that these were the four selected for interview. "Were there no more?" "Oh yes, many more, but they had been discarded". They were to be interviewed in about a fortnight. He was not allowed to see the others.

Usually, applications were sent to the department concerned. There, about eight or ten were selected, on the basis of qualification to do the specified work. These were passed to the Principal, who took up references and made a short list to be interviewed. The old Principal was still in office. It was explained that the Principal elect felt it vital that he should select *his* chaplain. Jeremiah took them back to his study. Not one had any special interest in the specified areas of work. Under the old regime, that would have ruled them out entirely. The Principal would have thrown them into the bin, saying, "I refuse to employ people who seem unable to read an advertisement".

The interviews would have been incredible in a Whitehall farce. Two said that they knew something of the areas of study needed, and would be prepared to read about it. One said that he had no knowledge of it, and did not see much point in it anyway. He had no great interest in the teaching side of the appointment. With the B.Ed degree it was important, as the University had to recognise the qualifications of staff.

The Episcopal Chairman was in the Chair, flanked by the Principal elect, and the Principal in office. Jeremiah was allowed to ask questions about the work of the department. He could give his opinion, but not vote. Three candidates were given cursory interviews. A young and personable clergyman was interviewed at length. He was the one who had no interest in the area of study specified. After all had been interviewed, the Chairman said, "I take it we are all agreed that there is only one candidate".

When asked his opinion, Jeremiah said that from the point of view of the department, it could put them into a muddle. He was concerned at their ability to continue with the syllabus advertised in the prospectus. "It is the chaplaincy that is vital". The fact that he would be paid as a senior lecturer in the department did not matter. The young man, pleasant enough as a drinking companion, was appointed.

Every year, there was an event known, prosaically, as Annual Day. The governors came to lunch. After lunch one of the Bishops, of whom, including the Chairman, there were four, would address students and staff. Sometimes it would be the entire student body assembled in the hall. On other occasions, the address was given to a selected body of students who came for lunch.

The lot fell on the Bishop of Lichfield. He was a well-built man with a florid face and a nose that looked as if had endured many rounds in the square ring. He rose to his feet in gaiters and frock coat. All knew what to expect.

He made no attempt to shew familiarity with current educational theory. Instead, he reminded the staff and students that, though they now enjoyed state grants, it had not ever been so. For much of its history the College had depended on gifts from the "man in the pew", whose generosity had built the place. To these men, who also paid taxes, they owed a duty. He was known as 'the man in the pew'; by some as 'Bruin'. This year, his eloquence knew no bounds. He threw down a challenge to the staff. They should stand firm on the Foundation Charter of the College and resist the evanescent theories of educationists. If any found themselves in trouble with the authorities, they need fear nothing, "We the Bishops will stand firmly behind you. Rest assured: you will lose nothing thereby". With that ringing call to arms, he sat down.

He was reported as having made a courageous stand. He had said what needed saying. Those, who understood the politics of these speeches, said that he was addressing a 'constituency' in his diocese, which objected to the waste of money on education. One or two things, he had overlooked. It seemed that he had not read the foundation charter, which had been framed and hung in the entrance hall to the Old Building; but a suitably pruned and 'politically corrected' version, that appeared in the College History, which omitted a commitment to the teaching of the "rites and doctrines of the Church of England".

He seems not to have heeded the parabolic advice of Jesus, who asked, "What King goes to war without first counting the cost?" Whether he had consulted his fellow Bishops on their readiness to make sure that none, who found themselves in trouble with the authorities for doing as he said, lost anything, is doubtful. Jeremiah, for example, was not yet 40. Most of the Bishops were in their sixties. He earned almost as much as one of them as a Principal Lecturer. Another oversight was that, for any member of staff, he and his fellow Bishops were the 'authorities'.

It chanced, in those days, that the Education authorities of Derby and Derbyshire joined with those of the Diocese, and said one to another, 'Come let us revise our agreed syllabus of religious and moral education'. As was their custom, they set up a committee, which 'took counsel together'. After much deliberation they produced the revision and, having done so, called on such as Jeremiah to speak about it to meetings of teachers, shewing them what materials are available and what changes had been made.

Thus it was that he found himself in Chesterfield, on a Saturday afternoon, to speak about the new syllabus in the Parish Hall. Usually he found about 20 people in a room, enabling him to make a few introductory comments and then allow the audience to look at a collection of books and other materials that he had assembled, with the help of the College Librarian. Thereafter there would be open discussion. The sight that confronted him filled him with panic. The Hall was packed. 200 faces stared up at him. There could be no moving about, or looking at anything. His informal introductory comments were useless.

The chairman said how lucky they were to have him. From what he had heard of their speaker's talks, they were in for a lively afternoon. He was unfortunately brief and sat down. What followed was an object lesson in the art of burying oneself, like his mother's fox terrier, which dug down a rabbit hole under a shed, then could not get out.

He stared at the audience, holding the syllabus in his right hand. Thinking he had something profound to say, they became hushed. The truth was that he had not an idea in his head. What they saw was not someone waiting for absolute attention, but a rabbit staring into the headlights of a car. He looked from them to the syllabus. It was grey blue. It used to be red, but that was hardly worth pointing out. He then noticed the title. It was not "Agreed Syllabus of Religious and Moral education", but Syllabus of "Christian Education".

"One change that you will notice immediately is the title". That was rich. He had had a copy for over a month and had only just noticed it himself. It sounded all right and he had made some noises. It is hard to say whether he was possessed of demons, or given what to say in that hour. "It raises the question of what determines what is 'Christian', if not the reported sayings of Jesus in the Gospels".

He could not resist a sniping throwaway, "unless, of course, the Bishop of Derby and his education officer, the education officers of Derby and Derbyshire have been into the wilderness and found a new Christ".

"There was but one basis on which they should be taught; that they happened to be true. If they were not true they should not be taught, so radical were their implications. If they were the truth, every child had the right to know what this man said. If not true, we had to face the fact that, as reported in the gospels, Jesus must be seen as the single most misguided and misleading figure ever to have lived. If the four evangelists had not reported him aright, they were guilty of misleading the world. It was no good shuffling. If what they reported was not substantially true, they were liars, while, especially in the case of the fourth, making much of the need for truth".

"One thing alone guaranteed the truth of the words attributed to Jesus in the Gospels. It is that there is, in truth and reality, God. If there is God, then all that he is reported to have said follows, as night follows day". He was not sure that Jesus should properly be called a religious teacher at all. "Most religions seemed to imply that what they called 'God' was an ultimately controllable being, who acted according to rules which, they claimed, he had himself laid down".

"If there was, in truth, God, there should be no surprise that the words attributed to Jesus were followed by mighty works, such as no man could do save God be with him. His words were no less miraculous than the things we refer to as miracles". He recalled the words he spoke to those who would have stoned the woman caught in the act of adultery. Having got this far down, he went on digging and, like his mother's terrier, piled up the spoil behind him, so that it had no escape, nor could even turn around. There was no rabbit in the hole.

"The syllabus, in the preface, says, three times, that its purpose is to produce mature, thoughtful, self sufficient, participating members of a democratic community. That seems somewhat at odds with Jesus saying, 'except ye turn again and become as little children, ye shall in no wise enter the kingdom of Heaven'. It seems that the demands for citizenship of the democratic kingdom of England are the opposite of those of the kingdom of Heaven. That is strange, since Her Majesty solemnly undertook that all law and governance in her realm should be subject to the law of the Gospel, when she received the orb set under the cross.........Come to think of it, the Kingdom of Heaven is unlikely to be democracy either, as I think that God has notions of being a dictator. He is said to have said, 'Let there be light and there was light'; no record of a vote being taken, nor of a committee being set up to discuss it".

He, later, suggested that, since the Queen and her ministers imposed the teaching of the syllabus, the Archbishop and the Earl Marshal should devise a ceremony, whereby the Orb set Under the Cross was solemnly handed back for safe keeping.

He had pictures in his mind as he stared, first at one then another member of the audience, his newly appointed Principal, the Chairman of his governing Body, the Diocesan Director of Education, his grandfather encircling heads with nooses, of his mother being left to light kitchen ranges while the family went to Church, the committee that revised the syllabus. "Put that in your pipe and smoke it", or, as Joy used to say, "Put that on your needles and knit it", less politely, "Either pee or get off the pot!"

He had got their attention. He then went back, more or less, to saying what he was paid to say. He sat down. The Chairman asked for any questions.

The open forum became an auction in impossible sayings in the gospels. One, above all, exercised many, especially head teachers. "What can one do about the sayings about marriage and divorce?" All of them end up with someone committing adultery. About 25% of the children in any class have parents living in roughly this state. There was no way out. "If we could be sure that Jesus said anything, he must have said that. It was the most oft repeated remark in the gospels. We may not like it, but if we are passing on what Jesus taught, he taught that. Take it or leave it. It would be a deceit to pass off any other view, as being 'Christian', if what Jesus said determined this".

"If you think of it, Jesus is ruthlessly logical. If I, as a married man, have an 'affair', that is what we all call adultery. If, then, I divorce my wife and marry the other, all I have done is to make adultery the permanent and recognised basis of my life from then on. It is ridiculous to pretend otherwise. It is as if a certificate from a magistrate can make adultery not adultery. You might as well apply to a magistrate for a certificate saying that a garden hoe is not a hoe. If, in that state, one goes off to church, what is one doing? One is assuring all that Jesus is wrong and his words may be disregarded, in the name of God".

He went on to point out that Jesus did not condemn the woman caught in the act of adultery, but said, 'Go in peace sin no more'.

He lacked the quality of mind to understand things until he articulated them. He found himself saying things, which he had hardly before thought. As I have described it, it is made to sound like a single uninterrupted discourse. It was not. It was punctuated with questions. The meeting ended. The Chairman said that they had had the kind of lively hour he had anticipated. He gave Jeremiah £5, expenses. He packed his wares into the boot of the car and drove home.

If he had dug a pit for himself, did it matter? The College governors, as upholders of the Gospel, could hardly object. The position he had taken was 'fireproof'. How could the L E A's object? What else could be the basis of 'Christian' Education? Chesterfield was far from the College. It would all be forgotten in a couple of days.

"Did you get on OK?" "I think so". I got a bit of a shock when I saw the size of the audience". They had tea. The telephone rang. "It's some man wanting to speak to you".

"Was it you that gave that most interesting talk in Chesterfield this afternoon?" He was a sucker for flattery. "It might have been. I did give a talk there this afternoon about the new syllabus........." "That is it. I was not there myself, but my wife was. I would like to meet you and ask some questions. Would that be possible?"

Jeremiah said, "Yes of course. What did you want to know?" This led to a string of questions, which he answered without inhibition. When the questions abated, he asked, "When would you like us to meet?"

"I don't think that will be necessary now. You have given me all I need." "What do you mean by, All you need?" "Oh," said the voice. Did I not tell you who I was?" "No" said Jeremiah, "You did not even tell me your name". "I'm Editor of the Sheffield Telegraph". "Shit", thought Jeremiah, "I've done it now. Oh well, Sheffield is a long way away. Nobody round here will read the Sheffield Telegraph".

He felt invulnerable on the ground he had taken. How could Bishops and Archdeacons, or any in the congregations committed to their charge, object to anything he had said? He even allowed himself to dream of the Bishop of Lichfield, shaking him warmly by the hand. When the Diocesan Office in Derby asked him to write a review of the syllabus, he wrote more or less the same. That was on his doorstep. So angered was the Diocesan Education Officer, that he demanded the right to publish a counter review. Jeremiah did not care if he produced fifty. One member of his department did. His name was George, a clergyman in his sixties. Academically, George could have eaten all the other members of the department at once. He had taught philosophy at Leeds University. He was massively well read, and had a tongue like a rasp. George feared no man.

It was monstrous to invite someone to review a book; then invite someone else, because you did not like the first. If Jeremiah disliked the Diocesan Education Officer, George did so in spades. He had a publication of his own, his Parish Magazine. Because of George's waspish comments, it circulated far beyond the confines of his parish. Not only did he not fear the Bishop or the Diocesan Education Officer, he did not fear the Bishop's wife. He took the matter up in his magazine. His editorial ended by describing the Diocesan Education Officer and the newly appointed Canon Theologian as, "these two grovelling and sycophantic creatures of a politically minded prelate who has all the qualities of the worst of the Borgia popes, except that he lacks their political savoir faire and the nerve to keep a mistress".

Only now did the enormity of what he had said, dawn on Jeremiah. His only way back would involve him saying that the words of Jesus in the gospels did not determine what was 'Christian'. Had he not spoken as he did, he could sit on the fence. Seen in terms of terriers and rabbit holes, it was foolish. Seen in the terms of the Gospel, he had said an unequivocal "Yes" to the teaching of Jesus. His livelihood depended on his saying "all else besides". If, having spoken as he did, he returned to that position, it was tantamount to saying that, having considered the words of Jesus, he had reached the conclusion that they were not 'of God'. He would then face the fierce indignation of Jesus, when confronted with those who had been his disciples, but had returned to the synagogue, "Ye are of your father the devil a murderer from the beginning and the father of all lies".

It seemed that this was, now, the position of the Church, which, over the past century, had produced lives of Christ, based on the gospels, knew them, and now backed away from them. While in ignorance of them, as was the Roman Church, for most of its membership, this dreadful saying did not apply. "Because ye say, 'We know', your sin abides".

The New chaplain was a pleasant man, but not much help in the department, often failing to appear when scheduled to teach, being busy with enquiries into the religious life of the College, at the behest of his master. He assembled four groups of students to discuss and report on it. One reported that they thought it 'immoral', in the 'latter part of the twentieth century', for the Chapel in the Old College complex to be a single purpose building. It cost too much maintain for only one purpose. The worship therein should not be of the traditional Christian kind, but should "reflect educational and social values". What the other three groups reported nobody knew.

The report of this group was circulated to all staff by the Chairman of the Governors, for free and frank comment. Jeremiah knew what Athanasius would have commented, and what Jerome, not one to mince his words, would have said. Before recalling the Bishop to some of their comments, he decided to take up the matter of the expenditure on the building. He went to see the man in charge of maintenance. "Do you have much to do on the Old Chapel?" "No", he said, "apart from cleaning the gutters we hardly touch it". The place that cost a fortune in maintenance was the New Assembly Hall. He was surprised to find that a good number of students attended morning prayers in the Chapel and a larger number, evensong. In a period of three days, hardly a soul entered the Assembly Hall.

Outside the Divinity lecture room was playing field, with a running track. As far as he could see it was never used. He went to see the head groundsman. Because it was so little used, it cost a lot to keep moss free. Armed with these facts he wrote his free and frank reply. He ended with Elijah's, "How long halt ye between two opinions?" He did not adopt a hostile tone, at least not openly. He wrote as if it was what the Bishop wanted to hear, so ended, "I think you will agree, My Lord, that this brings us face to face with Elijah's contemptuous question........"

He was summoned to meet the Chairman. The Bishop was conciliatory. "We are meeting as friends" he smiled. He was genial and maintained his affable manner. Jeremiah sat silent, which was unusual. For the first time in his life he realised how unsettling it was for the other, if their questions and arguments were met with silence. In the story of the Grand Inquisitor, Jesus says nothing, leaving the Inquisitor to justify himself against silence.

The Chairman's tone began to change. He said; "While I sympathise with your nostalgic desire to cling to Nicene orthodoxy as the basis of your teaching, I have to tell you that it is now outmoded, irrelevant and meaningless". Jeremiah stared at him. The matter of the syllabus had nothing to do with the case. It had the approval of the University. The Bishop went on, "If you do not see fit to come into line and realise that your first and only duty is to the state, which pays your salary and whose schools we use, then authority will have to be asserted. You know what that will mean. Think about it and let me know". He resumed his affable manner, "We can chat more at any time. This has been most interesting".

In one sense he was right. The state did pay his salary, the college depended on its schools; but the State claimed to be Christian, as was made explicit at the Coronation. When the students arrived they were solemnly given a Bible at an inauguration service by the Bishop himself, "Here is wisdom, here is the Royal Law. Here are the lively oracles of God". What now of the Bishop of Lichfield and his challenge?

Though taken aback by the Bishop's cavalier dismissal of what he called 'Nicene Orthodoxy', the interview did not worry him. Jeremiah had not mentioned it. It was as if the assertions of the Creeds had no connection with the Jesus of the Gospels. They and their 'doctrinal' assertions belonged in a separate 'conversation' from the words and teachings of Jesus. It was as if the one, whom all declared to be "God of God and Light of Light, Very God of Very God, being of one substance with the Father", was distinct from the One who said, "I say to you, Swear by nothing at all....". He was being, unwittingly, driven back to the opening of the Gospel, which he had read as a child, even more to the opening of the epistle of the same name, where, "That which our eyes have seen our ears heard our hands handled and which we beheld....", determines the truth.

His reaction was one of blithe assurance. No Bishop of the Church could publicly own such a view. He was not even greatly unsettled by the speed with which the Chairman had changed his manner from meeting as friends on Christian name terms, to making threats as Chairman. He had met this before, when he had attended a residential conference on religious education. One of the lecturers was a leading light in the evaluation of children's concepts of God.

Teams of teachers had questioned children about their ideas of God. He had a list of sample questions, and a scoring system, according to the 'maturity of their concepts'. At the end Jeremiah asked what seemed a reasonable question; "What were the criteria, by which you evaluated answers, as revealing mature or immature concepts of God?"

The lecturer said that he had submitted his scoring system to a list of eminent theologians and they had agreed. He listed their names. "Was that satisfactory?" "No", said Jeremiah, "I asked for the criteria on which you evaluated concepts, not the names of your high powered friends".

In the bar that evening, he was accosted by a man who had a label on his lapel, giving only his first name. In his opinion, people who asked silly and awkward questions were immature and unfit to be lecturers. Jeremiah had not asked for his opinion, and "if you want my opinion, you are a pompous twit!" The 'first name' became a College Principal, who would have words with his own newly appointed Principal.

Tom Hurdle had been appointed Education Officer for the Ely Diocese. A teacher of Divinity from that Diocese was present at the Conference. Knowing that Tom had been at the same College as Jeremiah, he had complained of his unhelpful questions. Tom had been unswerving in his loyalty. He said that he had known Jeremiah for many years, and that if he asked difficult questions he would not have done so without good reason.

Jeremiah's view of the Bishop's comments, about the irrelevance of "Nicene Orthodoxy", was changed by the Confirmation Service for the pupils of the High School, a day or two later. It was his duty to attend, as he had been made a governor, representing the Woodard foundation. He sat with his friend George. The service was conducted by the same Bishop, who gave the address. For five minutes he spoke about how unimportant were things like confirmation veils. What was truly important was that, in being confirmed, the girls took upon themselves the faith of those who stood for them at their baptism. They took on themselves the hallowed faith of the Catholic Church, expressed in the language of the historic Creeds. "Bloody humbug. It was another story yesterday!" Poor Hannah was uneasy at his increasingly aggressive language.

He felt that the integrity of his own teaching was at stake. Integrity was hardly a word that could be used in connection with anything he said or did. He had come to enjoy the time he spent with the group, who studied the early development of doctrine. He had spoken, with 'approval', of the position of Athanasius and his supporters. He did not know whether, in truth, Athanasius identified the one, who was "of one substance", with the one whose words the evangelists reported. According to his biographer, Pachomius, he had. Jeremiah had produced a duplicated life of the patriarch of Alexandria for the students, based on it.

He felt that Athanasius would have tarred all the Bishops with the remarks of the Chairman. He felt an urge to force this on the Bishop of Lichfield, like a poker player, saying, "See you"! There was nothing honourable in this. He was becoming increasingly irritated by the indirect attempts to undermine the basis of the teaching of the department. He had enjoyed ten happy years teaching. Now it seemed certain to end.

His folly was beyond belief. He lived in a world of dreams, among clergymen of the last century. Not only had they freeholds on their livings; many had incomes, which were enough to live on comfortably. Given that security, such as Sidney Smith could say that he had no doubts as to the apostolic descent of the English episcopate, as the only way to account for the Bishop of Exeter was that he was he descendant of Judas Iscariot. He went back to such as Athanasius, hiding in the desert. Hannah pointed out that he had no wife and family.

The Diocese had a conference. Now that Greek was in vogue it had become a synod, which met in the Assembly Hall. Students were invited to sit in as observers. There was a guest speaker, a Bishop from far afield. He spoke of maintaining Sunday as the "Sabbath rest". Having been long absent from England, he noticed the loss with sadness.

In the Chair was the Chairman of the governing Body. He spoke of being 'full members' of the Church. Only those who put themselves on the electoral roll and participated in decision-making could be seen as such. Jeremiah asked a double question. First, he wanted to know if being a member of an electoral roll had displaced confirmation as the sign of full membership, "now that we all played happy democrats". Second, if the Bishop was so anxious to restore Sundays as the Sabbath rest, should not he and his clergy give the lead?

The Chairman leaped up and seized the microphone, saying, "I know how to deal with these student revolutionaries". People who asked cheap questions like that were not fit to be members of a serious discussion. Jeremiah felt silly and sheepish, and began to make a shambling apology. As he did do, there came to him; "The Lord has delivered thee into mine hand this day". He was indeed sorry that the Bishop found someone, who spoke of the priesthood breaking the Sabbath, unfit for membership of a serious discussion. The question did not originate with him, but a man called Jesus who came from Nazareth, whom he thought to be of some significance in the assembly.

The last straw came, when the Academic Board met at the University. All members of the relevant department in each College could attend. Mostly it was left to the head of the department to do so, the others having better things to do. The meeting wound its way to 'any other business'. Everyone was putting papers into brief cases and standing up, when the Secretary, who represented the department of Education said, "I have been asked to put a proposal before the board by someone who would prefer to remain anonymous".

The Chairman, the Professor of Christian Theology, thought this irregular. Jeremiah objected. The secretary lent down and hissed, "You had best shut up, if you know what is good for you. It's your own Principal". The Chairman said that they might as well hear the proposal, but ruled that, if any objected, it should be held over and put formally on the agenda of the next meeting. It was that all colleges adopt the title "Religious studies".

Jeremiah objected. It made no difference. The discussion took place. He reminded the Chairman of his ruling. It was to no avail; so he packed his bags and walked out.

He had already written to the Chairman and governors. Some months ago, the Chairman had made it the condition of his future employment, as head of department of Divinity, that 'he abandon his nostalgic desire to cling to Nicene orthodoxy, as it was outmoded, irrelevant and meaningless'. He did not see how it was possible to teach 'Christian theology' in Church College, save on the basis of 'Nicene orthodoxy', to which all gave public assent. If this were to be the basis of his future employment, then he would have to resign. He did not think, for a moment, that a board of governors consisting of four Bishops, six archdeacons and a cricket team of canons, could accept his resignation on such a basis, without discussion. If they did, they would endorse that condition.

He phrased his letter carefully to force this choice. It was not a straightforward gesture. He had taken some care to cover both possibilities, and had been casting about for other forms of employment, in case the governors should, if he forced the issue, endorse the condition laid on him by the Chairman. He half wanted them to, as he was becoming tired of the endless manoeuvrings and the atmosphere of mistrust. He had been looking for some form of employment, in which this would not be.

There was a further motive, which was, perhaps, the only decent thing about him. Hannah's father was losing his sight. Jeremiah felt that it would be a good idea, if they could live closer to her family and that he should have some form of employment that enabled him to be at home, in case Hannah was needed to help care for her father. He had, therefore, started to look into the possibility of running some kind of guest-house. He still nursed foolish dreams that the Bishop of Lichfield and his like might find him some employment which would free him from all the 'political' manoeuvring that seemed to have invaded the College, with its dependence upon the state.

If the other governors stood with the Chairman, it would mean that he could hang the albatross round all their necks, but he did not think that they would. He was extraordinarily foolish. It should have been obvious, especially for one who had read of Ahab and Jezebel, that the governors had no choice but support their Chairman, and that the explicit condition would not be the issue. It would be a matter of authority, just as Jezebel had seen, "Who is King in Israel, you or this Jezreelite?" It never occurred to him that, if the other governors had refused to endorse the Chairman's view, his own position would be untenable.

He knew that, in the long term, he would not be able to sustain his position nor that of the department, if it was to be constantly eroded by the indirect methods that were being used. He feared that he would end up with the department of divinity as a branch of sociology and psychology, within a department of humanities. At heart, it is doubtful whether, in any positive sense, he himself believed 'Nicene Orthodoxy', as relating clearly to the reported acts and sayings of Jesus. He was a hypocrite. Insofar as he believed anything or in anything, it was on a largely negative basis. Insofar as it was positive, only his mind saw it thus. 'At heart', as we say, he did not feel that, for example, those who divorced and married others deserved the nasty epithet ‘adulterers’. 'At heart', he did not feel that one should not resist (him that is) evil. As long as other people did so for him, he was happy to enjoy the fruits of their having done so. He did not feel that, whenever anyone might pray, it should be in his inner room, behind a closed door.

These words served, usefully, as 'stones of stumbling and rocks of offence', to be used much as David used the smooth stones from the brook to stun Goliath, then taking Goliath's own sword to remove his head. He never thought beyond that. Had he contemplated what occurred thereafter, he might have seen that that was when difficulties arose. They would have done, for him, had the governors supported him. He never went so far as to imagine the consequences of living, or seeking to live on the basis of Jesus' words, in any positive way. It was 'all right' in novels like the "Idiot", or stories of yesteryear.

Beneath all the hypocrisy, other matters were beginning to seem important. The question of what might or might not be mature concepts of God seemed secondary and trifling in comparison with the objective question: whether there was in reality such a being. If God, as a being to be feared, was an infantile concept that got a low score, Jesus had a low score. That seemed ludicrous, both on that basis and on the basis of reason. If, as must be, God creates the universe, such a being is to be feared. He had begun to have such a fear, as distinct from being frightened. He was frightened by unpredictability. He was not frightened of Mr Blyth, he feared him. He was frightened by such as the Chairman, and the New Principal.

It seemed unwise, in view of Jesus' words, "I thank thee O Father, Lord of heaven and earth, that thou hast hid these things from the wise and prudent and revealed them to babes.....", to dismiss 'infantile concepts of God', just in case Jesus was indeed raised from the dead. Those, who spoke dismissively of such concepts as 'infantile', declared that he was. How then could their words be trusted?

He found it easy to throw out derisive remarks, but impossible to produce any positive or 'constructive' scheme. It is easy to see why his new Principal saw no point in discussing anything with him. When those in authority invited lesser beings to discuss something, it tended to be the easy way to get what they wanted by persuasion, rather than asserting their authority.

All of this had repercussions at home. It was reminiscent of war, without the danger of sudden death or physical injury. He was actively engaged in battles. He had his allies. Hannah, at home, had none of these things. She just had anxiety. She also, as she complained, had to deal with people socially. She could never know whether either Jeremiah or one of his allies might have offended them.

In the background was her family. Her father urged Jeremiah to apply for a post in one of the Colleges in his own area. He could not see that it would be disastrous if the same kind of issue were to arise again. Why should it? He would give him a reference. He knew the local Bishops, as friends. They were all affable men and stood by the Creeds. The Bishops on the governing body were affable men and stood by the Creeds.

Jeremiah had widened the argument, by writing to the Archbishop of Canterbury. He cited the condition laid on him by the Bishop of Repton, now endorsed by the three diocesans of Lichfield, Southwell and Derby. He asked simply, "Is it the view of the whole Church that 'Nicene orthodoxy' is to be seen as outmoded, irrelevant and meaningless, or just that of three eccentric midland bishops and one suffragan? If it is the view of the whole Church, should not the creed be removed from the Church's services, lest anyone be foolish enough to think that those, who led them to recite it, meant what they said?"

He was pleased and surprised to receive a prompt and friendly response from the Archbishop's chaplain. His Grace had had an exhausting year, and was about to take a vacation. So important was the issue that it deserved more than a quick response. The Archbishop would give the matter much thought and promised a full reply on his return. Jeremiah was exultant.

A month went by, and he heard no more; so he wrote again to the Archbishop, hoping that he had enjoyed his holiday, and reminding him of his promise. Another month went by and he heard nothing. He wrote again, enclosing a photocopy of his original letter and that of the Archbishop's chaplain. There was no reply. After a month he repeated the last letter, this time sending it by recorded delivery; waited a month and had no reply. He sent the same letter once more and no answer came. He then wrote, enclosing a stamped addressed envelope. By the time that Michael Ramsay retired, the Archdiocese of Canterbury was in the debt of Jeremiah to the tune of some twenty stamps!

He was contacted by Lady Playfair, who wrote of the matter to the Daily Telegraph. She was secretary of a society, which sought the retention of the Book of Common Prayer. The letters editor of the Telegraph was her nephew. She wrote of the affair in that paper, making one or two minor errors, giving Jeremiah the right to write of it in detail. The matter was even taken up briefly by an MP, one J Enoch Powell.

These things took place after he had lost his position. They had had to sell their home. The Archdeacon of Derby allowed them to rent a disused Vicarage. Given the acrimony that the matter caused, it was a courageous act. Hannah's steadfast loyalty was amazing. Jeremiah was unable to explain, to her or their respective families, why he had caused such a rumpus over a trifling matter, and that it was bound to recur if he found similar employment. If the matter was as crucial as he seemed to think, everyone else in the Church, especially the bishops and leading theologians would see it as such. "What makes you think that you alone are right, and everyone else is wrong?"

His dad saw it as a tiff with an apostate Bishop, saying that he felt sure that clergy and bishops, whom he knew, would not have behaved thus. They believed the Creed. Jeremiah asked what he would do, as chairman of the governors of a Church school, if a teacher said that the sayings of Jesus determined what was Christian. "I would support him, of course".

"Suppose that he followed this by saying that Jesus forbad anyone to swear an oath by anything at all, and said that those who divorced wives and married others made them adulteresses, and he had a deputation of parents complaining." "I would tell him to stop it immediately, or get out!" That was the position the Bishop was in. If Jeremiah were in the position of the Bishop, he would have done as did he; or be obliged to resign. He had a duty of care to the staff of the College.

The Archbishop could not answer such a letter. Jeremiah had succeeded in achieving much more than he planned. He was beginning to realise, but unwilling to see, that the hypocrisy of the governors was that of the Christian religion. The reported sayings of Jesus made it so, because, gathering up the words of the prophets, they articulated the logic of the word 'God', which meant, not religion, but the end of it.

Despite his dad's remarks, he preferred to believe that only politically minded prelates were hypocritical in that way. He deluded himself that parochial clergy and their congregations were not and, of course, that he was not being hypocritical himself. A more percipient person would have realised what his famous namesake was made to see, "the prophets prophesy wind in my name, the priests bear rule by means of them and my people love to have it so". He should have realised this, as the impossibility of explaining his actions became more clear. Try as he might he could not make even Hannah see why he had felt bound to act as he did. That put her into an impossible position, having to explain it to her own family. His subsidised lifestyle became a difficulty. But for that, he would not be in a position to act as he did.

Had he foreseen the outcome, he would not have written as he did. It was not only loss of employment that he failed to see. It was the consequential effects on his home life, and the fact that the whole Church stood with the Bishops. His dream was shattered. He imagined that someone like the Bishop of Lichfield would have come to his aid, or the Archbishop. What he thought they would do, he had no idea. His lack of integrity is perfectly summarised in the saying of Jesus about making tree corrupt and making also its fruit. He enjoyed the fruit. He depended upon it and was, therefore, unwilling to admit to himself that the tree was itself corrupt. If he did, it would set him against both his and Hannah's entire family.

Throughout this time Hannah's loyalty was remarkable. Here was her husband, with three children, throwing away secure employment, pension rights and all else; while refusing to seek similar employment elsewhere. He muttered about the same thing happening again, but why should it? He only need keep his mouth shut, and do what he was asked.

He wanted to turn his back on it all and forget all about what determined what was Christian, Nicene Orthodoxy and the "Law and the Prophets". As he read the books of the prophets, that seemed reasonable. Such as Amos had left his sycamore trees, gone off to Bethel and 'prophesied'. Then he went home and returned to trimming his trees. He forgot the of Jesus' fearful words of those who said, "Lord did we not prophesy in thy name?"

In truth there was greater worry, which neither his father in law nor his wife, nor his own family seemed ever to grasp, because he *feared* to explain. It was that the same was bound to happen again. If it did not, the entire dispute at Derby and his words would be made lies. It very nearly was. That it was not was through no fault of his.

At the end of the term, there was a final staff meeting, now called an 'academic board'. It ground on in its normal manner until 'AOB' was reached. At this a senior lecturer in the department of education, who had been Deputy Head of the High School, asked why it was that the head of very successful department, who had been happily employed on the staff for more than ten years, should have felt obliged to resign. A woman, who was 'number two' in his own department, courageously gave support. The fat went into the fire. The new Principal sought to explain. Jeremiah accused him of lying. It was an acrimonious half hour. The next day a notice went up saying that the Chairman of the Governors wished to meet the entire staff. Jeremiah did not attend. Faced with a hostile staff the Bishop had asked, "I suppose you think it should be I that resigned?" He was taken aback when there was a chorus of, "YES"

Hearing this, he donned his mitre and took his crook in hand. 'It is Christmas, the season of Peace and goodwill, and we are a Church College. Would it meet the objections of the staff, if he met Jeremiah and suggested that he write a letter withdrawing his resignation? This he would commend to the governors and all could return to work in peace and harmony'. The message was conveyed to Jeremiah, by the kindly Deputy Principal. Jeremiah was hesitant, but was soon to be out of work. The Deputy was anxious that he should not be tricked. He suggested that he come to the meeting as his 'friend', so that there was a third party present.

This was done and the letter written, Jeremiah making it clear that there should be no more attempts to undermine the syllabus of the department. With that the staff departed, 'each to his own home', for the festival of peace and goodwill.

Nothing more was heard. He thought that he had been reinstated. Two days before Christmas, they were invited to sup with a clergyman, who was the number three in the Divinity department. He had urged Jeremiah to fight the issue. It was a matter of 'academic integrity'. Jeremiah did not know what that meant, but it sounded good. He said, "we are all with you, but you are the one who is good at thinking on his feet". A few moments before they left for supper, the telephone rang. It was the College Bursar. He regretted to tell him that his letter had not, after all, been commended to the governors, so the governors had not 'received' it. Hannah was upset, Jeremiah angry. They had to put a face on it and go to supper.

What baffled them was that their host knew what had happened, before being told. He explained that he had been to the Chairman and spoken to some governors. He had agreed to take over as head of department, if they felt it was in the best interests of the College as a Church institution, in order to save them the embarrassment of having to advertise the post. He had taken this step to maintain the standards of 'academic excellence', for which Jeremiah had fought. He had fought for nothing of the kind. This made Hannah angry. She felt that he was too easily mollified.

The Bishop had acted with cunning worthy of Jacob. Faced with the hostility of the staff at the end of the Christmas term he had moved adroitly to pacify them with his appeal to Christian values, until all had broken up for the vacation. When they returned, they would be faced by a fait accompli. There would be no point in raising the matter again. One could not but admire the way in which he had so speedily changed his vesture from that of Chairman of Governors, to that of the devoted pastor, and reminded them of the season of goodwill. The outcome, against his wishes, had saved Jeremiah from making all had said into a pack of lies. He would have been happy for it to be so, at the time.

Had it been, his position would have been untenable. He would have humiliated the Chairman and new Principal. The fruits of victory would have been more difficult to deal with than those of defeat. He had a devious motive in writing to the governors as he did, in the apparent safety of having another occupation to go to. By doing so, he could not only fix the words of the Bishop of Repton about 'Nicene orthodoxy' on him in writing, but also on the other governors, if they endorsed it as the condition of his continued employment. He phrased his letter to this end. Had he been reinstated, he would have been indebted to his colleagues. That would have falsified the issue. Few of them were interested in 'Nicene orthodoxy', or whether the 'Only begotten Son', declared in that Creed should be identified with the 'Jesus of the Gospels'. Had he been reinstated, Jeremiah would have had to abandon that identification and, knowingly, become the hypocrite he was.

Neither the governors, nor the Archbishop and his chaplain, would see it thus. They did not see the declarations that roll from the tongue, 'God from God, Light from Light, Very God from very God, begotten not made', as referring, directly, to the one whose words the evangelists report. For them it refers to one "who had suffered death upon the cross for our redemption, and made there, by his one oblation of himself once offered, a full perfect and sufficient sacrifice, oblation and satisfaction for the sins of the whole world........". The 'Christ of Faith' was seen as something more than the Jesus of the Gospels. Until his impulsive outburst, when caught with an unexpectedly large audience, Jeremiah would have agreed, though he had a growing suspicion that, unless one clearly identified the "Christ of Faith" with Jesus of the gospels, 'theology' became a 'tale told by an idiot, full of sound and fury, signifying nothing'.

He could make neither his wife, her family, nor his own, understand, because he feared to do so. To them it was a quarrel with a particular Bishop and Principal whose ways he did not like. He quite liked the affable Bishop. What the Chesterfield talk made clear was that, if that which is Christian was determined by the reported words of Jesus, it would not be allowed in any school, not even, as he was to discover, one run by monks of the order of S Benedict.

The future of the College was in the balance. The governors needed more grant from the state if they were to expand as planned. If it did not, the likelihood was that it would be bypassed, and have to close. Such views, as those canvassed by Jeremiah, would not help. The Governors had a responsibility to the staff they employed, to safeguard their prospects. They had a duty to cherish and preserve the institution founded on the gifts of the 'man in the pew'. Caiaphas and the Sanhedrin had a responsibility to safeguard the interests of the people of Judah and Jerusalem, and to cherish the institutions and traditions of the people.

Neither they, nor the governors of the College acted as nasty men, but as 'responsible' and dutifully 'caring' men. Had not he been a protagonist, Jeremiah would have wanted them to act as they did. If he had been in a position to gain advantage from someone like himself getting into trouble, he would have jumped at it.

All they achieved was the postponement of the catastrophe they sought to avert, in both cases. The Sanhedrin appeared to have headed off the immediate risk of an uproar among the people, which would bring Roman reprisals. At the time the newly rebuilt temple was half finished. It had been in building some 40 years. Jesus was arraigned for speaking against it. Stephen was stoned for doing so. The prophet Jeremiah had spoken, 'Thus saith the Lord', of the temple as a "lying word". It was completed in AD 68-9. Completion, no doubt, gave rise to an outburst of religious and nationalist fervour. In A. D. 70, the army of Vespasian, led by his son Titus, ravaged the land and laid siege to the City. It reduced the newly built Temple to the state it is in now. It had lasted about a year.

They might have been better advised to listen to Jesus' words. As reported in the gospels, they are deceptive, becoming wholly different if heard as "finished". If he spoke and acted, as described in the IVth gospel in Jerusalem, then, by any accepted religious and political standards, Caiaphas was right to see a serious danger of trouble, with which the Romans would deal brutally. That nobody wanted. Faced with that, who would not choose Barabbas? Jeremiah knew that, while he might not have stood outside the Judgement seat and shouted crucify, but stayed at home; he would have been relieved that others had done so. He would have continued to enjoy the peace of the city thanks to their action.

He would have passed the payment to his children, as did those of Jerusalem. He could have indulged the supreme hypocrisy. Remaining at home, while others bayed "Crucify", he would have benefited from the fruits of their demand, while 'deeply regretting' that they had done so. He could even set aside a day of sorrow, calling it Good Friday, or, perhaps, Remembrance Day, when he fasted and mourned for the dreadful things that 'they' did, while, for the rest of the year, being, in act, if not in word, grateful to them. This, in effect, he had done for the past fifteen years.

From time to time, while these events took place, and for sometime before, Jeremiah had a strange awareness of what he was doing. He felt as if he was working for the counsel for the prosecution, against the College and the Church, seeking evidence to sustain an indictment. In many ways Jesus as described in the Gospels might be seen as doing that.

Chapter Fifteen

"Dreams come true"

They ended up buying a small guest house and restaurant, which had formerly been a cycle shop, before that a Saddlery and, prior to that, a pair of small cottages on the Norfolk Broads; property, then, being cheaper there than in the West of England. Jeremiah's insensitivity amounted to purblindness. He was in his home country. Hannah was not. He had grown up in homes that were open, like pubs and Vicarages. Hannah had not.

The domestic quarters were scruffy and basic. He was used to moving about from home to home. It did not trouble him. It did not appear to trouble her, but she put a brave face on it. It did not trouble the children. As a business the restaurant was amazingly successful, if hard work. At the time, serving Sunday lunch was not common. He decided to make this the feature of the restaurant. He bought enormous joints of beef and a saddle of lamb and carved them in the dining room. At the time both beef and lamb were cheap. The provision he made was lavish, so each customer could have two or three helpings. Within a week or two, it was packed on Sundays, largely by local residents.

Some, holidaying on the river, had money to burn. In the spring and early summer there were parties of businessmen taking second holidays, with little intention of using the galley. He got his wines and spirits from Peter Noble in London. He asked him how much expensive liqueur brandy he thought he should order. "One bottle will last you months", was the reply. It lasted two nights. It was called, "La Chatelaine". Some customers had ordered several rounds of it on almost the first evening of business. The next evening another party had asked for some of the brandy with the funny name. "How on earth did you know of it?"

They had met another boat full of people down river. They had said, "You must try the Restaurant near Barton Broad. Ask for some Brandy with a funny name".

One regular customer on Sundays was a solicitor, who had a taste for quality wines. He was a man of integrity and perfect manners, though reserved. One Sunday, he asked Jeremiah if he sailed. "Yes I do. I have a single handed racing dinghy, but would like to have a half decker so that the family could come out".

"Would you like to buy mine?" asked Mr Smith. "What is it?" asked Jeremiah. "It is a Yare and Bure One design, No 61, Golden Copper", was the amazing reply. She was the younger sister ship of Red Admiral, which he had seen as a child and set his heart on owning.

Mr Smith was a fair man, and a man of his word. "If you would like to buy her, have the use of her this year, provided you insure her. When she is taken out of the water in October, have her surveyed. If you think £450 is a fair price, she is yours!" Within a couple of days Jeremiah was taking his family out in his own One Design.

Nationally the economy was not flourishing. The stock market collapsed. Hannah's father congratulated Jeremiah on the wisdom of the investment. You have done better than the rest of us. Jeremiah was still enjoying his subsidy, through Hannah, but the congratulation made him feel good. The Ministry of Education returned his contributions to the occupational pension. It was £1700

The property needed much work and a larger kitchen. This money would pay for it. Hannah's father had a small bank for capital deposits. It needed deposits, he said. Would Jeremiah deposit the £1700 with him until he needed it? He could put it into Hannah's account. Of course he would. It would not be needed for about a year. Her father had a beloved Latin phrase, 'uberrimae fidei'. He tended to end letters and conversations with "uberrimae fidei, as always, dear boy". It seems that, even if one knows the meaning of such a phrase, its impact is less in a language, incontrovertibly dead. 'Credo in Unum Deum' seems more convincing than 'I believe in One God', 'Kyrie Eleison', than 'Lord have mercy', 'Hosanna' than 'Save, now'; unless, of course, it be assumed that God likes being addressed in obscure, ancient languages.

Their evening clientele not only included holidaymakers but local residents and others who had second homes nearby. Among these was a Minister in the current government, and the cast of a popular television series called "All Gas and Gaiters". Among the regular Sunday Customers was a Yorkshire family who, with their son, were in business, supplying food to the offshore rigs. They said that their son was overworked, had few friends, and no leisure activities. They would be glad if Jeremiah would take him sailing.

The first year went by. They even housed Hannah's younger brother and his wife for about four months, for which her father was duly grateful. All seemed set fair as summer became autumn and Christmas approached. Jeremiah enjoyed working with his wife and family around him. In the New Year work on the property could begin. The first job was to have a damp course put in; then re-floor the restaurant. In the spring they could begin the new kitchen and bar. The architect had been ingenious in his design, enabling the business to remain open while it was being done.

Chapter Sixteen

"A Cloud about the size of a man's hand"

Ecclesiastical disputes were forgotten. The winter care of boats was more important, as were bookings for Christmas parties and Christmas Day; when, on the front page of the local paper, was a large photograph of the Cathedral choir, singing Carols in the banking hall of Barclays Bank in the City.

Jeremiah tore off a derisive letter. He accused the Dean and Chapter of using methods of fund raising of a vulgarity unseen since Tetzel sold his indulgences in Wittenburg, put it into the post and forgot all about it; until Christmas Eve, when they were invited to a party at the Old Vicarage. He knew nothing of their hosts, but that they were regular customers. He and Hannah were standing just inside the door of the drawing room, when a bespectacled man and his wife arrived. They were introduced. He was the organist and Director of Music for the Cathedral. His face darkened: "Is it you who write letters to the paper?"

Jeremiah had forgotten all about his letter. "No; that would be my old dad in Sheringham complaining about the Gas Board". "It was not from Sheringham, nor was it about the Gas Board. It was about the Choir singing carols in the Bank". "Sorry", said Jeremiah, "that was mine, I forgot all about it. I never dreamt that they would print it, as it was a bit rude".

"A bit rude! It was deeply offensive and you know it! I was with the Dean, when he read it. He was so angry that he tore the paper up and threw it in the fire." Jeremiah recalled how Zedekiah had cut his famous namesake's letter up and burned it. The man did not find this amusing. "We are trying our best to take the message of Christmas beyond the Cathedral. We can do without such as yourself, who should know better, ridiculing us".

The room had fallen almost silent. Hannah was embarrassed. He had put his foot in it again. He thought it best not to make some such rejoinder as, "Do you think that the Temple of mammon the best place to do so?" They left as soon as decently possible. Hannah pointed out that his ill-considered letter had cost them five regular customers and possibly more. There was no gainsaying her. She was right. Unknown to him, their hosts were leading lights in the "Friends of the Cathedral Choir", and the party consisted largely of members of that society. It was likely that his letter had cost more than five customers.

Christmas and New Year came. They shut the business for damp-proofing and reflooring. The entire ground floor was torn out. Hannah decided to take the three children to stay with her parents for the rest of the holiday.

Jeremiah had nothing to do. For some reason, he returned to the book of his namesake. He would translate it. He was again riveted by the opening, "Behold me watching over my word to perform it". His entire life had been characterised by unfulfilled words. They were like dud cheques. Jesus spoke of the children of men being held to account for every empty word they utter.

One occasion, in particular, troubled him. In his last year at Cambridge, his girl friend wrote a letter in which she had said, "I would marry you tomorrow, if I could be sure of your love and loyalty". He thought of his reply, which he hoped would appear to say what she wanted, but did not quite do so. He had said that his love and loyalty had been ever hers. His duplicity must have shewn in his manner and actions, and he was dropped. Here was a word he could never watch over to perform. It was not so much the girl herself, but, almost as with Jacob and Laban; he did not feel that he wished to be involved with another family, who would direct him. It never crossed his mind to turn up at her door 'tomorrow'. No doubt, her words would have been made idle.

'Everyone' said or wrote things like that in their youth. How often did people sign letters 'with all my love'? Should all speak as Cordelia? Such thoughts evaded the point. Here was an idle word, and "for every idle word shall the children of men be called to account". Jesus added "in the day of judgement"; but that, given an eternal judge, would be the ever-present reality. He could see the logic clearly. If we used words as a currency, which we could devalue at will, we could hardly consider the possibility of a being, who is his word, and would watch over it. It would produce chaos for millions, if they based their lives on the assumption that a given word had changed, when it had not. A being that is perfect, in the sense of being complete, has no reason to change his word and, if eternal, that word cannot change. He thought of the fearful words in the IVth gospel about judgement, "Those that do the truth, come to the light....". How, now, could he ever "do the truth"?

He began to think of many situations, where we rely on others not watching over their words. How difficult it would be, if a wife or husband divorced and married another, and the discarded partner watched over his or her word. The one who had 'moved on' could hardly complain. They had been happy enough to accept lifelong promises. Everyone worried about the other not remaining true; not the other way round. It was ice creams all over again. This was the last thing he wanted. He had used words of Jesus as smooth stones to sling, without needing to believe much at all. They now returned like boomerangs.

What he read appalled him. He could see what he had seen fleetingly, when going through this book at the College. If the earth is created, its underlying logic will be the word of the Creator. If one buys a car and disregards the makers' handbook, but thinks that one knows better how to service it, one might expect it to break down. The opening words of Jesus' teaching of the Kingdom of Heaven are, "Blessed the poor in spirit". Such might not be destitute, but they would not pursue endless 'growth'. That was to make wealth the key to all things good. Might we not, then, expect the 'environment' to become degraded? He related this to the opening of the IVth gospel, "All things were made by means of *it*, and without it was not anything made".

He pressed on. It was like reading an indictment in a court of law, with evidence to sustain it. What good did it do? It enabled those, who came after, to see that the catastrophe was of God. If God did not maintain his word in judgement, he could not be relied on to maintain his word of blessing. They were one and the same word.

Hannah returned. The boys were back at school at Buckfast. Their daughter was at a small village school nearby, where she was happy, having been scorned at the local school. The incident of the party was forgotten. He told her that the Yorkshire family had telephoned to ask when they would reopen, as they missed their Sunday Lunch. In a few weeks they did. While weekends were busy, the early part of the week was not, so he pressed on with his translation. At half term Hannah went down to Devon to see the boys. She was only away for a few days. When she returned, he shewed her what he had been doing. She read the opening pages. She said; "If I really thought you believed that, I could not bear to be under the same roof as you".

"Oh God", thought Jeremiah, "I do. I cannot see how, if there be God, one can avoid that conclusion". Like others in Churches, Hannah declared belief in God who created all things. Best forget it all. It was fine when he was chatting with people, but when he was not, the dreadful matter of, "Behold I watch over my word to perform it" would, in one way or another, return to him. He was in two minds. It would be nearer the truth to say that what he 'felt' and what he 'thought' diverged. He felt, as did Hannah and everyone else, that words written over 2,000 years ago were irrelevant. On the other hand, all who went to services declared that they believed in the Holy Ghost, "who spake by the prophets".

Work started on the new kitchen. As a legacy of the old cycle shop they had two petrol pumps in the car park. Not knowing where the tanks were, the architect specified that all digging should be done by hand, the area having been probed with non-ferrous implements. The builder's interpretation of this was to use a mechanical digger. "It'll be fine", he said, "They are always six foot underground". Jeremiah was looking out of the window, when he saw the digger operator leap from his cab. He had struck the vent of one of the tanks. He contacted the architect and rang the fire brigade. It took only 20 minutes for an engine and many braided caps to arrive from Norwich, 12 miles away.

The tanks had to be emptied, degassed and filled with slurry before anything else was done. Standing nearby was a bulk cylinder of Propane. "Half the village would have been damaged if all this had gone", commented the senior officer, "Yours would have been the one building undamaged, I guess!" This set back operations for several weeks. The builder went bankrupt. He was last seen evading angry people in his minivan diving down country lanes.

Meanwhile, the young son of the Yorkshire couple was a more frequent visitor; not just on Sundays, but on many a weekday evening. They all went out for a meal one evening. Jeremiah felt that himself to be the outsider. So self obsessed had he become, that he saw it only from his point of view. It never crossed his mind that the young man was becoming the 'insider'. This made him yet more obsessed with himself, morose and silent. Desperately, he sought to explain himself to Hannah. She thought, as would anyone, that to find some ancient book a source of anxiety was weird. In her shoes, he would have felt the same. That it was one of the prophets made no difference.

It is easy to see her point of view. Everyone who went to church declared belief in the Holy Ghost "who spake by the prophets". They did not get worked up about God watching over his word, even if that word were Jesus, so why should he? Jeremiah could find no answer. She was right. In vain did he point out that he had been speaking thus when they met. "Yes", said Hannah, "but I thought you would change. You were young then, and it made you different". It must have been intolerable for her. She had put a brave face on accepting a way of life that was not to her liking, in the hope that all these disputes would be put aside. So had Jeremiah, who enjoyed being at home with his wife and family.

He told her of the example of his failure to watch over his word and his devious letter to the girl he was with, while a student. Hannah was slighted. She said, "What you mean is that you married me on the rebound". In truth, it was opposite. Had he not chanced to meet her at the Boat show, he might have made good his word.

It was as if they belonged in diverging 'conversations', although both spoke the same language. What he saw, more and more clearly, as 'obvious' and clear beyond doubt, she saw as abnormal and weird. His argument that "everyone declared belief in the Holy Ghost who spake by the prophets", made matters worse. Nobody else took all that so seriously.

The accepted 'conversation' became ever more empty. Even clichés like, 'on the rebound' seemed ridiculous. What basis had anyone to think that human beings behaved like rubber balls? What basis had anyone to think that human behaviour had any relation to lead acid batteries, but all spoke of the need to 'recharge one's batteries'. What of spoiling children? People would say of 'spoiled' children; "They get everything they want". Almost certainly they do not. Might not this cliché be as misleading as those about absolute power? Through this, Jeremiah began to see something else. It seems that we tend always to seek to understand human beings and their behaviour, on the basis of the most recent scientific and technological advances.

He also noticed that, when children wanted something; if they pestered for it, then got it, they seemed to have lost interest in it. Was the desired object as important to the child, as the spontaneous indication of its parents' devotion? If, in that way, a parent responded instantly, the child seemed less prone to want things. Children seemed to understand, when parents could not afford things. When a child was denied something, whilst the parent could afford new cars and other such things, it was otherwise. What he signalled to his elder son, when he forgot the ice cream, was that what the child wanted was of less significance to him than his own conversation. When children are said to be spoiled by being given all they want, was not the truth more likely to be that they were being denied what they wanted most? If the 'ideal' is Jesus, what would constitute spoiling?

It was abnormal for any sane man or woman to make a fuss about forgetting to buy an ice cream for a child, years after the event. That was the problem with the "Law and the Prophets" and the sayings of Jesus. What was insignificant in the accepted 'conversation', they made greatly significant. His failure to do as he had said to his elder son made that an "idle word". He had not "done the truth". That the normal 'conversation' of the world was based on such idle words did not change the fact that Jesus said what he did.

Some evenings, after all customers had been served, there would be an order for two steaks. When all was finished, he would leave the kitchen and go through to the front. The meal was for Hannah and the young man. On one occasion the young man asked if he would care to join them, as if he was kindly permitting the chef to sit with them. Still he saw it only from his own self-absorbed point of view. He became more and more morose. The building work was nearing completion. Hannah would go down to collect the boys, stay with her parents, and get the money from her father's bank. It was late July. She had arranged with some friends at Derby, that their daughter, about to leave school, would come for the summer to help. Jeremiah drove Hannah to the Station in Norwich to catch the train. As she got aboard with their daughter, she said, "I will decide if I am ever returning".

So distraught was Jeremiah, that he took from his pocket all the cash that was to be paid into the bank, and flung it into the carriage, "You might as well have this then", he said tearfully, and turned slowly away. Hannah picked it up and sought to hand it back. He left it on the platform.

If he had thought, he would have seen how dreadful was her position. She had remained steadfast throughout his seemingly needless quarrel at Derby. She had suffered the loss of her home and way of life. She had followed him to Norfolk, and accepted a way of life that was not to her liking, in the hope that all concerns with things said in Church would end, and they could enjoy a normal 'conversation'. She probably saw, more clearly than he was willing to, that if he followed his argument to its logical conclusion, it would not only indict individuals like the Bishops with hypocrisy, but the entire Christian religion and all who participated in it. That, as he made obvious, in bitter arguments with his own relations, would include her family and his. Now these abnormal concerns had come home. She probably felt, in a way truly, that they had always lain under the surface.

Her father had thought of ordination and spent two years at a Theological College. He was a lay reader. He was now Chairman of a County Council, Deputy Lord Lieutenant, a Magistrate, and a prospective parliamentary candidate. He was also prominent in the affairs of the Diocese, as well as being on committees at Church House. He had friends who were Bishops. One was a well-known translator of the New Testament. If they saw nothing to get worked up about in words uttered by the prophets, or sayings of Jesus about idle words, why on earth should he? She wanted a normal husband and conversation.

None of the Bishops, Professors of Theology or clergymen seemed to think these things greatly significant. She had been to a private school whose chaplain was now an Archbishop. She had been to services, as had everyone else. They all said they believed in the Holy Ghost who spake by the prophets, but none of them got into a stew about "watching over my word to perform it". They all believed in One Lord Jesus Christ. None of them made a great fuss about uttering 'idle words' over Ice creams, or having written deviously to a girl friend years ago. If he had thought in a less self obsessed manner, he would have understood.

His conversation became increasingly embittered. Those who made these declarations had cheated and deceived him, especially those who knew, or could know, what they were saying. Why stand up and declare belief in Jesus Christ, if you don't trouble to read what he said? If you really believed that he was all you say, would you not find out what he said? Does it not occur to you that some fool might think you mean it? Why declare belief in the Holy Ghost who spake by the prophets? Does it not cross anyone's mind that some idiot might go and read them? Though the logic of his complaint was clear, nobody else seemed to worry over these things. The young man from Yorkshire and his family were friends of their local Vicar, and spoke often of services. They did not worry about these things. What on earth had the poor woman married? Not even his own family, who were all deeply involved with the Church agreed with him.

She phoned him from Devon, asking sharply, "Do you want me to come back or do you not?" He said, "Yes of course I do", but was stunned at the abrupt tone of her question. What he did not then know was that the young man had followed her down there and that they went out together. She phoned again to say that she was coming back, but would be driving, as her dad had given her an old car that had been passed down by a teacher friend.

At about five o'clock, when they were busy in the kitchen getting ready for evening service, she walked in with their younger son and daughter, the elder son having gone to stay with a friend. There was a pile of unwashed cooking utensils. All she said was, "I can see my place as usual". Jeremiah did not help matters by saying. "It is all under control. We have almost finished preparation and have time to clean down".

She then said, "Dad has refused to release your money". "But he asked me to deposit it until needed, to help him out of a shortage........." "He still says that you cannot have it".

With that she went upstairs. Jeremiah followed her, asking, again, what had happened. "He says that you have used too much capital already. It should stand on its own feet". "Why did he ask me to deposit it with him, when he knew what it was to be used for?"

"I don't know. You cannot have the money and that is that. In any case more than half has came from me. She was right, at least, if the property were seen as his. This, he did not ever see. All he could say was, "He said to me that it had turned out to have been a very wise investment and that I had done the right thing." "I expect he has changed his mind".

At this Jeremiah said something more truthful than was intended. "What does he want of me? Would he like me to kill myself so that he can have the insurance? How else can I pay the builders?" He wept.

The evening was busy. He never left the kitchen until all was finished, then went through to the bar. There sat the young man and his parents. Hannah was with them. With them were their daughter and younger son. It was almost 11pm. They had overnight cases packed. "I am not leaving them in the house with you in this state of mind", she said. We are going with the young man and his parents". She opened the door and left.

The girl who had come to stay was worried. She would not leave the bar with Jeremiah in that state with gallons of spirits at his finger-tips. He told her he was all right. She departed. He wrote first to Hannah, then to the woman he had felt so guilty about deceiving. His letter to Hannah was bitter and sad. This was the only means left to him to repay everything that he had inadvertently taken from her father. He had not wanted it for himself. He never wanted the subsidy on the car and so on. He left it in the bureau. To the former girl friend, he said that this was the only way to make good the words he had written to her. With that took from the bathroom cabinet a bottle of phenobarbitone, long ago prescribed for his younger son, when a year old, but unused, a bottle of brandy from the bar, and a hosepipe. He got into the car and drove off, posting the letter through the letter-box of the former girl friend's parents. He drove to a spot there he was not likely to be found, washed the phenobarbitone down with the brandy, having put the hose pipe in the exhaust. As he felt drowsy he switched on the engine,

If this was the 'conversation' of life, as it had to be lived, then it was best over. If there were no life eternal, at least there would be silence. There would not be people standing up and declaring belief in One Lord Jesus Christ, or in the Holy Ghost who spake by the prophets, and then turning against him, if he "believed their report". So he passed into oblivion.

Chapter Seventeen.

Entering hell

He did not achieve oblivion, but came near doing so; being comatose for a week. The engine stalled when he was unconscious. The effect on his wife must have been shattering. It was made worse by the fact that the girl, who was staying, rebuked her, saying "What kind of a wife are you, leaving him in a state like that, and going off with your boy friend?" Fortunately, friends took her away before she could say more.

It is often claimed that those, who attempt suicide, seek attention and cry for help. Jeremiah wanted oblivion. He wanted silence from the empty words of those who reported belief in God and "One Lord Jesus Christ", but retracted it when it came to anything he had said. Why not declare, "I do not believe in God or in One Lord Jesus Christ? Seemingly scrupulous doubts about the dependability of the Gospel records made no difference. When read out in Churches, these are not mentioned, nor were they with the "Law and the Prophets". It seemed to him that, unless he abandoned this attitude, his family were better without him. He was in the way.

He was not entitled to oblivion. He had spent many years doing the same. It was only since being at the restaurant, that he came to see what he had blinded himself to, that this hypocrisy was essential to Christianity. It could not exist, as a religion, without it, once the gospels were available to all. To that, he had himself been a consenting and benefiting party for many years. He sought more than oblivion. He sought to be accusatory, as a child saying, "Now look what you have made me do".

When someone kills himself, it leaves those near to him with a nagging question. Was there anything I could have said or done, left unsaid or undone, that might have prevented it? If, however, someone seeks to end their life, and *almost* succeeds, that nagging question vanishes. Why should this be? In the case of Jeremiah, the fact that he was not dead was no thanks to anyone near to him. It was attributable to chance facts, the work of nurses and others.

The fact that those near to him were not left with finality was, as far as they were concerned, 'luck'. Whatever may have been said or done, not said or not done, which might have caused it, remained the same; yet the reaction is wholly different. How could this be? If, when someone dies in those circumstances, we feel 'guilty', why do we not feel the same if they come within a hairsbreadth of doing so?

If one nearly runs someone over, missing them by a millimetre, it gives one a shock, for a week or two. If we hit and injure someone, it is another matter. Is it not the same with stealing and all else? "Like as a thief is ashamed, when he is caught". No thief can afford to shew shame until he is caught, so to do would be to invite detection. Neither David nor Claudius, Hamlet's uncle, felt any need of forgiveness, until they knew they were caught. If, as both did then, they asked forgiveness of God, it could only imply that they felt that they had got away with it before God, until they knew themselves to be caught. That is insanity, if one believes there is God.

Where did it leave Jeremiah? With regard to the letter, which filled him with shame, he wanted the reassurance of forgiveness, while yet being possessed of the benefits of being happily married to Hannah. At the College, he wanted to enjoy the benefits of performing in the pantomime, as well as the sense of 'integrity', he gained from pointing out that it was a fraud. The many empty words that he had uttered cohered with that. They were like dud cheques. If he had not himself uttered empty words, he had said "Amen" to them, when others did so. He had countersigned their dud cheques. He had spent much of his youth and early adult life, saying "Amen" to a 'conversation', that was wholly alien to the sayings of Jesus, and "thereout sucked out no small advantage". He had every means of knowing what he was doing. He was one who said, "We see....". He was now complaining that others did the same.

He could see no means, by which he could redeem empty words, or clear the implied debt. The only way, in which anyone can know that a debt is forgiven, is by finding, or being given, some way of paying it in full, and more. If one were given a way of being forgiven one's debts, would one want it? In his case, the answer would have been "No". The version of the Lord's Prayer he was accustomed to using, made no mention of being forgiven one's debts, or of the condition, for forgiveness, being that we also have forgiven those indebted to us. He was without excuse. His Greek was amply good enough to read the Gospels. He knew enough of textual criticism to know that not a single MS of the Gospels suggested any other words. It was to take the words and works of a man, who had not a word of Greek, to open his eyes.

He was absorbed by one aspect of death, its finality, not so much from the point of view of the deceased, but of those left. The possibility of eternal life did not change that. Death put a full stop to anyone's words. There could be no argument, discussion, nor any attempt to persuade, or get around anyone. One cannot charm 'the dull cold ear of death'. It put an end to any chance of making good any empty words and, thus, 'doing the truth'. There was no more chance to make good any injury and discharge a debt, to a corpse.

The death of Jesus 'finished' his words. As long as he remained alive, there must ever be the possibility that he might retract and so, effectively, unsay much that he had said. Because he did not (save in a single explicit instance) 'unsay' anything, the order, in which Jesus was reported to have spoken things, hardly mattered.

The same applied, in effect, to the evangelists, collating the sayings of Jesus and making a written record. As long as they circulated in an oral, or even partially written, tradition, there would be fluidity. Nobody could know that someone might not appear with some word of Jesus that nobody had heard, which might change all that had been assumed. Once the written gospels became established, they would kill-off any such fluid oral recall.

Jeremiah was transferred from the general hospital to an acute psychiatric unit. Hannah came from time to time, sometimes with the young man. Still, Jeremiah saw this only from his own self absorbed point of view, though, towards the end of his time there, he noticed how affectionately they walked, hand in hand, when they thought themselves out of his sight.

His sister appeared one afternoon, having driven from Durham. She rebuked him. She said that his duty was to love his wife. "Thou shalt love thy neighbour as thyself". Was not one's wife one's neighbour? Jeremiah had no answer. He had read Soren Kierkegaard's "Works of Love". Kierkegaard's argument that, since love was commanded, it was not an emotion, but an act of will, was at one with what Mr Blyth said of the word 'lovingkindness' in the book of Hosea.

As she said this and turned to go, her eyes ran with tears. The uniting of thought and emotion made her words impossible to disregard. Whatever could he do? Very well, he thought, I will do as you say. I will go home and love Hannah. Thinking thus, he went to sleep. When he awoke next morning; what he had agreed to do became spontaneous.

He felt very silly and avoided leaving the building. In the end he had to go out. Nobody seemed to behave any differently. Perhaps they did not know. After about a month he was standing in the pub. The friendly landlord said, "We all knew what you did". This amazed him. It was also a great relief. He had made a complete fool of himself and everyone knew. There was no point in pretending to be anything else. For a couple of months he was as happy as he had ever been. He enjoyed doing what Hannah enjoyed, rather than trying to make her enjoy what he did. It was spontaneous. The young man appeared regularly and, when he was there, Jeremiah, again, felt an outsider. Hannah sometimes vanished for afternoons. Often she would seek to persuade him to go off and sail his boat, or attend a cricket match.

She said, "Do you know that for the past eight weeks, you have been the husband of my dreams". He was overjoyed, until she added; "But it's too late."

The boys returned to school, as did their daughter. It was now autumn and business quitened. Hannah said that she would like a holiday. She thought she would tour around the Lake District, staying in small hotels. Would he be able to run the business and look after their daughter for a week? That would be fine. Within a day or two she was off. The week passed quickly.

He enjoyed looking after their little daughter. She was happy, when she came home from school, to run errands in the kitchen. He decided not to ask her what she would like for tea, but prepare something, he thought she would enjoy and say, "Tea's ready". He then sat down and ate with her. Formerly, she had fidgeted about at meals and never finished anything. Suddenly she seemed to eat happily. She was as good as gold when bed-time came, would take herself off and call down for him to read her a story and say goodnight. The week became a fortnight. They had heard nothing. He began to worry in case there had been an accident. He phoned the police. One afternoon some friends opposite said that they had seen Hannah in the village in her car. That could not be true.

That evening she drove into the car park, and they ran out to greet her. The woman who came home was someone he did not recognise. She walked straight past them, saying, as she did so, "I am going away for ever". Stunned, he followed her into the house. He did not get tea for their daughter, thinking that Hannah would want to do so. She did, putting it on the table. Immediately the little girl started fidgeting. Foolishly, Jeremiah said, "Come on, we have not had a grizzle out of you at meal times for nearly a fortnight". He got some food and sat down with her. Hannah looked at him angrily.

There was no time to think of these things, as they had a full restaurant. He did not see Hannah that evening. When all was finished, he went upstairs. Hannah was in bed, with the counterpane pulled over her head. She was obviously distressed. He asked gently, "What is wrong?" There was no answer. It was about half past ten. He sat on the floor by her side, and simply held her hand, which was protruding from the bed. After some time he uncovered her face. She said nothing.

Outside the front of the restaurant was a sample menu with a bell. At about half past midnight the bell rang continuously. Jeremiah took no notice, thinking that it would be revellers, fooling about. It stopped.

A few minutes later there was a loud banging at the back door. It did not stop. He went down and switched on the lights. There stood the young man. Jeremiah unlocked the door, but only opened it partially as the young man tried to push his way in. "Hullo. What brings you here at this time in the morning?" "I want to see Hannah. Is she all right?" "Of course she is all right, she is tired after a long journey, and has gone to bed". "Is she hurt? I am going up to see her".

At this, he tried to force his way past Jeremiah who had a foot against the door saying, "She is asleep." With that he forced the door shut and locked it. As he did so he looked past the young man into the car park in which there was a floodlight. He was shocked to see that there were two cars there. One was the young man's Jensen, the other a large traveller, driven by his father. On the ground beside the cars was a pile of suitcases.

He went back upstairs to find Hannah sitting up and alert. "Who was that?" she asked. When he told her she said coolly; "You were not very polite. You might have asked him in".

His mind was in a whirl. Whatever was going on? For the first time he began to see the relationship between Hannah and the young man other than from his own self-obsessed view.

Next morning, he had to drive into Wroxham and took the car, which she had used for her holiday. The previous owner had been punctilious. He kept a diary of every penny spent on the car. He even noted when he replaced a light bulb. The notebook happened to fall out of the glove box. As he picked it up he noticed the last entry. The car had done little more than 500 miles, since he had fitted a new bulb, yet it had been driven from Devon two months before. If Hannah had been to the Lake District, she did not seem to have used that car. She had said that she had indeed driven through the village earlier the previous afternoon. She had hoped to find their daughter in the car park on her own. She had intended to pick her up and drive off with her unseen. It seemed to him that the holiday might have been a kind of advance honeymoon, and that some arrangement had been made whereby she would be collected on the previous evening.

Hannah remained upstairs all day, apart from a fleeting appearance in the afternoon. She appeared late in the evening to fetch a bowl of soup, which she threw away as far too salty.

Jeremiah seems ever to have been driven by a lemming like urge for self-destruction. He went upstairs and sought to evoke pity. Instead he provoked contempt. Again he sat by her bedside. She told him abruptly, "For goodness sake get to bed". He went down and got some brandy. He did not, in fact, drink very much, but pretended to, to emphasise his state of hapless bewilderment. He let the bottle slip from his grasp, as if hopelessly inebriated and miserable. Hannah did not react with pity, but leapt up and went to the phone. He then began to get into bed, but, as she was long on the phone, he followed her. He thought she was phoning the young man so pulled the phone out. She was not. She was phoning the police who arrived some ten minutes later, followed by a doctor. The policemen took him downstairs, and chatted, saying, "Don't hit the bottle". What amazed him was that they knew of the affair between his wife and the young man. When the doctor arrived they left. The doctor talked to them both and left. Jeremiah went to sleep.

He awoke next morning to find a note in his hand. Hannah had gone. She was sorry. She felt that he would be better without her. She felt that there was, "something that had to come out", which her presence impeded. Jeremiah had hardly time to take this in, when there was a knocking at the bar door. He went and opened it. There stood the doctor. He came in and sat down.

"There was something wrong last night", he said. "Of course there was, I was drunk, and my wife was frightened". "You were not drunk, you were only acting to get sympathy. She was not frightened. That was what was wrong". "She has left.......".

"I know", said the doctor, "that is why I came. She telephoned me earlier. That was what made me realise what was wrong last night".

"Whatever do you mean?" "It was what she said on the phone. She told me that she had left you, and could not be responsible for what you might do. I said that I had the impression that you were a man of impulse and action, and while you were unlikely to harm anyone else, you might be inclined to harm yourself. It was her reply to this that made me realise what was going on last night".

"She replied, quite coolly, 'I realise that, but have discounted it'. It was as if she was telling her stockbroker why she had decided to dispose of some shares. I realised that she was 'playing' with you last night, and so providing herself with a witnessed excuse to leave you".

When Jeremiah told him of the events of the previous night, the doctor seemed to think that they confirmed his view. "It's much easier that way. I daresay they had arranged to go away together, but she found it hard to face you with it directly". Jeremiah felt that, in like circumstances, he would have done the same.

It would be, if not frightening, a source of perpetual anxiety to live with someone who tended to injure themselves, especially fatally. Suicide could be an ultimately aggressive act. He had no idea where Hannah was. He was distraught. He was fortunate in having some friends who kept a hotel for fishermen, a mile down the road, Alec and Tricia.

They suggested that he came down and slept in one of the rooms in their hotel rather than remain on his own at night. He did so. Eventually he learned that Hannah was with her parents. Her father, 'Uberrimae Fidei', advised that he write to the boys, as if nothing had happened, and their mother was at home. Whether 'Uberrimae', for so he will be known, was playing games or not, he did not know. While the boys received letters from Norfolk, as if their mother was there, she was visiting them in Devon.

After some weeks, Alec had a call from Hannah's mother. Hannah was returning. She and Uberrimae asked him to tell Jeremiah to expect little from her and to treat her very gently. Alec did not inform Jeremiah immediately, but waited some hours, then phoned back, seeking confirmation. He explained to Uberrimae and his wife that 'the poor chap' had been through a lot, and it would be cruel to build up his hopes, if he was to be let down. He was assured that Hannah would be home within a day. Thus reassured, Alec gave the good news to Jeremiah, who set about preparing the home to welcome her. Nobody arrived. Next day he waited expectantly. Nobody came.

Some days later, Alec had bad news. Hannah had returned to Norfolk, but was living in a flat some miles away. She had asked Alec to act as a go between. To this he had agreed. Jeremiah was not to try and find her. For some weeks silence reigned. Then Alec and Tricia spoke to him. They had withheld news, which they did not think he could stand. Alec had driven to Hannah's address, one morning, at about half past nine. Outside he had found a black Jensen, which had obviously been there overnight, as it was covered with dew. He had gone back later when the car had gone, and told Hannah that he was not prepared to act as a go between, while she was 'two timing' Jeremiah. She and her mother had deceived him once. Alec was not prepared to be a party to another deceit. Jeremiah went into a tail-spin. He would drive round places trying to get a sign of Hannah's residencc, or a sight of their daughter at a school.

The boys' headmaster was anxious. The only way to set their minds at rest was for Jeremiah to appear in person. He intended to drive down, but the local policeman heard about it, "You are overwrought and tired, and we don't want one of our colleagues to have to scrape you off the road". He took a late train from Norwich. It stopped at every station. The more he thought of what lay ahead the more miserable he became. He went down the corridor and tried to open a door to jump to his death. Having got the window down he looked out, to see that the train was travelling at little more than walking pace. "Bloody typical", he thought. "All I would end up with would be a broken collar bone, feeling silly." He returned to his compartment. The train stopped. A jaunty man with a rucksack got in.

"Evening everyone". "Oh God," thought Jeremiah, as the man sat down opposite him, "This is just what I need, some hearty fellow who says, 'Evening all', at one o'clock in the morning". To make matters worse the other two occupants left. The man sought to engage him in chat, and persisted despite abrupt and hostile replies.

"How long have you been in pain?" "I am not in pain". Eventually, after many such questions the man asked, "What is the matter?"

Jeremiah tearfully told him what had happened. When the man responded, saying that he knew, Jeremiah told him not to be silly. The man said that he did not know the details; only that, when the train arrived, he felt sure that there was someone in trouble. He got aboard and, as soon as he saw Jeremiah, knew that it was he.

What followed represented everything that Jeremiah's 'high and dry' upbringing made him hate and suspect. The man said, "Kneel down and I will lay hands on you". There was nothing to lose, so he did so. No doubt there are adequate psychological reasons for the effect. It was nonetheless amazing. Up to that point he had felt like an over-inflated tyre. It was as if the pressure was released and cool fresh air flooded through him.

"You feel better, don't you." said the stranger. "It will not last for long." He then told him of the occasion when Peter tried to walk on the water and sank, when he saw the waves about him. His companion advised him to recall that story whenever he felt despair, and to look up. He said that the sense of assurance would not last long, but that the more often he did this, the longer it would last.

The man travelled to London with him and waited through the night. He would travel down to Newton Abbott with him, but thought that he was all right now. Jeremiah said that he was. The man gave him a telephone number to ring if he felt desperate. He did ring it once. On the other end was a cheery, plump, West Indian voice. She was a lady who spent her time listening to phone calls from people in trouble. Jeremiah asked her of the man whom he had met. The woman told him that he spent much of his time doing as he had experienced, but never allowed people to know who he was, as that would not help anyone. They should not rely on him, but on the one in whose name he did these things.

Some weeks later, when a former student, David, a clergyman's son from Yorkshire, was staying, there had been a phone call, when Jeremiah was out.

David said that a man had phoned to ask if he was OK. He said that he was fine. The man said, "Tell him to remember the night train to Liverpool Street".

He saw his sons. The headmaster lent him a car to take them out to supper. He was about to tell them of what had happened, when his elder son said, "We knew what was going on dad, we tried to warn you in our letters, but you never got the message". He returned home, travelling on the night sleeper. He had never slept on a train before.

Half term came and with it something of an adventure. Hannah wanted them to go to her parents nearby, where she would stay. They refused saying, "we are going home". The headmaster rang Jeremiah to say that they were steadfast in their determination. The problem was that there was a strike at Liverpool Street. They could reach Norwich, travelling via Bristol, Birmingham and Leicester. Jeremiah would meet the train at Norwich. If they were on it; well and good; if not, he would assume they had gone to their mother. He met the train. Out jumped two triumphant smiling faces. They were given an extended half term.

He heard sounds upstairs late at night. There was Hannah in the boys' bedroom. She was not pleased to see him. She was now living in a flat with the young man. She made no bones about the fact that it was a 'love nest'. She did, however, think that they should put on a show of being a family for the children's sake on November 5th. This revolted Jeremiah. When the time came he again gave way to his emotions and behaved stupidly. He even tried to pour paraffin on himself and jump onto the fire.

He was bewildered. How could anyone who had been a close companion for fifteen years, become so hateful, as he had become? How was it that the person, who had been someone's close companion, could suddenly become the most despised person in the world? It was not peculiar to him and must be so for millions. It did not make it any less bewildering.

He took his sons back to London. He took them to hear the first part of a Concert at the Festival Hall, where an aged Annie Fischer played a Mozart Piano Concerto. Next day he went with them back to Buckfast, and came home. At eleven o'clock that evening, the telephone rang. A leering voice with a Yorkshire accent spoke. "Go and kill yourself you silly sod, that is what we want, or sign papers making me the adoptive father of the children". There was a mocking laugh: "She is in my bed tonight. You won't stand this for long. Go and kill yourself". Jeremiah was tired and dozed off; to be woken by the phone ringing. It was the same again. At about two hourly intervals through the night it was repeated. The same happened on the following night. The next night, he picked up the phone at about eleven p.m. He was overjoyed to hear his wife.

She spoke with great affection and sorrow for all the pain she had caused. She assured him that she loved him dearly. "Can you ever forgive me and let me come home, I love you....." She must have realised that things had gone too far and that she had to stop it all.

"You know that you need only open the door and walk in; there is nothing to forgive. Nobody on earth could be more welcome". He was overflowing with happiness.

The leering voice took over, saying that she was in his bed, and that he was about to remove her nightie. "Go on, save us all time and kill yourself, that is what we both want. You won't stand this for long". This was a new touch, making the calls much more distressing. The phone calls interrupted sleep again at intervals through the night. It was obviously futile for Hannah to repeat her opening regularly. It was done at intervals, though on later occasions, Jeremiah thought it was not she, but someone pretending to be her. How many times it was actually Hannah is impossible to know.

It was very distressing for the first few weeks, during which time it was repeated, nightly, several times, though seldom throughout the night. He dared not leave the phone off the hook, as he would be sure to forget to replace it and thus there would be no bookings made. The exchange could, then, only intercept every call and ask the caller to identify himself. That would not encourage people to make bookings.

After about a fortnight, he drove the kitchen help and waitresses back to their homes. As he dropped one of them off, the local policeman pulled up and told him that one of his rear lights was not working. He would follow him back down the lanes so that nobody ran into him from behind. When they reached the car park, Jeremiah thanked him: "Like a cup of coffee?" "Love one," said David.

As they went in, the phone rang. Knowing who it would be, Jeremiah handed the receiver to David. He listened for a full three minutes, as the same routine went on, saying nothing until the young man had finished his leering mockery. He then said that he had not been speaking to Jeremiah but to P. C. Sayer. He asked the caller to identify himself. There was silence. The operator's voice said, "Sorry Constable the caller has rung off".

David Sayer smiled. "Silly fool", he said, "He should know that there are no male operators except on Sundays".

Even though he knew that the police now knew, the young man persisted. After this, it seemed that Hannah decided to take no further direct part, though she was there in the background.

The phone calls were distressing, but less acutely as time wore on. Having an upstairs extension, Jeremiah had anyone, staying in the house, listen in. His niece, a sharp-witted, diminutive young lady, interrupted the young man disdainfully, "This is very boring. Have you nothing better to say?" Despite a policeman, his niece and others, making it clear that others knew, Hannah and her lover persisted. He learned later that, on one occasion, or more, his elder son, aged twelve, had picked up the phone and heard it all. They must have known that, had Jeremiah been driven to kill himself, as they hoped, there would have been an inquest, and the story of this sustained attempt to drive him to do so would have come out. The need to prevent this seems to have become significant in later events.

The boys returned for the Christmas holidays, refusing to go to Hannah's 'love nest', even though their little sister was there. She had been miserable at the school she had been sent to. She used to hope that her dad would appear in the playground and take her away. Jeremiah would have done so had he known her whereabouts. Hannah decided to return, but without a scintilla of remorse. It was more as if she were condescending to do so. The calls persisted in a desultory way. She would generally try to pick up the phone, if it rang late in the evening. She would then, ostentatiously, speak to a Mr Smith. As Mr Smith was a regular customer, it was not a very original or wise name to have chosen.

Chapter Eighteen .

Guardian Angels.

Those who propped Jeremiah up, over the next years, had no white wings. Most were not, in any accepted way, religious. He knew nothing of the stranger on the train. All, in one way or another, even if unconsciously, led him to sayings in the Gospels, by their actions rather than their words. Two we have met, a former grain dealer and his wife, who kept a fishermen's hotel nearby. The kindly publican down the road gave much advice.

Ernie kept the old mill in the village and milled chicken feed, ground bait and other such things. Before the war he had milled flour. He also supplied fertilisers to farmers, and eggs to anyone who could not afford to buy them. Ernie was a walking chuckle. His old face was creased with lines left by his smile. When Ernie delivered flour, chicken feed, eggs and sundry things to homes, he knew to be poor, he would leave the motor running, jump out, leave the goods on the doorstep, knock, run back to his motor and be off. The only way to pay was to pay his wife.

One evening, Jeremiah was standing in the pub, gazing forlornly into a glass of Guinness, when a large whisky appeared. From behind him came a merry chuckle: "Have a drop of short, my friend, and Cheer yew up. Yew ain't the only bugger who's done wrong, and they aren't half as clever as they think they are". Jeremiah could have hugged him for those words.

A problem with giving advice is that it makes the givers seem much more clever than the recipients. Another is that someone might take it. Had Jeremiah been capable of following it, he would not be in the muddle he was. Ernie did not give that kind of advice. He did, later, give Jeremiah one piece of advice, but of a wholly different kind. In his later life, Jeremiah came to think that everything that had happened was made worth it, because he met such as Ernie Cole.

Over the road was another pub, which had a run of cottages. They were like the one in which he had spent years of his childhood, having the same sanitary arrangements, even in 1975. In one of these lived a widow, known as Sam, though her name was Daisy. She used to work in the little shop over the road. Sam had had a very hard life as a child. She told how, one morning, she was so hungry, on her way to school, that she pulled up a 'swede-turnip' from a farmer's field and gnawed it, to get rid of the hunger pains. The farmer saw her from the window of his house, got in touch with the head teacher, and she was beaten. She also recalled the kindness of others who passed on shoes and clothing to her.

Sam was not religious, and never went near a Church. Her generosity and hospitality were boundless. She kept her house like a new pin and the door was ever open. Anyone, who walked in, would be sat down to a cup of tea, a plate of bread and butter, patties and cakes, followed by a fag and a glass of 'toddy'. On one occasion, when Jeremiah was bitter and angry at the way his wife and her father were behaving, Sam said. "My boy, I have been thinking a lot about what the Good Lord said. He said, 'Father forgive them, they know not what they do'. I think you should remember those words. I don't think that old bugger knows what he is doing".

Sam had five children, three sons and two daughters. All were very intelligent. The eldest son was Derek, known to his mother as a 'Dead loss' and a 'Dog'. But for Derek's appearance in Jeremiah's life, later, he would certainly have ended it. A more loyal friend, he could never have found, nor a more resourceful one. It was Derek who brought the telephoning to an end, in a way that the policeman could not. He said, "Jeremiah has had enough of this. Any more of it and it wont be the law, but the 'heavies'....Got that?" What happened, Jeremiah dared not ask. All he knew was that two large and sinister men appeared in the restaurant about a week later, and asked directions to the village where the lover lived. The phone calling stopped abruptly.

If one went to buy fish in the bridge shop in Wroxham, one would be served by an elegantly spoken man. It did not take many minutes to realise that one's plaice was being filleted by one, whose pedigree made that of the English nobility a thing of yesterday. Here was one, of the 'seed' of Abraham. John Jacobs had a gentle smile that seldom became a merry chuckle. It had a sad resignation about it. A more gentle man one could not meet, but, true to his ancestry, John could never resist a deal. He would never accept anything for nothing. Often, when he came for a meal, Jeremiah would say that it was 'on the house'. "No", said John, "business is business". The most he would ever accept was a bottle of wine. He would inspect the bill to make sure that he had been charged for everything.

It was John who took steps to ameliorate the effects of the phone calling. He would ring Jeremiah up at about eleven p.m. in the evening, saying, "Go and have a large whisky and get a good night's sleep. Take the phone off the hook, and don't worry. I will give you a ring, when I get to the shop tomorrow. If you are repeatedly engaged I will hop into my van and drive over. It's only 3 miles".

John's family had lived and prospered in Norwich, since the seventeenth century. They were in the leather business, and prominent members of the synagogue. John had disgraced himself by marrying a gentile. For this, his mother never forgave him. She was the incarnation of the Jewish matriarch, a large, handsome, woman of considerable wealth, who wore a jewellery belt when she went to bed, much to the amusement of John and his beloved daughter. During the war, John and his brother served in the Navy. The brother was killed. His mother used to say openly that it should have been John. This, he accepted with a wry smile. In his early, married life, John and his wife, Joice, had lived among the well to do, holidaying with well-known film stars; but his wife had developed Huntington's disease. John had said that it was very painful for her, when the symptoms first manifested themselves, as her mother had suffered the same degenerative illness.

One morning Jeremiah went to the fish shop. John looked ashen and drawn. "What's the matter, John? You look awful". "Oh God," said John, "It's Joice, I go to see her every weekend, but she does not even recognise me. Whatever is the point in it all?" Jeremiah wished he had not asked the question. He had no answer. Who could have? John was far too wise and intelligent to be fobbed off with the usual banalities. If, brought up on the book of Psalms and books like Job; clichés about one door closing and another opening, challenges, and the like, seem what they are: empty noises.

After wandering about doing not much, he went upstairs and got a sheet of high quality paper and his pen. In his best handwriting, he copied out the opening words of the Sermon on the Mount. He avoided the word "Blessed" and used the word "fortunate", and made one or two other small changes, continuing to, "Let your light shine, in this way, before men, that they may see your good works...."

On the back, he wrote, "Thank you for letting your light so shine before men, that, at least one can see your good works and glorify your Father which is in heaven". When the restaurant closed that night, he drove to John's house and poked his document through the letter-box. He felt so silly that, for the next week, he bought no fish.

In the end he had to; so went to the shop, hoping that John would not be working that morning. He was. As a trade customer he went round to the back. John flung his arms around him. "Thank you", he said, "What you said was perfect, just what we needed to hear". "They were not my ideas," mumbled Jeremiah.

The butcher in Hoveton was a man of vastly different stamp. He was small and had black hair; a sharp witted, very intelligent, son of truly rural Norfolk. His education had, he said, ended at the age of eight. He read prodigious amounts. The back of his shop, where the meat was boned and cut, was full of backchat and merriment, most at the "Guvnor's" expense. Clifford would be found, knife in hand, dressing out a side of beef, pipe in mouth, under a large notice saying "No Smoking". Of course he was not smoking. His pipe was out.

Clifford proved another loyal friend, as did his brother Richard, who kept the accounts and ran the front of the shop. Clifford spoke, as did many, including Sam, contemptuously, of those he called "Half Sixers". "Who are, "Half Sixers?" "People like you!" was the reply. "People who are not a full dozen." "It's you educated people who go off to public schools, whose parents and grandparents did too. You think you are better than the rest of us, but can hardly wipe your noses without help. We are working on you, but it's so engrained that it will take time to make you a human being again".

To walk into the back of the shop was a tonic, with its badinage and laughter. Even to phone with an order was a source of merriment. Sometimes he would ring and order pheasants, adding, "no shot", as customers tended not to like finding lead pellets. There would be a shout to the back of the shop; "There's a bent chef on the phone wants bent pheasants, Guv'nor." "Tell him we don't deal in bent gear, here!" "How many does he want, just in case we find any?" (which, of course, they did not)

He found other friends at this time, among them a wealthy couple, who were regular customers, called Charles and Joey. Charles was a quiet man with a limp, and a great sailor, who tended to look down on those who messed about under sail, on rivers and broads. In his youth he had sailed J class yachts at Cowes. He had much sadness in his life. His family owned a once famous firm in London, which transported luggage between the mainline stations, in yellow carts. His first wife had died suddenly in her twenties. He had married again, and his second wife died of cancer. He had a daughter who had been diagnosed with lymphoma. This had been treated. When she went for a check up, she said that, apart from feeling very tired she was all right. They diagnosed leukaemia.

They had a friend called Bertie Wooster, a former London banker. Bertie was also a keen sailor, and spoke like an Archbishop. His father had been a Norfolk clergyman, and knew Jeremiah's grandfather. He told how, as a young banker, he came out of one of the city pubs at lunchtime, wobbled on the pavement and was almost run over. The car stopped. In the back was Queen Mary. "She", complained Bertie, "was not in the least concerned for me, only that her bloody Daimler was not damaged". He would tell of the agony, when a customer to whom he had lent money would stand in a bar and say, "Drinks on me! No, on the bank!"

When Jeremiah told Bertie that he had bought a One Design, Bertie said, "Oh do be careful, you can easily buy a lot of half rotten timber. They are old boats. What number is it?" Jeremiah told him. A couple of weeks later Bertie came in. "You have done well. I looked up number 61, and as far as I could tell, there is no rotten timber in her".

Bertie had contemplated buying one years before. He had gone round the yards, where owners stored them in the winter, at night, with a torch and penknife, poking the timbers under the waterline to see where there was any rot.

He spoke of the time when his family had hired a cottage at West Runton, during the first war. It was full of trainee soldiers. "The poor sods were being trained to go over the top with hardly a bloody rifle between them..."

One of those who helped him was a real aristocrat, Jo Dashwood Howard. Jo's father had been the Marprelate King of Arms. He had been the first customer in the restaurant, the night they opened. Jeremiah asked him if he was local. "Yes", said Jo, I live down the road at Threehammer Common. "Did you come from far away?" "Oh yes, from Ludham". That was all of three miles away. "Did you know my great uncle who was Vicar there? His name was Boycott." "I should think so. He baptised me! He was a keen sailor. He had a One Design, it was "Purple Emperor".

There was one other party in the restaurant at the time, and elderly man and his family. Hearing this, the man said, "No it was not. It was White Ermine, number three. I should know; I used to crew him. On Sundays, after evensong in the summer, he would ask, Who wants a sail? He would always look back up Womack Water, as we sailed away, saying, Look there my boy, you won't see a more beautiful sight on the face of the earth. You don't need to travel. He had been out in China and other places".

This conversation of no shot pheasants, half sixers, and even the seed of Abraham, eccentric clergymen who burnt off their noses, when giving 'magic lantern' shows with an acetylene lamp and seemed to spend more time racing 'One Designs' than taking services, was one that Jeremiah felt at home in. Hannah did not.

What he failed to grasp, for many years, was how much more difficult it made life for her, after the 'love nest' and all that went with it, when those of that 'conversation' closed ranks around him. Whether it would have been otherwise had they lived in Somerset or Devon or Yorkshire, is hard to say. It is easy to see why her father saw it as essential to remove Jeremiah from that area, and return him to some professional form of employment, among those whom such as Clifford called 'half sixers', if the marriage was to be restored. That may have been more essential than the location.

If they remained in that area, the lover was always on the doorstep. Having a restaurant meant that he and his family were liable to walk in at any moment, or pick up the phone and book a table. Jeremiah had spent his life, in childhood and youth, as a semi bedouin, constantly moving about the country, and living in a vast array of homes. In terms of 'class' and education, he was also semi bedouin. He was happy as such. He enjoyed the badinage of the butcher's shop and felt at home in it. He did not mind being derided as a half sixer. Whether natives of other areas of the country looked on their 'betters' with this underlying contempt, he did not know.

There seemed to be a uniting factor among those who befriended and propped him up. They were all, in one way or another, 'renegades'. Jo had fallen out with his aristocratic family, and had gone off to sea, not in the Royal Navy, but as a merchant seaman. He despised them. He had married a girl from Glasgow, who had been brought up in great poverty, such that the malnourishment of her childhood caused her untimely death. Jo never forgave his well to do relations, who lived in the 'Hall', for the way in which they patronisingly humiliated his wife. He hated the yacht racing fraternity on the broads, and would sail his old and formidable estuary cruiser, with its huge bowsprit, among them when they raced.

The heart of the difficulty, however, lay in the poem of the later Isaiah, about the one who 'believed our report'. This, as Jeremiah came later to understand, is that of the Gospel itself. It was the problem of belief in God, as being what the word implies. If God is not what, logically, the word implies, all 'conversation' that derives from this, must be of 'confused language'. The sayings of Jesus in the gospels make this clear.

Any fool can understand and do as he says. It takes no wisdom or prudence to go two miles when commanded to go one. It takes no great intellect to ‘give one's cloak as well', if sued for a coat. Any fool knows how to forgive those indebted to him. One needs no great religious understanding to pray as he demands. Any idiot knows how not to swear an oath, or give not the smallest indication of having given to charity. One needs a lot of intellect to find reasons not to do such things, while declaring belief in the one who demanded them. The only basis, on which anyone might do such things, would be an assurance that there was indeed God and that, as one's heavenly Father, he would care for one.

Those who rallied around Jeremiah seemed more open to such words than others. It had nothing to do with their living near Wroxham. In one way or another, they encouraged him, as Ernie Cole and Sam, and later, her elder son to "abide in them". Some years later, the 'Dog' asked Clifford why it was that he had been so loyal a friend to Jeremiah. Clifford said, "I'd like to believe what he believes to be true". Jeremiah felt like a tipster who had commended a rank outsider in a race. For the first time since childhood he was beginning to see a positive aspect in the sayings of the Gospels. Was it worth it? It seemed more like being put into detention for failing to attend in normal lessons.

Chapter Nineteen

Betrayal with a kiss

The Christmas Holiday, with Hannah home, was not easy. The telephoning went on in a desultory way. Understandably, she seemed more kindly disposed to "Mr Smith" than to Jeremiah, having returned only because the boys had refused to go to her. As Christmas came, she became more friendly. After Christmas she seemed glad to be home and was almost affectionate. They went out for an evening in Norwich. At the end of the meal Hannah went out for five minutes, returning a different woman, speaking as had Auntie Gladys; making excuses for him, which were accusations. She had discussed him with many people. From what she said, chief among them was Uberrimae.

It was no wonder that he was as he was, given his ancestry. His dad had no business to leave his family and go to the war. He should have done as her father. Jeremiah thought that her father had been exempted on health grounds, being diabetic. That was not so. He had been in a reserved occupation. The war, or its immediate aftermath, had, as he had said, been of great benefit. His office was one of the few undamaged buildings in the centre of town.

Jeremiah's father need not have gone into the army at his age. He rang his dad and asked why he had volunteered. "Your uncles and I may have been wrong, old boy, but we felt that the values that we were fighting for were worth it. None of us need have joined up. It would have been a poor look out, if nobody had volunteered. We did not do it for fun". Jeremiah felt ashamed.

Hannah's accusatory excuses went on. "No wonder you are as you are, having been away from your parents, brought up by all those adoring women". It had the stamp of Uberrimae. He should have met Miss Hubner and Miss Butcher, Aunt Edith and the rest. Adoring they were not. No doubt, what her father said of him was right. It seemed unfair. It was as if he had personally arranged the war, chosen his schools, chosen his parents and chosen his ancestors.

More disturbing was the sudden change in Hannah's manner. It was as if she were an agent in a hostile country, who realised that she was becoming too friendly with the enemy. He felt that she was acting under advice. They went home. Next day she was friendly again, so he put the matter from his mind. She became increasingly so, as the time came for returning the boys to school. Their daughter went back to school some time before them. She was happy at her old school. Hannah asked why it was always he who went with the boys, when they returned. It was because she did not want to. She was welcome to do so. He would keep the restaurant open, and look after their daughter so that she could settle back in her school.

"Let's both go", she said. "It would greatly reassure my parents to see us all together". Jeremiah said, "Not yet. We are hardly a united family, in any case, our daughter should not be taken from her school again". Uberrimae telephoned, speaking in the same vein. He was full of congratulations for Jeremiah's strength of character in holding things together and reuniting the family. "Your mother in law and I are full of admiration for what you have done, dear boy. Please come down as a family. It would greatly reassure your mother in law." Jeremiah spoke as before. "Think about it, dear boy", said Uberrimae.

Hannah, again, tried to persuade him. She said, "Let us make it a really new start. We'll go back to the Isles of Scilly and have a second honeymoon". Feeling slightly uneasy, Jeremiah relented. Somehow it did not ring true, but he loved being with his wife, and wanted above all to restore the happiness of the family, for his own, not their sake.

A few days later, they drove to Norwich, bought tickets, and boarded the train for London. Once aboard Hannah became remote. He was left to occupy the children while she sat staring fixedly out of the window, a look of determination on her face. As the journey progressed her remoteness became more pronounced. Her parents met them by car. When they arrived home, her mother told Jeremiah to sleep at the other end of the house from his wife. He was bewildered. After two days, he was returned to the train, Hannah drove him to the station. He was tearful. She was affectionate, squeezing his hand, saying, "I hate seeing you like this". He was deposited on the train for London. She turned away.

He arrived at Paddington miserable, and went to the Samaritans. He could not face returning alone, his buoyant hopes dashed. He felt as if he had been lured onto a stage where the rest of the cast knew what parts they had to play, whereas he alone did not. Having reached Liverpool Street, he collected a mass of 10p pieces and phoned his in laws.

His mother in law answered. She was gently reassuring, but it was she who had twice reassured Alec of Hannah's return. "You have nothing to worry about, love, Hannah is devoted to you; she loves you dearly. She is sorry that things did not work out. All she wants is a few days rest. She is upstairs, I will fetch her; she will want to tell you herself". With that she left the phone. He could hear a conversation in the background.

Hannah came to the phone. Never, in his life with her, had he heard such words of tenderness, love and affection. She only wanted a day or two's rest. She would be back at the weekend. Could he manage all right till then? "Yes of course". With such words of love and devotion ringing in his ears, he returned happily. At the weekend she phoned again. She was almost as affectionate as before. "Could he manage for a few more days?" "Yes, of course. It is not busy, though we are quite heavily booked for next weekend".

"Don't worry, I'll be back by then". She would phone him from London to tell him what train she was going to catch, so that he could drive into Norwich.

On Friday afternoon Alec and Tricia dropped in for a chat. The phone rang. "That will be Hannah". He picked it up. It was not. It was her father. He snapped orders like a sergeant major. "You are to cancel your daughter's place at her school. We have 'put her to' a private school in Plymouth. She has been there all this week and has settled in well. She will need......". Jeremiah was stunned and mumbled something about her promised return.

"Do as you are told, boy". Down went the receiver.

Jeremiah's mind was in a spin. He walked out of the place, flinging open the door with such force that one of the aged hinges snapped. He walked round and returned, feeling silly, to find his friends still there. They calmed him down. Alec said that he would come up and run the bar. Not only was he very good at this, he was good, reassuring, company. Fortunately it was a busy weekend. Jeremiah wondered whether Uberrimae had contacted Alec, saying that Jeremiah was about to receive bad news, and would he be there to see that he did not do anything silly. Years later, he asked Alec if this were the case. He said that it was not.

Uberrimae said that their daughter had been at school for a week. When Hannah phoned, it must already have been arranged. Had the whole escapade, the promises of new starts and honeymoons, even Hannah's return, been part of the arrangement? Later events made this seem probable. Living in a love nest with a lover who had sought to drive Jeremiah to kill himself, would not greatly appeal to Uberrimae, either as a Lay reader, or Magistrate.

On Sunday afternoon, he telephoned his in laws. Hannah answered. She seemed entirely at ease with all that had happened. It was the sensible thing to have done. "What were all those words of love and affection, when he had phoned her from Liverpool Street?"

She said, quite jauntily, "Oh *we* had to think of something to tell you to make you feel happy, otherwise, you might have gone and done something silly, and we would have lost money. It was the sensible thing to do". The cool matter-of-factness in her voice horrified him. Of course it was sensible. This was what the doctor had noticed.

It was more or less what Machiavelli advised, when he counselled the Prince. It was better to eliminate an enemy by befriending him, gaining his trust, until he laid his head on your shoulder; then slip poison into his wine, than have a war; probably better for the enemy too. As Hannah spoke, it was not Machiavelli that came to his mind. He was taken, in heart and mind, back to the story he had read at seven. He was in a garden with Jesus and eleven of his disciples, when the twelfth appeared, said, "Hail Master", and kissed him. He said, "What you are saying is that you used pretended affection and love in order to *betray".*

He said this to shock, not to offend. He hoped that, by putting it in such terms, she and her dad would be so aghast at what their scheming had led them to do, that they would stop and think, "This is going too far." It had no such effect. She said calmly, "Of course, it was the only sensible thing to do. It is what any sensible person would have done".

Jeremiah had to admit the truth of this. He would have been happy enough to enjoy the benefits, if someone else had done such a thing for him, preferably without his knowing. Whether he could have done so himself was another matter. The reason he might not, would have been an inability to sound convincing. He said, "That has a famous precedent."

"Go on", said Hannah, in a voice of tired disdain, "I suppose you will tell me what it is". He said, "There was once a man called Judas who used false tokens of love, to betray". The line went silent. She did not hang up. He waited a minute and replaced the receiver. Some hours later the telephone rang. It was a very angry Uberrimae. "What did you say to my daughter, you little swine?" He replied, "Fifteen years ago you responded to the question, "who giveth this woman......? You had better ask her". With that he put down the receiver.

That brief telephone conversation told him more of poor Judas than all the commentaries ever written. Was it his fault? Might he not have been of an ancestry and upbringing that made him likely to behave thus? They could not risk approaching a former publican or a Galilean. Such might say two words and the second would be 'off'. They had, as Jeremiah knew all too well, to approach one who 'spoke their language'. He had experience of this; "You are one of us".

No doubt Judas thought that he was being sensible, having his Master's 'best interests' at heart. He could persuade himself that, in Jerusalem, Jesus had gone 'too far' and should adopt a more moderate attitude. Faced with the assembled Sanhedrin, Jesus might have seen 'sense'. If he had done so, he would be in Judas' debt. Judas would be the 'sensible one', who had saved his life. It was not unlike the occasion, when Peter told Jesus that he should not think of being crucified, and was told, 'Get thee behind me, Satan'. For the first time Jeremiah began to see the impossible position, into which, Jesus, as described in the gospels, put everyone. If he alone spoke truly of God, he left all with only one choice, to cast him out, or become his disciple. He could hardly expect the High Priest to do that.

Nothing had changed. How, today, could anyone expect someone in a high, or even modest, position of 'responsibility', in church or state, to become a disciple of Jesus, as the four evangelists reported him? One had to learn of anyone but him. However did these four men come to report him as they did? It could only be that he spoke as they described. Jesus was the most dreadful man ever to have lived. To one possibility, Jeremiah was blind. Had the positions been reversed and Hannah adopted his 'position', he would have run a mile.

Of all the events in his life, only this gave him nightmares. They were surreal, but the crux was always the use of pretended love and affection to deceive and, having done so, to see it as sensible, in an unconcerned way, as if anyone who was taken in by the empty words was insane. It was enhanced by the fact that she participated in the phone calls, explicitly designed to secure his death, in the same way. He realised that he reaped as he had sown. He did not mind, when Hannah disposed of her former boy friend with similar decisiveness. Is it easier to speak words of undying love convincingly when they are false?

It frightened him that both Hannah and her father felt so convinced that what they planned was for everyone's good, that even the use of false tokens of love was permissible. Persuaded of the ultimate good of the plan, they were possible to see as almost genuine. If Jesus had relented, made concessions and 'come to terms' with the Sanhedrin, it might have made Judas' tokens of love true. In a sense they were. Judas could have been persuaded that he was acting in his Masters' best interest. "Thank you Judas, you have saved my life". Even members of the Council could persuade themselves of this. If their leader realised that it could not be and was determined on a ruthless course of action, he could persuade himself that Jesus had been given 'every chance'.

The more Jeremiah pondered such events in the light of the gospels, the more shocked and frightened he became. What shocked him was that the reported words and actions of this single man would oblige almost anyone to act in this way. What frightened him was the seemingly limitless capacity of men and women to find self-justifying arguments against his words, while making declarations of belief in the one who spoke them.

If publicly declared believers, who knew the story of Judas, were, in no way, constrained by the realisation that what they did led them to emulate his mode of betrayal, what would constrain them? It horrified him further because he realised that it was, as Hannah had said, the sensible way of doing things.

The conviction that a planned course of action was seen as good and in everyone's 'best interest', made it nigh impossible to abandon, especially if it was argued as being so, 'in the name of God'. The more arguments were devised in its favour, the more one convinced oneself and others, the less was it possible to reconsider. He saw that this was the permanent effect of the words of Jesus. They forced almost everyone to argue against them, again and again, as if being prodded to move further and further towards the outer end of a branch, until it would no longer bear their weight. By doing so they were led to put themselves into more and more untenable positions. Uberrimae would see it as being in everyone's 'best interest'. It was, provided that nobody asked of the basis, on which it was decided what anyone's best interests were. Had it all worked out as Uberrimae hoped, the deception would have been made 'good'. Jeremiah would have thanked Uberrrimae for making him see sense. He began, dimly, to see these stories as 'cautionary' and protective.

If he sought to restore the marriage, it was desirable to put the maximum distance between Hannah and her lover. It was also sensible to move them away from an area where people, especially Jeremiah's friends, knew of the discreditable business of the telephone calls. Hannah's younger brother had not formed a very high impression of the lover, his family, or their business methods. Then, there was Jeremiah's attempt to kill himself. While his friends seemed to take that in their stride, and he did not mind the loss of face, nay, was glad of it, it was not the kind of company that Uberrimae thought suitable either for his daughter, or their children. "Publicans and sinners" are fine in ancient tales, but not here and now. Worst of all, Jeremiah was becoming impossible to deal with, because he kept falling back on words in the gospels, when he felt cornered.

He had to be 'got off his high horse'. Had this been discussed with reference to anyone else Jeremiah would have agreed. He only got on his 'high horse', because it was the only one he was capable of sitting on. For him it was anything but a *high* horse. In referring to the betrayal, he completely misconstrued the effect. If Uberrimae was raising the stakes to coerce Jeremiah for his own and his family's good; by referring to that episode he had, unwittingly, doubled them.

Having persuaded themselves that a planned course of action is 'for the good of all', many feel free to fall back on coercion when argument fails. 'We' know what is good; if you cannot see it by argument, we will take steps to make you do so, just as children are made to attend school. It is a deceit, since to argue implies that, if one's arguments do not convince, the other is free to disregard them; even more if his or her counter arguments prove more cogent. How can devoted Churchgoers argue with someone, who likened their action to that of Judas? It was.

Once again, Jeremiah had dug down a rabbit hole, and buried himself in it. Once he had said that the sayings of Jesus determined what was Christian, he could not unsay it. Now, having fallen back on the sayings of Jesus and those of the marriage service, he was stuck with them. That such as Sam, Derek, Clifford, Ernie and others had stood by him, because he had said such things, made turning round even more difficult. Seen from Hannah and Uberrimae's point of view, it would be an indication of his having greater loyalty to his friends than to his wife. He feared the derision, "He set out to build a tower, and only managed to lay the foundation". He was beginning to fear God.

For Uberrimae, it was embarrassing for obvious reasons. Neither he nor his daughter wanted to discover that life was easier, when everyone knew what a fool one was. That is not possible if one occupies a prominent position, directing, 'judging and dividing' over others in church or state. In such a position, Jeremiah would have agreed that it was best for all, that such as himself should be separated from the company of those who had supported him, and returned to professional, churchgoing circles and the 'conversation', in which they belonged.

With Hannah in Norfolk, Uberrimae was not in a strong position to use coercion, even if convinced that it was for the good of all. With Hannah and their daughter down there, he had cards to play. That may seem coldly cynical. It is not, if one has convinced oneself that one's overall aim is good. His aim was to restore the marriage on what he thought a sensible basis, for the good of his daughter and their children. That one in his position should feel wholly convinced that he was right, and that, in his words, "you should be advised", is not surprising. If he did not believe that he knew best, he would not assume a position in which he directed the lives of others 'for their own good'.

Hannah had put herself in his hands. In her position, Jeremiah would have been economical with the truth. Uberrimae would not want to know about the love nest or the phone calling. Knowing would have put him in a compromising position. Such economy made for difficulties. One could never know how much the other knew; so played blind man's buff. Hannah would not have told her father of the sustained attempt to drive Jeremiah to kill himself; still less that she had, on some occasions, been an active party in it. As the policeman knew, it could have laid them open to a humiliating charge. Uberrimae was both a magistrate and deputy Lord Lieutenant.

She could not know whether he knew of this from other sources and, if told, he believed it. If Uberrimae knew and believed what he had been told, he could not let Hannah know, if she did not tell him. If it were open between them, what, as a magistrate and deputy Lord Lieutenant, could he say to her? She with her lover had done that, which, in those capacities, he would have condemned in anyone else. Whereas nobody down there would know of these things, or be prone to believe, if they heard of them; there were plenty of people of unimpeachable repute about Jeremiah, who had first hand knowledge of the business.

If he said to Jeremiah, with his Christian hat on, "You should forgive", it would imply that there was fault on his beloved daughter's part. By combining with her lover in the sustained attempt to secure his death, she had committed an offence. Whereas the law of the gospels was that all should be forgiven, he had not the same assurance when it came to the law of England, of which he was a sworn upholder. Had he been sitting on the bench, when a woman was accused of such an offence, having succeeded in driving an unwanted husband to kill himself, he would not say that it should be forgiven.

Jeremiah began to see an aspect of forgiveness, which had not occurred to him. The forgiven is ever in the power of the forgiver. "There is mercy with thee; therefore shalt thou be *feared"*. If one forgives someone indebted to one, they remain indebted. Whether one or another has more to be forgiven for is an unquantifiable matter. What was crucial was the awareness that both stood in need of the forgiveness of an eternal unchanging authority.

Even if forgiven, could such a thing be forgotten? No-one can control his memory. In many conversations, Jeremiah would be an ever-present source of potential embarrassment. Even if he said nothing, all would know that he could. As long as these things remained hidden, he would need only to look at Hannah or her dad, if they took the moral high ground.

The tale of Judas was truly tragic and was, like many tales in the Old Testament, cautionary. Having set such a process in motion, he could not stop it. Is this what Hannah had herself done? It is easily done, especially if one has powerful relations and friends. Perhaps Uberrimae had advised her to persuade Jeremiah to come down with their daughter, 'then we can put her to school down here, and he will see sense'. In Uberrimae's position, with his money and influence, Jeremiah might have done the same. He could see that it would be very hard, if not impossible for his daughter to resume a respected life in the middle class professional 'conversation', in Norfolk. If his beloved daughter found her friends among those who stood by Jeremiah, she would be in a 'conversation', in which her own family would not be at ease. Those who stood by Jeremiah were all, in one way or another, 'rogues'. They laughed at things, which should not be laughed at in Uberrimae's world.

He began to think of friendship. If he had done as she, and used words of love to betray; he could gain credit by telling many of his friends about it, especially clergymen. "Do you know, I once did a dreadful thing. I feel ashamed. It makes my declarations of belief in Church hypocrisy. I used pretended affection to deceive one who trusted me....". They would give him credit for his candour, and 'knowing himself'. Those, in whom he confided, would feel that they must be very special, ...and have something on him!

He knew whom he would not tell of such things. One would have been his old Supervisor at Cambridge. He would have no patience with such unburdening of the soul; but would have sighed and said, "Whatever is the use of telling me of things like that? If you feel ashamed of what you did, do something about it!" It is humbug to unburden one's soul, while still enjoying the benefits of the action, for which one feels shame. If one enjoys the benefits of an action, one is glad of having done it, in act, if not in words. Words of regret are made idle. 'If you don't intend doing anything, then stop moaning about how bad you feel! What you want is the best of both worlds, the credit for having shame, while enjoying all the advantages that your deceit gained'. No wonder Mr Blyth could talk of the prophets, as if he had met them. He had.

He would not have told Jimmy. If he had he would have got no sympathy. He would not have told Sam, or Ernie, or anyone, like the Baker, who would have seen the hypocrisy involved in expressing sorrow or regret for some action, while continuing enjoying its benefits. Much later, Jeremiah chanced to meet John Carey. He would not have made such 'empty' confessions to him either. This told much of friendship. He would not have told anyone whom he respected, anyone who might speak truthfully.

All would change, if an act, for which one felt shame, were *publicly* known. If such an act of deceit and betrayal were publicly known, those, in whom he had felt it safe to confide, would distance themselves, not wishing openly to associate with a known betrayer. Such as A C Blyth would be unaffected. If he met him on the street, he would, as he often did, blossom into a beaming smile and say "Good Morning," as if nothing had happened. The *hypocrisy would be no longer.* Mr Blyth had nothing to loose by associating with a blackguard. Most others had.

He came to feel sorry for Hannah, if this were the truth. She lived a highly respected way of life amid a circle of friends, most of whom enjoyed good positions, and were members of the established Church. Was she ever aware that their friendship depended on the maintaining of appearances?

How could it be that, even when he said to Hannah, "you used false words of love and affection to betray", she did not see what was coming? She was in her mid thirties, the daughter of parents devoted to the Christian religion. She had been expensively educated at a boarding school, whose chaplain became Archbishop of York. Here was the archetypal tale of betrayal with false tokens and words of love, yet it might as well never have been told. He had used the word betray, deliberately, to evoke that story. How had she failed to recognise the allusion? It was not just a matter of services on Good Friday. It was echoed at every service of Holy Communion, the Eucharist, Mass or Lord's supper, in the prayer of consecration, "who in the same night that he was betrayed...". It was embedded in our culture.

Tom's reference to the verse from the psalm, was enlightening. If one used false words of love to betray, and someone recalled the act of Judas, one would almost certainly rebut the implication with anger and vehemence. We, then, confuse warnings of danger with condemnatory judgements.

He had not spoken to offend, but to shock. He thought that, so appalled would both Hannah and Uberrimae be, that she would return home, as she had promised, and they could live happily ever after. That she did not, made him miserable. Had she done as he hoped, he would have forgotten all about Judas, and the one he betrayed. He would not have seen any value in poverty of spirit, meekness, or anything else that the Gospels taught. The notion of giving one's cloak as well, if sued for a coat, would have seemed preposterous, as would forgiving those indebted to one.

He would have made a lie of every word he had uttered. It was, again, no fault of his that he did not. It would be wholly erroneous to think of him as a 'faithful' believer. He was nothing of the kind. He could not cope with anything 'better'. He was in the wilderness and needed manna. He did not, therefore, want to offend the supplier. He did not want to remain in the wilderness, but get out of it as soon as possible, when all thoughts of manna and the supplier would go to blazes. Roast beef would be the order of the day.

Chapter Twenty

"In the corrupted Currents of this World"

It was at this time that the one known as a Dog appeared. A man of great intelligence and ability, he had left a famous North Norfolk grammar school with an illustrious alumnus and been signed by West Ham as an apprentice. Having been found propped against a bar at the dog track, on a Friday evening before a match, he was told that his services were no longer required. For a while he became an upholder of the law, as a policeman. Finding, as he said, that 'his sympathies lay with the other side', he had become a seller of Insurance, first for the NPI, the Norwich Union, then for the Royal Group; then for a company that offered a large salary and bonuses. It went bankrupt, leaving the Dog out of work.

Sam asked, "Would you like my eldest boy to give you a hand?" She thought that Jeremiah would like him and, whatever else he might be, he would be a loyal friend. A more loyal friend, in good times and bad, nobody could have. Thus it was that Derek, heavily built with thinning hair, disarming smile and more wiles than a cartload of monkeys appeared.

He would need no pay and would only take any if he asked for it. He transformed the place from being quietly viable into a gold mine, and was driven nearly mad by Jeremiah's untidiness. As a compensation, for which he never quite forgave him, Peter Noble gave him a taste for fine wines. Derek's watchword was, "Have no care for the morrow". He would chide Jeremiah. "I suppose it is for you to say and the rest of us to do". Derek made him see why Jesus had cast out those who said, "Lord, did we not prophesy in thy name......?" and why he took such an equivocal attitude to the Baptist.

Before his appearance, Jeremiah was in a desperate state. His elder son had sat a scholarship. Jeremiah had taken the train, walked in to collect his final papers, and taken them out to supper. Uberrimae had been in touch, saying, "be advised dear boy". He should sell up and return to join his family in Devon. He would fix him up with employment. He told his friend Alec of this. Alec said that he would buy the place for £30,000 tomorrow.

"It's less than its worth. I would put a manager in and run it and sell it again and make a nice little profit". Jeremiah was becoming less trusting of Uberrimae, particularly when he used that phrase and called him 'dear boy'; but he liked him. He phoned him, immediately after Alec had spoken, saying, "That is fine, I can get £30,000 tomorrow. I have had a firm offer, so I will do as you say, and should be able to reunite the family by the end of the month".

It was not the first priority after all. "You are very strong, dear boy. Let your old father in law advise you. Hold on for a better price. Hannah will respect you, even more, for doing so". Whether Jeremiah trusted him this time or not is hard to say, or whether he intended accepting Alec's offer. He was in two minds. His elder son had made him promise not to sell the place. Uberrimae was in an untenable position. He gave advice, probably sincerely, not expecting it to be followed speedily. His advice involved speaking for another, and effectively making promises on her behalf.

Having been to evensong every day at school, Jeremiah should have learned to suspect flattering words. Assertions of frankness, honesty and truth tend to accompany economy with it, especially when sworn on oath. The Dog said, "I promise to tell the truth, the whole truth and nothing but the truth", would be more fittingly phrased, "I promise to tell as much of the truth and as many lies as I can get away with, as will assist in winning a case".

He received a strange letter from Hannah. Her father had been looking over his insurance policies and investments, which he had deposited at the bank, whence, she said, they had been sent to Uberrimae's bank for him to look at. He thought him over insured. The policies were part of a school fees plan. Uberrimae suggested that he surrender one of considerable value. He had asked his own bank in Plymouth to send it on to him, with the necessary forms. Jeremiah wrote that, as far as he was concerned, they were jointly taken out, and were nobody else's business. In the last resort there was only one comment, "be not anxious for the morrow". A few days later, an envelope, marked Natwest Bank, St Andrews Cross, Plymouth, arrived on the door mat. Since he had no business with them he left it there. He knew that it contained the policy in question and the form for its surrender.

A week or two later, he received a letter from the manager of his own bank in Derby. He enclosed a form *requesting* the release of the securities he had deposited. Jeremiah wrote back that, since they had already been released and transferred to his father in law's bank at Plymouth, it was nonsense for him to request what had already been done. If they needed his request, they should have sought it before doing so. Only if the manager could assure him that all were where he had left them, would he sign the request. This could not be done, as one lay on the doormat. The reply was a letter, containing the same form, a week later. He replied in the same way, receiving no answer.

The lover was still phoning every evening. Sometimes a woman who sounded like Hannah would open the call as before. He did not think that it was her. He did not know whether she kept the love nest going on a part time basis. One morning he was pleasantly surprised to receive a friendly letter from her, with her love. It was a Thursday. At about ten a.m., his pleasant surprise ended. There were two men at the bar door holding an impressive looking envelope. He had to sign for it. In it was a summons to appear in the Magistrates Court in Tavistock in the following week. She had applied for custody and control of the three children.

It seemed strange that he was given only a few working days' notice. The shortness of notice did not suggest that there was any great wish to discern the 'best interests of the children', if anyone knew what they were. There was little point in attending. She was among friends. Tavistock was their local town, her father was, by far, the most well known citizen, Deputy Lord Lieutenant of the County, and himself an honorary member of the bench. All in the business establishment knew him, as did those of the Church.

There was no time to arrange a solicitor. He did not even know one who would be in a position to act on his behalf. He did not want anything that the court could provide. He did not want 'his' children, under license from a court. Such an act would be an admission that men had the right to put asunder. In a childish way he felt that only one authority could give him what he wanted, his family reunited in love and fidelity. All he could do was "seek first the kingdom of heaven and its righteousness". That he thought in this way was far from a positive belief, or great faith, it was the only source of "manna". He was in the wilderness. "Acts of God" are fine in the wilderness, a nuisance out of it.

Whatever meaning had life now? Whom could he trust? A loyal friend who had been the sub manager of his Bank and had lived almost next door, came to stay. Bill, who now had his own branch, was shocked at the way his former manager had behaved over his securities. He had doubts about the genuineness of the summons; it being on crudely duplicated paper. He was wrong. The reason was that the county Boundaries were being changed.

It began to seem that Uberrimae was a man of great duplicity. If sure that one is right, duplicity is allowable, like bowling a googly to get a wicket. First he had asked him to deposit the returned pension contributions and then refused to release them. Then he invaded his bank and removed his securities. He was not going to touch the letter from S Andrews Cross. Its contents had been deposited for safe keeping with the Cornmarket Branch in Derby. He had refused to sign a form releasing it; as far as he was concerned, it was where he had left it. It proved an expensive gesture. While lying on the mat, the policy lapsed.

He went upstairs and wrote to the court. There was almost indecent haste in their action, hardly conversant with seeking the best interests of the children. He thought it doubtful that they would have consulted the boys, or their headmaster, who had told him that under no circumstances should he allow this.

He would not "render unto Caesar that which was not Caesar's". The test was "whose image and superscription", the coin bore. His children did not bear Caesar's image, but were made in the image of God. Their superscriptions were not those of Caesar either. They might take them from him, but no man could take them from the hand of their father, 'even in heaven'. He recalled the saying of Jesus, "none shall take them from mine hand". This, as servants of the Defender of the Faith, he would expect them to know. As to their demand for maintenance, he would not vary the undertaking he had given on his marriage under the Prayer Book of the Church, of which her Majesty was supreme Lord and Governor. He undertook to endow his wife 'with all his worldly goods'. That was unchanged. As far as he was concerned all that he had was hers. He would do nothing that implied a variation of this, nor anything that implied a recognition of the court's right to "put asunder". He enclosed £100, as they did nothing, but for a fee. He recalled them to the parable of the "Good shepherd". Those who enter the fold, by climbing over the wall, not by the door, were thieves and robbers who scattered the flock. The one who told that parable said that he was himself the door. Did they, or Uberrimae, or his wife's lover, enter through that door?

He sat down and wept bitterly. It was the end. He recalled Hannah's words at the restaurant. He was not only born, but bred for disaster. If Uberrimae were right, and he was as he was, thanks to his parents' upbringing, it had to go back from them to their parents, thence to their parents. So it went back, generation after generation, to 'Adam and Eve'. It was as if he had been booked on a down going escalator to the pit of hell before the foundation of the world. He wished he had died, not just when he tried to kill himself, but when he had suffered an acute collapse of his lungs after having his appendix out. Why did the nurse have to find him going blue?

He had passed into blissful sleep with a needle prick. He was happy. He had been given a miniature diesel engine for an aeroplane. At that age, he had harmed nobody; he was 'innocent'. How different it was now. He thought of the Ice Cream again, and how many empty words he had uttered. He thought of Hamlet, "There's the respect that makes calamity of so long life". He wished that he had never been born. He felt deceived, especially by those who made him listen to their declarations of belief. He felt at one with Job; why not curse God and die? He did not feel that 'his redeemer liveth'. Even God had deceived him. He had led him to say and do things, in a foolish assurance that they would turn out well, but it never did. He felt alone in a world, where everyone spoke a different language.

He felt alone no longer. His famous namesake had made the same complaint. "Lord thou hast deceived me, and I was deceived, but Lord, thou art mightier than I and hast prevailed". He too had cursed the day of his birth. He recalled Hosea. A similar situation had led to his indignant indictment of the infidelity of Israel.

Gomer's infidelity was, in Martin Buber's words, transparent into the life of the nation. (Buber wrote this of the prophet Jeremiah) He recalled the curse at the end of the Deuteronomy, in which the infidelity of the people resulted in their being afflicted with what we know as adultery. He could do what Hosea did. At least it gave some purpose to his life. A dim light began to shine ahead at the end of the tunnel. The escalator on which he seemed to have been put, 'from the beginning of creation', became enlightened, if not very brightly. If at the future end of the tunnel there was a dim light, the down-going escalator led to it.

Soren Kiekegaard provoked the beautiful Regine to break off their engagement. She married another. In his diary, Kierkegaard notes that he met her pushing a pram and doffed his hat. The outcome was that Regine is known, not for being the wife of the man she married, but for having been engaged to Soren

Kierkegaard. For over 2,000 years all that is known of Gomer is that she was Hosea's wife. Hosea wrote of his marriage as commanded of God. It seemed likely that he saw it thus, after the event. Kierkegaard made a curious comment about his decision to part with Regine, "He was in eternity too old for her".

Submerged in such thoughts, the day of the hearing arrived. Early that afternoon, the telephone rang. It was Hannah. "I need your help. I cannot cope with the control of the children. I never wanted it. I only wanted to make sure that I could see the boys. I never thought that the case would happen. I wanted to make you come with a solicitor, so that you did not get all emotional". That had been made impossible by the shortness of notice. Did she not know that he had been given only a few working days notice? Had she been deceived by a wily solicitor, who led her to believe that he was carrying out her wishes, when he was not? He did not know, then, that, had he consulted a solicitor, the case at Tavistock would have been stopped. It was 'illegal'. A lawyer would have insisted that more notice was given, and that the children be heard.

The case should never have been heard at Tavistock, which, given Uberrimae's position, would be seen as far from neutral. If the case were heard in the nearest court, there was the risk that the matter of the love nest and the planned attempt to circumvent the need for any legal actions by securing his death, might emerge. Hannah might not know of these things.

Had he known this at the time, and been given the chance to have a lawyer, Jeremiah would not have done so. He would not have wished to appear against his wife in court, still less have a lawyer do so for him. If the matter of the sustained attempt to drive him to kill himself had come out, he would not have wanted it.

This gave rise to an animated discussion, late one evening, in the bar. A friend was exasperated and said, "Who do you think you are, God?" Jeremiah was surprised at the cogency of his answer. "No, if I were God I would make the rules, since I am not I am content to abide by them. Its much easier!" The friend laughed, "Trouble is, the bugger's right!"

Hosea had gone into the wilderness and met his wife, and spoken to her heart. He would do the same. To the Dog's annoyance he went down to Dartmoor and sat on the moor outside her house. There he would remain, even if he died of starvation. He felt confident that he would return with her. Then all that Hosea had said would be forgotten. Though summer, it was cold on the moor at night. He wandered about to keep warm at night, sleeping by day. He achieved nothing but hunger, until his sister in law, who lived nearby, left sandwiches for him in the shed at the bottom of the garden. He had been there over a fortnight when a car drew up. Out got the Dog with his wife and family. They took him off to Plymouth for a meal and a clean up. The Dog had been in touch with Uberrimae and arranged a meeting with Hannah that evening. He was returned to his place. He waited. Nobody came. Whatever she might do, he would wait, as he had said. He waited all night. She appeared the next day with her brother.

Next day the Dog arrived. He had suspected this. He went to the phone and spoke sharply to her father. When Uberrimae started getting high and mighty, he got a surprise. "You can keep a civil tongue in your head......You are nothing to me!" He told the Dog to warn Jeremiah that they had taken counsel's opinion. Unless he returned immediately to run the business, they would bring an action under the Law of Property Act, because he was failing to 'safeguard the asset'.

The Dog withheld this information until Jeremiah was a hundred miles away, on the way home to Norfolk. He still deluded himself that, if Hannah was led to do more extreme things, she would think, 'This is going too far'. He had forgotten that she had participated in the sustained campaign to drive him to kill himself, which was still going on, and would not, herself, forget it. She would also be aware that the staff in the restaurant knew. She knew that the local policeman and sundry others knew.

They drove back to Norfolk in an aged, borrowed Simca, with not £1 between them. It was an amazing journey. By the time they reached Thetford, the fuel gauge was resting at zero. "Be not anxious for the morrow," said the Dog; "O ye of little faith!" They reached Norwich. The old car negotiated the city. They were on the Wroxham Road; then sitting by the riverside, where the Dog and his family lived. He even felt confident enough to get into the car and drive Jeremiah the four miles back to his own home.

The Dog had a lot going for him, when it came to living without anxiety for the morrow. He had many ways of earning a few quid, in three card brag schools, on the dartboard, or at the dog track. If anyone suggested a game of brag and he was playing, wise men went home. Everyone else left penniless. Derek left smiling. He could work out probabilities. Apart from that, he had a great asset. He allowed people to disdain him, as Goliath disdained David with fatal consequences. He would slump up against a bar looking as if he were the village idiot, or, as one barman described him, "A fat old man with piles!"

In a pub that was off the roadside, when time was called; the landlord had locked the doors and declared a private party. He suggested a darts match. Seven were keen to play and produced high quality tungsten darts, while the Dog slumped over a pint of beer. "Will you join in, then?" "All right. Can yer lend us some darts?" The landlord fished under the counter and produced an ill-assorted handful of darts. "They'll do fine."

The landlord produced an exercise book, "We'll have a book on it". Looking over his shoulder, the Dog asked, "Who's that you've got at 50 to 1?" "You, of course" "You cheeky sod. I'll have fifty notes on myself!"

In his heyday, only a full time professional could live with Derek on a dart-board. He could rely on putting three darts in triple twenty at least once in a game. Unlike Jeremiah, he was a generous hearted man. He would never have dreamed of demanding £2,500 from the landlord. "I'll take £20. That'll larn you", was more his way.

Having sent the cheque book to Hannah, Jeremiah yet received bank statements. He noticed a regular weekly payment of exactly the sum awarded by the court. He was fully prepared to do as he had said. He was not prepared to recognise their authority to put asunder. He wrote to the bank saying that he did not wish such cheques to be honoured. Nothing happened. The Dog, having been in the police, knew about such matters. "The court wont be bothered," he said, "They wont do anything unless someone lays a complaint".

Meanwhile, since there had been a court order, the headmaster of the boys' school had changed his mind about who was the fit guardian for the boys. Jeremiah reminded him of this. He reminded him also of what he had written when he had entered the boys. He was sending them to be educated 'in the faith and fear of God'. The head had written back, saying that his letter made him feel ashamed. The only parent, who sought from the school what it was set up to teach, was a non-Catholic. Jeremiah wrote that, until he could explain how his endorsing of the right of men to put asunder fulfilled his undertaking, he would not pay the fees.

He received a patronising letter, such as ministers and priests are prone to write to lay people, recalling words of St Paul, "All have sinned and fallen short of the glory of God". The "apostle Paul" did not simply assert, "All have sinned". It was a subordinate clause, beginning with 'because'. If he was going to cite the scriptures, he should do so accurately. He took the Head line by line through the Greek text. As he was a Catholic, he added the Vulgate version. He received no reply, so reiterated his original letter. There was no reply. He recalled the head to his founder's rule.

He wrote to the Abbot, asking him to tell his subordinate to answer letters. There was a long delay before he received a reply. The reason the head had not replied was that he had been on holiday. This saddened Jeremiah, who admired Placid Hooper. He wrote back angrily saying, "You know that is a lie, unless members of the Order take four month holidays". He received no answer. He wrote again, "Is the headmaster back from his holiday yet?" He received no reply from the Abbot; but received one, from his father in law's deposit bank. It enclosed a summons.

The Bank had 'subrogated' the bill for the fees, and was instituting legal proceedings to recover the cash. Jeremiah had not the means to pay. His securities had been removed. The current balance was nothing like enough. He was not going to touch the policy lying on the mat.

His Bank Manager friend came for the weekend. Sitting in the bar, Jeremiah told him of the mess he was in. "You're not in a muddle, lad. It is a disputed account! All you need do is write to the directors of the Bank. Tell them that you do not wish the account to be paid until the dispute is sorted out, and that you have withheld the fees because the school is in breach of contract". His eyes twinkled...."That will put the buggers into a muddle. They have already paid it!"

Hannah was a director of the bank. She explained that the Abbot was very lax in replying to letters. Her dad had given them a large amount of money, about £5,000, and it had taken him a month to write and say thank you. "Oh", thought Jeremiah.

He wrote to the Abbott a short postcard. "Would £5,000 be roughly the equivalent of 30 pieces of silver, allowing for inflation?"

He then wrote in Hebrew Greek and Latin. In Hebrew he asked Elijah's famous question, "How long halt ye between two opinions?" In Greek he asked that of Jesus, "The teaching of John the Baptist, was it of heaven or of men?" In Latin he asked, "should not the motto of the order/school, be changed from "Pax et Scientia" to "Non habemus regem nisi Caesarem?" (We have no king but Caesar). He heard later that Placid had resigned his Abbacy. His respect for the man soared. Had his letters been the cause of this good and honourable man's resignation?

Not many weeks later, he received a further summons, this time for uttering threats. The case was being brought by the headmistress of his daughter's school. He had made it clear that he was in no way party to her being there at the outset. Now that the court had made its order, the Head thought he would have come to a better mind. She wrote him a conciliatory letter, enclosing a term's report. It had the condescending tone of a matron speaking to a recalcitrant child. He noticed that she taught his daughter 'Scripture'. Jeremiah wrote what amounted to a catena of none too polite sayings from the scriptures, which seemed apposite. This had so upset their client that she was unable to continue as a teacher. They had instituted proceedings against him for uttering threats.

He wrote back, saying that, as their client was unable to read, it was perhaps best that she was unable to teach children. He had threatened nothing. All he had done was to draw her attention to warnings in the very scriptures that she taught. If there was no truth in them, she had nothing to fear. That being so she should not teach them. If, on the other hand, they had truth; neither he, nor such as Elijah threatened anything of themselves, but warned of what another might do. Again, he heard no more. Later, he learned that the head had ceased teaching altogether, and the school had been closed. This made one of his warnings seem extraordinarily fitting. He had reminded the head of how the ship on which Jonah sailed was caught in a violent storm. Jonah realised that the only way in which they could avoid shipwreck was to throw him overboard. He warned the headmistress that unless she did that, her school might face shipwreck!

The local Vicar was blind. He had expressed a wish to hear some works of modern theology, especially the writings of the famous Swiss theologian Karl Barth. Once a week, Jeremiah went to read these to him. A day before the custody summons arrived, he had become hostile. He had summoned him to the Vicarage. There he had told him that it was his duty to give his wife and her father all support in bringing up the children in a suitable home.

"But they love living here," said Jeremiah. The Vicar replied, "You come from a long line of educated Norfolk gentlefolk. That restaurant is no place to bring up children. You are exposing them to working class influences. What do you want for them, that they should be brought down to that level?"

"If as a minister of the Gospel you are putting me up against it, I suppose I should want for them, that they learn to be poor in spirit, meek, sorrowful........". The Vicar became angry and drove him from the house. It is doubtful if Jeremiah wanted anything of the kind for his sons and daughter. In that way the Vicar was right, or was he? There would be no room for such as Sam, the Dog, Clifford and John in that world. Still less could he have written as he did to John.

He may not have been quite as hypocritical as he seemed. He was beginning to find better friendship than he had ever known. He could see that by urging children ever to better themselves, one put a burden on them. The fact that someone had education, training or expertise, did not mean that he should ascend above his fellows, or even deserve a vastly higher salary. He was beginning to see that the "beatitudes", alone, were prescriptions for a merciful way of life. If nothing else they would provide a safety net, for such as might fall catastrophically.

One Friday evening, two policemen walked into the bar, shortly before they opened. "What can I do for you?" he asked them. "We have a warrant for your arrest, but we can see that it is not a good moment to arrest you". There had been a complaint that he had failed to pay some £45 of maintenance, ordered by the court. It was decided that Monday morning would be a suitable time. He was bailed to appear in about a week. Derek and another friend drove him over. He was confident that all would be well. They would meet for a drink in the pub and have lunch afterwards. He took to heart what he had read in the gospel and gave as little thought to what to say as possible.

He was called to the witness box. The usher handed him the New Testament and a card on which the oath was written. He was silent. The Chairman asked if there was anything he did not understand.

"Yes, there is". "What is it? We are here to explain things". "Is the book you have given me sacred in the eyes of the court?" "Of course it is", said the Chairman, echoed by a lady, sitting on his left, but if you are not a Christian.........". "Is the God, of which this book speaks, the same as the one referred to in the arms above your head?" asked Jeremiah. "Of course", said the Chairman, "what is the problem?" "It is exactly that. The card asks me to swear by Almighty God to tell the truth. The book, which you tell me is sacred, forbids me to swear by anything at all, could you explain?"

The lady on the bench seemed to be losing her patience, and said, "You can affirm if you wish". Not wishing to cause offence, he did so.

"Can you afford to pay this money?" asked the Chairman". Do you agree that you owe it?" "Yes," said Jeremiah. "You need only pay part of it".

He said that, in the marriage service, he had undertaken to endow his wife with all his worldly goods. This he had done. She had the cheque book; she owned everything as far as he was concerned. He had told the court this. Her

Majesty the Queen, whose laws they dispensed was Supreme Lord and Governor of the Church of England, under whose Prayer Book he had been married.. Thatbook, enforced by act of Parliament, imposed on all the duty, when they married, to endow their wives with all their worldly goods. That he had done and would do no other.

He went on to point out that the same marriage service ended with the strict prohibition, "those whom God had joined together, let no man put asunder". The service claimed to represent nothing less than a divinely ordered union. The situation arose from men putting asunder. At her Coronation, Her Majesty had solemnly undertaken that all law and governance in her realm would be subject to that of the gospel. The words that ended the marriage service were taken from those of the man, whose words were the 'gospel'.

Did the lawmakers, the Queen, her judges and magistrates, now, know better than the man whose words were the gospel? Were they not men? If so, unless they knew better than the one whose words were in the very book they had given him, they had no right to put asunder those whom God had joined together. It was tantamount to bowing down to the image, which Nebuchadrezzar had set up, or, in this case, Uberrimae Fidei.

If, as men, they knew better than the one, whose words were written in the book that they had given him, why did they not open the eyes of the blind, heal all manner of sickness and disease? Why were they not 'clothed with light as it were with a garment?' Why did God not say of them "these are my beloved sons, hear ye them?" Until, they could do all these things and more, he would stick with the one who said, "those whom God has joined together, let no man put asunder".

The Clerk was shouting, "Send him to Prison". The three on the bench filed out and filed back. They asked him if he would obey the orders of the court? "No", he said, "When the one, whose words are written in the book you gave me, was offered all the kingdoms of the world, if he would acknowledge an authority higher than God, he was content to remain obedient to the words of an ancient lawbook, saying, "It is written........". All he would say to them was, "It is written, those whom God has joined together, let no man put asunder. If that meant going to prison, it was an honourable place to be".

For Jeremiah, it was like an 'out of body experience'. He spoke with quiet, assured, disdainful, calmness and fluency, never hesitating, but slowly and deliberately. The tone of quiet disdain in his voice shocked him. It was as if he were the prosecuting counsel. All changed in a second, when he was led away from the court to the cells. As he went he tossed the keys to the Dog, saying, "shut the place up. It's all over".

Once again he deluded himself. He thought that, if he spoke as he did, the court would be bound to accept what he said. He had taken to heart the promise of Jesus that, when led before magistrates, it would be given him what to speak, and that no man would be able to answer. That had been true. They could respond with, "Go to Prison". He had overlooked that warning. He felt sure that, if sent to prison, Hannah would feel 'this is all going too far'.

He had tie and shoelaces removed, was brought some lunch and awaited the van to take him away. He was fearful now. It was no longer a game of words. On the van the accompanying policeman said, "A man of your background and education might not find it easy in there". His heart sank. The policeman said, "I'll have a word with the warders...."

Chapter Twenty One

'In the court of the guard'.

To be driven through the gatehouse of a prison is not a happy experience. Reception is not pleasant either. One is scrubbed in a bath and inspected to see that one has no lice. All one's things are taken away and one is kitted out in brown uniform, as a civil offender; given a roll of bedding, a plastic chamber pot, shaving utensils, a stamped envelope and sheet of paper and led off to a holding cell. One has no idea what is happening. The cell gradually fills with others, who have come from court, until it is packed like a sardine tin. Food is brought in. When all have returned from court, the door is opened, orders are shouted, names called out, and one is led onto the floor of the 'wing'.

All around were pale green cell doors with spy holes. An iron stairway led up to iron balconies with nets hung across. He was led up the stairs and along the 'landing' with another, who had been 'weighed off' with him, into a cell, in which there was already one inmate. It measured about 12ft by 6ft. There were two iron-framed bunks; the third was the base frame of a bed, the head of which rested on the footrail of the lower bunk; the foot on a folding chair. There was a table, a small cupboard and two chairs. They were told to make up their beds and the door was slammed behind them. Jeremiah was given the upper bunk.

The resident inmate explained the routine, and about slopping out. It seemed grotesque, but not unlike the first day in the army. The officers did not seem unpleasant, nor the resident inmate, a lad serving a sentence for GBH. He immediately produced tobacco, cigarette papers and matches, split into three, and offered the newcomers some 'burn'. When the bed was made, Jeremiah wrote to Hannah, telling her not to worry. He was fine, and everyone seemed quite pleasant. Again he thought that she must feel that everything had gone too far. He could not believe that she would have laid a complaint over £45, if she had thought it would lead to this. After what he had written to the court, she must have known that he would refuse to acknowledge its authority.

He suspected that others were pulling her strings, but felt, erroneously, that his incarceration might make her say, "No", to any more of it. He later learned that there might well have been a more devious reason for manoeuvring him into such a position. If he could be coerced into compromising, it would be possible to talk 'sensibly'. He had, however, come to feel ever more secure, when he fell back on the words in the Gospels. He was less inclined to abandon his 'high horse', since the friend had become so exasperated with him in the restaurant. Those sayings had a massive coherence, as if each was the focal point for all. If one contradicted one, one found oneself contradicting all. Behind the individual sayings of the first three gospels, came the fearful emphatic either/or of Jesus in the fourth; then the words of Elijah and the prophets. The words of Jesus were like a magnifying glass, concentrating the rays of the sun, so that it would burn a sheet of paper.

They were wakened at six, shaved, slopped out, and had breakfast shoved through the door. They had to be inspected by the doctor; then appear before the governor. The Governor seemed a pleasant man. Flanked by the Chaplain, with a senior officer behind him, he sat at a table, with papers in front of him. He said to Jeremiah with a smile, "My advice to you is to pay five pounds, say you are sorry, and go back home, but from what you told the court, I think my words will fall on stony ground". He asked the Chaplain if he had any words of wisdom. He had not.

The rest of the morning and early afternoon was spent lying on the bunk looking at the ceiling. Half way through the afternoon, the cell door was opened. He was called to the visiting room. There was the beaming smile of the Dog. He had much to tell. With the help of Sam in the kitchen, and Jo, he had reopened the restaurant. As a civil offender Jeremiah was entitled to a daily visit. Derek saw to it that he got one. One or other of his friends, often the Dog, himself, appeared every afternoon. He saw that prison sentences, like many punishments, fall on the families of offenders as, or even more, heavily than on those inside. After a day or two he and the other newly admitted inmate were allowed what is called 'association'. One is allowed to eat one's meals on the floor of the wing, and remain there for about two hours, before being returned to one's cell. Once he grew accustomed to the routine, it was not a bad existence, as long as one did not fret to be released, or long for the things one might do 'on the out'.

On his third morning, he received a postcard from his sister. It said simply, "Our mother would be proud of you". Jeremiah could not remember whether she had added, "for the first time in your life!" In a sense his sister was right; though their mother would have indicated that, had he been a more thoughtful husband, he might not have been there. Oddly, he would have felt more at ease with her in prison, than living in a well appointed home in the country, drawing a large salary as a Principal lecturer in 'Christian Theology'. She would, herself, have been in two minds. On the one hand, she would have been glad that her son found himself in a secure and well-paid job. On the other, she would have felt that there was something bogus about expounding a gospel, which began with, "Blessed the Poor in Spirit...", while earning a handsome salary.

One evening, when it was time for the lights to be turned out, the resident inmate became excited. It was an old prison, with the switches outside each cell door. "It'll be Arthur tonight", he said.

Jeremiah had noticed messages scratched on the cell door saying, "God bless you Arthur." It never occurred to him that any such person existed. What was so special about Arthur? What was special about Arthur was that he stopped at each cell door and said goodnight to each inmate, by name. He told them not to worry. If someone was to appear in court, next day, he would push fags through the little spy hole. If there was glass in it, he would knock it out with a broomstick. The lad said, "I'd like to be like Arthur".

Here was a lad who had been in and out of approved schools and juvenile prisons. He was now in prison for GBH, and had no intention of 'going straight', when released, only making sure that he did not get caught again. If he could have fulfilled an ambition, he would have been like Arthur, the night screw in Norwich prison. It was an ambition that required little educational attainment, yet was beyond the reach of most.

On his second night, the Chaplain had made his routine visit to new inmates. He spoke to the resident occupant of the cell. He spoke at length to the other new occupant. He would not even say 'good evening' to Jeremiah. What could he say? He, after all, conducted weddings and ended with the words, "let no man put asunder". He knew that it was for asserting this that Jeremiah was in the cell. He could hardly shake his hand and say, "Well said", nor could he say that he had been a fool to do so. He symptomised the parlous position of the Christian religion.

As the chaplain turned to depart, Jeremiah asked him if he could let him have a Bible. His reply amazed him. "Sorry, I have run out. I could let you have a Hebrew Bible if you want". He said this disdainfully. Jeremiah said, "That will do fine". The other inmates sniggered and the Chaplain left. Whatever did this religion mean? Here was an ordained minister of the gospel, chaplain to a prison, asked for a Bible, the very Gospel, which he was ordained to preach. One would have thought that he would have been pleased to provide one, even if it meant going to a second hand bookshop. He never produced the promised Hebrew Bible.

Jeremiah was given work as a yard cleaner. Except on canteen days; there was nothing much to pick up. In charge of the yard cleaners was Paddy Lapsin. He was in for being drunk and disorderly. Most of the time was spent in a disused greenhouse reading ancient yellowing papers. There had to be occasional excursions, to be seen to be doing something. Paddy was a cheerful rogue, using the prisons of England as doss houses in winter months. A cell, in one of her Majesty's penitentiaries, was better than a bed in a hostel. It was more orderly and you did not have meths drinkers around. When discharged, he told the governor to keep his cell for him. He would be back at the weekend and got on well with the other two inmates. He was as good as his word. He was discharged on Wednesday morning. He was back, mop in hand, on Friday.

Paddy was angry. He had hoped to be in Norwich Nick for Christmas. As prisons went, he considered it a 'nice little drum'. It seemed that the Governor, the magistrates and social workers had discussed his case, and he was being sent to stay with his sister and her husband in Liverpool. This did not please Paddy as, "They're f---ing teetotallers." Jeremiah could not understand why others, sleeping rough, did not do as Paddy and use the prisons as winter hostels. All Paddy needed to do, to secure a month's shelter and food, was to get hopelessly drunk, wave down a police car and offer the driver a half eaten beefburger.

The whole business of punishment seemed futile. In the first place it fell as heavily on the families of offenders as on inmates. In the second it seemed to encourage few to 'reform', only not to get caught. The culture of the prison was that, 'There is nobody in here who does anything half as bad as those that send them here', the only difference being that they hire others to do things for them and make the laws, so they don't apply to them. There was also the matter of what became a 'transfer of guilt', if the penalty exacted 'by society' was excessive. Governments and their agencies were essentially nothing more than highly successful 'protection racketeers'. If they wrongly incarcerated someone for ten years, he or she would be set free with a token apology, and perhaps some compensation. If any private citizens, or a 'gang' did so, for a couple of weeks, they would be prosecuted.

How might it be, he wondered, if those in prisons came to accept their lot? The food was not nice to eat, but one got used to it. It was very boring, but so, for most, was life. One had no responsibilities. There was little point in worrying about things on the outside, as one could do nothing about them. It was his time in the nick that made him reconsider of the exile of Isreal.

As a civil offender, he was transferred to the open wing. It was the old Britannia Barracks, where he had last resided as a commissioned officer. Life was more amenable. They were in dormitories and could wander about. There were separate kitchens and the food was better. In the next bunk was a man, who had been a restorer of pictures for a leading London gallery. He had sought to use his technical skills, to produce his own 'old masters'; but was not quite skilful enough. He spoke enthusiastically of water colourists, their techniques, the paper they used and so on. Jeremiah listened intently. It was to prove very useful in years to come. Another, in the open wing, opened his eyes to a further aspect of the effects of punishments.

They obviated the need for any 'moral' consideration. If one committed an offence, for which there was a penalty, it became a 'bargain'; if one was caught. Unless every malefactor were caught, all claims of justice were rendered meaningless. It became a lottery. This man had enjoyed a life of crime since leaving school. He was very intelligent. His crimes were forms of fraud, committed against institutions. By no other means, could he have enjoyed the lifestyle, he had in his youth. He needed to get caught and to have every offence taken into consideration. The eight years he was to spend in prison were his 'working life'. He had plenty salted away to live very well for the rest of his days overseas. If every offence was taken into consideration, he could retire in peace to enjoy it. He had paid his debt to society; whatever that may mean.

While in the open wing the Dog brought him news. Hannah, her father and a business adviser, with an accountant, had visited the restaurant. He had persuaded her to come and visit him. Whatever he did he was not to get emotional. She would be coming that afternoon. He was not permitted a second visit; but the screws were a kindly and understanding lot, and ready to bend the rules. He awaited her arrival with great expectancy. She sat down and tenderly held his hand in hers. She explained that they had come up to help him run the business more profitably and get him help with the accounting. His emotions got the better of him. She seemed not annoyed by this, squeezed his hand, gave him a kiss, and left. The next day the accountant came to introduce himself. His name was Alan and he seemed friendly. The Dog was wary, but Jeremiah was in high spirits. He felt sure that his family would be restored, that Hannah and her father had seen that it was the only way.

He was surprised to be summoned to the visiting room, in the middle of the morning, on the following day. There stood two men, a sheaf of papers in their hand. They asked his name and handed him the papers. The Officer said, "Don't go back to work, go up to your dormitory and read the papers". It was another summons, this time to appear in the Chancery Division of the High Court. He was to appear about five days after being discharged. Two of them were a weekend. He was summoned under the "Law of Property Act", for absenting himself and not "safeguarding the asset", exactly as Uberrimae had threatened in the summer. That was the purpose of the visit to the business. The accountant was not there to help him make it profitable, but to take over as the Chancery Court's receiver. Hannah had come to arrange the delivery of the summons. It is odd that we feel happy to hire others to do those things, which we could not do ourselves, as if, in some way, it absolves us.

He was no soul of truth, but this kind of deceit was beyond his comprehension, unless someone did it for him, preferably without his knowing. He turned to the attached affidavit, sworn by his wife. As he did so, a young acquaintance came up to him and warned, "Whatever you do don't let anyone see that you are upset. If you do someone will put a note in and you will be taken back to the cell block".

The affidavit was too much for him. It was four pages of foolscap, a catalogue of his faults as a husband, not all of them by any means. There was, of course, no fault on the part of the swearer. It was no good trying not to be upset. There was his entire life with her over fifteen years, nothing to be said in his favour, and not a scintilla of fault on her part. This was the truth, the whole truth and nothing but the truth. He wept, in no small part, because it was substantially true. All the faults were his, although there was no mention of the affair, the love nest or the sustained attempt to drive him to kill himself. He could see that he had driven Hannah to do these things.

It was not long before two screws appeared. He was told to roll up his bedding and was led back to the cell block, via the hospital, and put into an isolation cell on the ground floor. There, not unkindly, he was told that he could weep as much as he wanted. It would not 'wind up' other inmates. That evening, a screw came round with large doses of vallium. He refused it. He spent the night going over the affidavit again and again. It broke his heart. He did not sleep. The next day was the same. That night, exhausted by misery, he slept. When he awoke, he was not happy, but felt, somehow, that all would be well. When his door was opened he said a cheery, "Good morning". His refusal of vallium meant that he was taken back to the doctor and thence to a psychiatrist.

He read through the affidavit again. It was full of trifling errors of detail. They were the kind of errors he had been taught to notice in the narrative of the gospels, indicating that the writers were unfamiliar with the background they described; as when S Luke had the man on the stretcher lowered through a tiled roof. It was obvious that, whoever provided the material relied on second hand information. If one had lived in a village for five years one would hardly get its name wrong. One error was glaring. How could a devoted wife of fifteen years not yet know her husband's first names, or even his initials? He had been endowed with Uberrimae's second name and initial. 'The hands were the hands of Esau but the voice was the voice of Jacob'.

That morning, he was again summoned to the visiting room. It was not visiting time. "Oh, God! Not another summons". When he got there, he saw a clergyman, with whom he had been at school. Henry had been asked to visit him by the blind Rector. His relief was such that he wept again. Henry was understanding and kind. He produced a packet of little cigars; Jeremiah smoked almost all of them. Henry, later, became Dean of Carlisle.

In charge of the ground floor was a senior officer, Mr Proudlaw. Some of those, in the isolation cells, were in a bad state and were civil offenders, for whom this life was unbearable. One had killed himself by cutting his wrists with the serrated plastic knives they were given. He was only a lad. His offence had been to sell a piece of agricultural machinery he had bought on credit. He had maintained the payments, but was in breach of the agreement. He had, so the story went, found Guy Fawkes' night more than he could bear. He had looked out of his cell window, seen the rockets in the sky and thought of his children. What a horrid world this was. Would we not, in truth, be better without the festive occasions, weddings, funerals, Christmas, Remembrance days and all the rest?

If one was genuinely sad at the loss of life during the wars, one would feel so all the time, or at any moment, when one recalled it. The sorrow felt on set occasions was engendered. Given the sort of music played, the Nimrod variation, the Dead march from Saul and so on, any assembled company would mourn a dead rat. Such engendered mourning could be turned off, when the music stopped; then everyone could forget all about it, and return to normal life; perhaps indulging in a further act of public mourning in the evening.

The man in the next-door cell moaned and shouted. The officers gave him fags and mugs of tea. It was 'bang up' time. Mr Proudlaw came to the cell. "I have a job for you, if you don't mind". Jeremiah did not mind at all. He followed Mr Proudlaw to the kitchen and was given a mug of tea to carry. He followed him back to the adjacent cell, where the officer gave the tea to the distressed inmate. Jeremiah felt that even a senior prison officer could manage to carry a mug of tea unassisted, and returned to his cell. Mr P came in and sat on the chair.

"They tell me that you were once a Professor of religion." "No", said Jeremiah, "I was never a professor of anything. That's way above me".

"Explain this to me", said Mr Proudlaw. "I've always been taught that it was a gospel of love. If it is, how did he say those awful things to the scribes and Pharisees?" "Oh God", thought Jeremiah, "This is just what I need, and I did not even get a mug of tea!"

He said, "If you had young children, and you saw them running towards a cliff edge looking back over their shoulder, would you not shout at them, even throw things at them, to try and make them look where they were going, especially if they were encouraging others to follow them?" "I see, said Mr Proudlaw, "He's saying, For God's sake stop it". Jeremiah thought that Mr Proudlaw had made him see much more than he had enlightened Mr Proudlaw.

The morning after his transfer to isolation, his cell door had been opened slightly, at about 6am. A hand appeared round it with yesterday's papers, and threw them on the floor. A familiar voice said, "Here you are mate, I thought something to read might help. Try and cheer up, it will be all right". "Are you Arthur?" asked Jeremiah, "I would love to meet you." "Can't stop now," said Arthur, "they'd sack me if they knew that I opened a cell door on my own". With that he was gone.

They offered Jeremiah a transfer back to a normal cell. There seemed little point, as he was due for discharge in a week. "It's up to you, I don't mind". They left him where he was.

Those discharged are given an early breakfast so that they don't 'wind up' others. There was Mr Proudlaw, holding out his hand. He said. "I would not wish it on you, but we'd like to see you back!" They were led to the gate and it shut behind them. Standing in the gateway was a small balding man. He held out a hand, "I'm Arthur, he said." Jeremiah told him how much his "goodnights" meant to the inmates, especially the youngsters. Arthur smiled, "You do your best to make life a little better for people. They are not bad lads, you know, far worse than they could ever be sit on benches and send them here!" One of the most oft read books, in the prison library, was Dostoevsky's 'House of the Damned'. Jeremiah had sought to read it, and was told, "It's out. You'll have to wait a long time to get hold of it".

Outside the gate were the Dog and Jo. Jeremiah took the train to see Hannah. How foolish he had been, if he hoped for the restoration of his family, had not yet dawned on him. The fact that he had spent time in prison as he had, would, itself, become a source of embarrassment in the future, had it come about.

Chapter Twenty Two

"Offence's gilded hand"

Hannah had moved to a flat. Her brother was there, shortly to be followed by her father, then her solicitor. They went into a huddled conversation in another room. The solicitor emerged saying, "Your wife does not want to know". One by one they departed. At about four o'clock his elder son, who had left the school at Buckfast, returned. Jeremiah was shocked to see him so cast down and dispirited.

Hannah tolerated his presence and said that he could stay the night. The case in Chancery was only three or four days away. He pointed out the errors and the erroneous names he was given, in her affidavit. It was implausible that a wife of fifteen years did not know either her husband's names or initials. Clearly it was her father's handiwork. Her attitude seemed to soften. She became almost affectionate.

"Please don't involve poor old dad. He is not a fit man. If you dragged him into it, and questioned him in court, it would kill him. You know what you are like when questioning people. You never let go. You seize on their answers and fire questions at them. Dad could not stand that. Please let the case go through. That is all I want. All I want is to be sure that the place is sold. As long as I can be sure of that, I promise that I will bring the family back by Christmas and stay with you until the place is finally sold. Then we can all make a fresh start". She seemed truthful. She may have been, for herself, at the time.

Reassured he returned to Norfolk. Again he travelled overnight, arriving in the restaurant as Sunday lunch was being served, with Sam in the kitchen. It was early November. The case was heard without his being there. He would not have appeared anyway. Alan, the receiver, told him what went on. Though not yet officially appointed, he began, in a general way, to supervise the running of the place. All accounts were taken over by the court. He received a copy of the judgement. Jeremiah did not. One thing amazed him. The judge gave Jeremiah an unlimited right to appeal, at 24 hours notice. "That's extraordinary", said Alan. "Normally they set a time limit. They must have been unhappy at the case going through by default". No doubt, this was why the plaintiff's solicitors had not sent Jeremiah a copy. That was their way. The principal partner made speeches in the House of Lords, about the duty of the law to safeguard the weak.

All had now to be run on a cash basis. It was not easy. There was not much business in mid November; but they had a stock in the bar and on the wine racks, enough to last them a couple of weeks.

Alan's appointment was ratified. He was empowered to receive and manage the premises. 'Very well,' thought Jeremiah, 'you can receive and manage it'. He served a final lunch on Sunday, locked up and walked away. He spent the night with John Jacobs and his daughter Mandy, who gave him a reflective groundsheet, as he had nowhere to lay his head. The next day he walked west as far as Downham Market. It was cold. He was given shelter, in the barn between the presbytery and church, by the Roman Catholic Priest.

The old man invited him in for a night-cap of Malmsey wine. They chatted. The priest was in trouble for refusing to abandon the Latin Tridentine mass. His objections were not, primarily, linguistic; though it seemed odd that they should ban Latin, having, for years, told people that Latin was the proper language for the liturgy. When the old man had mentioned some of the changes, Jeremiah said, "Those words have been used since the days of Hippolytus' father".

"What sort of vagrant are you? Not one in a thousand has heard of Hippolytus". He invited Jeremiah to hear the last ever saying of the Tridentine Mass in England. The postman arrived bearing the eviction notice. It was a horrid document. As a memento he gave Jeremiah the envelope in which it had been sent. Years later the irony and hypocrisy of that eviction struck him. The Church of Rome had once again allowed the use of the Latin Mass. The upholders of the Christian religion seem capable of any disingenuousness, and always had a bowl to hand in which to wash their hands. They learned much from Pilate, more, it seemed, than from the one he crucified.

He made his way west to Northampton and stayed with his bank manager friend and his family, having stopped at Cambridge, where Charlie Moule gave him lunch at Clare, and allowed him to use a bath. Thence he went to stay a night with Tom Hurdle. Bill told him that what had been done about his securities had been highly irregular. He made his way back to Hannah's door once again. He was, again, miserable at the sight of his elder son. He had a pound note. He put it into the envelope given him by the old priest, and wrote, "Happy Christmas". His sister and her husband in Durham had suggested that he reopen the restaurant, and had given him a cheque for £50. He said good night to his son and got as far as London by train. In his pocket, as he sat on the station, he found his pound note. On it was written, "your need is greater than mine". He had only a few shillings left. It was cold, and dark. He got to the northern outskirts. He would have to walk, but the roadside was a sheet of ice. A lorry stopped and the driver asked him aboard. "Where are you heading?" "Norwich" he said" "You are in luck", said the driver, "so am I".

It was warm in the cab, and Jeremiah dozed off. They were approaching a town. "Where are we?" "Norwich", was the reply. "Had a good sleep?" The driver said that there was an early train to Wroxham. He would be catching it. If Jeremiah had not enough money for the fare, he would pay for him. He found that he had just enough and walked the three miles to the restaurant. The place was locked up. Nothing had been moved. The sweet trolley stood where it had been left, with mouldering sweets on it. He climbed in through a window into a lavatory, and his first task was to light a fire. The next was to phone the Dog, who said laconically, "Finished going walkabouts then, have we?" The next job was to wash up; then see what there was by way of stock. The bar had almost nothing left. There were some wines; the freezers were quite full.

It was not long before Derek appeared. It was not hard to guess what he would say, "Spare no thought for the morrow, sunshine. That is what you tell everyone, it's time you started doing it". He was ingenious at restocking a bar with £50, or somewhat less, as food also had to be bought. The pub had changed hands. Its new landlord was a cockney called George, who had had a window cleaning round in the east end. If any moved onto his patch, George described how he waited till they were up their ladders; then kicked them away. George and Pat became wonderful friends. They inched their way to Christmas. If three or four customers came, the takings were promptly turned into stock for the next day. If they could reach Christmas, they might survive, as long as no large bills arrived.

One did. It was for a quarter's electricity, almost £300. The red reminder came, with the threat of cut off in a week. Whenever they had an evening that produced a surplus, Jeremiah became 'mean'. Derek noticed this, telling him that his face and eyes became all mean and nasty. Being tight with the odd £20 would not help in paying a bill of that size; so he might as well forget it.

Two days before the cut off, the phone rang. It was Norwich Number One Round Table. They had a crisis. The place, where they had booked their Christmas guest night, had closed, "Could he possibly produce a Roast Beef Dinner for about forty five people, tomorrow evening?"

There would be one or two other customers who had booked. That did not matter. The Round Tablers drank freely. The other customers also ordered roast beef. Next morning, Jeremiah wandered into the Post Office and counted out £300 in cash. "What did I tell you, said the Dog. You never listen to me".

They reached Christmas. Catering Turkeys are cheap, and one can charge a lot for a meal on that day. Clifford was appalled, "You should be ashamed of yourself, expecting people to eat that old tack". They had fresh birds. There was money in the safe. Having served the customers, Jeremiah prepared a meal to welcome the family home. Whether he believed Hannah's promise, or made himself act as if he did, is hard to say. Two customers, known as the Arabs, from the name of their boat, stayed with him. They did not think that she would keep her word, but did not say so. The evening wore on. They promised to leave as soon as there was any sound in the car park. Eight o'clock came, then nine. It was obvious that nobody was coming. Jeremiah collapsed into a tearful heap.

He cannot truly have believed that she would keep her word, as there had been no communication; but 'make believe' can become almost as compelling as belief, if one tries hard. On Boxing Day they were shut. In mid afternoon Hannah phoned. She apologised for not having done so the day before. The children wanted to wish him, Happy Christmas. He asked, "Where were you all?" "We had a lovely day, Mum and Dad invited us over."

"But you promised that ......". "When Mum and Dad asked us, we could not refuse. We had arranged to go to them. We could not let them down". "When did you agree to go to them?" "Oh; about a fortnight ago".

The fact that she had promised to spend Christmas in Norfolk and stay there, at the beginning of November, seemed not to matter. Nor, it seemed, having made such a promise, was there any need to cancel it. This was "Uberrimae Fidei" in practice. He realised that this is the 'conversation' of the world.

When she made her promise, he was the one who carried a possible threat. Had he questioned her dad in court, he might not have only humiliated him, but led him to admit knowledge of the love nest and all that was consequential on it. The court might have taken a dim view of his drawing up an affidavit for his daughter to swear to.

Faced with such an implied threat, she probably felt momentary affection for Jeremiah. Once that threat had been eliminated, her affection was transferred. He could hardly blame her. One tended to creep around those whom one feared. Was that love? If the Deuteronomist be right, the "Fear of the Lord" was the first step in learning to love the "Lord thy God". He could begin to see how a greater fear cast out a lesser. Fear would be a permanent condition, fright temporary. Like it or not, it is the 'conversation' of this world. It is the 'conversation' of business. If one verbally agrees to a deal, but signs nothing, and a better offer comes along, that is fine. Nothing can be done about it. There could be a shocking corollary. If one acted on a given word, saying nothing more, allowing everyone to assume, 'e silentio', that one would not do so; it could produce chaos. How might it have been, had he assumed that she was not going to keep her word, and she had?

He went back to the word God and the word of God. He spoke once, and was silent. It was the same with Jesus in the gospel, as the 'word made flesh'. There it is, take it or leave it. He thought of the events declared in creeds, the virgin birth, death, and resurrection, ascension and return. It could only be said once. Given those 'signs', it could not be retracted. What more could be done to certify one man and his words as of God? You could hardly have two resurrections! If asked what were the gospels about, they were an exposition of the reality of absolute power.

No doubt, in the moment of saying what she did, under the apparent threat of Jeremiah hounding her father in the witness box, Hannah was sincere. As soon as the threat was removed, all changed. She then faced other, more pressing threats, from her parents. How could she tell them that she had promised to return and reunite the family, in order to buy off Jeremiah? She had signed the affidavit, sworn that it was the truth. She would have known also, that, if she returned until the place was sold, it probably never would have been. Apart from that she would not have wanted to live under the direction of the Chancery Court and its receiver. It is seen as sensible, when a Chancellor decides to devalue the currency, to assure all that he has no intention of doing so. Those, who trust his words, lose. Those, who realise that they are a necessary falsehood, gain.

She probably sensed that he would not go to court anyway. She might even have been aware that, having repeatedly got onto the 'high horse', refusing to acknowledge the right of men to put asunder, he could hardly now get off. To have gone to court would have meant recognising that right. Here was an extraordinary irony. She and her Dad needed him to be guided by the very words and sayings, for adhering to which they despised him. They needed him to 'believe their report', in Church. How much they did so, he did not then realise.

There is a curiously worded saying that follows the well-known words, "God so loved the world....". It is about judgement and choosing the light or the darkness. Jesus speaks of those that *do* the truth coming to the light, that it may be seen that what they have done is 'wrought *in* God'. Almost always, it is the case that, as with Hannah, whether one is able to do the truth of one's words or not, is out of one's hands. One is either *enabled* to do so or one is not. One could be led to utter words which, in the moment of speaking, were sincerely meant, but which were made into falsehoods within hours.

New Year came and went, and they survived. Alan, the receiver, was helpful. If they could make the place prosper, which, under the Dog's guidance, it did, he might be able to help. He had come to the conclusion that the people who had appointed him were not being truthful. Little by little, they were clearing accounts with those who would accept payments, by endorsing any cheques in favour of an account holder.

There was a small wooden barrel of draught beer on the bar. The Brewery did not accept payments. When they could, they bought a replacement for cash. One Sunday it ran out. Jeremiah slipped down the road to George, for a large jug of beer to pour into it. It was a despised, pasteurised, brew. He was standing behind the bar, when three men came in. "You deserve three stars", they said. "Why?", he asked... ". "You have cask-conditioned beer in a wooden cask and no pumps! Let's have a pint all round." "I am sorry. We can only serve drinks if you have booked a meal". They said that they were members of CAMRA.

"We'll book in for lunch then". Jeremiah was out of his depth. "I will go and see if we have a table", he said, and rushed out to the kitchen. "What the hell do I do?", he asked Derek. "Leave it to me".

They were pleased to have found room for them, and here were three pints of beer. They held them to the light and were amazed at the clarity, tasted it and declared it, "magnificent!"

One evening, a party had come in; a woman among them drank brandy. They had only about a single glassful left. Jeremiah ran down to the pub. Pat unhooked the bottle and optic and handed it to him. After her meal, the woman had another; then said, "I think we will all go down to the pub again!". Laughing merrily, she held out her hand, saying, "I think I'd best take their brandy back to them!". She slipped it under her coat, went down to the pub, walked in and ordered a large brandy. Pat was about to explain, when the woman produced bottle and optic and said, "I think you need this back!".

Such sprees contributed to a sense of joie de vivre about the place, which the customers began to enjoy. Per capita spending doubled. If they were not fully booked by 11 o'clock on Sundays, Jeremiah invited people living alone to come free, paying for their own drinks.

Alan came with bad news. He had a letter from the solicitors telling him that a man, whom I will call 'Slope', was coming to view the property with a view to buying it. He was a well-known and respected financier in the City. "Whatever does he want with a tin pot place like this?"

Alan said that it was an old dodge, to save the costs of prolonged actions in major courts. It not 'kosher', if there is collusion. He felt sure that there had to be. Of course there had to be collusion. The place was not on the market. Here was a prominent City financier, suddenly wanting to buy a tin pot restaurant in the country, and, for some reason, taking it into his head to contact a firm of solicitors in Plymouth, in order to do so. What will happen, Alan explained, was that Slope would make him an offer that he could not refuse. He would hang onto the place for a year and sell it. Any loss and expenses would be made good, discreetly. It was a practice used all the time. Chancery cases soon ran up costs of tens of thousands. Slope was coming tomorrow.

Having got away with it for four months, Jeremiah was undone. He phoned the Dog. "Don't worry about Slope", he said, "He's as bent as a nine bob note." "That's no help. He's coming tomorrow".

"Listen to your Uncle Derek, and do as he says. Just ask him if he has seen 'Ken Boater' lately. Slope will be off as if his arse is afire!" Jeremiah knew that he would not get away with asking a question like that convincingly. He passed the message to Alan and went to see Jo. When he returned, Alan was amazed, "Whatever did the Dog have on Slope?" He was very interested in buying, until asked the question. He then turned round, got into his car and drove away. What did the old Dog know?

"I didn't *know* anything, but I bloody well do now! I bet Slope's arse is like a Smartie, and so's Uberrimae's, if he's involved". Three days later, Alan arrived clutching a letter from Hannah's solicitors. The Dog was there. The letter thanked him for shewing Slope round. He no longer had any interest in buying. The final paragraph made Alan's eyes pop out of his head. "Mr Slope wanted to know whether a 'Mr Derek......' had any connection with the place". Whatever it was that he knew about Slope must have frightened the hell out of him, as not only had he remembered it, but knew that the Dog alone knew.

Some years earlier, Slope and Boater had met the Dog wanting to buy a number of single premium endowments. The sums involved were so large that Derek felt curious. He played the village idiot, and plied them with beer, until they had to go and relieve themselves, then he had a quick look through their papers. He got an impression that they were hiding money, they should not have. He later told Jeremiah that he had enough on 'Slope' to have him put away for ten years or more.

This was the time of the Jeremy Thorpe scandal. A man called Norman Scott alleged a homosexual relationship and that the 'heavies' had been sent to frighten him. They had killed his dog to shew that they meant business. In the background was a mysterious figure whose initials were GW. He was offering Scott, so it was said, 'hush money', in the form of civil service jobs in the West Country. Jeremiah had been given a large colour TV by Charles and Joey. On this were shewn the letters, with the "G W" referred to. On one was a hand written Postscript, initialled "G W".

It was alleged that "GW" was a South African journalist, who had spent some time on one of the London papers, but hotly denied anything to do with the matter. Thorpe and his friends said that he had no connection with them. How he could offer jobs in the West Country was not explained.

What struck Jeremiah was that his handwriting was extraordinarily similar to a "GW" he knew, who was in a position to offer such jobs. The "GW", he knew, was a friend of Thorpe and the party grandees. How easily those with ambition could find themselves compromised in such circumstances! One needed only to find oneself standing among important people, who might say, "We've got a bit of a problem. You might be able to help us", for anyone to hear himself saying, "Of course, you know that I'll do anything I can". The next thing that the unfortunate man would know was that he was being referred to in letters.

He was touched, in the second week of March, to receive a parcel from Hannah. It was his birthday. In it was a present from herself and the boys. She wrote an affectionate letter. He was happy for about an hour. As before, two men appeared with a summons. It was for divorce. He was gutted. This time he received proper notice, with plenty of time. He knew what he would do.

Chapter Twenty Three

Crimes, Misdemeanours, and Arthur Ransome

The weekend before the Divorce Hearing, Jeremiah took the train to Plymouth and arrived at his wife's door. He was invited in. His elder son was there, so was his daughter. The younger son, who was still boarding at Buckfast, was due home in a few days. On Sunday, Uberrimae arrived to take everyone to church.

This was, no doubt, thought fitting. All could petition God to facilitate the putting asunder of those, whom he was declared to have joined together. Given the fawning sycophancy of ministers of the Gospel, when dealing with the mighty, it would not be beyond imagination, that the very minister, who had pronounced these words, would wish them well in court. The lay reader and his daughter would attend the 'Holy Eucharist' in the very Church, in which, fifteen years ago, she and Jeremiah were solemnly told, "Those whom God has joined together let no man put asunder".

It could be, though it was not, the same Minister of the Gospel, who would say, "who in the same night that he was betrayed took bread and when he had given thanks, he brake it and gave it to them saying, Take eat, this is my body which is given for you, Do this in remembrance of me". Anyone might think that the one, who would be remembered, would be the very one who said, "Let no man put asunder". In cultic re-enactment, they "ate of his flesh and drank of his blood", as he commanded, declaring to all that they are those who abide in his words. With due reverence they would, "Take and eat this in remembrance that Christ died for thee, Feed on him in thy heart by faith with thanksgiving", in 'anticipation' of a felicitous 'putting asunder' on the following day.

All are comfortingly assured that there is no need to remember Jesus or his words, by the Minister. It is as if 'Christ' is some other, when he says, "As our saviour Christ has commanded and taught us, we are bold to say, Our Father........". Hearing such words anyone might think that the prayer would be as Jesus gave, but as the Minister of the Gospel and any, who can read, know, it is not. If the amenable version is, as all upholders of the Christian religion are sure, the work of the spirit of truth, it cannot be said to "bring to remembrance all that I spoke unto you". It hardly glorifies the one, whom all declare to be Very God of Very God, to imply that he managed to provide only one prayer and got it wrong. It makes the entire process a suitable prelude for what was to take place on Monday morning.

It is not beyond imagination that the lady Judge, herself, attended the Holy Communion on Sunday, before spending Monday, and probably the rest of the week, putting asunder, those whom, according to the Prayer book, "God has joined together". This, she would be empowered to do by the Defender of the Faith and Supreme Lord and Governor of the Church of God by law established, "duly knowing whose minister she is", whose Prayer Book makes that solemn declaration.

The Judge gives additional assurance that Jesus' words may safely be disregarded, since, as all know, he said, "Judge not, lest ye also be judged......" One must assume that this does not apply to any who do so, as their trade, profession and vocation, and are highly paid for it. Jesus also refused to settle disputes between a man and his neighbour, not having the authority. Thus it is that all, in one way or another, from the Defender of the Faith, the Judge and the Minister of religion, the Lay Reader and his daughter, set themselves above Jesus and his words, which makes declarations that he is God of God and Light of Light, a trifle odd. It might be more fitting to declare belief in themselves. Jeremiah wrote of this to the lady judge, was rebuked for his scurrility and threatened with proceedings for contempt.

Few can doubt that societies and kingdoms of the world need provision for divorce. Hannah could not be expected to endure a life with Jeremiah. What those words make clear is that no such kingdom and its rulers, nor its religion, can claim to be of God, unless Jesus and his words are not. He and his words must be assumed to be "of the devil" and so, his miracles "by Beelzebub Prince of Demons". The Gospels make the entire business almost farcically hypocritical. What makes it anything but farcical is the possibility that there is God and that He raised Jesus from the dead.

In the Book of Common Prayer is a section, "PRAYERS AND THANKSGIVINGS, on several occasions". Since the book is subject to sundry revisions, Jeremiah thought that there might be some suitable additions. There could be a Prayer for those seeking divorce.

O Almighty and most merciful Father, who didst send thine only begotten son into the world to redeem mankind, and who said that no man may put asunder those whom God has joined together, Send into the hearts of thy chosen people the spirit of truth and compassion, that those who minister justice under our sovereign lady Queen Elizabeth, who, when crowned and anointed in thy name, undertook that all law and governance in her realm should be subject to thy holy gospel, may put asunder those whom thou hast joined, with care and diligence, seeking only thine honour and glory and knowledge of thy truth, and this we ask through Christ our Lord, to whom be all honour and glory with thee and the Holy Spirit, Amen.

There might also be a special Prayer, "For those setting out on a life of Adultery; to be used when those who have divorced partners seek the blessing of the Church on their marriage to others".

"*O Lord, who hast given as grace, as at this time, with one accord to make our common supplications unto thee and dost promise that where two or three are gathered together in thy name, thou wilt grant their requests, Fulfil now, O Lord the desires and petitions of thy servants as may be most expedient for them, sending into the hearts of all men the Spirit of truth, lead us to all truth. Take from the hearts and minds of all men, hard sayings, that may set husbands against wives and children against parents, that they recall no more the words of him who said that those who divorce partners and marry others commit adultery, that family life may abound and children be brought up in love and compassion to serve thee, the only true God. For Christ's sake, Amen.*

In keeping with the spirit of the age, it might also be fitting to add a thanksgiving for, "The Joys of Fornication and those who provide it".

Almighty God, the Father of all mercies and giver of all blessings, we, thine unworthy servants give thee humble and hearty thanks for all the gifts of thy creation and the blessings of this life, for the spirit of love and of love making between man and woman with which thou hast, in thy bounty, endowed us. Lead thy people, and all people in the way of truth, that they may see that it is not that which proceeds out of a man, evil thoughts, fornications, adulteries lasciviousness, but that which enters his mouth which makes him ordinary and defiles him. We thank thee that, through the operation of thy Holy Spirit, we have been led see all in the light of thy truth, that we are what we eat, and above all, for thine inestimable love in the redemption of the world through Christ our Lord, who led us out of bondage and fear into freedom from fear, giving us the understanding that thou, O God, Almighty and most merciful, art no longer be feared by those who have put away childish things, as thy Holy Apostle has taught us, but full of compassion, understanding the ways of men and their needs. Grant that we, thy servants, may be given boldness to go forth in freedom from fear of thee and thy words and those of Jesus our Saviour, and so attain an ever higher knowledge and understanding of thee, our Father and our God, for thy great name's sake. Amen.

Jeremiah hid. His elder son refused to go to Church. The following day his wife gained her divorce. A few days later, the younger son returned from school. For a day or two the family was reunited.

His wife decided to take their daughter and stay with her parents, leaving Jeremiah with the boys. He noticed that the visit to the restaurant, while he was in prison, had been something of a raiding party. One object taken by the raiders struck him as odd. It was a Georgian silver salver bearing his family Crest.

The next morning Hannah rang up and spoke to the elder son. When she asked what they were going to do today, he had replied, "I think we will go back to Norfolk!" Hannah said, "Enjoy yourselves then". Jeremiah put the salver into a bag, took the boys to Plymouth, sold the Salver, and went to the Station. He bought tickets to Norwich. At Liverpool Street he telephoned the Dog, asking him to light a fire and expect three. This time it was the Dog who was anxious; so was Jeremiah. They reached Norwich without being apprehended, and got to Wroxham. Clifford was hesitant, but transported them in one of his vans. Immediately they reached home, Jeremiah sent a telegram to Hannah saying that all had arrived safely. Nothing happened. He realised that she might hesitate to bring a court action. This time, he could not avoid being present. He did not yet realise how vulnerable she and her lawyer were.

It was Easter. Business was improving. There was a source of anxiety: a bulk cylinder of Calor Gas. They were on a 'no Gas order', there being an unpaid account for its installation. He checked the dial on top of the cylinder. It registered 3/4 full. In relief he slapped the tank. The needle fell back to less than 1/4. That was not good. He wrote to Calor Gas, explaining the position. He had no collateral except that offered by Elijah to the widow. A day or two later he received a phone call from a Mr Dance, the director of credit control for the company. He had never had so original a letter in his life, and was prepared to do a deal. If Jeremiah would pay half of the outstanding bill, he would authorise a drop of gas: half a tankful, if he paid for it. Every cheque was endorsed in favour of Calor Gas.

It was almost Whitsun. The gauge registered empty. Every time he lit the cooker he watched for the flame to die. He telephoned Mr Dance. Mr Dance seemed to have had lessons from the Dog. "I thought you were the one who said, "Have no anxiety for the morrow. Did you not recall me to the promise that the cruse of oil would not waste?" Mr Dance was enjoying himself. Even Jeremiah found it funny. "I am not talking about oil, but gas, Mr Dance!" "Ah," said his adversary, "we deliver it in liquid form!"

"Have I paid enough yet?" More than enough, Oh ye of little faith", said Mr Dance. I authorised a drop three days ago. It comes from Thetford. You should get it any day now". As he put down the receiver Jeremiah heard the sound of a diesel engine. Into the car park rumbled a tanker labelled CALOR.

Peter Noble was as good as his word. The wine racks were full, all paid for, the bar well stocked. The place was booming and they were settling accounts, frozen by the court; when Alan brought some extraordinary news. He was about to become bankrupt himself, so was resigning the receivership. "Join the club, mate", chuckled Derek

Late one evening Derek sat with a man and his wife having a drink. She had gone out for a few minutes, when the man started talking about having found the Lord. The Dog had said ,"I am not so sure.....I prefer, Get thee in front of me, Satan, and lead the way. I am not too keen on, If a man divorces his wife and marries another, he makes her an adulteress!" The man jumped up as if a Jack Russell had nipped his ankle. "I wont have you calling my wife an adulteress".

"Not me", said Derek, "It was the one you found. Sit yourself down, and join the club!" It was not a club that the man wished to join.

The court appointed another receiver. An elderly partner in a well-known firm of accountants, who specialised in such work, came to present his authority. He explained that it would be in everyone's 'best interest' to co-operate, to make the matter as painless as possible. The better the place ran, the better price it would fetch. The new Broom handed him his letter of authority. It empowered him to receive and manage the property and the business. Jeremiah handed him the key, saying, "You have received it. Now get on and manage it, and, by the way, there are 56 people booked, this evening".

"Whatever do you think I am?" exploded the new receiver, "I have better things to do than run a place like this?" I did not undertake to do that". "That's what it says here! I cannot help it, if you cannot read". "It's not what it means", said the exasperated receiver. "If the High Court of Chancery cannot express themselves clearly, it's not my fault. If you undertake to manage a business, then it is up to you to hire staff and pay them, and have the license transferred". More significant was the failure of the court to provide the Receiver with insurance either against fire and theft, or public and employee liability.

The new receiver proposed an arrangement whereby he would exercise general oversight, with Alan acting as go between. To this Alan agreed. It was the last that they saw of the new receiver, who not once made any contact with his go between, or Jeremiah. He seemed to be the agent of the Plaintiff and her lawyers, not the High Court.

All means were tried to remove the boys without a court action. First there was a visit from an Inspector of education. Jeremiah had arranged a teaching timetable for them. The Inspector thought it satisfactory. His elder son made a comment that Jeremiah never forgot, when he was urging them to read and study.

"Think of all the friends who have stood loyally by you, dad, and those who have turned their backs. Those who have been loyal have hardly an O level between them. All education does is to teach you how to make good excuses for letting people down, not keeping your word, and doing things you know, damn well, you ought not to do!"

They had a visit from a policeman, to make sure that they were being properly looked after. He too was satisfied.

It was Thursday evening. They had cash in the till, and a single £5 note. His elder son asked what he could sell to the man who kept the little shop opposite. "I don't think there is anything he wants to buy off you! What do you want to buy from him?"

He wanted a pair of dark glasses. Jeremiah gave him their last £5. His elder son went and bought them. "You'll get it back dad", he said. Thursday was normally busy, but not a customer came. At about eight o' clock, he went down and switched off the grills, telling the staff that, if nobody came in half an hour, it was not worth hanging on. He went upstairs disconsolate. Up the road, appeared three holiday-makers. They looked too scruffy to be coming for a meal; but they walked past the pub. He ran down stairs to switch on and called to those outside. The three holiday-makers were followed by the rest of their party, making six in all. More came and yet more. They had the best takings ever. It was the last time his son ever asked him to buy anything for him. This incident, Jeremiah never forgot. It seemed that, if children knew that a parent was prepared to spend their last £5 on something they wanted, they wanted no more. It was this that made him think again about the matter of 'spoiling' children.

His younger son wanted a puppy. They bought what was said to be a Labrador-collie cross. It turned out to be a collie whippet cross. She was called Sadie.

One morning a car drove in. Out of it got Hannah. She had a court order demanding the return of the boys. How she obtained the order without Jeremiah knowing of a hearing, he did not understand; but he knew little of the law. She spoke to the boys. If they did not want to go, she would not enforce the order. She stayed the rest of the day and they had a happy lunch together. In late afternoon she went. The main holiday season was approaching. They had heard nothing of the court or the receiver, were making money as never before and paying off accounts; when they received notification from the Sheriff that they were to be evicted. There were not only his two sons there, but also a Belgian boy who had come over to learn English, his parents being friends of Jeremiah's sister. The eviction was to be on Monday morning.

They served lunch on Sunday. Jeremiah decided to leave that afternoon. Alec lent them his sailing cruiser. In the interval between the warning notice and the event, they made sure that none of Peter's clarets and 1959 burgundies fell into the hands of the receiver. They drank them, gave them to customers, and the remainder George hid away. They took to the water. It never occurred to Jeremiah that Sheriffs needed court orders to take possession of a property. It never crossed his mind either, that when Hannah obtained her order to remove the boys, he should have been issued with a summons.

While such as Mr Dance might be as good as his word, Hannah was not. With the Sheriff's men, came Hannah with two court bailiffs to seize the boys. It was only when they sailed down to Horning and met Bertie Wooster, that he realised that they were being actively sought. They had little food with them, and not much money. They sailed about for three or four days and made their way back up the Ant. About the only place on the river, where there is road access, is Irstead Shoals. There, unknown to them stood Hannah and two process servers. Also on the staithe, was a lad called Robert and his girl friend Judith. They had worked in the restaurant. Robert was a sharp-witted lad. He had never seen Hannah in his life, but he knew what 'process servers' looked like, and he did not like them. He looked down river and saw the boat coming into view. Without hesitation, he engaged Hannah in conversation, so that she had her back turned to the river until they were safely past.

They returned the boat to its moorings and wandered up the path to Alec and Tricia's hotel. As they did so, a large black car came down the lane. Jeremiah did not like the look of the occupants. All four jumped into the reed bed, thence into the carr behind it. The car waited awhile, turned round and went away. They went back to Jeremiah's own half-decker and sat on board, till it seemed safe to move. They went to the hotel. Alec and Tricia were worried. They had been under siege by process servers for most of the day. They could not stay there. They phoned the Dog. Angela, his wife, was there to fetch them within the hour, and they were taken back to Caister for the night. They lived in a small council house with three bedrooms and had two children of their own, but happily accommodated four more for the night, plus a dog.

That evening his brother in law phoned. He was responsible for the Belgian boy. Jeremiah should drive him up to Durham, and, if his sons asked to stay, they would be welcome, but they must ask. If Jeremiah suggested it, John and his sister would be acting as his agents. Next day they got into the old Vauxhall Viva that he and the Dog had bought for £40, and drove north. Behind them was a black car that looked like the one he had seen, the afternoon before. It followed them all the way through Kings Lynn and up the A 17. He knew that, if they were process servers, they had not the authority to stop a car, but the boys needed to get out.

He had driven this way many times and knew of a short cut, down a lane. Luckily, he happened to have a couple of tractors and trailers between him and the black car, when he dived into the lane. Nobody followed. They stopped for coffee, and the boys relieved themselves.

Jeremiah returned to Caister. It was lucky that they had left when they did. Not ten minutes after they had done so, the process servers were at the door. He could not stay there. If they served court orders on him, he would be forced to go to Durham and hand the boys over. All he could do was to take to the water again, in his One Design. It had a canvas awning and he had a camp bed on board. There was a sleeping bag and a primus stove. The awning was shower proof. He had almost no money and no food, beyond a few tins that Angela gave him. He set sail down the Ant. The Process servers knew that he had used Alec's boat. It would not take them long to identify Golden Copper, with a large 61 on her sail.

Next day he sailed down to Horning and went to the grocer's shop, bought some baked beans and half an ounce of tobacco. The woman behind the till recognised him. She and her husband had been customers. Would he like to come up to their flat for coffee? Up he went, drank coffee and tucked into biscuits. They asked him if he would help carry two boxes of dented tins, they could not sell, from their warehouse. Of course, he would. "Where do you want me to take them?" "Back to your boat, of course. Its our way of saying, we think that you are right, that is all".

He had food for over a week. The next thing was paraffin for his primus stove. There was a DIY shop up the road. He had enough money for a gallon, and had a container. In the shop he found yet another customer, an Italian named Nando. He would not take a penny for his paraffin. "Why not come home with me, for supper tonight? Margaret would love to see you". Be here at about six and I will pick you up. Jeremiah went back to the Grocer and asked if their two lads would like to come sailing for the afternoon. They would love to, so they sailed down river and back. Nando took him home that evening. He was a tonic. He told of his childhood during the war and how they survived between the occupying Germans and the patriots. At midnight he drove Jeremiah back to the boat.

He crawled under his awning and started making his camp bed. A hand appeared and dropped £20 onto the floor. By the time he could get his head out, there were two rear lights disappearing up the road.

One of the River Inspectors was a friend; the other was Sam's nephew. They hailed him as he sailed by, shouting, "Go up north". They would be the first people the process servers would contact. Although he now had the disadvantage of a large No 61 on his sail, he had the advantage of being under sail. When he saw a motor boat with two men aboard clutching official looking papers, he bore down on them and called for water, whereat he would put about and sail away. Up at Hickling and Horsey there is almost no road access. He got down to eating dog biscuits. He could find food for the dog in dustbins. She never had a moment's anxiety. The weeks passed into months. He spent days without any food.

Mooching down the road, one morning, a familiar looking blue van stopped. Out jumped 'Taff', one of the lads who worked for Clifford. In his outstretched hand was a bag of special sausages..."The Guv'nor said I was to give you these if I saw you!" A couple of days later he and the Guv'nor were sailing on Hickling Broad. Near where he moored, was a dingy public lavatory, which enabled him to shave. Walking up the path, Sadie jumped onto a large yacht and helped herself to some dog food in a bowl. A lady looked out.

"Sorry" said Jeremiah, "she is very hungry". He explained his position. The lady offered him coffee and cake. Every morning, for over a week, he had coffee aboard and Sadie had a tin of Pal. He had been afloat for three months. He learned a lot about sailing One Designs, single-handed. One morning, he was sailing about near the Pleasure Boat, when he saw a blue cruiser sail onto the staithe and pick up a mooring with considerable skill. The ease with which the skipper handled her made him envious. It annoyed him even more when he recognised Alec. Half a bottle of wine and some quiche did much to mollify his envy.

Alec had a motor and suggested that he sail with them down river so that they could tow him through the bridges. It was now late September, so he did so. They parted company. The wind was freshening. As he sailed he noticed that the wire halyard on the peak of his sail was fraying. He watched, horrified, as one by one the strands of wire snapped. He turned into Womack Dyke and moored up. When he inspected the damage, he saw that there was little wire left. He was in a fix. There was a boatyard at the end of the dyke but he had only a few shillings. He found a couple of old pork chops in a dustbin for Sadie, but nothing to eat for himself. The next day he took the halyard off and went to the boatyard. They told him that the galvanised wire was as old as the boat and, having served for 40 years, it did not owe him much. That did not help. He remained there for a couple of days, finding food from dustbins for Sadie, but nothing could he find to eat himself, apart from blackberries.

'I can hoist the sail, by tying the rope halyard directly to the gaff'. What a fool he had been. He wondered what to do about food. He knew that if he telephoned Clifford, he would gladly send out some sausages. Nando would give him a meal. He thought of Jesus in the wilderness refusing to make stones into bread. He did not do that, so he would not ring up friends. It seemed silly, as there was little connection between the incidents. Jesus had refused to use what power he might be thought to have, to save himself.

If he asked for help from someone like Clifford, he could hardly refuse to take whatever advice he offered. If he put himself into Cliff's position, he could see what advice he would feel bound to give. He could only advise him to see a lawyer, go to Social Security and so on. It would be tantamount to admitting, "Your way does not work". He did not want to admit that to himself, let alone someone who had been so faithful a friend, as had Cliff.

There was a deeper reason now. He had flung the words of the gospels in the teeth of judges and magistrates. He had told a packed hall that the sayings of Jesus determined what was Christian. He was coming near to believing that they provided the best way to live. If he went to social security, he would be seeking help from the very people, whom such as Uberrimae represented. He could hardly expect them to support him while he openly defied court orders. Having driven him into prison and had him evicted, would it not be fitting that Hannah should cause him to die of starvation? He thought that it would. She and her lover had made no bones about the fact that they wanted him dead, and had set out to make him kill himself. What was there left to live for anyway?

What a horrid world it was. How could one trust anyone? Central to the mistrust was the Christian religion. How could upright citizens go off to Church and make solemn declarations, leading children to believe that they meant them, and then make it a crime to do so? How could the Queen and the Archbishop undertake that all law and governance would be subject to that of the gospel, and then condemn him for pointing out what that gospel said? He should not have found it puzzling. He had done so himself, and been well paid for it.

Full of such thoughts, he hoisted his sails and sailed down to Thurne Mouth. It was Saturday. The wind was freshening. As he turned into the Bure, it was ahead of him. Not only had he to tack all the way, the new hirers were leaving the boatyards, so, in a fresh gusty wind, he had to thread in and out of them. He found a 22 foot 'One Design' a handful, tacking single handed, on a three day empty stomach. As he passed S Benet's Abbey, he was irritated by a man on the bank with a child strapped to his back, trying to engage him in conversation, every time he reached that side of the river. He asked, "Is it fun sailing a boat like that?" None too politely, Jeremiah replied, "If you are so damned interested, why not come and help me?"

, The man called to his wife, handed over the child, and ran down the bank, to jump aboard at his next tack. "I have always wanted to sail one of these", he said. He explained that they were emigrating to Australia in a week. He was the doctor at Martham. They sailed down to Ranworth. There he suggested that they should have a cup of tea. Jeremiah could just about afford a cup of tea. To his horror the doctor ordered sausages eggs, bacon, tomatoes, chips and beans, an apple pie and cream and sat down with his trayful of food. Jeremiah could not bear to watch it vanish into an already well-fed mouth, so gazed out over the broad. When he looked back there was the plate of sausages and beans in front of him.

"This is for you," said the doctor. "I realised who you were. My secretary was a customer of yours. She told me about your eviction and everything that had happened". Jeremiah tucked in voraciously. He thanked the doctor and they sailed back to South Walsham, where he was to meet his wife. The wind had eased, so they had a sail on the broad with her. They said goodbye and he sailed away, intending to leave the broad and sail up the dyke. At the mouth of the dyke is a boatyard. It was Saturday evening, changeover day. It might be worth inspecting the dustbins. He moored up, saw that there was nobody about, and lifted the lid of the first large bin. On the top was a grocer's shop of food, discarded by holiday-makers. There were loaves of bread still wrapped, untouched half-pounds of butter, dog biscuits and even unopened tins of food. He restocked his lockers. Truly there was manna in the wilderness...."You might have left a bottle of gin, Lord", he said, and cast off. Sailing into the dyke, he heard someone shouting behind him.

There was a grey haired man in a motor boat. He put about. It was Jimmy Hipwell, the City Coroner. He followed him back to his motor cruiser, lowered his sails and jumped aboard. "Like a drink?" said Jimmy. "I could murder a gin and tonic!"

The reason for his being invited was that Jimmy had a couple of girls on board, one of whom knew Jeremiah, or did when he was about eight. Her father lived in his grandfather's village. The large 61 on his sail had proved useful. Jimmy Hipwell had recognised it, and said, "That's Jeremiah". Jimmy suggested that he should get legal help. When told what had happened, Jimmy said, "I think you are causing more trouble in the courts than anyone could with legal help. If I were you, I would carry on as you are!"

The girls had a house near the broad. They took Jeremiah back for a hot bath and a meal. He returned to his boat with a full stomach, wondering where to go. Perhaps he would go and see Bertie in Horning. He thought that he had best not do so, as Bertie would be bound to advise him. Instead he sailed back up the Ant and arrived back at his mooring. He went straight to the hotel where Alec and Tricia lived. They were full of laughter and he stayed for supper. "Why not have a bed here?"

He would stay on his boat. That night, there was an unfamiliar sound. Rain was falling on the awning and falling heavily. The awning was more or less waterproof, but, once thoroughly soaked, tended to drip. It rained all night. The evening before, it was announced that the Government had appointed a Minister for drought. Jeremiah thought of the second psalm. In bad moments over the past three months, he had prayed for many things. One that never entered his head was the weather. Two wet days would have made his life aboard the boat impossible. The year was 1976. The prolonged drought was not good for most people. It was a life-saver for him.

He thought of praying for things in Churches. How dangerous it would be if, as religions suggested, there was, 'power in prayer', especially when lots of people did so, or did so for a week. It would be bad luck on those who did not want whatever it was that was prayed for. Nobody said, over whom the power was exercised. If over God; God was a puppet. If it was thought to act directly on people and things, then God must have laid down such a system. Provided God maintained the system, he she or it could be forgotten. It was a very dangerous system, if, in either case, those, who knew how to do so, could exercise power over people and things. When people said, "We will, pray for you", Jeremiah felt uneasy. What might they pray for on his behalf? Praying for things in public was also a means of 'subliminal' suggestion, which could be used to implant horrendous ideas in people's minds, like hijacking airliners, in the name of God.

Those of the Christian religion seemed to be of one accord that, in one way or another, it is in everyone's 'best interest' to acquire wealth. Jeremiah knew, as well as anyone, that life was easier with cash in one's pocket than without it. The trouble was that the more one had the more one seemed to need. One soon began to trust in riches. 'Acts of God', then, became a nuisance. He began to see that, if you did not see your 'best interest' in those terms, people would find you difficult to deal with. If the pursuit of increased wealth was anyone's object, those, who could supply the means to this end, had you in their power.

The next day he returned to the hotel for breakfast. The land around the mooring was a quagmire. Bacon and eggs, sausages and tomatoes, toast butter and marmalade vanished. The telephone rang. Alec sounded grave. It was the beginning of the fishing season and it was a fisherman's hotel. The kitchen help had contracted mumps and would be away for two months...."Could you possibly help us out?" For the next six weeks they housed and fed him and gave him a few pounds each week. Whenever he could, he put ten pounds into an envelope and posted it to Hannah. She never acknowledged it.

That winter, and most of the next year he was on the move. Often he went down to Hannah's flat. He walked hundreds of miles. The incidents he could recall, but the intervening narrative became confused. Looking back, he found it impossible to cram so many events into so short a time. That all these things happened within a fixed period he could not doubt. This was of interest on an 'academic level'. It revealed much of the narrative of the gospels, which is seemingly confused. If he, as the person to whom all these things happened, having first hand knowledge of the geography, found the order of events confusing, how much more would the evangelists find it so, without maps or calendars and little knowledge of the culture they described, with the possible exception of the fourth, or his source. He found that, when he set about recounting the events, he began with he one that seemed most significant, and appeared to summarise the whole.

This was so with others. They would return from a holiday, with an animated account of what they had experienced. Never did this follow a chronological sequence. They would begin with the most significant occurrence that seemed to encapsulate all. From this the narrative would develop, in both directions. How might it have been had someone gone to Nazareth and asked about Jesus in his childhood and youth?

At Ludham Bridge is a shop. Sitting at the cash desk was a lady with a limp. He had met her many times there, but knew nothing of her. She looked at him fixedly, and asked, "Are you Charity Boycott's son? Does the name Bertha Davey mean anything to you?" "Oh yes," he said, "my old mother often spoke of her, she had a sister called Annie". "She is still alive. She talks of nothing but her time with the Boycotts. She is 96, so make sure you go and visit her, and don't put it off, mind!"

Next day he went to call on Bertha. Her family had been 'in service' with the Boycotts, at Burgh, or five of six generations. Bertha produced old sepia photographs of bewhiskered gentlemen, and their wives. She said that she was the nursery maid when his grandfather was a child. She told of their eccentricities, and how, on one occasion, after dark, she was walking up the lane from Church, alongside a hedge, when a black-cassocked figure jumped up on the other side of the hedge and shot a pheasant. She ran home terrified, saying to her mother, "I have seen the devil or the Rector or both!" She explained that 'this was his great grandfather;---not him', as she pointed to another man in the photo.

"That's Cap'n Charles. He brought your granddad up, but he was your great, great uncle. He was a 'rum lad', crazy on tobogganing. He had some trouble in Ireland". She then looked at him fixedly. "Do you sail boats?" "Yes I do" "Hmm. They all did. What's born in the bone comes out in the flesh".

Bertha was full of these anecdotes, and spent two hours telling him tales of his eccentric forebears. That night he pondered what he had heard. "Wait a moment", he thought, "She is 96. If my grandfather were still alive he would be over 120. How could she have been nursery maid, when he was born? If she knew Cap'n Charles, as a boy, she would have to be over 170". Bertha was passing on stories told to her by her mother and grandmother. They had been told so vividly that she took them to herself. Years later, his godfather and cousin wrote of the Boycotts and of how the eponym entered the language. Many of Bertha's reminiscences were apparently accurate. What people said seemed to be fixed in her mind, if it typified their 'conversation'.

He began to doubt the literary and form critical criteria, which cast doubt on the veracity of the gospels. He was also beginning to see that it was a secondary matter. Whoever spoke those words, one possibility alone made them true, that there was, in reality, God. If there is God, those words singly and exclusively give expression to that reality. If there is no God, they are the most misleading words ever uttered. Even if there is no God, we were still left with the word. God must exist as a word and, as such, carries a clear logic. That logic Jesus articulated, as the prophets before him. He was getting ever nearer the opening of the IVth Gospel; but a 'postulate' did not perform mighty works, or raise the dead.

He thought of his own position, vis a vis Hannah, Uberrimae and the courts. Only one possibility sustained the position he had found himself adopting, that there was, in truth, God, and that the gospels' report of Jesus' words was the truth. It had to be, if there were God. What, most of all, made him doubt this were religious beliefs.

He had not adopted that position from good faith, but because it, alone, seemed able to give him what he wanted. He did not want anything the courts could give. All he wanted was the return of his wife's love and the reunification of his family. The courts could not provide that. Now it seemed that God would not, either. Had he acted 'reasonably', he might be better off. Perhaps, it is best that there is no God, and so, whoever spoke the words, attributed to Jesus, was wrong. That would (a) not get rid of those words nor the word 'god' (b) whatever he thought would not get rid of God. If God existed, the words attributed to Jesus had to be right. That being so, if he stuck with them, in one way or another, he would be all right. He was applying to himself, something of the assurance he had felt about Jesus, when he read the Gospel as an infant. Whether he would be 'all right', in the ways he hoped and wanted, was another matter.

If there were no God, atheists would be right. Even the word atheist involves a difficulty. It means maintaining a negation. The only ones who had to be wrong, either way, were those of religion. They needed to have it both ways. On the one hand they declared belief in God and Jesus. On the other, they needed all that Jesus was reported to have said to be wrong. If those words expressed the reality of there being God, there could be no 'having it both ways'. On that Jesus was remorselessly clear.

Chapter Twenty Four

Ernie Cole.

"As we also have forgiven those who are indebted to us"

The only way to buy Ernie a 'drop of short' was to invite him into the bar, when he came to play bowls. Jeremiah listened to Ernie as he chatted. One evening he said; "I can tell you one thing my boy. Never chase a debt. Let the buggers go and you'll let your troubles go with them".

This was the guiding principle of Ernie's life. His remark made Jeremiah realise, for the first time, the significance of what the evangelists reported Jesus as saying, in his only prayer. Ernie, sitting on the hillside when Jesus taught, would say "Yes, Yes". He saw the effect of Jesus' teaching in a new light. Instead of gathering people to himself, and retaining them in dependence on himself, as do religions of necessity, Jesus did the opposite. If they heard and did his words, they had no need of him, 'in person', any more. In the gospels he speaks of gathering a harvest, rather than sowing and planting. The sayings attributed to Jesus gave belief in the one true God final articulation. If anyone believed truly in God, as a being who is what, logically, the word implies, they would arrive at thoughts, to which the sayings of Jesus gave fixity. Anyone who truly believes in God, as the eternal creator of all things, would have no need to chase a debt.

Whatever benefits modern life might bring, it makes it harder to hear and do as Jesus commanded. Most obviously is this the case when it came to having no anxiety for the morrow. Being dependent on services, paid for quarterly, means that people could get into deeper trouble, than when they paid for them weekly. It is not only that it is easier to run up debt, there is also the greater inconvenience that resulted, if one was unable to pay. Having care for the morrow becomes a duty. Being incessantly told of the apparent long term effects of diet and the detailed contents of foods, the assumed effects of activities on the environment and other such things, causes much anxiety for the future. If, to echo Martin Buber, mankind loses, or has taken from it, the perception of being a 'living soul' and of eternal life, the only sane response is to seek to prolong one's life; while also 'building barns', so that one can 'take one's ease'.

Oddly, it seems not to 'work'. It is impossible to believe that a modern composer of music, who extended has active life for a hundred years, would come anywhere near to achieving what Mozart did, either in quantity or quality, in 35 years, or Schubert in 31, or that a writer would come near achieving what Aquinas did, in 44.

Jeremiah asked, "Were you born and bred here, Mr Cole?" "Lor' no, my boy, my home was any old London station, where foster parents dropped me with a luggage label, to be collected by the next lot". It seemed, as later, when he met Bobby, that the lack of a 'father on earth', was more likely to make anyone conscious of a heavenly Father, than having one.

Eventually, a family had collected him at Liverpool Street and brought him up to Norfolk. There he had remained. He had hardly ventured out of the county. Ernie had no envy for those who travelled, took holidays and enjoyed a well to do life style. It was the reverse. "It must be hard for such as you, who need all these things. The likes of me are lucky".

Neither Ernie nor Sam ventured far. Holidays were things unknown to them. They did not need them. Norwich was about the limit of their travel, even if they went as far as that. Those, who needed all these things, also needed the likes of Ernie and Sam. Ernie did not need boats to sail in. He knew the river was down the road. Occasionally he might have looked at it. That it was there was enough. He did not need music, or 'cultural heritage'. He lived in a spotless prefab-like bungalow, without carpeted rooms. There were rugs on the floor, curtains at the windows.

Many owed him quite large sums of money and had done for years. Some had been unwilling or unable to settle his account long ago; but had subsequently prospered. The fact that Ernie did not chase the debts might have stood between them and bankruptcy. One soon got to know that, when creditors demanded payment, Ernie's bill could be left till last, and then left altogether.

There comes a time when debts become nigh impossible to repay. Being subsidised led one into a way of living that would be impossible without it. Often it led one to take on more commitments and more debt, making Ernie's account more difficult to pay. Even without inflation, simply to have paid, such as Ernie, what had been left unpaid over 20 years would be to insult the man. If, thanks to his forbearance, one had prospered, one wanted to say that, "mine hand and the strength of mine arm hath gotten me this wealth". One could hardly say that one was, now, wealthy, thanks to having failed to repay an inconsequential mill owner what one owed him. If one became a pillar of society and a magistrate, one joined a 'conversation', from which such as Ernie must be excluded. One could never know how much it may have cost such as Ernie to forgo payment, at the time when he did so.

It is easy, whilst going to Church, to justify such things to oneself against the words of Jesus. People who failed to demand payment of debts were immoral and irresponsible. People should learn that they have to pay for things. One could say that such as Ernie would not know how to use money properly. He would only waste it buying drinks for wasters in pubs, or allowing people, whom he thought poor, to have flour, eggs and chicken food without paying. "A fool and his money are soon parted". In any case, what did he want with any more money? He lived in a prefab. He would not appreciate wall-to-wall carpets, nor a holiday overseas; 'I put money to good use. I can expand my business and thus provide work for others'. Jeremiah knew, all too well, how easy it was to spend money on the expectation of payment.

Ernie might have forgiven those indebted to him. He did not forget. When he was much older, he went each week to collect his pension. Often he would sit and chat with Sam over a cup of tea and a 'toddy'. When a large new car swept past the cottage window, Ernie said; "You would not think that bugger owed me thousands from years ago. I could do with that money now, but he wont even give me the time of day".

It was through Ernie, that Jeremiah began to see what would be the effects of Jesus' words, at the heart of his one prayer. All 'trespasses' against another put one into the debt of the other. Idle words were like dud cheques. A prayer with that clause in it would be unusable in any public act of worship. That it should be so, is at one with Jesus' insistence on prayer being in secret. Taxes were collected, 'On Her Majesty's service'. If all knew that the Defender of the Faith would forgive those indebted to her, revenue might fall sharply. Such a clause could only be used, provided all were assured that it was an empty repetition. One did not need Scribes or Pharisees to tell one how to forgive a debt. A Bank Manager could tell one, no doubt adding, "but not with the Bank's money!" One could forgive those indebted to one, without any 'nice feelings' toward them. One might do so while spitting with anger, as an act of obedience.

Ernie kept chickens and, for years, had given free eggs to those whom he thought poor. As he got older he could not manage them any more. One morning he went into the shop and asked for two large trays of eggs. Sam asked why he needed so many eggs. It was because some, to whom he had given eggs for many years, had complained, when he failed to do so.

Ernie provides a suitable introduction to a sequence of incidents that followed the adventure on Golden Copper. Jeremiah wandered about England, often sleeping in telephone boxes, cardboard boxes and the like. He made his way up to Durham to see his sons. His sister and her husband, John, had sent them to Durham School, the younger winning a King's scholarship. Jeremiah felt shamed, knowing that, he would not have paid fees for his nephew and niece.

John had been trained as a barrister after leaving Oxford, but had decided against continuing in that trade, before the war. He hated corruption and freemasonry. He joined the 'Charter Company', in effect the Colonial service, in what was then North Borneo. He had spent the war in Japanese internment. He had had to dig his own grave and kneel down to have his head removed. He was saved by the news of the dropping of the second atomic bomb. After the war, he continued in Borneo, rising to become Chief Secretary and was a magistrate, also sitting on the court of appeal. Much had happened since the boys had been there. There had been a battery of letters from Hannah's solicitors, demanding their return. John replied courteously, pointing out that he was not acting as Jeremiah's agent, as they alleged. When they replied, he would seize on any obscurity and ask for clarification, knowing that the longer the boys were established in a school, the less firm would be the grounds for removing them. Any case should be heard at the court nearest their residence, so that they could be heard.

One evening, a lawyer, claiming to be Hannah's cousin telephoned. John asked Jeremiah if he knew of such a person. This man had threatened him with instant committal to prison, if he did not immediately return the boys. He claimed to have taken counsel's opinion.

It was easy to imagine such a thing happening. The nephew would be with his influential uncle, whose daughter had entered a plot to dispose of an unwanted husband by driving him to kill himself. She had committed perjury, as had her lawyer, (Jeremiah did not yet know this). His grandsons were living with Jeremiah's sister, whose husband was running circles round her lawyers. Jeremiah could imagine himself acting as, it seemed, her cousin did. "I can help you with this, I think. What is their phone number?" He would have stopped short of that.

The man he would telephone was a lecturer in Oriental studies and Bursar of a college. Hannah had met her brother in law. It was surprising that she did not urge caution. Intellectually he could eat her cousin. Nothing daunted, the cousin apparently picked up the phone, and made his threats.

He picked the wrong man. The threat of instant committal to an English prison did not strike terror into one, who had spent five years in a Japanese camp, where 4,000 were interned and less than 1,000 survived. If John, after careful thought, had decided that his course of action was right, no threat would deflect him. He commented, "I have drafted more laws than that silly young man has read!" His bogus threats were met with, "Your office seems to keep very late hours. The proper way to deal with this matter is in writing. If you would let me have your name and the address of your firm, telling me, also, what is your locus standi in the case, I will be happy to deal with the matter". It was not in the highest traditions of legal practice, to remain anonymous.

Hannah's cousin preferred to do so. He said that he would not to reveal his name, still less his professional address, and rang off. The frightening aspect of such near criminal behaviour is that, if the person he telephoned not been experienced in matters of the law and less sure of the ground on which he stood, such bogus threats might have succeeded. It seems never to have occurred to the cousin to apologise for his action, which was certainly not within the standards demanded by his professional body. He did not thank John for his forbearance, in not complaining to the Law Society, or his firm.

The other event, of which he told, was more disturbing. Having been in practice for ten years before her marriage, Jeremiah's sister continued to practise in her maiden name. This, it seems, was overlooked by Hannah and her father. A police officer had arrived at the College where her husband was bursar, enquiring after a doctor of his name. The porter sent him to the bursar. The officer asked about this doctor, not knowing that he was speaking to her husband, thinking that she was employed at the College.

John asked, "Why are you not recording this in your notebook? Should you not have another officer with you?" The officer told him that he had been asked to make 'off the record' enquiries about the doctor. John pointed out that this was highly irregular. He was told that he would be wise to co-operate as it came from the, "Very Highest level". John picked up his phone and demanded to speak to the Chief Constable. He suspected that Uberrimae had got onto his own Chief Constable, or high-ranking officer, and set the process in train.

It chanced that, while staying in Durham, his rich aunt telephoned to say that his uncle, whom he greatly admired, had had a major operation for cancer of the bowel, but was not expected to recover. His sister asked if they needed any help in the house, Jeremiah having offered his services. He spent the next three months acting as cook, housekeeper and part time sick room attendant for his Uncle, who recovered for a short time. It was an extraordinary experience. His sister told him that what his Uncle needed, first, was a high protein diet to enable his body to repair itself after major surgery. This he determined to provide. His aunt was a woman of wealth and had taken Jeremiah under her wing in his youth. She had introduced him into a social life he had never before known, with hunt balls, coming out dances and all the rest of it. He was in her debt.

He found that little by little, since he spent most of the day in the kitchen, he was spoken to in a way appropriate to that station in life. He did not mind. He found, as his mother at the rectory, that he was more at ease in the kitchen than in the drawing room. He managed, while there, to collect about £5 per week from the DSS. His sister had told him that albumen was first class protein. He made foods with eggs, and was called to order by his aunt, for wanton extravagance. Thus it continued, until he returned to Durham for his sons' birthdays.

His Aunt was a devotee of the Church. She wrote to his sister saying that Jeremiah had been a wonderful help. It was, however, a pity that he seemed unable to get over a man who had lived 2,000 years ago! The irony made him gasp. Whatever is all this Church going about, if not some man who lived 2,000 years ago? But for that man, he would not have thought of going there in the first place. He then thought of Ernie Cole. In a curious way he felt that he was no longer in his Aunt's debt, nor indebted to her 'conversation'. The only way anyone can *know,* that their debts are forgiven, is by being given some means of repaying them.

If it were made possible, would one think it worthwhile? If, as he now found himself doing, despite himself, he was redeeming empty words, so paying his debts, was this a matter for rejoicing or not? On the whole, he thought not. He wanted them magicked away. He could see that it did not pay to utter empty words. One was likely to be stuck with them.

The uncle had a trout farm. Some fifteen years before, he had sent Jeremiah 100 shares in the business. He explained that the purpose of the gift was not that Jeremiah should make a capital gain. He needed someone in the family to be a shareholder in case there was an emergency and documents needed signing. The nominal value of the shares was based on the valuation of the assets when the business became a limited company long before the war. Since then, there had been much inflation and the business had more than trebled in size; so the shares were worth many times their nominal value.

He pondered again the curious wording of the saying, "those that do the truth come to the light that their works may be seen to have been *wrought in* God. It was as if God enabled one to make words true, or render them empty. He had no such intention, when offering help. It was a spontaneous impulse. In performing a duty to his uncle, his six months as a ward orderly in a paraplegic unit had been useful training, well in advance of need.

He made several visits to Hannah in her flat. Once he went at her request. For a few days she seemed happy to have him there. One evening, she said that the Vicar of the major Church in Plymouth was coming round. "Don't antagonise him". The Vicar came. He explained that, being the Vicar of the major church in a town the size of Plymouth, he ought to be a Bishop. Hannah said that her husband had somewhat unusual views about Christianity.

"I have been driven to the conclusion that the sayings of Jesus as reported in the gospels must determine what is Christian". The Vicar found this fascinating.

A few evenings later there was another guest, "an old friend", a huge Australian, who had left his wife and family in Australia and had set out back packing round the world, fetching up in Plymouth. He and Hannah referred to each other in terms of intimate endearment. Jeremiah made a fool of himself, flung down his drink, splashing it all over the place and breaking the glass. He said to the Australian that, he was not there to meet him, but because he fancied, "my wife". The Australian said that Hannah was not his wife any longer.

Hannah said that she had to go away for a day or two, 'Will that be all right?' He found it touching that she should ask. Then she said, "Don't let anyone see you here". He would not leave the house. One afternoon he was standing in the kitchen, when Hannah's brother came to the door and saw him through the window. Immediately he ran off. Hannah returned, a different woman.

"I have been talking to people about you". Chief among them was the Vicar, who had warned her against having anything to do with anyone who had such attitudes. "We get such people all the time. Have nothing whatever to do with him". It was not so much that a minister of the gospel should say such a thing, but his two-facedness that shocked him. There he had sat, a few evenings before saying how interesting it was and how refreshing. A day or two later that was all made into a lie. In his position, Jeremiah would have said the same. The Vicar was right. One could not advise any woman to live with someone like him. Jesus said that he and his words would break up families. He was coming, even more, to see that this hypocrisy was not a matter of individuals, but was essential to religion.

If, as all who attend any services declare, "he shall come again in glory...." Jesus would say nothing that he did not say before. If there was truly God he could not. The Vicar would have to advise people to have nothing to do with *HIM*. If it had not been serious, it would have been laughable. What made it truly serious was that there might indeed be God.

Uberrimae and his wife appeared. She said to Hannah, "We have spent a fortune getting rid of him, why do you have to have him back?" She took their daughter home with her. Uberrimae told Hannah to tell Jeremiah to go away. She did, never mentioning that she had suggested that he come down. He then told Jeremiah to leave, saying, "You are now going to get a lesson in where authority lies. The Bishop of Repton tried to teach you; but you refused to learn".

"Where is that?" Uberrimae referred him to a book by someone called Haldane, called something like "English Law and Practice." He replied, "It is written, a man shall cleave to his wife. It is better to obey God than man".

The effect on Uberrimae was staggering. He crumpled. He had been the dominant man of power. Suddenly he looked a pitiful shrunken little man. Whether it was the substance of what was said, the dismissive tone, or that, for the first time in many years, his authority had been swept aside on the basis of a higher one, is hard to say.

He soon recovered and, picking up the phone, summoned the police. They came and escorted Jeremiah away, dumping him with Sadie at the gateway. It was late afternoon and was beginning to rain. He rolled himself in his coat putting Sadie inside as a warmer, and lay down on the pavement. There he remained most of the night, with much coming and going in cars. Two police cars arrived. He was bidden to get into one of them and was glad to do so. It was warm. There was a sergeant and, with him, a constable. The sergeant asked many questions.

He said, "I can fully understand your position, but I don't think that our Master would want you to mess a young constable about. Will you go with him and not cause trouble?" Amazed at the sergeant's reference to "our Master", Jeremiah agreed. It would be a lot more comfortable in a police station than in the wet. He was driven to one. A social worker appeared with a tin of dog food. Then came the police doctor, who questioned him at length. He knew what was likely to happen. They would 'section' him. A hospital bed in the warm was much to be preferred to homelessness. The doctor said that he would not do this. Jeremiah asked why. The doctor explained that his logic was incontrovertible. If you set out from your position, you must end up as you now are.

Next day, he was taken to another doctor. This time it was the psychiatrist at the Nuffield Centre. It was warm and dry, and there were cups of coffee and biscuits. He also refused to section him. The police let him go. He took up residence on the bus station. After a few days, the police cleared all the dossers out. "Where can I go now? "Go up onto the Moor out of the way", said the policeman. It was about midnight. To the Moor he would go. He hoped his corpse would be found there. It was pouring with rain as he trudged, the ever-faithful Sadie at his heels, towards the moor. He was very tired. He decided to shelter in a telephone kiosk and fell fast asleep standing up. It was daylight when he awoke. The door was open. There stood a woman with a tray, a pile of bacon sandwiches, a pot of tea, a mug and a bowl of food for Sadie.

"Here you are love. My husband saw you with your dog when he went off to work". She told him that she lived only three doors away, and cleaned the kiosk, so he could leave the tray there when he had finished. A hot breakfast made him feel better, so he trudged on. Driving towards him came a car. It was driven by Hannah. She was taking their daughter to school. He walked on, and was amazed, some 20 minutes later, to find himself offered a lift to her house by his wife. She wanted to go with him up to Durham to see the boys. She drove him to Uberrimae's house, where he would be welcome to spend the night. He was made very welcome. His mother in law was fascinated by his story of the phone box and called Uberrimae to come and listen.

She left. Uberrimae questioned him earnestly. The poor man was now almost totally blind. "Tell me, dear boy," he said, "Do you think the gospels could be the truth? Is there really eternal life?" "Oh yes", Jeremiah heard himself saying in a voice of quiet assurance.

Whatever was he saying? He felt no such certainty. What dreadful books they were. The more one knew them, the worse they became. They held out this dazzling hope, yet there were always pages one feared to turn, knowing that over one might lurk the story of the Rich Young man, over another the parable of Dives and Lazarus, over another the words about marriage and divorce; then the parable of sheep and goats. If one found oneself uttering words of condemnation of some offence, one recalled, "let whoever is faultless among you cast the first stone", or "Judge not, lest ye also be judged". Jeremiah knew only too well, as the Dog had pointed out, that one needed very little in the bank for 'one's heart to be there also'.

The next day, they were to drive up to Durham. It was the last time he saw Uberrimae. He met him in the lane; "What will you do with your life now, dear boy?" Jeremiah said, "I will try and live so that Hannah can walk back into any home I may have, as if she had only been out to the shops". Uberrimae Fidei held out both of his hands and grasped Jeremiah's.

Poor man, he was in a terrible spot. He had to protect his daughter from exposure. He had his own position to maintain, with a son in law, who seemed ready, flagrantly, to flout court orders and commit contempt. He seemed genuinely to want to restore the marriage, especially when Hannah was not there. It seemed that she, when not influenced by others, half wanted the same. The one thing that seemed to stand in the way was Jeremiah's fixation with something that happened 2,000 years ago. He wished he had never read that wretched book as a seven year old. Why did people take him off to Church, without seeing that someone might identify the Jesus, about whom they sung hymns, with the one, of whom those four men wrote? If one stands up and announces belief in a man who lived 2,000 years ago, declaring him to have been raised from the dead, surely, one would be at some pains to find out what he said? Had he come on this 'way out' view, because he had read that gospel at seven, instead of picture books of Jesus for Sunday schools?

Why did those four men take it upon themselves to write of him as they did? The argument that they did so, to assist the spread of the new religion was unsustainable. Aside from the story of Christmas, the Virgin birth and the temptations, the Christian religion, as a religion, had all it needed in the writings of St Paul, which antedate the gospels by more than a decade. As far as the virgin birth was concerned, it was better without the gospel narratives. Two never mentioned it. It did not, nor could have, featured in the teaching of Jesus, even if he could have known of it himself.

The Christmas story bore little relation to anything reported in the gospels, nor the season of Lent to the story of the 'temptations'. The narratives of the resurrection appearances were more of a nuisance than anything. It defied belief that these four men could have concocted such a tale. The crux was what they reported of Jesus in word and act. That gave single expression to one logic, that of the word God. Jesus, as reported in the gospels, and God were inseparable. Was it not best that there was no God? That amounted to the same, as saying "Was it not best that Jesus never existed or spoke as he did?" The problem was that he did. Nothing would change that. Whatever the critical positions adopted by the upholders of the Christian religion, they are stuck with the four gospels. The human race is stuck with the word 'God'. The problem presented by the writing of the four gospels was intractable. However much might be discovered of Jesus and his life, it would not get rid of what those four men reported.

The prayer given by Jesus is hardly a prayer in the ordinary sense. To ask "Thy kingdom come, Thy will be done, as in heaven so on earth", is, if there be God, a prayer for that which is inevitable. The Christian religion would be better off without the gospels; as, in effect, it had been for most of its history. It could not do without the appearance of Christ any more than there could be the "millennium". Judaism could not do without the expectation of a promised redeemer, 'Christ'. Neither could do *with* Jesus as reported in the gospels. The 'catch' seemed to demonstrate that there is indeed God.

The germ of a wholly different purpose in the writing of the gospels was beginning to infect his mind. It was not to forward the expansion of the new religion, but to drive it back to those words, as its bedrock. That would accord with the opening of the First epistle of John, with its emphasis on "that which our eyes saw, our ears heard, our hands handled...". If the evangelists feared God, they would be careful not to misrepresent Jesus in anything that he said. Jeremiah had become careful not to misquote his words. It was no sudden concern for truth. If one has only the manna to depend on; you don't offend the supplier! If better fare had been available, he would have jumped at it.

He remained in Durham. Their daughter wanted to stay there. While there, his sister received a letter from Uberrimae. He passed on to her the Nuffield clinic doctor's opinions of Jeremiah, some of them none too complimentary. His purpose was to persuade her that her brother needed treatment for schizophrenia. That, she felt sure, was Uberrimae Fidei's opinion, not that of any doctor. That a doctor was prepared to divulge information, gained in a consultation, to influential people, provided the patient was of no consequence, shocked her. Uberrimae's elaboration amused her for its mistakenness. "You may be all sorts of things, but schizophrenic you are not! You exhibit all the opposite symptoms, as any doctor would see at a glance".

John got Jeremiah to write a letter to the doctor. Just ask a simple question, "Would you tell me what else you passed on.?" A very evasive reply came back. That is fine said John..."Now ask another". This continued, until a reply came back which made him laugh, "Now we've got him, and he knows it; that was composed by a lawyer. We'll give him the fright of his life. Nobody told him that you have another member of the profession in the family!" He received a sharp letter from Jeremiah's sister.

While with Hannah, Jeremiah had a further experience with a psychiatrist. He had found himself sitting, with Hannah, her mother and father and a noble Lord, the head of the firm of lawyers, used by Hannah, arrayed against him. As a means of achieving reconciliation, the noble Lord had suggested that Jeremiah should go and see his 'shrink', whom he often consulted. Jeremiah agreed, on condition that he and Hannah went together. He made an appointment. Hannah drove him there, but, when called into the office' the 'shrink' shut the door, leaving Hannah outside. When Jeremiah said that he had only agreed to attend, if both were seen together, the 'shrink' said, angrily, that it was unthinkable and that he insisted on seeing Jeremiah.

For over half an hour he submitted Jeremiah to interrogation. He was more like an inquisitor than a physician. Jeremiah asked if he might ask him some questions. "Of course, you may". "You have asked me many questions about what I have said and done. I have tried to answer truthfully. By what authority did you do so?" The shrink was not prepared to answer, saying, "I would have thought it was obvious". Jeremiah said that if it had been obvious he would not have asked. "You are a psychiatrist. As I understand it, 'psyche' means soul. If you prescribed medication, how would it reach my soul?" The 'shrink' replied that it was not the health Jeremiah's 'psyche' that troubled him. It seemed robust. What troubled him was the fundamentally seditious nature of his words and ideas. He would write letters that drove respected head teachers to breakdowns, commit contempt of court, flout their orders, and say, as if it justified all, "If it's good enough for Elijah, it's all right for me".

He even said that Jeremiah was one of the most dangerous men he had ever met. "Oh, you are not likely to injure anyone physically. People like you are worse than that. It would not take many like you to render any civilised form of society ungovernable".

That was ridiculous, but it taught Jeremiah much about the likes of Elijah and even such as Kierkegaard. It made him fearful of men of word. Their words echoed down centuries, with the power to set men against one another, thousands of years after they had been spoken.

He returned to Norfolk, once again finding work with Alec and Tricia. He went up to Durham when his elder son was confirmed. Hannah also came, with her brother, who was godfather. This was strange, as he had never shewn the remotest interest in any thing like that. John was suspicious of there being an ulterior motive. He and Jeremiah's sister made sure that the brother was never in a room with Jeremiah, without one of them being present. Their suspicions were well founded. Jeremiah did not attend the confirmation, thinking it ludicrous for a husband and wife to do so as strangers. Instead he went on a coach to Edinburgh to find his old friend, Roland Walls. Roland saw instantly that, at the heart of Jeremiah's story, was the hypocrisy of the church. Whilst staying with Roland in his tin hut, he renewed his acquaintance with his friends from the Gold Coast who lived nearby. It was wonderful to see them again. His Goddaughter was there. They too had fallen on hard times.

That they had done so was a relief. He would not have dared to face them, in his state, otherwise. Elisabeth had surreptitiously put a folded five-pound note into his tobacco tin. Arnett drove him back to Roland's hutted home. He got out of the car flung his arms about Jeremiah, saying, "You have been the first breath of hope we have had for years. It was wonderful hearing you assert, simply, the truth of words like 'Blessed are the Meek...". He pressed a further £5 into Jeremiah's hand. With that he was back in his car and away.

Jeremiah made his way back to Durham thence back to Alec and Tricia's hotel. There was a party of policeman, who were fishermen. One morning, he received a large envelope, a summons to the Chancery Court for the authorisation of the sale of the restaurant. Attached to it was an affidavit, sworn by Hannah's brother, in which he related a conversation that he had had with Jeremiah in Hannah's presence, in which he had refused to sign documents permitting the sale of the property. That was a lie. They had had no such conversation; though Jeremiah had said such things to others. One question would have exposed the falsity, but it was after 9am when the letter arrived. The hearing was set for eleven o'clock, that day.

He apologised to the senior policeman, and asked what he should do. "Don't worry." said the policeman, "give them a ring and they will delay the hearing". He telephoned the court. "It is up to you to ensure that you receive your summonses in good time". When he told the Police Inspector of the court's reply, he said, "That is about what you would expect from that lot"! It does not make our job any easier. Now you know why people do not hold the law in respect".

It had been deviously done. The summons had been sent to him at Durham. His elder son had answered the door and was persuaded to sign the recorded delivery slip. It had been forwarded that morning. Had he been in Durham, he would have had only two days notice. Hannah knew he was not there, as he had sent her money from Norfolk, and even telephoned her from there. The false witness made little difference. They would have sold the place anyway.

At Christmas, Jeremiah was again homeless. He walked sadly by his old home, boarded up to prevent his gaining access. He felt bitter at the brightly lit homes proclaiming good will to all men. It was then that he thought of Jesus' words, after he had spoken to the Rich young man, "All things are possible for God". He remembered exactly his feelings, when lecturing at Derby, and imagined a needle's eye obligingly expanding to allow one rich man into eternal life. "I overlooked the more obvious possibility. He can make one destitute!" It made him laugh.

He found temporary work at another hotel. In the bar, one evening, a woman, sitting with her husband, said, "You don't remember me, do you? Remember Hickling Broad?" It was the woman who had fed Sadie. Her husband was a police sergeant, who had been asked to look for Jeremiah. He laughed at the thought that the man, he was looking for, was being given coffee by his own wife.

One morning, sitting on the reception desk, the phone rang. It was Hannah. She said that her father had arranged to buy her a house in Durham, as a basis for reuniting the family; would he come for Christmas? He was hesitant to put himself in his debt yet again. She said, "Think about it". Nando walked into the bar a few days later, and said that he was about to open a restaurant. 'Would Jeremiah act as his chef?' "Of course I will!"

He decided to go up to Durham, but could only afford a fare as far as Doncaster. The rest of the way he would have to walk. It was bitterly cold. Having walked for hours, he decided to try and get some shelter and rest. Finding the trailer of an articulated lorry in a lay-by and a discarded dustbin bag, he pulled this around him and stuffed Sadie inside for warmth, curling up in the lea of the double wheels at the rear of the trailer. He must have gone to sleep, as the next thing he knew was a powerful jolt. The tractor was hitching onto the trailer. He and Sadie shot out from under the wheels, as if from a gun. The lorry moved away.

He walked back to Easingwold. Passing the Church, he knocked on the Vicarage door. He asked the vicar, "Have you as much as a cup of cold water....?" The vicar said that he could provide a mug of tea and a marmalade sandwich. What day it was he knew not; but at that moment an elderly lady came by and said, "Oh good; we are going to have a dog in Church this morning!" Jeremiah trailed behind them into a little side chapel. It was many years since he had heard the cadences of the Prayer Book of 1662. After the service the Vicar said goodbye to the congregation, but when it came to Jeremiah and Sadie, he shut the door and asked him to sit down

"What have I done wrong?" "Nothing", said the Vicar. "Hearing your voice behind me, as we said the creed, was almost like hearing an exposition of its meaning. I have never heard it said with such understanding in my life". He went to the poor box and took out a five-pound note. If I were you, I would get a bus to Thirsk. There is a cafe there where you will get a lot of food for not very much. "Do sit here and rest, sleep if you like".

Jeremiah rested for a couple of hours and did as he was bidden. The cafe was all that Canon Smith had said. As he came out, he heard a phone ringing in the kiosk outside. He went in and answered. It was Canon Smith. "I hoped I might catch you", he said. He asked many questions, said goodbye and they never met again, though Jeremiah wrote to him later. He thought it sensible to phone his sister in Durham. She had heard nothing of any house being bought. The boys were in Devon with their mother for Christmas. He had best return the way he came, at least he would have the wind at his back. "If you had a German soldier with a rifle behind you; you'd walk!"

His old student, David, rescued him and took him to his home for a couple of days, then drove him south for several miles. He made his way to Derby, stayed with the College Librarian, for a night or two, and made his way back to Norfolk on foot with Sadie, as ever, at his heels. He was given a lift by a passing lorry, whose driver, a man from Old Gride, near Boston, was kind enough to buy him a cup of tea and buns. Alec and Tricia's son in law let Jeremiah live in his cottage. While there he had a communication from the cousin, who had taken over the trout farm. If Jeremiah was willing, he would buy his 100 shares, so that his wife could take over his role. He would send him the £100 nominal value 'by return', as soon as he received the certificate; then have them valued, and send the balance. Jeremiah sent the certificate, and received the £100, but heard no more.

The boys came for their Easter holiday. Hannah paid a visit with their daughter. She left saying that 'deep down' she loved him. They spent the rest of the holiday on a houseboat. She came up that summer to say that she had decided to marry the Australian, who had unexpectedly returned.

Nando found him a small council flat. His younger son resolutely spent his holidays with him. It must have been very boring for him. His loyalty was touching. Nando told him of the wedding, and how his elder son had phoned to ask Jeremiah to stop it. There was nothing he could do. Jeremiah felt strangely relieved. A 'false hope' had been extinguished. He came to see a further reason for Uberrimae's dislike of the Australian. He had no carrot to dangle any more. This is not to imply that he was cynical; he genuinely wanted to restore the marriage, but, at the same time, he would not want Jeremiah to become a 'loose (and loaded) cannon', over whom no control could be exercised. How strong were his reasons, Jeremiah had yet to discover.

Meanwhile the wheels of Chancery ground on. He received notification of the awarding of costs. All were awarded against him. Nando was anxious. He made an appointment for him to see his solicitor.

Chapter Twenty five.

"Thieves for their robbery have authority....."

The solicitor was a partner in a large firm. He was the matrimonial specialist and, in barrack room terms, a real 'pox doctor's clerk'. He was sure he could help, but only if Jeremiah paid £1,000, up front. Jeremiah explained that he had not a thousand pennies and earned £35 per week. He had no chance of legal aid. He suggested that he should do all the donkey-work, writing letters and so on. That was not allowed. With that, he went off to the firm his dad used, with the same result.

He returned to the first firm. He asked the receptionist if there was anyone, who cared for fairness and justice. The receptionist phoned round several offices. There was a member who might be able to see him in a fortnight. That was no use. She returned to the phone. Jeremiah sat down. He was ready to sit there all night. Eventually the receptionist told him that there was a newly joined solicitor, who would see him. He was led up a back staircase to a sparsely furnished room in a garret.

Behind the desk sat a young man with a shock of dark hair. He spoke quietly and reassuringly. His name was John. Though Jeremiah did not know it at the time, this was his first case. John listened patiently as he told his story. He did not want any money in advance. Jeremiah could make enquiries, writing letters and so on. He warned that, if he did so, he might not receive replies. "The easiest way to deal with a difficult letter is to leave it unanswered".

When told of the custody hearing, John gasped, "My God, how did they get away with that?" He explained that the case should have been heard at North Walsham, or in a neutral court, if North Walsham was thought likely to have been prejudiced. He could see no reason why it should be. Tavistock, with Uberrimae's connections, would not be considered neutral. But there was the matter of the attempt to drive him to suicide, which might well have emerged at North Walsham. The shortness of notice was also, if not illegal, "somewhat irregular". It should have been a month at least.

Could Sheriffs evict one without a court hearing? "Of course they can't," said John. "How can I discover what court authorised it?" "You might start by asking the Sheriff's department".

Nando bought him a typewriter. He wrote to the Sheriff's department, asking if they would be kind enough to tell him which court had authorised them to take possession. He received no reply; so he wrote again, and received no reply. He wrote by recorded delivery. No answer came. He wrote four times. Not a letter was acknowledged. He contacted John. "That was what I feared". The old Dog explained that they were civil servants, and would not want trouble. There were only two possibilities, one that he was just messing them about, the other, that he had not been notified of a court hearing. If it were the latter, all sorts of complications might arise. "Try asking the plaintiff's solicitors".

They were a well-known firm in Plymouth. Jeremiah wrote to the member of the firm who acted for Hannah. He did not answer. He wrote several letters with the same result. He wrote to their London agents. They remained silent. The principal of the firm was a noble Lord, his party's spokesman on Home Affairs in the upper house, a man known for his integrity. Jeremiah wrote to him asking him to instruct his partner to reply to legitimate enquiries. He received no reply, though he thrice repeated the letter.

This was what John feared. There was obviously something, which they would prefer not to be known. They knew that Jeremiah could not afford to pay a lawyer to write for him. He sat bewildered in the foyer.

Idly, he picked up a copy of the Times. It fell open at the page reporting proceedings in Parliament. There, in capitals, was the name of the noble Lord, who had made a speech in the Upper House, denouncing a court, which had failed to safeguard the interests of an unrepresented defendant. This, said the eloquent and impassioned peer, was a threat to the historic liberties of the citizen, cherished since Magna Carta. 'Bloody Humbug', thought Jeremiah, as he caught the bus back to Horning.

He wrote, not to the noble Lord, but to the leader of his party, detailing what had happened, and asked the leader to tell his spokesman to put his own house in order before making such speeches. The leader replied that he could not instruct his spokesman in the upper house, all he could do was to shew him the letter.

The result was instant. A large brown envelope arrived two days later, containing details of not one, but two cases, which had been heard without his knowledge. The second he disregarded. It was a case in the County Court, in which Hannah had obtained authority to remove the boys. He knew of this, as Hannah had arrived with the authority. It had no relevance to the Chancery court and the costs, or so he thought.

He read the details of the case, in which the possession order was granted. It was in Chancery. Attached to the papers was an affidavit, sworn, not by the plaintiff, but her solicitor, "a true and trusty friend of the Court". No wonder they had been at such pains to prevent him knowing of the case! That, to which the 'true and trusty friend of the court' had given his oath and did swear, was a pack of lies. If the courts esteem such people as their 'true and trusty friends', it is small wonder that few hold them in any respect. He had sworn that, 'to the best of his knowledge and belief', there were no other persons residing on the premises to be possessed, other than the defendant. He knew that the two boys were there. He had phoned them, himself, and spoken to them. He had sent a policeman to make sure they were being properly cared for. He had sent an Inspector of Education. He had two receivers overseeing the business, both of whom knew they were there. Hannah had herself come up to try and persuade them to come back with

her.
"I bet minors are not persons in the eyes of the law!" "Of course they are", said John, "They would be seen as vitally significant persons", adding; "I think we may have something to work with, after all". The difficulty might be in establishing that, when he gave his oath and swore to his affidavit, the solicitor knew. "I think we should put an affidavit into court".

Jeremiah had drafted one before, so set about doing so again. He raised a serious criticism of the second receiver, who had never been near the place, and had refused to receive and manage it, made an arrangement, but not carried it out. When he took possession, he had not made an inventory of what was on the premises; but had allowed the Plaintiff to help herself to whatever she wanted, sending him a suitcase of clothes and a dustbin bag of odds and ends, in which was a pile of dog's turds. Many articles were missing and not accounted for. One was of great value. It was a cavalry officers 'pouch belt' of the Penninsular War, belonging to the Leicester and Derbyshire Yeomanry. There was also a scale model wherry made by his dad, and a mass of books, some valuable first editions, which had vanished.

He then turned to the matter of false witness, adding a catena of quotations from the prophets and the gospels, including the words of the prophet Jeremiah at the Temple, 'How long will ye kill, steal, commit adultery, and bear false witness, and come to this place which is called by my name to buy more time to continue these abominations'. He ended by pointing out that, as all law and governance in Her Majesty's realm was subject to that of the Gospel, Judges had no right to put asunder. Since they had arrogated to themselves this right under the law, the nation will be filled with a spirit of lawlessness, family life would break down. They would not have enough room in their prisons. In substantiating the allegation of perjury he cited the conversation on the telephone, Hannah's arrival, and the knowledge of the receivers that the boys resided there.

He still had no documentary evidence, shewing that the solicitor knew that the boys were there, when he swore that, "to the best of his knowledge and belief", they were not.

He picked up the details of the other case. Hannah had sworn the affidavit. It related to the occasion, when he had arrived on her doorstep, the weekend before her divorce petition. She had sworn that he had forced his way into her flat, in her absence, moved in, and refused to leave, when she returned and asked him to go. That was a lie. She said that she had immediately removed herself to stay with her parents. That too was a lie. It made no difference to the present matter. Then he noticed the date at which this application was made. It was made only a day or two after the Solicitor had sworn his oath. He had represented her in the county Court. If, a day after swearing that no others were residing on the premises, he appeared in another court, demanding their removal, he must have known that they were there. Here was documentary proof, sworn testimony that he was lying. No wonder they had sought to keep the details secret! No wonder the noble Lord had felt that, in this case, the interests of an unrepresented defendant should not be safeguarded.

"That should give them something to think about", said John, as he had the affidavit engrossed and attached 90 pages of documentary corroboration.

Jeremiah wrote to the Master, saying that he wished to put an affidavit into court. The Master replied that he was glad that he had decided to do so. He should send copy to court and a copy to the Plaintiff a fortnight in advance. The fitting time for him to present it was at the hearing of the Final Account. For this he would make arrangements. It was to be in about six weeks.

Jeremiah caught the train to London. Peter Noble was not allowing him to hang about, worrying about appearing in court. He was to meet him for lunch at "Balls Bros and Co.'s Wine Bar". Peter was himself on hard times. The new owners of the Wine Merchants, a brewery, had not fulfilled their promises to him when they bought the business. The Directors had assured him that they wanted it to be run as before. Once they owned it, things changed. Peter was himself on the dole, with a CBE as his only reward.

Jeremiah made his way to the Law Courts. He had been there before, and knew where the Master's chambers were, but was directed up a side staircase to a room, whose furniture consisted of three stacking chairs and a chipped Formica table. Leading off it, was a larger office, full of clerks doing accounts. Stretched out on one of the chairs was a tall well-dressed man, who was Hannah's counsel. From the adjacent room appeared a short, rotund, man, wearing a white linen jacket.

The new arrival introduced himself as the chief accounts clerk and asked what Jeremiah wanted and who he was. He said that he had come to present his affidavit. "Don't be silly" said the Clerk, "You can't do that here. I am only a nuts and bolts man. I am not empowered to hear evidence".

"But the Master told me to ......" "Of course he did not," said the Clerk. "The Master knows that we cannot hear evidence".

By the grace of God, and unusually for him, Jeremiah had brought the Master's letter. As soon as the letter was produced, both the Clerk and the barrister produced copies of the affidavit. "We had better hear it then"; said the Clerk.

Jeremiah had an urge to remind him that, only a minute before, he had said that he was not empowered to do so, and that the Master knew this. He had no chance to speak. The barrister sat up and took over.

He spoke in the self-assured drawl of a long-suffering tutor commenting on a poor essay. "Our friend had failed to read carefully what the 'true and trusty friend of the court' had actually said". "Shit", thought Jeremiah, "Typical me! But John read it, and he is as sharp as a needle".

The barrister began to explain the distinction between knowing and believing something to be true. "I don't need you to tell me that", thought the defendant. He admitted that the Plaintiff had visited the boys, but that was long before. They only had his word for it that the true and trusty friend had spoken to them by phone. He had made all possible enquiries; before swearing to his affidavit and, 'to the best of his knowledge and belief', it was true. "Of whom did he make his enquiries? They had two receivers, both of whom knew that the boys were there".

Jeremiah fumbled in his pocket. To his relief he felt a sheaf of papers, and pulled them out. "If he did not know that the two boys were residing on the premises, how was it that he appeared in another court, on the following day, demanding their removal?" He put the details of that case on the table. The barrister had not read the mass of attached documentation.

At this, the Clerk intervened. "You are alleging perjury". "Not only alleging, but demonstrating it, beyond reasonable doubt". "It was two years ago," said the Clerk, "Have you thought how much inconvenience you would cause, if we heard your evidence? You should have brought it to the court's notice at the time".

Jeremiah said that he had, at the time, no knowledge of the case being brought, and had only, with great difficulty, managed to extract the information a few weeks ago, as the Plaintiff's solicitors refused to reply to his letters. "It's your responsibility to ensure that you get your summonses in good time".

It was the Mad Hatter's tea party, without tea.

The Clerk said that perjury was none of the business of the Chancery Court. It was a civil, not a criminal court. Perjury, being a criminal matter, had no bearing on the case. It was all a long time ago. Jeremiah asked whether, if he stole the crown jewels and kept it concealed for a couple of years, melted them down and sold them in bits and pieces, the same would apply? It would inconvenience many people to restore them.

The Clerk ruled that, as it had criticised the work of a servant of the Court, the second receiver, the entire affidavit should be seen as an act of contempt. He warned Jeremiah that any further reference to it would render him liable to instant committal to prison.

Jeremiah had visions of the Clerk pressing a bell, calling for a tipstaff ,and of his being led away to Wormwood Scrubs. Norwich Nick was one thing, a big London prison another; so went to the door. Having opened it, he asked; "Would you tell me what distinguishes this court, which was set up to put right abuses in lower courts, from a Mafia Tribunal?" He felt like saying, "A Masonic lodge". With that he made his way, with all speed, to Liverpool Street and the train to Norwich, half expecting to be arrested for contempt on his arrival.

Next day he spoke to John. "It does not shew English Justice at its best. They were just messing you about. They knew that it was not an act of contempt, but knew that you would not know". It seemed that the Master had welcomed his affidavit, feeling sure that there could be nothing substantial in it, but found otherwise. It had all been a waste of time. In about a fortnight he received a bill for costs. They had deducted the price obtained for the sale of the property, which, including fixtures and fittings, had realised £21,000, at auction. Jeremiah thought of the time when Uberrimae had urged him to hold on for a better price. He was faced with £85,000, to be paid somehow, by attachment of earnings, 'garnishee orders' and so on. In panic he went to the phone box and rang John.

The quiet, reassuring, voice said, "Leave it with me. I will ring your wife's solicitors. Don't go away. I'll ring you back in five minutes. Within three, the phone rang. "You can forget all about that bill. I can assure you that you will hear nothing more of it". He achieved more than that. Jeremiah's dad had sold the large house he lived in, when his mother was alive, and moved to a smaller one. With the spare cash he had taken over the bank loan they had taken out when buying the restaurant. The plaintiff's solicitors had refused to recognise it as a business liability. John made them agree to do so.

"Whatever did you say to them? "We won't go into that now. Just take it that I told them that you had not the means to pay." "Suppose that in years to come I had?" "You will hear no more of it, so don't worry".

Later, he learned that John had said more, and seems to have said something to the effect that, "If you want the money, come and get it. There are one or two matters we will then have an opportunity to go into". He promised Jeremiah that, should he be sued for libel, he would defend him for nothing.

There ended Jeremiah's experience with the laws and practices of England to which Uberrimae had referred him.

It left him sore amazed. It seemed that those of the Christian religion, who enjoyed positions of power and influence were ready to act, not only in ways that were at variance with the teachings of the one they declared to be God from God, but in ways that were wholly at variance with the principles of their statutory office. Under the gospel it was straitly forbidden to swear an oath. Under the laws of Sinai, God took a dim view of bearing false witness against one's neighbour. It seemed that it was fine to swear an oath in order to bear false witness, 'in a good cause'. Both God and his only begotten Son overlooked that. The laws of England also took a dim view of Perjury, unless, it seems, it was used in the furtherance of a civil case. Then it had the approval of almost the highest court in the land, provided it was concealed for a suitable time, and was performed by 'true and trusty friends of the court'.

It frightened Jeremiah for the rest of his days. If those, who publicly declared belief in God, were in no way constrained by his laws, to which they publicly assented, what limits were there to what any might do, once assured of their own rectitude? If men of wealth and power could play 'skipping stones' with the laws of the land, what protection was there in any legislation? How could such as the noble Lord make eloquent speeches, voices breaking with emotion, when a court failed to safeguard the rights of a defendant, while knowingly conniving in a systematic attempt to do exactly that in his own business? If people with wealth and power could persuade doctors to divulge information, gained in a consultation, provided the patient was of no consequence, and feel so assured that they did not hesitate to write of this to another doctor; then arrange for policemen to make 'off the record' enquiries; whom, in any position of authority, could one trust? A lawyer could be persuaded to do that, for which he might well prosecute anyone else. His experience in the High Court confirmed his fear. A court, set up to right the wrongs in lower courts, was happy to act on false evidence, and declare an affidavit, that established it as being so, an act of contempt; when it was nothing of the kind.

Jeremiah could understand why the 'Screws' said, "There's nobody in here who has done anything half as bad as the ones that send them here". Dostoevesky reached the same conclusion in "House of the Damned".

Peter's choice of "Balls Bros" was apt.

All served to confirm his childhood fears of authority, which centred on the declarations of the Christian religion. How could anybody let themselves be deceived by them? The emphatic teaching of Jesus about being as a little child should tell anyone that they could not be genuine. If those who solemnly made public declarations of belief in God and his only begotten Son, could find it worthy of condemnation that anyone should be childish, within five minutes of doing so, everything had to be a lie. One would hardly act in such a way if one feared God. If one did not fear God, one did not believe that there is God. Nobody could have been more vehement, on that matter, than Jesus himself. If one feared God, it had the effect of making one fear others less. To be fearful seemed distinct from being frightened. The only being, who could always be consistent with his word, would be God, because he needed nobody and nothing.

Jeremiah had amazing luck, most obviously in finding John the solicitor, who was not only kind and understanding, but intelligent, reassuring and calm, and a very good friend. Fortunate, he was, in his sister and brother in law. It was not only their loyalty and generosity he had to be thankful for, but the fact that one happened to be a medical practitioner and the other knew his way about the law.

It is worth, even if it means reiteration, reviewing impossible position that Jeremiah had put both Uberrimae, his daughter and the lawyers into, by, in effect, 'giving his cloak as well'; whereas, if he had contested the cases, he would have not have had a prayer. By being the inept loser, which he did not like, he had, without realising what he was doing, led them into positions which were indefensible and without means of withdrawal. Sam had phoned him, recalling, "Father forgive them, they know not what they do". Jeremiah was ready to do that, and wanted to, but neither Uberrimae, Hannah, nor her lawyers, nor her silly cousin wanted, or were in any position to seek forgiveness. Doing so meant admitting a fault. That becomes difficult, if others are involved, and the actions, for which forgiveness is sought, involve misdemeanours, if not crimes, and transgressions of professional codes of conduct, which have been the means of winning cases. This is not to suggest that Jeremiah had not much, for which he needed forgiving.

The problem was Hannah's act of folly, not only in having her love nest, but being an accomplice in the sustained campaign of phone calling, which had the boasted purpose of securing Jeremiah's death. This would be a matter that nobody, especially someone in Uberrimae's position, would want dragging out in court. It would be humiliating. Uberrimae doted on his daughter. He knew from independent sources that it had happened and that Jeremiah could produce a dozen witnesses to testify to it. He would not have told his daughter that he knew. It is likely that the case in Chancery was planned as a threat. Had Jeremiah been to a solicitor, he would have advised an out of court settlement. It would be crazy to go to the Chancery Court over a property worth £35,000.

It would not have affected the outcome if Jeremiah had attended. The Master said that the only relevant fact in Hannah's affidavit was that he was in prison. It looked as if he was manoeuvred into prison to facilitate the case, but that was not the court's business. The casual manner in which the affidavit was produced suggested that Uberrimae and the lawyers did not expect the case to be heard. There was no doubt in Jeremiah's mind that Uberrimae sincerely sought to restore the marriage. Whether Hannah did is another matter. She might have done so, on what she and her father considered sensible terms. In those terms, Jeremiah had got 'worse not better'.

The matter of the 'love nest' and telephone calls would have been crucial. While Uberrimae might dismiss this as an outrageous defamation of his beloved daughter's character, and a lie, he knew that it was not. He was wont to adopt a highly moral view of such matters. With him, at theological college, there had been an old friend, who had formerly been a chemist. He had 'a nice little earner'. He bought the materials and made up his own cosmetics. There was little likelihood of the Tax Inspectors knowing, so he pocketed the cash. On the eve of his ordination he had confessed it to the Bishop. The money, which was due to the Inland Revenue, should be given to charity. Uberrimae often said that this was disgraceful. His friend should have told the Inland Revenue, and paid whatever fines and accrued interest they imposed. He even muttered that there was 'bad blood' in the family. Suppose that he applied this to his beloved daughter? She and her lover had done that which he would have condemned as a magistrate. Had they succeeded, he might have sent them for trial at Crown Court.

Most are prepared to do things, but are unwilling to articulate them Hannah might be aware that her doting father knew; but would, at the same time, be unwilling speak of the matter, nor would he want her to do so. Such things are best left unsaid. Articulating them seems to give then fixity. Hannah knew what her father said about his friend and his failure to inform the Revenue. She knew what his attitude would have to be as a magistrate. If it were articulated, she would be obliged to admit that he was being shifty and hypocritical, as would he. Being left unsaid, whatever may have been done seems less culpable, almost not to have happened.

In addition to the 'love nest', there were now irregularities and downright illegalities in cases, unless it is permissible for 'true and trusty friends of the court' to commit perjury. The daughter and son of a Deputy Lord Lieutenant had 'gone and done likewise'. In the case of the true and trusty friend of the court, there may not have been intent to do so flagrantly. If Hannah, when she came to Norfolk with the court order, allowing her to remove the boys, had done so, there could have been no other persons residing on the property, when the affidavit was entered in court, even if it was untrue at the time it was sworn. How the plaintiff's solicitors got away with not properly issuing summonses, Jeremiah never knew. Alan said that it was easily done. All they had to do was to send them to him c/o Hannah, to obtain a recorded delivery slip to display in court.

The consequence of all these illegalities was that the possibility of restoring the family was made almost, if not wholly, impossible. It would have been difficult enough in view of the love nest and the attempt to secure his death, and his own attempted suicide. It seemed to be Uberrimae's intention that Jeremiah was made a lifelong 'client'. To say that is not cynical. It was the only way. Jeremiah had become a 'loose and loaded cannon'. He, in the Dog's words, 'had something on' Hannah, her father and many of their esteemed friends; now that he knew of the illegalities in the court cases, beginning with the Custody hearing. On top of that there was the attempt to conceal it all, by the refusal to reply to letters. This involved not only Hannah's own solicitor, but also a major party's home affairs spokesman in the House of Lords, a close friend of Uberrimae.

Words flung out, as insults, can reveal much of the one who uses them. Often, Uberrimae would say angrily, "You are a dirty little blackmailer". Jeremiah had never hinted or suggested that he might reveal discreditable information. Aside from the phone calls, he did not, then, know that there was any. Clearly, Uberrimae did.

Ernie Cole forgave those indebted to him, but he did not forget. If anyone is to be forgiven, there has to be something to forgive. Jeremiah had much to be forgiven for. He was lucky not to be involved in the legal matters. He could admit things. Hannah could not, without compromising others. In all her affidavits she was faultless. If, for the sake of argument, there was anything, which needed Jeremiah's forgiveness, and she sought it, she would, then, need forgiveness from such as Uberrimae, her mother, her brother, her cousin and the true and trusty friend of the court; as they would be compromised by such an admission.

The petition in the one prayer given by Jesus seems crucial, "forgive us our debts, as we also.....". Hannah was indebted to all these people, just as her mother had said. She was also indebted, in other ways, to Jeremiah, to whom she had made many promises in order to gain what she wanted and avoid potentially difficult situations. She was caught between two 'masters' as it were. The only way out was the one towards which Jeremiah had been stumbling. She could have said, "I will stand on the words, Let no man put asunder". That would have had the effect of, "Let whoever among you is faultless cast the first stone". All would have been obliged to walk away in silence. Had she done so, it would have put Jeremiah on the spot.

Jeremiah was fortunate in not attending court. Had he done so, John would not have been in the position to force Hannah's solicitor to forgo costs of over

£80,000. It would be well over half a million in current terms. Solicitors do not forgo such sums of money unless they are forced to do so, even if they do so on behalf of their clients. The speed of John's reply made it clear that Hannah's solicitor had no time to consult either her or Uberrimae.

In other ways, he could hardly be said to have been fortunate. He had lost his wife, his family, his home, and was reduced to penury, having spent a year with nowhere to lay his head. Only in one respect, could he be seen otherwise. If he had sought experiences which might lead to his perceiving, as the truth, that which he had read, when a child of seven, he had been given them. He even had a sharp lesson in listening to what Jesus actually said. All along, he hoped that if he lost wife children home and land 'for my sake and the gospel', he would, in this life, have them all back.

He omitted to note that Jesus has spoken of wives, children, homes and lands, in the plural. This, in a curious way, had come about. He was treated as one of the family by many of his friends. On the other hand he was becoming more and more of an outcast among those who went to Church, even his own family. Among the churchgoers, he was seen in the same light, as by his well to do aunt, who wished he could get over 'something that happened 2,000 years ago', particularly, what someone said, 2,000 years ago.

A comment by Roland had opened his eyes. When staying with him in his 'tin hut', they had gone for a walk in the park. Others had doffed their caps deferentially to him. "They think I'm the laird who owns the place. I might as well be", said Roland. Jeremiah thought, 'If God is your Father, you are the son of the entire 'estate', without having the trouble of looking after it'.

Jeremiah had great respect for Uberrimae. He would never have taken the risks with his position that Uberrimae had taken, in order to safeguard his daughter from humiliation. If all that John had said about the illegality of the initial magistrates' hearing were true, and if, as seemed obvious, Uberrimae had somehow arranged for the 'off the record enquiry' by the police sergeant, he might have forfeited his DL and JP and much else besides.

There was another extraordinary 'chance' occurrence. Jeremiah had a cousin who was his accountant. His son was at Exeter University. He had visited him, staying in a hotel; when in walked Uberrimae with another man, obviously a barrister. This cousin had met Uberrimae and recognised him, but Uberrimae was almost blind.

John Boycott went to say, 'Hullo'. As he waited for a pause in their conversation, he overheard him speak of the problems they were having with a difficult son in law in Neatishead in Norfolk. Knowing who this was, he waited for Uberrimae to sit down, then went and sat behind them, overhearing all about the planned High Court action. It did not help Jeremiah to know. Uberrimae had already threatened such an action if ever he left the premises again. It seemed to illustrate the line from the psalm, "He that watches Israel, neither slumbers nor sleeps".

Central to the matter was the Christian religion, and the public declarations of those who attended services. Whether people, themselves, made them, or not, was almost incidental. They were made for them. That Hannah and her father thought it wholly fitting to attend the Holy Communion service, on the day before she applied to men to put asunder, seemed perfectly to illustrate the hypocrisy in this. But for that there would be no purpose in telling the story.

Hannah and her father, with many of her friends, were regular attenders on the services of the Church. Here was an ambivalence, which takes one back to the question asked by Isaiah, and the shocking answer he gives. Jeremiah's repeatedly 'getting on his high horse', as she described it, annoyed them, her above all; but, when it came to the court actions, she needed him to remain on it. She needed him not to appear, and 'to give his cloak as well'. Nobody, including Jeremiah, saw, then, that doing so put the 'plaintiff', ultimately, into a worse position than ever. It was like forgiving a debt, so making it permanent. She, or her solicitors, may have even have needed him to confront the court, as he did, and go to prison. That provided the ground for the Chancery action.

Hannah complained that he was like an armour-plated man. In all the things that he had done, many of them seemingly foolish, he had set out with high optimism; whether it was sitting on Dartmoor, making visits to Hannah, confronting the magistrates, or letting cases go through. Always they ended in disappointment. He was reduced to being a despised and tearful idiot. He thought, often, of the words to his namesake. "To whomsoever I shall send thee thou shalt go, whatsover I command thee thou shalt speak. Be not afraid of them, for behold I am with thee to deliver. Be not dismayed because of them, lest I dismay thee before them". Always, he ended up being 'dismayed before them'. Each time, he echoed his namesake's complaint, "Thou hast deceived me....." .

Afterwards, it seemed different. Each time he learned much, as, for example, when Hannah had begged him not to challenge the Affidavit in Chancery, promising to restore the family by Christmas. It would be more truthful to say that he was taught much. Had he not felt a false sense of optimism, he would never have set out to do these things. Never, in the accepted sense was he 'depressed'. He felt stronger, when apparently in the 'vale of misery', with only the sayings of the gospels to stand on. He began to learn from the psalmist, "Those going through the vale of misery, using it for a well....". When he was, in the words of Isaiah, 'cut off from the land of the living', he felt stronger not weaker. "He feared not those who could destroy the body and then could do no more". It was almost a reversion to being a little child. Everything said by Jesus was self evidently true.

His namesake was promised, "Behold I make you this day, brazen walls and a defended city...."

If Hannah had done as she promised, and restored the family by Christmas, it would have been futile. She would have done so under threat. Whatever, then, would have been the relationship, either between themselves, or between them and their respective families?

If, after all he had written to the magistrates, he assented to their right and authority, and not been sent to prison, he would have wallowed in uncertainty. He never, for one second, thought that he would be sent to prison, any more than he thought that the governors at the College would accept his resignation on the grounds he gave. He thought his argument so incontrovertible that the court would recognise it. His friends 'knew' what he would say from all that he had previously said. They realised how it would end. In Jesus words', he would have abandoned the 'rock' foundation of his house, the rock against which 'the gates of hell' would not prevail. This, he was becoming less and less willing to do. As long as he stood on the 'rock' of the sayings of Jesus, however miserable he felt, he felt secure. The ground under his feet was solid.

They needed him to be the 'outcast'. That they lived at ease and in prosperity, surrounded by friends, most of whom were devotees of the Church, drawn from the professional classes and, in one way or another, 'judges and dividers' over others, whereas his friends tended to come from those who were 'judged and divided', demonstrated to all the rectitude of their position. Ministers of the Gospel held out their hands in welcome to them. They tended to shun Jeremiah. If he raised such matters as the sayings of Jesus about men not putting asunder, or the declaration that, 'If a wife divorced her husband and married another she commits adultery', they would tell him to learn that the gospel was one of forgiveness and mercy. Hannah and her man were welcomed at weddings. He was not.

They would tell him that his words and ideas came from the Old Testament. The 'God' of the Old Testament was one to be feared, that of the gospel was the God of Love, who demanded that one love one's neighbour. This was the 'new commandment'. In vain did he point out that it was a quotation from Leviticus. Jesus did not share that opinion. He spoke of the need to fear God with emphatic vehemence. How could one not fear a being, which is the infinite Creator of all things?

It was uncharitable and insulting to mention Jesus' words about those who divorced husbands and married others. God understood our weaknesses, and forgave all our sins. Jesus said that, whoever was ashamed of him and his words, of him will the Son of Man be ashamed. This was what they demanded. As to the matter of forgiveness, nobody wanted forgiving, apart from Jeremiah. This took him to the answer that Isaiah gave. It was necessary, among churchgoers, for him to be seen as the one who was 'stricken'. It demonstrated that they, in their churches and as 'judges and dividers', were right.

They prospered and were held in esteem by all who were 'of account'. He was not. The plump geese, in Kierkegaard's parable, had their divine worship, in which a gander preached of their great destiny to fly off to distant pastures. At every mention of the divine name, the ganders bowed their heads and the geese curtsied. They grew fat, plump and delicious and, at Michaelmas, were popped in the oven. There were among them, a few thin, ill-favoured geese. As they waddled home from Church the fat ones looked, knowingly, at them, saying, "You can see what comes of taking seriously the promise of our great destiny......". 'Isaiah' describes the one who believed our report: "We did esteem him stricken, stricken of God, but he was stricken for our offences, the chastisement of *our peace* was laid upon him".

In relation to the sayings of Jesus, any public avowal of belief would lead to this. It is in him and his words that all, who attend services, declare belief. They declare that they are his disciples, those who abide in his words. To be 'left in peace' to do this, it is necessary to esteem any who, however feebly and for whatever reason, seek to do this, so 'believing their report', as being stricken of God, just as with Kierkegaard's geese. The prosperity and respectability, of the lives of such as Hannah, were the equivalent of 'signs', proving the truth of the Christian religion, *against* the sayings of Jesus.

The motives, for Jeremiah's behaving as he did, were, at best, mixed. One might have been his reading of the fourth Gospel as a child. That would provide grounds for seeing anyone, in later life, as being 'stricken of God'. A fundamental reason was his inadequacy and immaturity. There was another. He had used the sayings of Jesus and the prophets, and the biting sarcasm of Kierkegaard's parable, flinging them in the teeth of churchgoers. There was justice in his being so reduced, that he was left with them, alone, as the basis for his life. That, at least, gave truth to his words. He was, unwillingly, being obliged to do the truth. That was not his intention or wish. He had overlooked the fact that Jesus had said that it was blessed when men hated and despised one and said all manner of 'evil' against one falsely, for his sake. He averted his eyes from words like, "He that hates his life in this world shall have eternal life". Yet there is clear sense in this. Death is the only certainty.

Uberrimae seemed to be caught in two minds; more so, it seemed, than his daughter. As his last words with Jeremiah shewed, much of him wanted to believe as Jeremiah had come to do, or speak. He had striven to restore the marriage, but it had to be on his terms, with Jeremiah as his 'client', indebted to him for everything. Otherwise, as I pointed out, Jeremiah would ever be in a position to cause embarrassment. He had to be brought back within the accepted conversation of the 'judges and dividers'.

The inevitable lack of openness between Uberrimae and Hannah made things impossible of resolution. He might use 'stick and carrot' and advise Jeremiah, with the promise that, if he took his advice, the marriage would be restored, but Hannah would not go along with that. On the other hand, Hannah might, in the moment of utterance, as when she promised to restore the marriage if Jeremiah let the case go through, genuinely have sought a restoration. She, then, would have to justify it to her parents.

At the heart of all was attendance on the services of the Church. If Jeremiah went about pointing to the hypocrisy of such activities, he implicitly alleged it against Hannah, her father and friends. He could understand why Uberrimae, according to his elder son, hated the Australian, and hated the idea of Hannah marrying him. Jeremiah would then have nothing left to lose. Hannah would be stuck. She, with her Churchgoing friends, would provide a perfect symptom of the hypocrisy of the Christian religion, especially that of the established Church.

Those who upheld the Christian religion would speak easily of such hypocrisy. "Of course", they would say, "We are bound to be hypocritical. We all are, but God understands our weaknesses". They would speak of the many reforms that had taken place, shewing progress in eliminating the hypocritical ways of the past. There was shiftiness in this smug optimism. Those who spoke thus, tended to speak of returning to the ways and beliefs of the primitive Church. This to took them to the teachings of S Paul, rather than those of the Jesus, conveniently by-passing the gospels. The sayings of Jesus in the gospels were now available in accessible form to most, if not all. Were those of the Christian religion any more inclined to 'learn from him', than in the past?

Jesus did not regard hypocrisy lightly. It his one sustained indictment against the upholders of the religion of his people. If, as those of the Christian religion assert, there is forgiveness for all our sins and wickednesses, what purpose was there in Jesus crying Woe to you Scribes and Pharisees? Jesus did not say that there was forgiveness for every sin. He was clear that, for one, there was no forgiveness, neither in this world nor that which is to come. It seems mysterious; or can be *made* to seem so. "But for the blasphemy against the Holy Spirit of God there is no forgiveness....." . In the ten commandments, one is without forgiveness, "The Lord will not hold guiltless him that takes his name lightly".

If those, who declare themselves to be his disciples, set aside his words, while declaring him to be God of God and Light of light.......being of one substance with the Father", what else are they doing? They are led, in doing so, by the Ministers of the Gospel, the Scribes, Pharisees, Sadducees and teachers of the Law of the Christian religion.

The hypocrisy in the position of Hannah and those around her, because they went to Church, while enjoying and advertising the benefits of men putting asunder, and a life whose foundation was adultery, the swearing of oaths, the bearing of false witness against a neighbour, seemed to trouble nobody within the Christian religion. It irritated and upset Jeremiah, but seemed nothing very 'serious'. It took his acquaintance with a man who said that, while he could not believe in Jesus, because he found it impossible to believe in the supernatural, to make him see it otherwise. The same man said that he regarded Jesus as the greatest teacher the world had ever known. When Jeremiah told some of this story to John Carey, his reaction was unequivocal and vehement. He was shocked at the *hypocrisy* of Hannah and her friends. He was shocked at the hypocrisy of the Christian religion. It seemed that this man, who did not believe in God and, therefore, not in Jesus, learned more from him than those who declared belief. How could those who made public declaration that they believed Jesus to have been raised from the dead, not only refuse 'learn of him', but advertise the fact that it was better not to do so?

Jesus' words, about blaspheming the Holy Spirit of God, were provoked by the allegation that he cast out demons by Beelzebub, prince of demons. Those making this allegation faced an acute problem. The words of Jesus were 'followed' by 'works such as no man could do, save God be with him'. Theirs were not.

What, then, of his being raised from the dead? Those of the Christian religion, who led and encouraged such as Hannah, openly, to advertise the benefit of setting aside his words, must imply that he was raised from the dead by Beelzebub. Jeremiah came to see the truth of Jesus' fearful word to those who had once been his disciples, "Ye are of your father, the devil......".

Carey's comments, in a letter to Jeremiah, in which he also expressed his disgust at the 'shifty accommodations' made by the upholders of the Christian religion, in order to appear 'multi-cultural' and achieve 'political correctness', entirely changed his perception of the matter. He said that, 'as he understood it', Jesus claimed, exclusively, to be the way to God. There could be no doubt that he was right. Jesus said, clearly and unambiguously, "no man comes to the Father except through me". Pondering this letter, Jeremiah recalled the late Anwar Sadat, assassinated by Muslim fanatics for being a peacemaker. On that basis, if all that one knew of Anwar Sadat was that he died as a peacemaker, had he not been 'brought to the Father' by the one who said, "Blessed the Peacemakers, they shall be called children of God?" Jeremiah decided that he wanted to know no more of the late Anwar Sadat.

Jesus spoke of two ways, one of which was entered by a narrow gate and was, itself, narrow. He did not say that it was steep and rugged. He said, "Take my yoke upon you and *learn* of me, for I am meek and lowly of heart and you shall find rest unto your souls; for my yoke is *easy* and my burden is *light*". He accused the Scribes and Pharisees of loading men with burdens grievous to be borne. The narrow way led to life everlasting. The alternative was a broad way, which led nowhere but to the vile dump, into which putrefying carcasses and detritus were flung, in the valley of Hinnom; where maggots did not die and fires always smouldered. Seen in those terms, the hypocrisy of the Christian religion and its upholders appears in a different light. They were leading men and women into a broad way, promising many ways to God and eternal life, while pretending that it is the narrow way prescribed by Jesus. That is a cruel deception.

Hannah and those around her were *used* as standing proof that Jesus was wrong to have suggested that a wife who divorced her husband and married another commits adultery. That such a respected 'lady' should be thought of doing any such thing was disgusting. Alternatively, she might be seen as proof that 'adultery' was not a dangerous minefield to be avoided. Here was demonstration to all that both God and his 'beloved son' were wrong. One effect of the words and actions of Jeremiah was to rob them of their 'innocence'. Thanks to his behaving and speaking as he did, neither Hannah, nor those associated with her, could claim to be ignorant of what the one, whose disciples they publicly claimed to be, said about these things. Jesus had been vehement, "Because ye say we see/know, your sin abides".

Hannah and her circle were symptoms, as Gomer, of the faithlessness of 'Israel'. Jeremiah's attitudes forced the accredited upholders of the Christian religion to argue against the truth of the words of the very one, whose representatives they claimed to be. In retrospect, he came to see the shocking effect of his constantly being reduced to a shambling idiot. It led his adversaries to advance their arguments against the truth of Jesus' words with greater and greater assurance. To substantiate their own words, they need those, such as Hannah, whose works provide 'signs' that the sayings of Jesus had 'passed away'. They do not need any who might imply the opposite. Jeremiah did not wish to be cast in the role he found himself playing. It was the only one he was capable of. He knew that, 'prophesying in my name', brought no gain to those who did so. They were told, "Depart from me, I know you not.....". If he had found it possible to play any other role, he would have done so.

It was a meeting with some, who had formerly been his disciples, that draws forth Jesus' greatest indignation. He provokes them, saying, "If ye abide in my words, then are you truly my disciples". They reply with words, designed to offend. His response was a tirade, "Ye are of your father the 'devil', a murderer from the beginning, and the father of all lies. When he speaks a lie he speaks of himself". Such words are shocking and offensive, no less today, than when they were spoken. If it be the truth, that one narrow way, alone, leads to eternal life; those who declare belief, are assuring all that there are many others. If the other ways lead only to the dunghill, are such words not justified, however offensive they may be?

These thoughts cascaded into Jeremiah's mind, in the years following the events I have described, but into his mind alone. All other 'senses' found them repugnant, as he found the vehement denunciation of his former disciples by Jesus repugnant, with any other faculty but his mind. It took a letter from John Carey, and the events that followed, to make him see it with 'heart and soul and strength' as well.

Chapter Twenty Six

"Going two miles"

Having been led to see what problems were caused for a plaintiff and the administration of 'justice' by giving one's cloak as well, Jeremiah was taught what problems were caused by going two miles when bidden to go one. He continued to work in the restaurant for a couple of years; but the happy relationship, on which it had begun, became soured, when the head waitress sought to direct it. There had been something of a contretemps, and he had been summarily dismissed. He found work with Clifford, supplementing his income with water-colours. He then obtained work as breakfast cook at a big hotel on the riverside. It belonged to a huge brewery and catering company, but was managed by an Austrian called Fred, one of the kindest men alive.

Fred came from Linz. With some friends, he had come to Britain, not long after the war, and settled on Herm. At one time there were more people from Linz on the Island than natives. There he had met his wife, Pat, who came from Norwich. They had moved up to Norfolk and settled there. Fred took no great trouble to acquire an English accent, but both he and Nando understood everything that was said. Jeremiah learned from them that there were great advantages in being a resident alien, one of which was that one was not burdened with heritage, one could enjoy as much of it as one wanted. Another was that one was not burdened with involvement in politics. Knowing Fred and Nando confirmed what he had learned through Derek. There was an advantage in being disdained. Because they had obviously foreign accents, many Englishmen took such people as being stupid.

Fred made him see was that it was futile to adopt postures of defiance with huge companies. Other managers would bluster about standing up to them. Fred did not indulge in this. He noted that, when they met senior management, the bluster evaporated. He worked at running the hotel, as if it were his own, and did all that 'those in Moses seat commanded', while not doing after their works. He delivered good profits, but while doing so, made a burrow for himself under their rules and regulations.

There was a large bar, with three tills. When he cashed up every evening, Fred never counted the floats. All he did was to 'ring in', to get the day's takings, remove that amount, and let the float 'care about itself'. It saved counting all the small change, and meant that his day's takings were always right. The company bought a lot of electronic tills, which were not designed for use in bars. On these, one could not obtain a figure for the day's takings without first counting what was in the till, and ringing it in. The till then told one what one should have taken. This not only meant that the takings were no longer bound to be accurate, it involved Fred in having to count the small change every night, which could take an hour. Instead of raising objections, Fred set his mind to finding a way round it.

He noticed that there was a button on the till for a half penny. Pubs do not use half pennies. In adapting the tills, the half penny did not register on the till roll. He rang in one half penny as his day's takings. The till obligingly told him what he should have taken.

One evening, Fred told Jeremiah that it was necessary to attend confession once or twice before being married. Jeremiah was incredulous. "You mean to tell me that you went to confession, Guv'nor?" "Of course not", said Fred, "You pay a taxi driver to go for you and come back with a certificate!"

Jeremiah began cooking the breakfasts, also acting as relief chef. Just before Whitsun, the head chef left and went to a bigger position. Fred walked into the kitchen, "Would you take over?" Jeremiah felt honoured; but it was a kind of catering of which he had no experience. There was a monthly audit and stock check. They had to meet percentage targets. The rule of thumb was that 60% of the turnover in food had to be profit. There was a restaurant, serving breakfast, lunches and dinners. There were also bar snacks, and food had to be supplied to a river boat, moored outside. Fred was well organised. He had a list of everything ordered from each supplier, so it was only a matter of going round the stocks each week and making a list. Even with this, it was beyond Jeremiah. Fred went round with him.

He decided to behave childishly. Any idiot could go two miles when told to go one: if he did that, he thought that his Heavenly Father would take care of the profit margins. Sweets and other things, previously bought in, he started to make himself. It cost the company little. The materials used were not expensive, but the labour was costly, or would be if it were paid. It meant that they could either cut the prices, or, since the brewery printed the menus, make a greatly increased margin of profit. On some occasions the profit margin went up to over 80%.

There was not a lot of business in the winter, so he decided to use a few pounds of his own money to provide some unusual dishes. First, he laid on additions to breakfast, as they had regular business residents. It cost only a few pence to offer additional items, which customers enjoyed. He started doing the same in the evenings, buying things like pheasants from local poachers. These were put on as special dishes, very cheaply. As he bought the birds or game, the profit margins were enormous. The regular residents found it fun, and one or two more from the same company came. The result was, Fred said, that, for the first time since the war, the hotel carried a profit forward from the winter. Jeremiah learned from this that if, even in a large company, someone worked on that basis, it could lead the higher management to misconstrue the situation.

Imagine a business, which depends on skilled work. The man in the workshop is paid a salary, and given a key. Unknown to the owners, he does many hours for which he is not paid. The owners will feel that the high productivity results from their policies. They can either undercut rivals, make larger profits, or both. On this basis they might borrow money to expand. All might be well, until the man in the workshop moved away. Then there would be a problem. They would either need to raise their prices, or accept reduced profits. If they did the former, their customers might be driven away. They would not control their own business.

An owner might be angry with the worker, who had led him to misconstrue the facts. "You have put me into a muddle. You had no business to work all those extra hours without telling me. I took on a bank loan, on the strength of the profits we were making; now I have either to raise prices and turn work away, or take on an extra worker". The owner had been glad enough of five years unpaid work. He would be in a position analogous to someone hiring staff from an agency, who worked according to the standards set by the agency. Whatever the owner may pay them, the agency says, "Do twice the hours you are paid for, and we'll take care of you". Imagine the son of a vastly wealthy parent being told, "Do double what you are paid for. Don't worry, I will see that you are all right". That was the basis on which Jesus gave such instructions. It would leave everyone in a managerial position in a muddle. In the same way, it would leave them in a muddle, if highly qualified employees 'took the lowest place'.

It would be the more embarrassing, if managers were to go about, giving talks to others on their successful methods of running a business. If they were upholders of the Christian religion, the departed worker, who 'went two miles', might say, "I only did what you say all should do." "Whenever did I suggest that you should do twice as much as you were told to do?" The employee could reply, "You say that, every time you declare belief in One Lord Jesus Christ".

Those who rule might be led to misconstrue evidence. It appears that England was, in days gone by, a law abiding and forbearing society. Rulers would attribute this to their policies. It might, however, have been that they were given a forbearing and law abiding people, because people "feared God and walked in his ways", nothing to do with the antics of their rulers, "performing such tricks before high heaven as make the angels weep". These were the high days of Mrs Thatcher, 'Victorian Values', and the law of the market. She decreed that schools and hospitals be put on a market basis. If independent schools could be self sufficient, why not those in the State sector, if, as it were, the government paid the fees? Anyone thinking in that way could be misled by a handful of people believing in God, and following the instructions of his only begotten son.

The head of classics at Jeremiah's school had died after lunch, aged 92. Two hours before, he had been teaching the sixth form Greek. He was a considerable scholar of exceptionally lively mind. For the past 25 years and more he had probably cost the school virtually nothing. He knew of a school, whose headmistress worked for an assistant teacher's salary. Others had to be told to pay in their monthly salary cheques. They were unmarried and lived in the College. Mr Hart, not only gave such as himself free tutorials once a week, he taught in the faculty, he was Dean of Chapel in his College, and admissions tutor, as well as running sundry clubs and societies. He could have held a Chair in almost any

University in the English-speaking world. The finances of the school, of which Jeremiah was a governor, were run by one of the governors for nothing. Though they would not have made much of it, such people would have expected anyone to realise that, as they had received freely, they gave freely. So far from robbing others of earnings, they seemed actually to facilitate prosperity for those around them, as did the Abbey at Buckfast; as, in a small way, did Jeremiah at the hotel. The dining room remained open throughout the winter.

The same could be replicated in hospitals. Many a nurse had been paid a pittance, but came from a well to do family. Others, less fortunate, would give freely of their time. No planner could take this into account. Rulers of people are in no position to turn their servants to the sayings of Jesus. They would risk having them returned on them. Having a patronised Church, whose clergy were upholders of the established order, telling the labouring poor of the blessing of poverty, meekness and of hungering and thirsting for righteousness, might have contributed much to the country's prosperity. For investors and collectors, it is useful to have lesser folk warned against 'laying up for themselves treasure on earth'. What, then, if such teaching were taken away?

Jeremiah began to see, if dimly at this time, how extraordinary was the grasp of the 'law and the prophets', in the sayings of Jesus. It is of a different order from that of the evangelists themselves. In this aspect alone, he manifestly gathered up the insistence of the Deuteronomist, that Israel was the least of all people and that the Lord set his love upon them for that reason. If they prospered, it could be thanks to God alone. They were not even to 'say in their heart, Mine hand and the strength of mine arm hath gotten me this wealth'. The prophet Jeremiah wrote to the exiles telling them to seek the good of the land in which they dwelt. No great power wants to find that its economic well-being depends on people, dwelling among them, who do not share and uphold its beliefs and are regarded as beings of a lower order. This has, it seems, ever been the problem of Israel, as a dispersed people. The Egyptians found it so. So, if Tacitus be right, did the Romans. The Nazis resented the economic influence of international 'Jewry'. As found in the Gospels, Jesus translated this perception into a language that was 'exportable'.

It seemed that there had been almost a 'trick' played on mankind by the writing of the gospels. The Christian religion had established itself and spread rapidly, before they appeared. As a religion it did not need them. They had been carried in its hold as smuggled cargo, almost explosive devices, buried in its foundations. The more that was built upon those foundations, the more disastrous would be the consequences of their detonation.

Until the latter part of the nineteenth century, few seemed to see the gospels, as, in any way, exceptional within the New Testament, or even the Bible. Then came a flurry of lives of Jesus. Many of the less critical ones had been written, as if, rightly understood, the life and teaching of Jesus led inevitably to the established Church of England. It was a captivating delusion. Thanks to such as

Kierkegaard, Tolstoy, Schweitzer and others, the figure of Jesus in the gospels came to be seen as altogether less amenable than anyone thought. Upholders of the established Christian religion seem, then, to have backed away. In so doing, the Church's worship became much more 'religious', the largely instructional services of Matins and Evensong, falling into disuse.

Israel yearned for the coming of the Lord's anointed, but decisively refused to identify that one with Jesus, as found in the gospels. The Christian religion asserts that the 'Christ' had come, and would return in glory, but refuses to identify the promised one with Jesus, as described in the four gospels, whose teaching might have been said to have been rediscovered in the nineteenth century. There were sects that took fundamentalist views with regard to almost any words in the Bible. None applied this to anything said by Jesus. His seem to be the only words, ever reported, that were not of God.

Aside from being hard work, life was good. Fred allowed him to keep Golden Copper on the mooring assigned to the manager. He went sailing whenever he had a day off, often sleeping aboard. Pat said that, while moaning about the loss of his wife, he was a walking argument in favour of divorce. After Christmas in his second year, Fred had to lay off staff. Since most were on short time anyway, the saving was small. Jeremiah suggested that he laid him off instead. Fred jumped at it. Jeremiah had not had a break of any kind for almost two years, so abandoned his flat and went to stay with his old dad. He was now in his eighties, but fit and strong. Derek transported him and Sadie to Sheringham. As the old Dog turned to go, he said piously, "I think that it is my duty to ensure that the old man lives out his days in his own home". It was easy to say. Little did he think that his old dad, a heavy smoker, would die of "old age" at 98! Thus he ceased working at the hotel on a full time basis, but returned for three days to help at the weekends and give the new chef a day off. Living the rest of the week with his dad, he was once again in the ambit of the established Church, surrounded by devoted churchgoers, for the first time in over ten years.

Among the extra staff taken on for the summer at the hotel, was a lass in her twenties. One evening, when he was cleaning down the kitchen, she came in and said, with some fervour, "You used to be a professor of religion, or so they say. What does it all mean?" He pointed out that he was never a professor of anything. She had been upset by something and had been to the football ground to hear Billy Graham. It was after 11pm, and Jeremiah wanted to get finished.

When he got home he pondered the matter, and decided to write an essay, which he felt was unquestionably true. He had little understanding of religion. What he did understand of it he did not care for. On the other hand, faith in Jesus was simple. If anyone believed in him, all they need do was to acquaint themselves with what he said, and seek to act on that basis. They need not have any great knowledge. It was only necessary to act on the basis of what they did understand, as each saying almost contained all others. The more one did that, he thought, the more anyone would come to understand. The crux was to regard his words as final and incontrovertible, whether one understood them or not. If, for example, one heard him say, "As we also have forgiven those indebted to us", there was an end of it. One simply acted on that basis. If one did one would understand its significance.

An incident with Fred in the bar had led him to see this. Fred had told him that his school had a famous alumnus, Adolph Hitler. There had been some cheerful badinage about the latter, in which Pat had said that they often felt that Fred was a descendant. Jeremiah had thrown in the comment that the Guv'nor and Adolph were old school chums. Since Fred was only a couple of years older than himself, he thought the remark so preposterous that nobody could believe it. An hour later, time was called, but the bar was still quite full. One or two asked if they could have another drink. Fred said "No". This had given rise to some nasty comments about gutless little Nazis. "If you had stood up to him" we would not have had to fight a war to sort it out for you...". Fred just smiled. Jeremiah wondered whether his badinage had given rise to these nasty comments.

Such thoughtless remarks, made without malice, might easily lead to someone scrawling graffiti on Fred's walls. That could lead to even nastier things. If he and Fred been ten years older, they would have been aiming bullets at each other. The same applied to Nando. Here were two men who had been good friends to him. They needed only to put on uniforms, and be caricatured as Nazis or Limeys, for them to have been killing each other, as in Hardy's poem. Jesus' said, "You have heard it said by those of old, "Thou shalt not kill"......but I say to you that whoever calls his brother, 'Moron'......".

There had been chat in the bar about penalties. Fred had argued that anyone taking a life should pay with his life. This greatly disturbed Jeremiah with his memory of his grandfather's nooses. He could not gainsay Fred's argument. Whatever was the truth? He lay awake thinking about it. It occurred to him, "Let whoever among you is faultless cast the first stone." There was nothing more to be said. Nobody was faultless, especially if Jesus' comment about being angry was heard. He fell asleep.

It was on that basis that he left his essay in an envelope for the young lass. The result was not what he had expected. A week or so later, she reappeared, having obviously received a fairly savage blow on the side of her face. It turned out that she had been out one evening and returned late. Her stepfather had rebuked her, saying, "We have tried to give you a good Christian home." The lass had replied, "In that case before trying to remove a speck from my eye, should you not remove the plank from your own!" Jeremiah had not foreseen anything like that. She had obtained a copy of the Gospels and simply read one. As soon as he sought to back away from what he had written, she rounded on him. "If that is what you think, you're a fake".

She was right. She went on to speak of what she had read, as if she were there. "Don't tell me that he did not say it, because he did". It was as if, thanks to his essay, she had gone to Capernaum and heard Jesus speak, seen him heal a leper, open the eyes of the blind and cast out a demon. It was like a boomerang returning and striking him in the face. She taught him more of the consequences of the gospels, in a couple of months, than anyone, before or since.

It would be so, for anyone who actually heard Jesus speak, sitting on the hillside, or at a lakeside. Whether or not, as we have it, the Sermon on the Mount represents a pastiche, it is doubtless representative of his teachings, and is a complete 'package'. It ends "whoever hears these sayings of mine and does them is like one who built his house on rock....." Anyone hearing those words would be entitled to think that he or she needed no more. What, then, of the Christian religion, in the midst of which he now lived? If such as the lass at the hotel had done as she read or heard, for the rest of her days, saying simply "Yes, yes", it would not gain her membership of any sect or denomination of the Christian religion. She would need much more besides. She would need to learn hymns and prayers, creeds and all sorts of other things. This would apply to any who had heard Jesus speak, and done as he said.

If any followed Jesus and learned from him, and abode in his words, no religion, or other society that upheld any kind of belief, would accept them. No religion on earth would find Jesus' words acceptable. No political party could do other than cast them out. Those concerned with the environment would find them the most unacceptable words ever uttered. The seemingly careless attitude towards the immediate future would be anathèma to any concerned with the long term future of 'planet earth'. For the next month or two the lass attached herself to him.

The stark contrast between the demand of the gospels and that of the Christian religion, led him to buy an old duplicator and produce a stream of papers. He sat at his typewriter, and typed directly onto stencils. He would continue all day, sometimes falling asleep as he did so. He would waken and continue where he had left off, without even reading the last sentence. The first, he called "Let's play Monopoly". It was a parable of life in the accepted 'conversation' of the Christian religion and the world. While the game is being played, the money and properties took on reality. If a player did not enter into this 'reality', it spoiled it for the others.

Successful players always wanted to prolong the game, and would lend to those losing. When 'Mum' put her head round the door saying, "Bedtime in five minutes", those with good properties would beg for longer. The one with only the Old Kent Road, Waterworks, and a couple of stations, would long to pack up. All was put back in the box, and others would play with equally strong belief in it all.

The next was entitled, "Let's play charades", and took up the pantomime quality of the observances of the religion. Another took the view that the Rich Young man did sell all, and went and followed Jesus. In writing this he felt he had solved one problem. He felt sure that he did as commanded, and that this was the beloved disciple, the source of the IVth gospel. In another he asked how it might be, if someone went and did as he heard Jesus say. Receiving a summons for his 'coat', he 'gave his cloak as well'. It would set him against his wife and in laws, his own parents and children as well. Hearing what Jesus said about praying, he refused to pray in any public place, but only secretly in his inner room. He would be at odds with the members of the synagogue and his own family. If, then, he rebutted their arguments by appealing to the Rabbi from Nazareth, he might end up saying, "How is it that, if he is wrong, he opens the eyes of the blind, whereas you do not?" He would be in the position of the man born blind in the IVth Gospel.

It would be somewhat different in the churches today. The signal difference is that, whereas those of the synagogues did not declare belief in one Lord *Jesus* Christ, those of the Churches do. That led to another paper, which recalled Jesus' words about those of Chorazin and Bethsaida. If the men of Sodom and Gomorrah had seen the mighty works that they had seen, they would have repented long ago in dust and ashes. Those of Judea and Galilee had seen the eyes of the blind opened, lepers cleansed, the lame walk. Those of the Christian religion claimed to have witnessed the empty tomb, seen Jesus transfigured and clothed with light, heard the voice from the cloud saying "This is my son, the beloved, hear ye him", and been left with Jesus *only.* They had seen the storm stilled, and bore witness that they had seen the angel Gabriel visit the Virgin Mary. It was a short step to translate the events of the gospel to the contemporary world of belief.

He wrote of the amazing reply of Jesus to those who would stone the woman, caught in the act of adultery. Given the circumstances, such a reply was no less miraculous than stilling a storm. He imagined it being the Gospel read out at the Holy Communion, and the subject of a sermon. After the service a group met for discussion. The subject was 'crime and punishment'. The assembled company produced all manner of arguments to shew that transgressors should suffer penalties. After half an hour of such argument, someone, hitherto silent, recalled them to the words, "Let whoever is faultless among you ....". So far from silencing all, it would provoke more argument, against those words. All present had, an hour before, thanked God for 'this, thy glorious gospel'. Having done so, they stood and declared belief in the one who spoke those words, as "of one substance with the Father....". Those who were driven away in silence made no such declarations. The more anyone is provoked to argue against those words, the more deeply entrenched becomes their hostility toward them, and whoever upholds their truth. "They would esteem him, "stricken of God". He would be 'stricken for our offences.......'. That was the effect of Jesus' teaching on his contemporaries. It is so today.

He circulated his papers around every Bishop and Churchmen of all denominations, who had their names in official year-books. The responses saddened him. Three Bishops, assisted, it seems, by their wives, returned his letters in unstamped envelopes, with notes on the back, "You can pay for your unsolicited mail to come back to you, and you won't know who returned it!" The address on the front was in different writing from the note on the back. One

Bishop wrote favourably and enclosed a cheque, asking him to be sure to send any further papers, as he considered them the most honest theology he had read; John Baker of Salisbury. Charlie Moule wrote that he found them awesome, for the power of language and that of truth.

Down the south aisle of Norwich Catheral, they were busy selling certificates, which proclaimed that a named person had contributed a number of pounds; so had maintained the cathedral for so many seconds or minutes. There was much chatter and clatter. He produced a paper, recalling the eviction of those that bought and sold in the Temple. This he deposited in the Cathedral, interleaving it into the piles of newsletters stacked on tables. The response of the Dean was indignant.

He wrote that if he ever did such a thing again he would take legal action. What followed baffled and saddened Jeremiah. "Do you not realise that, if there were no money changers and dove sellers, there could be no house of prayer for anyone?" Jeremiah replied, asking the Dean if he thought Jesus, himself, too stupid not to have realised that. If that were the case, it did not say much for God either, since by the Dean's declaration, he raised this man from the dead. As to threatening legal action, he reminded the Dean that Jesus had done rather more than leave a few duplicated papers around. He repeated this in S Paul's, Westminster Abbey, and Canterbury Cathedral, relating the pantomime nature of the observation of Christmas to the accounts of the birth of Jesus in the Gospels. He also circulated them round various parishes in the Diocese of Norwich. The Vicar of Bale returned his paper, re-using his own envelope, with no stamp. He wrote on it, "unsolicited communication, return to sender". Jeremiah replied that this was apt. It was the clergyman's attitude to the "Word made Flesh", an unsolicited communication. Return to sender.

Meanwhile his dad, aunt and their friends were going off to Church. He was expected to wake his dad up and get him ready, and got told off sternly if ever he failed. All rejoiced, when a new rector reverted to the old Prayer Book, with its solemn recitation of the Ten Commandments. It was "high time that the young were given proper moral guidance". "Do you mean that all should learn to do no manner of work on Saturdays?" "Don't be so damned silly". "But that is the law, you pray to be written on your hearts. Do you mean that all should be discouraged from making or bowing to any kind of graven image? Your church is full of the things and you bow to them. It's a veritable shrine to the art of the image maker!" "Don't be such a bloody fool. They are reminders of the truth".

He went and got a Prayer Book, "It adds, 'Nor the likeness of anything in heaven or earth, or in the waters under the earth'. Should I stop doing that?" "Of course not: you silly fool. He went and fetched one of his paintings. "Is not this an attempt at a likeness of something in heaven or earth?" "Well of course it is." With that he destroyed it, and ceased painting pictures. Doing so in a house that belonged to someone, who declared these things forbidden of God, was like living with a judge, and storing stolen goods in the garage.

A retired clergyman, whose wife had been in hospital, used to call on his dad. He was diabetic; his wife needed a special diet. Could Jeremiah help? He ferried meals up to their house. The wife had taken up painting, finding it therapeutic. She had been a Sunday school teacher, and sent him a note drawing his attention to a remark in a commentary, which explained that graven image making did not apply to making statues, still less to making pictures.

When he went up to their house to deliver something, she took the matter up. "God", she purred, "Does not intend people to waste their talent. Surely you know the parable". "Yes" he said, "but the *parable* concerned money, of which a talent was a large sum. All you do is to change the terms of the metaphor, and 'leave it in a parable'. The parable is a description of a well-known business practice. A man with money sets people up in business, tells them how to trade, then returns for an audit. It's a perfect metaphor for the word of God. Trade with it and more will be provided, put it aside and all will taken away". This was waved aside. "You cannot believe that God forbad the making of any likeness of anything".

"No, of course I do not, nor does the Hebrew imply that. It implies that the image is the likeness, "Thou shalt not make to thyself any kind of graven image, the likeness of anything......." "Why are you being so silly about it then?" "Because it is what *you all say* in Church. Those commandments were given to Israel...You say that we live under the New Covenant". "Oh don't be silly, you must understand that, when God says that we must not make a graven image or likeness of anything, he does not mean that we should not make images or likenesses........".

The purring smugness of the woman incensed Jeremiah. He replied, "Are you telling me that *my Father* in *Heaven* is like a third rate student who cannot put his thoughts into words?" The effect of his use of that phrase on the former Sunday School Teacher was electric; "You blaspheming little beast". Outside the house he stood and wept bitterly.

The confrontation taught him more of the early years of Jesus, than could all the commentaries in the world. The former Sunday school teacher had, doubtless, assured many that all were God's children, as did the Rabbis. It took him back to his confirmation. He thought of the words of the opening of the Fourth Gospel, "to them gave he the power to become the children of God", the words of Jesus in the Sermon, "Ye shall be children of your Father which is in heaven", and his injunction to "Call no man on earth thy Father, for all have but one Father which is in heaven". He related all of this to the story of the virgin birth. It became the subject of more papers.

His daughter wrote a touching letter, saying how horrid it must be to lose one's children, especially one's own, (she having been adopted). Jeremiah was stunned. What could he say to her to assure her that it made no difference whatever? He wrote several letters, but threw them away. He wrote, "Call no man on earth thy father, for all have but one Father even in heaven", and, having done so, put the matter from his mind. He was beginning to see that the words and life of Jesus were 'redemptive', or a 'ransom'. His death sealed them with finality.

There was an ironic aftermath. Some days later, the clergyman husband dropped in on his dad for coffee. He said that if Jeremiah was not going to continue painting, his wife might be glad of some of his sable-hair brushes, as they were very expensive to buy!

Chapter Twenty Seven

" Paracetamol, Broken Legs and salvation by the Poll Tax"

Jeremiah became more and more disillusioned. All that he had been driven to see in the gospels provoked angry argument. No churchgoer would give any positive assurance of their truth. Having declared belief, they retracted it, when it came to anything Jesus said: 'If people did that sort of thing, it would be the end of civilised life'. He would drive up to see Roland. He took his old dad as far as Durham, leaving him with his sister, and set out for Edinburgh. It was as if he stood with Elijah, when he went to Horeb, "What are you doing here?" He turned his car around and headed south. The next day he collected his old dad, and they returned.

He stayed a night with his elder son, then a medical student in London. His son was not feeling well at the time, but went out with some friends. Jeremiah took them in his car. He, then, put his papers in Westminster Abbey, S Paul's and Canterbury Cathedrals. His son hoped, above all, that he had not inherited his dad's genes. Jeremiah returned, disconsolate. Was there nobody, who would give any reassurance of the truth of the words of the one, in whom all declared belief? Nobody seemed even to think that anything said by Jesus, the single most determinative figure in the history of mankind, had final significance. Could all be sure that there was, in reality, no God, while standing and declaring that he had raised Jesus from the dead?

Those, who set up the ancient hospitals and medical schools, had done so in an attempt to follow his teachings. The same was true of the ancient universities and many schools. The establishment of the health service, as indeed many industrial reforms, owed as much to people who sought to follow the teaching of Jesus, as to any socialist doctrines. Mr Churchill had said that the war had been fought to defend 'Christian civilisation'. Bertie Wooster had recalled the words, "To him that has (faith) shall be given. From him that has not shall be taken even that which he has". Jeremiah recalled the warning in the book of Deuteronomy, "Beware lest thou begin to say in thine heart, My hand and the strength of mine arm that hath gotten me this wealth". He trembled at the thought that, as a society, even that which we had might be taken away.

People are ready to turn to the Gospel when all else fails. It changes when the crisis is over. When the brother of one of his son's friends had a serious accident and was long comatose, his son asked Jeremiah to write to him to give him hope. When Jeremiah was working at the hotel, his elder son was travelling about Europe picking grapes and tomatoes. The barman told Jeremiah that he had phoned him from France. He was in difficulty. That evening, he rang again. There had been chatter with the women, who helped in the kitchen. One had asked, "Do you see anything of your elder boy now?" "No", said Jeremiah, "He will be in touch when he wants something". "He should learn respect. You should teach him a lesson". Jeremiah wondered what lesson she had in mind.

Thieves had broken into the car, in which his son was travelling, and stolen his money. "Could you help, dad?" Jeremiah transferred two or three hundred pounds to his son's account. He could then use his credit card. "You should have taught him a lesson". Jeremiah thought that he had. When there was a famine in the land, the prodigal had returned to his father. Why had his son had phoned him, not Hannah? She was a hundred times richer than he. Was it that his son 'knew where he was' with Jeremiah and could have the 'last word'. If Jeremiah had demanded to be repaid, he could say, "I thought you believed in one who said, "Lend, asking for no return"?

The story told by the evangelists was grotesque. What harm did Jesus do? People were glad to turn to him, when they had diseases that no physician could cure. In films, such people were shewn, bewailing his crucifixion. It would not be thus. In many cases they would have added reason for wanting to be rid of one, who spoke and acted, as did Jesus. He was a threat, or so it would have seemed, to their cherished way of life, as Caiaphas warned. Incurably sick people would have little to lose if there were trouble and the Romans destroyed the city. Restored to health, all would change. They would have a vested interest in preserving the peace. The miraculous healings certified the words spoken by Jesus. Those words were a threat to their cherished traditions, as they are to all such traditions, even to this day. They would see it as, 'in their best interest', to distance themselves from the one to whom they owed their health.

It would not be hard to do. "I saw through him. He was a charlatan. Such diseases get better. It was God who healed me, not that man". That, in a sense, is true. It could give 'theological' justification. "God would not have restored my sight if he did not intend me to make use of it". They might even say, that he cast out demons by Beelzebub. It would provide a ready means by which one join the crowd who cried, 'Crucify'. That others knew that one had been healed by this man might give anyone a stronger urge to dissociate oneself.

Many, attending Churches, are glad enough of those, who might be called, the "least of these my brethren", when all else fails. Once 'on their feet', it pays to dissociate from them. Jeremiah knew this all too well from himself. If Hannah returned, or he had found it possible to resume the kind of employment, he had at the College, he would find it 'in his interest' to distance himself from the friends who had stood by him, without whom he probably would not be alive. The rich young man, alone, sought of Jesus what he came to give, 'eternal life'. That was far from being what Jeremiah sought. He sought the restoration of his family. Once that had been provided, the last man on earth, whose words he would have wanted 'never to pass away', would be Jesus of Nazareth.

He was made to see much by an old dosser, he met in Durham, queuing up for a hand out at the Dole office. Twenty minutes later, he was standing outside a stationer's shop, trying to sell ball-point pens for a high price. Behind him in the shop window were the same ball-points in bargain packs. Having invested all in these packs, the old man could not buy food for himself, nor even tobacco.

When he talked; so far from being poor in spirit, he was vastly rich in spirit. He spoke of becoming wealthy. He would bear down hard on any whom he employed. His desire to be rich increased the pain of his poverty. The 'conversation' of the world tells all that it is blessed to be rich, not just for oneself, but one's children. Was there any other sane 'conversation'? Rich, one could buy a better home, better schooling for one's children, better health care, better holidays and food. One could keep a One Design. One could drive about in a Mercedes, not a rusting old Allegro. The entire sensible 'conversation' came with the package. One could argue that, by buying private health care, one was releasing beds for others in the NHS, for one paid one's taxes too. The same would apply to education for one's children.

One could speak of making a contribution to society, participating in the rule and direction of the lives of others. If one gave much to a school, one might become a governor, and a magistrate. One could do a 'service' by seeking elected office as a councillor. Meekness went out of the window. One had a vested interest in maintaining the 'conversation' and the institutions that upheld it. Any world, in which the pursuit of endless economic growth was the law, must collapse in ruins. There could only be peace in one populated by the meek. In one of his papers, he told of Arthur in Norwich prison. It was used as the basis of a sermon in a Church in Glasgow.

If one sought poverty of spirit, meekness and to 'mourn', might it not be best to find oneself, repeatedly, facing misfortune? Jeremiah recalled the interpretation of the parable of the Sower, and those who, for a while believed, but were choked by the cares and riches of this life. He thought of the terse comment of the IVth evangelist, that Jesus needed nobody to tell him what was in men. What a horrid world this was. He thought of his mother. Well to do relatives were glad enough of her services, when someone was sick. Thereafter she was seen as a lesser being. Even the lass whom he had met at the hotel soon changed her mind. He had no money left. He would end it once and for all. He bought a huge amount of paracetamol. His elder son had told him that if nothing was done within a few hours it was fatal.

He shovelled over 100 pills into his mouth washed down with alcohol, which he was told would enhance their effect. Having done so he hid himself away for several hours, then set out, somewhat unsteadily to walk home. He was accosted by a policeman, and taken to hospital. There he delayed matters further. Eventually they pumped him out, took him to another hospital, where he was put to bed with a drip, containing a blocking enzyme, in his arm. Every day they took samples of blood for tests. After two or three days the infusion was finished. The Registrar drew the screens around his bed. He told him that the overdose was too massive and the treatment too late to have had any effect. He was sorry but he would be in hospital for a very long time. The next day a doctor, a long time friend of the family, visited him, and explained his position in even more blunt terms.

Jeremiah was content. He wanted to die. He felt deceived and cheated by those who stood up in public and declared belief in One Lord Jesus. Thanks to them he was alone in this world. When shovelling the pills into his mouth, there came into his mind, the promises of Jesus to 'those that believe', in the disputed ending of the second gospel..."If they take of any deadly thing it will not harm them....". That was the last thing he wanted to find true.

The blood tests continued, with the same result. A few days later the house physician returned seeking a further sample. "You had one a few hours ago", said Jeremiah. "There has been a mix up in the lab", said the young physician, who was Singalese. "Your sample shewed 100% perfect liver function and that is impossible". With that he took another. A couple of hours later, he returned. "We cannot believe it, but your liver is perfect". They took further samples and, a couple of days later Jeremiah walked home. It was not what he wanted.

Some time later he received a message from his elder son. He had been unwell and was being sent 'home' for a rest. The medical staff at the hospital suspected either leukaemia, or lymphoma. They were performing tests. Jeremiah could not sleep. At about 3 am, he felt assured that all would be well, and dropped off. He was woken by a loud knocking at the door, but was not pleased to find two 'Witnesses' standing there, holding their Bible. They had called about a fortnight earlier. "Would you be glad to know that everything in this book is true?" "You asked me that last time. Do you believe that yourselves?" "Of course we do".

It chanced that a gallery had sold one of his pictures a few days earlier, so he had a £50 note in his pocket. He produced it, saying, "Have you anything that you've got to do today?" "Only the Lord's work". "Good", said Jeremiah, "Take this and catch the coach to London. It only costs £7 return. You can keep the rest. Get off at Aldgate, cross the road and you will find New Street. Go to number 24 where you will find my son, who is thought to have leukaemia. Lay hands on the sick and they will recover". The witnesses became experts in the manuscript tradition of the gospels, busily consulting the notes in their Bible. "Those verses are absent from all the ancient MSS". Jeremiah was furious. "I thought that you said that you believed everything in this book. How many ancient manuscripts is it missing from?"

"O hundreds was the reply". "I think you'll find it's more like three". With this they turned and left. Jeremiah followed them, asking, "How many more people are you going to batten onto when they are feeling vulnerable?" He returned and consulted such books as the receiver had left to him, producing a paper on the textual variants of the passage. This he deposited in the 'Kingdom Hall'. He then produced a further paper, warning of the way in which people, not only the 'Witnesses', would batten onto people with their doctrines. Once they had their claws into anyone they would not let go. Do not be 'led astray'. There was only one, whose words were those of eternal life. This he posted through almost every letter-box in the town. It gave rise to some unpleasant phone calls, the callers preferring not to say who they were. One young man was so incensed that he flung Jeremiah's paper, wrapped round a clod of mud, through his front door.

He produced two further papers, which he circulated as before. Both related to the disputed ending of the second gospel. In one he argued that, on the basis of the rule of textual criticism, that the 'more difficult the reading, the more probable', those verses would have to be seen as genuine. There were many reasons for scribes in the fourth century omitting them. There were no cogent reasons for adding them. Although these verses were absent from three or four manuscripts of the IVth century, it was unlikely that they were 'made up'. The likelihood was that they stood in earlier manuscripts, from which those that included them, were copied.

He also noted the curious use of the word 'follow', suggesting that those, whom they followed, had no control over the occurrence. This was almost as Jesus himself, where the signs served to certify his words as of God. The promise was, therefore, 'logical.' If the words of Jesus were certified in this way, it would be so for those who spoke and did likewise. He asked, "Would anyone want this to be so?" The answer would, almost certainly, be 'No'. If anyone spoke in such a manner as to recall Jesus' words as true, and found himself 'followed' by such occurrences, whatever would he or she do?

The second paper took a different approach. Such signs could only be 'of God'. The signs, to which the upholders of the Christian religion pointed, as following those who believed: improved 'moral standards' and such like, could be engendered, contrived and even enforced by the thumbscrew and the rack, the stoning of adulteresses and so on. These could be used to uphold the kingdoms of this world, and their rulers' claims to be benefactors. Those promised by Jesus could only be 'of God', and would serve to undermine such claims. The words attributed to Jesus could not be used as the basis of any form of service, at which healings were performed. One favourable response lifted his spirits. It was from his old Hebrew Tutor.

Writing these papers led him so see a crucially important fact in the four Gospels. They were of one accord: the miraculous events followed Jesus, only, as the one who proclaimed the 'Gospel of God'. They certified his words. There was no suggestion that he was, in any way, a miracle-working prodigy beforehand, as was the case in some of the 'apocryphal' gospels, and in Mohammed's account of his childhood.

Those of the established church were happy that the Witnesses were put to shame, but what of Ascension Day? In the Book of Common Prayer, the 'Holy Gospel', set for that day, consists of those disputed verses. The people respond, "Praise be to thee O Lord for this thy glorious gospel". They, then, stand and declare themselves to be those who believe, in words that make the 'faith of the Centurion' seem as nothing. The Centurion did not believe that Jesus was of 'one substance with the Father'. He did not believe that he was conceived by the Holy Ghost and born of the Virgin Mary, or that he was raised from the dead. Once again, there was an answer for everything. 'You must distinguish between faith and belief'. They the same word in Greek. Did it occur to none of those, who assented to these things in public, that some silly child might believe their report? This was the subject of another paper.

His dad had a moped. One Friday morning, Jeremiah was awakened, by much bumping about. His dad was getting up and going out. It was about half past seven. Half an hour, later a policeman appeared. His dad had driven his moped into the back of a parked car, flown over the handle bars through the rear window, to be found unconscious with his head between the front seats. He was in the local hospital. Jeremiah found him in bed, with sixteen stitches in a cut running from the side of his face to the base of his neck. Apart from that he seemed fine, only demanding his pipe, tobacco and matches. Three days later he was home again. He had mistaken the day. Thinking it was Thursday, he had set off to attend the early service for Ascension Day.

An elderly cousin had written to him, many years before. She had no children, but had a few bits of silver that belonged to his grandmother's family. The name had died out, and he had her surname incorporated into his. She, therefore, felt that he should inherit it. He had never met the cousin in his life. He had forgotten all about it, when her god-daughter telephoned him, saying that there was this silver which he could collect, if he came to London.

She lived at Ascot and kept a racing stud. Her husband had a very up-market shop, in Bond Street, where he could collect it. He thought it would be a few odds and ends, so went with a small hold-all on the bus, stopping for lunch with his elder son. When he arrived, there were two hold-alls full. There were enough spoons and forks to sit eighteen people down to a meal, all in Georgian fiddle pattern silver. There were soup ladles, gravy boats and ladles, chafing dishes, sliver jugs and a lovely 'bullet teapot'. Whatever should he do with it? He rang his sons. Neither of them wanted it. The elder suggested that something of value should be given to their sister. He sent her the teapot. Other small items he gave to friends. What about the bulk of the silver? It was the time of the Ethiopian famine. Very secretively (not because of Jesus' instructions,) he decided that it should be sold. Such was its quality; it should go to a London Auction House. He gave it to a friend to take to the Oxfam shop in Norwich, telling her to say not a word.

Unfortunately she told his aunt. Jeremiah found himself facing a rebuke from both the aunt and her daughter. They were family heirlooms. He had no right to do as he had. Both had just returned from Church. He pointed out that Jesus had warned against 'laying up for oneself treasure on earth'. That was dismissed angrily, as was a reminder of what Jesus had said to the rich young man. Jeremiah had not sold *all* that he had and given to the poor. Whatever did this churchgoing mean, if one then turns on anyone who, however feebly, seeks to do as the one, in whom all declare belief, demanded? His younger son said that he was wicked to believe, as he did, that the words of Jesus, only, were those of eternal life, not those of S Paul or anyone else.

One evening, there was a knock at the door. There stood Peter Noble. It was not the immaculately dressed, urbane Peter that he remembered from the Wine Merchants, but a somewhat dishevelled figure. Peter said that he had been very silly and knew of only one man, who was himself such a fool, that he could not look down on him. He had had some difficulty 'domestically' and had taken an overdose. He could not face returning home, he felt so foolish. All that he had left in the world was piled in his car, which was not very large. What Peter said was to have great significance for Jeremiah. I will return to it in another context.

His dad was taken to stay for a few weeks in Durham. Jeremiah had been with him for about five years. All said that he should keep his marriage vows. How could he do this? It was, as with everything else, a good idea in general terms, but not when made specific.

His sister left him some money to have a break himself. He spent it on a coach fare to Bristol where the Baker now lived. He intended to go on from there to see Hannah, taking the faithful Sadie with him. Having no money left, he had to walk from Bristol. He would see his daughter again.

He reached Newton Abbott. It was autumn and cold at night. He was hungry and had no money; sat on a park bench, with his dog beside him. On the opposite side of the road were fish and chip shops, take-aways and burger bars. The smell was painful. A shadow fell on him and he looked up. There stood a lad in his twenties holding out a bag.

"Here you are mate, I got you this". In the bag was a double cheeseburger. "You did not get that for me, you bought it for yourself," said Jeremiah. "No, I didn't; here's my supper", he said, producing another bag. "How very kind of you", said Jeremiah. "No it's not", said the lad, "I know what it's like".

He would have been happy to have given him a blanket on the settee in his room, but dared not risk it, as he had only moved in that day, and did not know how the landlady would react. He had £40, Jeremiah could have £20, if it would help. He would get another giro in a day or two. He had been released from nick that morning.

Here was a lad just out of prison, who was ready to share half of his entire wealth. Jeremiah knew well that he would never have done such a thing for anyone, though the old Dog might. What of those who sent the lad to prison? They would be the kind of people Jeremiah would associate with, had he not been reduced to such a state. What of those who went to Church, and spoke of eternal life and of the parable of the sheep and the goats? If there were to be judgement, that lad, whatever those who condemned him said, had given food to one who was hungry, and offered half of all his money to one who was poor. He imagined the terrible day of judgement. There would be the lad, with the righteous speaking against him. Jeremiah could be the witness for the defence. "When I was hungry he fed me. Where were all of you?" Jeremiah knew full well. They would be as himself, slipping down to the take-away in their cars, oblivious of a hungry vagrant.

He saw a new and fearful aspect of the parable. The sheep knew not what they had done, nor did the goats. They asked, "Lord, when saw we thee hungry?" He said, "Inasmuch as ye did it to the least of *these my brethren,* ye did it unto me". That would be impossible for any, like himself, who knew the parable. Knowing it, he could buy a passport to eternal life by giving food to a single hungry man or woman; but they had to be the "least of these my brethren". He could not ask, "Lord when saw I thee hungry?" He would know perfectly well when. How amazingly careful were such words. Had he been shewn a different role for those of the Church of Jesus, to be the least of his brethren? He went back to the marriage service. What a lie it was to declare, "let no man put asunder, when meaning, "let those duly appointed by the Defender of the Faith put asunder, with our blessing". Perhaps, this was the time to force the issue by sitting on his wife's doorstep.

Next day he went to where his wife worked, having first called at the place where his daughter worked. She was away at lunch when he arrived. His daughter was on holiday. The porter told him to return in the afternoon. When he did, the porter said that his wife had decided not to come into work that afternoon and thrust him from the premises. A day or two later he met his daughter. She told him that his appearance had so upset her mother that she had lain on her bed crying, for over a day. He should never do it again. He had a problem with regard to forcing a court case. It was black and white and had four legs, and had been with him, faithfully, through everything. If he were sent to prison, what would become of Sadie?

He continued to wander about, with extraordinary luck keeping him alive. One evening, sitting on a bench outside Totnes Church, a policeman told him that, while he could sit there, he could not sleep there. "If I nod off, will you come and wake me up?" A man getting into his car, parked nearby, heard the exchange. Twenty minutes later he returned with a dish of dog food, a pile of sandwiches and a blanket. He would meet him there, with the woman he lived with, on the following evening, for a meal at the pub. A couple of days later he walked to Dartmouth. There he chanced to meet a man called Cranmer, a descendent of the famous Archbishop, who allowed him to sleep in a sail loft, which he was converting into a flat.

From there he walked to Buckfast. He wanted to meet Placid Hooper, and make peace. He reached the monastery, knocked at the door and asked to see Placid, whom he had not seen for twenty years. The porter said that he was shewing people round the Abbey. It would be easy for him to spot Placid in his habit. Coming round the apse into south aisle he saw him at the far end and walked towards him. Amazingly, Placid recognised him from afar off and ran to greet him.

One sunny afternoon, wandering down a lane a car stopped. It was driven by a woman, who asked, "Do you want a lift or don't you?" She drove him to her house, and gave him a cup of tea and cake, while feeding Sadie and her own dog. "Where are you heading?" He found himself saying, "I am going to Salisbury, to say thank you to the bishop". "In that case", said the woman, who turned out to be a doctor's widow, "I'll run you down to the main road after tea". She took £20 from her bag and gave it him, "If I can afford to spend money on a fortnight in the Canaries, I should be able to pay your bus fare to Salisbury".

The next afternoon he walked through the Cathedral Close to the Bishop's house. The driveway was full of cars, when he knocked at the door, dirty and unshaven. A very grand lady opened it and asked what he wanted. He explained that he had come to see the Bishop. He was busy in a meeting. At this, another lady, very well spoken, but not so grand as the first appeared. It seemed that she was the Bishop's secretary. She explained that the Bishop would be tired, and would not wish to be prevented from putting his feet up. Jeremiah said that he only wanted to say thank you to his face.

He was led to the kitchen, given tea and slices of cake. The one whom he took to be the secretary turned out to be Jill Baker, the Bishop's wife. Sadie, meanwhile, stretched herself out in front of the stove. Bishops, Archbishops, Popes and Cardinals, came all alike to her. The county lady looked at her saying; "That dog has a lump, it should see a vet!"

Vets cost money and he had none. He had consulted a vet about it some time ago and was told that it was harmless. Jill Baker, who had no experience with dogs, was worried. All was forgotten, when in walked the Bishop. He shook Jeremiah by the hand. The evening before, Jeremiah had telephoned Peter to ask how he was. Peter did not answer, but Penny did. Had Peter returned? "Oh yes", said Penny reassuringly. "It was a silly psychiatrist who had said that he should do something wildly extravagant that had led to his taking an overdose". He was now in St Thomas's, having had a bypass operation. When John Baker asked, "What are your plans?" Jeremiah had said. "I'm going up to London to see my friend in St Thomas's".

Jill said, "I think we ought to take Sadie to see a vet. There is a scheme for free treatment". With that Sadie and Jeremiah were bundled into the car. The vet said that he thought it was nothing to worry over, but that, if it would set minds at rest, he could easily remove the lump on the next day. Jill insisted on this being done. She wanted instructions about looking after dogs. Jeremiah was sent on his way to London.

He went to the bus station in Salisbury, but had not enough for the fare. In any case, there were no buses till next morning. He would walk overnight to Basingstoke and catch the bus there. He was very tired. He had plenty of time to find a suitable spot, sit down and have a short sleep. There were banks sloping down to the road. If he lay down and slept, he feared sliding down onto the road while asleep, so he walked on to find a bus shelter.

There was a stone in his shoe. He sat down to take it off, walked on, found a bus shelter, had a sleep and took the bus to London, just as he planned. On the bus he had a nasty dream. In it, he had dropped to sleep while removing his right shoe and had his legs run over. Even in a dream it hurt. One leg was bent through a circle and the foot was upside down alongside his knee. His dream continued after the accident, when he was taken to hospital and had his legs pulled straight and put into plaster. One hurt a lot, the other not so much. He was then put into an ambulance and taken to another hospital. They would have to operate on it, drill a hole into his ankle and fix a pin in it so that it could all be stretched out. All this was in his dream, and he was lying in a hospital bed, as the coach rumbled along. Into his dream came two ambulance men. They had delivered another casualty to the same ward.

"Hullo", they said, "How's your dream? "When we picked you up last night, you told us to go away. You were only dreaming!" Reality dawned on him. He had inverted dream and actuality. He had been so tired that he had fallen asleep when removing his right shoe and slid down the bank, just as he feared. He was in hospital, his ankles were broken and one was tied to a wire with weights on it at the end of his bed. "My God", he thought, "Sadie!"

A nurse went past. "Is there anyone you want us to ring?" First he asked that a message be sent to Hannah, his next of kin. Then he said, "Please ring Mrs Baker in the Close, and explain what has happened. She has my dog". The nurse came back, saying that there was no Mrs Baker at the address he had given. "She'll be under, Salisbury, Bishop of....", said Jeremiah.

The nurse went away. He asked a staff nurse to phone the bishop and his wife, with no result. After pestering everyone, including the sister whose name was Pam, someone came back saying that all was well, and that the Bakers would look after Sadie. It was now Sunday. The lunch was excellent. He tucked into roast duckling with orange sauce. That evening he had a visitor, the Bishop of the Diocese, who said that he looked very much better than when he had seen him three days before.

The consultant had been dismissive of Jeremiah, speaking of him as if he were not there. When he came around on Monday, he said, "Good morning, I believe you know the Bakers. Are you connected with the well-known family in Salisbury of your name? Did you know that one of them was the first medical officer of this hospital?" The sister was not having her ward turned into a club and said, "They spell their names differently".

She was a wonderful woman. No job was beneath her. She would scrub floors and empty bedpans, sweep up and move beds about. Jeremiah had a strange sense that he had been there before, whenever he heard her voice, but he had never been to Salisbury in his life. One day, when he had been there for some time, he asked the sister where she came from. "Up in your neck of the woods", she said. "I come from Suffolk". The feeling of having been there before was nothing more than hearing a trace of an east-anglian accent. It was not many days before he received a postcard. A glance at the picture told him whom it was from. It was a picture of a blue Gresley Pacific.

The postcard was from 'the Baker'. He might be in the area, as he had heard that Mallard was going to steam over a bridge nearby. If he was around he might pop in. This was typical of his kindness. He never let anyone think he was being so. He and Sally arrived. Sally has, among her many gifts, one for giving presents. She takes infinite trouble over choosing them, especially for children, when ill. They brought all the things that would make being in hospital enjoyable.

His daughter came. John Jacobs drove down from Norwich and walked out of the ward with his pipe in his mouth. One afternoon, who should appear but Charlie Moule, whose family came from that area. A man from Horning, he knew as 'Uncle George', also appeared. A friend of his mother's family, whom he did not know before, visited him regularly. She brought a sketch-book and pencils. He drew his way round the broads in Golden Copper. It was better than sailing her. It never rained, the wind was always perfect; he found moorings wherever he wanted. The man, who owned the Gallery, where he sold his pictures, sent him a pack of drawing materials.

The consultant said, "You are enjoying yourself far too much in here, you will have to go. The Baker collected him. He had arranged for him to lodge with a mutual friend who had a large house, with all necessities on the ground floor. Meanwhile Sadie had established herself at the Bishop's house, where he stayed overnight, when returning as an outpatient. Jill had visited him, one afternoon, and said that, if he wanted, they would love to keep her. Since Sadie had been there, she had felt wholly at ease in the evenings, when John was away. Sadie was in a dog's paradise, with a huge garden, a river and rabbits to chase. There she died, and had a tombstone carved for her by the Cathedral mason. On it was written "Sadie for all the happiness you brought us." The kindness of the Baker and Sally was amazing. It would take too long to tell of it. Always they made him feel as if it were he who was doing them a favour.

Meanwhile he had heard that his dad had had a heart attack, and was in a 'home'. On his last visit to outpatients, they had established that 'slow healing' had set in. The badly broken ankle had reunited with gristle, but had failed to produce bone. He was shewn the X ray with a thick black line through the bone. The registrar had gripped his ankle in both hands and wrung it about to shew him that the union was flexible.

An appointment was made for him to return in three months and, if need be, have a bone graft. With that he returned on crutches to look after his dad, who hated sitting in a nursing home, with food that he found disgusting. Jeremiah told his doctor that he would have to make arrangements for him to return, when he went to Salisbury for his operation. When the time came, however, he was told that it was unthinkable to move his old dad about, so he cancelled the appointment and remained in plaster for over a year and would have done so for the rest of his days, which he did not wish to be prolonged. If one found oneself alienated from the 'conversation', while one might have moments of enjoyment, one would come to hate life in this world.

His bitterness was overflowing. He was penniless and hobbling about on crutches. All seemed to think that it was what he was fit for. He was spoken to as if near half witted. He was silly to have given up painting; he should know that, when they prayed for these laws to be written on their hearts, they did not intend anyone to take them 'literally'. Meanwhile he had no money. His father had only his old age pension, and a little extra income from some investments. It was enough to feed and maintain one. Jeremiah began to be seriously undernourished. He did not care. He more or less collapsed, and was taken off to a short stay psychiatric hospital. The Doctor, a kind and understanding man gave him some pills to make him feel lazy. Jeremiah asked if they would have any side effects. "Would I do anything like that?" replied the doctor. "The food is far from delicious, but it is wholesome and there is plenty of it. Unless I give you these pills you will fret to return home. What you need is food". Meanwhile, he and social workers at the hospital set about getting him some money. They secured an attendance allowance for his dad. That was something. One of the nurses noticed the plaster on his leg.

"However long has that been there?" "Just over a year?" "It will have to come off. You could easily get an infection there. With the reduced circulation, it could become gangrene or septicaemia". 'Good', thought Jeremiah, 'at least I will be dead'. The nurse did not agree. He was taken off to the general hospital to have the plaster removed, revealing a leg like a matchstick. They insisted that he be X-rayed. It was quickly done. "The consultant will see you now".

The consultant sat behind a desk with papers from Salisbury in front of him. He looked a gloomy man, with half glasses. "Do you want my professional opinion?" "Not much, but I daresay you are going to give it me". "In my opinion, your ankle has been perfectly reunited for at least thirteen months".

It was thirteen months, almost to the day, since the Registrar had demonstrated that the bone was only united with gristle. When he had waited to have his leg re-plastered at Salisbury, he had wondered about all things being possible for God, and how easy it would be to cause confusion by making a mark on an X-Ray plate. If indeed there were God, he could make the bone strong in a split second.

"It must have made bone that long ago", went on the consultant, "as the bone has reshaped itself to a smooth contour. There is no sign of a callous at the point where it was broken, and that takes a good year". "In fact", he continued, "If I had not your papers in front of me, I would have given my oath that the break in your ankle took place before you were four years old, as there is almost no trace of it. That is usually only so, when children break bones when very young". Jeremiah returned home.

His dad seemed to have recovered from his heart attack, and simply took a pill every day, but found the effort of getting off to Church on Sundays too much for him. That was a relief. Now that he stopped praying for a law, which forbad the making of any form of likeness to be written on his heart, Jeremiah resumed painting.

During the past years he learned something of what it was to honour one's father and mother, and what was implied by 'being Abraham's children, if you do the works of Abraham'. His dad would go out with friends to lunch and would return with them saying, "Coffee for three, boy." He would produce the coffee and return to the kitchen. He could hear his mother laughing, "Now you know what it's like, you little beggar. That'll larn you!"

The poll tax came, which he had to pay. He had no means of doing so. He wrote to the council, saying that they were welcome to send him to prison for failure to pay, provided they found someone to care for his old dad. They rang him as soon as they got his letter. "How is it that you are not receiving Income support?" "I have written many times but my letters are unanswered", he explained. "I will ring them", said the woman from the council

She was as good as her word, and within a few days the forms arrived. They back-dated his claim for a few weeks, so he got a cheque for about £500. It did not take long for 'his heart to be there also' again, and he resented having to pay poll tax. In the end he did not have to. The fact that, thanks to it, he was better off by some £1500 a year was soon forgotten.

Meanwhile he found a friend, or rather, two in the town. He had hardly spoken to a soul outside his dad's circle in eight years. Then he met Molly and, through her, Philip, her seaman husband. He had actually known Molly, by sight, for many years as she worked in a greengrocer's shop. Every day she would come over, as his old dad was coming down for breakfast, greeting him with a cheery "Hullo". She would take his arm and escort him to his breakfast. She was the only person he ever allowed to assist him in this way. Philip, knowing that he had been in Malaya, would bring back a selection of Malay and Singapore papers for him. Molly left the greengrocer and went back to work in a jewellers shop.

One afternoon, she returned from work with a bag, full of shirts. The owner had brought them in to use as rags. Molly said, "I know someone who will wear those!" There followed trousers and suits and ties. He was not to say, "Thank you". Molly kept the most spotless home in the town, and a weed free garden. One afternoon, he saw her gazing at a pansy. She had bought a packet of a single variety. The bed was full of them. "I think that is really clever", she said. "They have all got the same face, yet they are all different. How do they know how to do it? I think it's wonderful. Don't go and say anything or you'll spoil it, and it will make me cry!" Jeremiah envied Molly. She understood more of what it was to live in a created world than he ever could. The fact that plant breeders had spent years experimenting with crosses, arriving at the particular hybrid that so fascinated her, was bypassed.

From Molly, Jeremiah began to learn a further aspect of the hypocrisy of Christianity. It was hurtful. Salvationist friends would invite her to go out for a meal with them. She paid for her own lunch. Often they went to a licensed eating house. If she ordered a glass of wine for herself, they would tell her that doing so was needlessly offensive. Why, then, go to a licensed restaurant?

When there was a fund raising tea or barbecue, Molly was roped in to move chairs, cart furniture, bake cakes, and prepare things, while the uniformed membership looked on and talked of important matters. When the tea took place, Molly stood at the gate to collect the money. They knew that she would get it. Then she could help wash up. It was as if they did her a favour by permitting her to 'hew wood and draw water'. Those, not quite up to wearing a bonnet and banging on a timbrel, should feel fortunate to be permitted to help, thus obtaining a lesser share in the Kingdom of God. No doubt those, heaving stones to build Pharaoh's giant coffin, were made to feel the same.

Aside from being a good badminton player, Molly had another quality. She could nag! 'Poor Philip' often came in from the garden to face a tirade. He was wonderful. When the storm abated he would smile broadly, and say, "Can we go and play now?" When Philip laughed, it was total. From Philip, Jeremiah learned another thing. Never to have him on the helm of a sailing boat in a strong wind when there is an aeroplane in the sky! All else would be forgotten, and an expensive mast could be crumpled against a branch. Philip was among the kindest men on earth.

Through Molly, Jeremiah met Joy and her husband, Jimmy. Molly and Joy had been at school together. Joy had decided to do an "A level" in English. She could not understand her Tutor's grades. Down the margin he put a series of ticks, yet he only gave her "C". They were reading Hamlet, some poems by Thomas Hardy and a play by Tom Stoppard, 'Rosencrantz and Gildenstern are Dead'. Jeremiah was no man of letters. He found himself having to read such books. They also had to read poems by Ted Hughes. The combination of the Stoppard play and Hamlet was fascinating. By knowing 'Hamlet', it was as if one were in an all knowing, almost God-like, position with regard to the action. Stoppard played with the notion that God could overturn the laws of probability in the tossing of coins.

Though only 40, Joy and Jimmy were grandparents. She had her first child, when only 17 and unmarried. Their granddaughter had been born with a serious heart defect, involving major surgery at Gt. Ormond Street. As a young unmarried mother, living in a town that had a large church and chapel-going population, she had suffered much at the hands of the righteous. Joy was no shrinking violet, and when catcalled, was not one to be as a lamb led to the slaughter and was dumb. Had she known that Jesus was also born of an unmarried mother, the exchanges over the street would have been worth recording.

The hurt that the righteousness of the Christian religion and its hypocrisy could bring, he had hitherto seen only in terms of himself. Molly and Joy made him see otherwise. The disdain for such as Joy and Jimmy was wholly alien to the attitude of Jesus. Both his teaching and actions identified him with such as might do as they did, but alienated him from the righteous, who condemned.

At this time, divers found the wreck of Titanic. Before being in the wilderness, Jesus had spent years as a prominent member and preacher in the synagogue. Jeremiah thought of his own days teaching at Derby, and how everything had fallen about him after his dismissal. Having spent years, teaching as he did, he could not simply 'retire', and enjoy the benefits, if he had 'second thoughts'. It would be like selling tickets for Titanic and, having noticed that there was a shortage of life boats, deciding not to go oneself; but allowing all those, to whom he had sold tickets, to go to a watery grave, while keeping the commissions one had earned. What then of Jesus, when he returned from the wilderness?

If one took the direct, general, teaching of Jesus, not only could it never be made the basis of any system of law, no preacher, who enjoyed a socially responsible position could conceivably commend it to a congregation. He or she would ever be forced to find arguments against it. No minister could stand in his pulpit and commend a congregation to give their cloak as well, if taken to court for their coat. Someone might do so. Where would that leave the minister? The man or woman might return saying, "I did as you said; now I am penniless and my wife and family have turned against me. What shall I do?" The Minister could hardly say, "Come and follow me"! It would go beyond the minister to the 'community'. If any church expected individuals within it to act thus, it would, as a 'community', have to do so. It was the same, with the commandments given to Israel, where 'Thou' addresses the community, seen as one, which is what the word community means. How could any institution that owned property and had corporate status exist, if it acted thus? .

How did this man come to speak words, which obliged those, making public declarations of belief in God and in himself, everlastingly to find arguments against the truth of all that he was reported to have said? The more one produced such arguments, the more one entrenched oneself against those words and their finality, while influencing others. The more convincing the arguments against the finality of Jesus' words, the more people could be persuaded to erect structures on that basis, making the possibility of receiving them ever more impossible. The argument that the words, attributed to Jesus in the gospels, had been modified through the needs of the early community seemed less and less compelling. Jesus must have spoken as they reported.

Jesus had, apparently, made much of the matter of divorce and marriage to others. On a domestic scale it mirrored the same process. Having married another, one inevitably built a way of life on that foundation, which drew in others. If one attended services, one assured all present that the saying of Jesus had 'passed away'. The tree, to whose root Jesus and his words laid an axe, became large and 'the wood hard'.

Jesus himself expected it to be thus. Jeremiah, for the first time; began to see the horror of this man and his reported words. He said, "Blessed are the Peacemakers; they shall be called children of God". He also said, "Think not that

I have come to bring peace on earth, not peace but the sword". It could not be otherwise. If 'everyone' found themselves obliged to argue against his words, they were obliged to argue against the only words of peace for mankind, in order to preserve cherished ways of life, over which wars would be fought.

By any religious, social or political standards, Caiaphas and the Council were right to see, in Jesus and his words, a threat to the continued existence of the nation under the Romans. Yet, had they heard and done as Jesus said, not only would it have enabled them to live quietly under Roman rule, or that of any other colonial overlord, it would have made obsolete the two centres, which generated nationalist/religious fervour: the synagogues and the Temple. It would hardly have troubled the Romans if people went two miles when told to go one, or turned the other cheek. The Romans would not have bothered, if all abandoned the synagogues and prayed as he said, in their private room with the door shut. If that had been, Judaism, as a religious and ethnic tradition would have ceased existing. It would have been replaced by an unknowable number of people who simply did as Jesus commanded. Those, who came later to call themselves, or be called, 'Christians', would have been among that number, whether or not they were of gentile or Jewish origin. Not only would there have been no Jewish religion. There would be no Christian religion either, hence no Islam. There could have been no holocaust.

Jeremiah's old dad was becoming less and less able to look after himself. He was over 95. Thanks to the Jeweller, Jeremiah had clothes to wear, and was selling paintings, to the point where he was no longer entitled to claim Income support. He had had a dispute with the gallery where he used to exhibit and buy materials, and moved elsewhere. After an exhibition at a little gallery, which sold his pictures, they went to the pub for a drink. There, in the corner, sat a girl with a mane of auburn hair, whom he knew as "Ginger Jo". She had worked on the framing desk of the former gallery. He had not spoken to her for years. He took his drink and said, "Hullo".

Ginger Jo asked abruptly, "Did you know that I was pregnant?" "Yes, he had heard a rumour of this". She said in a voice of great antagonism, "I suppose that you disapprove like the rest of them". "I don't see why I should, and I don't see why my approval or disapproval matters anyway. It's not as if I judge the earth". "All the Christians do!" said Ginger Jo, obviously angered and hurt. "They say that they thought better of me, and that I let them all down".

That is strange, said Jeremiah, "I had the impression that Jesus was the son of an unmarried mother". Tension evaporated instantly. Everyone could laugh. The conversation eased. He could enquire about things that mattered like, "Will you be all right for money?"

At the age of 98, his old dad died. On the death certificate the doctor wrote, under 'Cause of death', "Ia, Old Age". He had longed to enter that on a death certificate. Molly and Philip were wonderful. Molly dealt with the removal of his corpse from, the house, saying, "You wont like this bit, its horrid to see him carted off in a body bag". Philip took him to their house for a whisky. They took him to the Registrar in Cromer and the Probate Office in Norwich.

The probate officer, a man of about fifty, was kind and helpful. When all was done, he led Jeremiah into a small room, with chairs and a table in the middle. Piled on the table were all manner of books and other objects. "Do sit down, said the officer, "you now have to swear an oath. I take it that you won't mind using the New Testament. If you prefer something else I can provide most things", he said, waving his hand towards the pile of books and other things on the table.

"I hope that you will not think I am being awkward", said Jeremiah, "but I would rather not. In the Gospel, Jesus is reported to have strictly forbidden the swearing of an oath by anything at all".

The probate officer jumped from his chair. Jeremiah thought that he had said something to annoy him. Instead, he held out his hand. "Thank you very much", said the officer. "I have been doing this job for 30 years and have longed for someone to say what you have just said. You are the first person to have come here who's read the book".

It offended him, whenever anyone came in to obtain probate, wearing clothes that gave public indication of membership of the Christian religion. He would say that he understood that they might prefer not to swear an oath, especially using the New Testament, because Jesus forbad it. Always, they said dismissively, "Don't worry about that. Give me the book", and swore their oath on a book that forbad the very thing they were doing. This shocked him, as they had no need to swear at all. They could simply 'affirm'. Here was yet another example of the impact of the same hypocrisy. How could those, who went out of their way to make public declarations of belief in Jesus as God from God, and dressed in ways that drew attention to their belief, dismiss what he said with such disdain? There is nothing obscure in the instruction.

Through these random encounters and experiences Jeremiah was driven to see the truth of Jesus' saying, "Believe me that I am in the Father and the Father in me, or else believe me for the works' sake". The Miraculous events that "followed" him, as the one who spoke words, which clearly and singly derived from and articulated the word God, did not serve as the prime assurance of the truth of his words, only as a 'fall back' confirmation, when one was given to doubt. The primary basis for belief was the 'logic' of the word God. If such a being existed, the sayings of Jesus gave single and exclusive expression to that one reality. Seen thus, all must be seen as of God, whether apparently explicable on other grounds or not. The problem with miraculous events is, that, with the affluction of time, what seems inexplicable is explained on natural grounds. In the recall of any event, one has only the impression it made upon one at the time.

In recall it would be impossible ever to know, for sure, whether an event, which seemed corporeal, was visionary in nature or not, as with the appearances after the resurrection, the transfiguration, and even the stilling of the storm. How readily that, which was actual, could seem visionary, Jeremiah knew from first hand experience.

His sister and her husband were as good as their word. They had said that he should inherit their dad's house when he died. They wanted nothing. Jeremiah said, "I am deeply in your debt". His brother in law said, "You owe us nothing". His sister had confirmed this, saying that, if he had not spent 14 years looking after father they would have had to pay for him to go into a home. Few can have been as fortunate as he in their relatives.

Thanks to Molly, he had yet another outlet for pictures. The Jeweller had agreed to have them in his shop. He went further. He bought half a dozen of them unframed, and so provided cash for materials.

A year or two before his old dad died, he had been watching TV. Jeremiah had been in and out of the room to light his pipe for him and see that he was all right. A book was being discussed. The book was about a group of writers in the early part of the century, such as Virginia Woolf, D H Lawrence and T S Eliot. The author seemed to think that the received opinion of these people needed revising. Jeremiah thought, 'I'd like to read it'.

The programme ended, he rushed in to see the name of the author and title of the book. All he saw was "Merton Professor of English, University of Oxford." He wrote to the "Merton Professor, Merton College Oxford", asking the title of the book. It was late June.

He received no answer, but had spoken to the Baker, who went round bookshops in Bristol, discovered it and sent him a copy. In November he found a letter on the mat, with "Merton College" on it. Professor Carey apologised for not having replied earlier, but had been away on a lecture tour in the States, and came back to find a mass of letters to answer. He told him the name of his book and hoped he would enjoy it. He would value any comments! Jeremiah had already read and enjoyed it.

He wrote to Professor Carey saying that he found his book fascinating. There followed a sporadic correspondence, largely as a consequence of another TV interview, in which Carey had adopted a highly critical view of a once famous book by Aldous Huxley, called, "Doors of Perception." This book Jeremiah had read. Carey's critique was impossible to controvert. In one of his letters Carey said, "If ever you are in Oxford, do let me know and come to dinner". At the time he could hardly leave the house, so there was no question of doing anything of the kind. In any case Professors would see how bogus was his knowledge and how stupid he was.

A year later, he had to pass through Oxford where his cousin lived, so he wrote to Carey, saying that he would be in Oxford on the following Friday. A letter came by return of post, saying simply "what good news, see you at Merton at 7.30!" Carey's monumental erudition was fearful, his clarity of mind almost more so. Augustine of Hippo was mentioned. Jeremiah remarked that he had never been able to find any mention of the explicit nature of the one forbidden tree in any of his writings. "You would not," said Carey, "He says that it is irrelevant!"

Chapter Twenty eight.

"I go a fishing."

Thanks to the encouragement of Molly and Philip, the Jeweller and others, Jeremiah, who had never had a lesson and found books on the subject beyond him, was earning a living from his water colours. They were not, 'art'. He found himself having to pay tax. Once, he would have thought himself fortunate to be in a position to do so. When it came to writing the cheque, his views about 'rendering unto Caesar' changed.

Now that he seemed financially secure, he wrote to the cousin, who had asked him to transfer his shares to his wife. He made it clear that he did not seek any payment, as that had not been the intention of the gift, but would be interested to know what valuation had been put on the shares. His cousin and his wife had sold the business and bought a farm. His reply was extraordinary. He wrote that the accountant said that, if a shareholder in an unquoted company, which was still trading, *wanted* to sell his shares, he was only entitled to the nominal value. Jeremiah had not wanted, or asked, to sell his shares. His cousin had asked him to do so. He could not but wonder whether the cousin knew of this before asking Jeremiah. He said that another minority shareholder, whose holding was larger than Jeremiah's, had raised the matter angrily, on receiving only the nominal value. Jeremiah wrote that he hoped that his cousin had not approached the other shareholder, after writing to him. If he had, he would have known that he would only pay the nominal value. The promise to 'have them valued and pay the difference' would have been empty

From this incident he learned two valuable things. First, how easily one misconstrued what one read. His cousin had said that, once he received the certificate, he would have the shares valued. That would apply to an antique or other object, but not to a shareholding. One did not need to have a share certificate to obtain a valuation. The second was more important. He had been led into 'temptation' but delivered from 'evil'. Had his cousin had the shares valued, and paid the difference, as he implied at the time, Jeremiah would gladly have pocketed the extra cash. He would then have acted falsely towards his uncle's gift. From his cousin's point of view, he could see that, if he and his wife sought to buy a farm, they would need to realise the maximum from the hatchery as an asset.

He had lent a friend some money. The loan had been for a short time, but repayment had not been possible. Both knew Ernie Cole. Out of the blue came a cheque. Soon after his Dad had died, he had been over to Horning with some friends. Uncle George had seen him. Within a week there was a message from the young man, to whom he had given Golden Copper, "Get on that boat and sail her! He did so with delight. Ginger Jo and some friends had said that they wanted to learn to sail. Once a week he took them sailing in her. Nick, the new owner, had lavished care on the old boat. She was now over sixty years old, but looked as though she was built a week ago.

Jeremiah spent the money on a boat of his own. He would feel free to let others use it. He could not afford a 'One Design' any more. Instead he bought a newer boat, called a Reedling. There were only ten of them. He had friends about him. He took Philip out, also Jimmy, as well as Neville. He even entered races, and fulfilled a near lifelong ambition to compete in the annual 'Three Rivers' race. He completed the course four times, twice with Neville and Ginger Jo, twice with a highly expert sailor, a friend of Neville's, whom they knew as the Ancient Mariner. He was enjoying life. Neville agreed with Pat. Hannah had done him a favour! Next door lived a dentist and his wife, who were helpful, when his old dad was dying, washing linen in their machine and so on. He could almost forget the past. His younger son and daughter were married, the elder was doctoring out in Newfoundland. He was free to do things as and when he wished.

He went out to spend Christmas in Newfoundland, staying a fortnight with his son, who was senior medical officer in the local hospital. He and his girl friend, a native of the province, gave him a wonderful time, and he made friends out there. He found the whole way of life in rural Newfoundland so attractive that he could hardly bear to drag himself away. It was a relief not to have a great cultural heritage and all that went with it. It was suggested that he make it a tradition to spend Christmas with them. He could not wait to return next year, when he stayed almost two months.

Back in England his pictures were selling well. His son's girl friend, whom he liked, sold them in Newfoundland, so he had a bank account out there. It seemed that all the fuss about marriage and divorce was best forgotten. Hannah was happier than she could ever have been with him. If it was hypocritical, did it matter? His son came to stay for a couple of days with the girl from Newfoundland, whom everyone made welcome.

The tale of Peter going fishing troubled him. 'Could they put all that they had learned behind them, *after the discovery of the empty tomb*?' It was all too easily done. It was an amazing discovery, but so was the incident of his broken legs. What difference did it make? Thousands of people every Sunday declare that, in effect, they were witnesses to its discovery: still, they seem to know better, than did Jesus, how and what to pray. What did it all matter? He talked of these things with Neville in the pub. He had a habit of pushing questions back farther than anyone wanted to go.

Neville worked at the Gas terminal on the coast, having worked off shore. The explosion on Piper Alpha made him conscious of the detail of safety procedures. If he noticed malfunctioning equipment, he reported it. This did not please his superiors. It passed responsibility up to them. On 'crisis management' courses, instructors, explaining procedures for controlling potentially catastrophic events, enquired, from time to time, "Does everyone follow?" Always, one hand went up, "Could you explain something you said, which I did not follow?" Everyone else seemed to have done so. The lecturer would turn to the rest of the group, when it became clear that nobody else had. This was typical of the man. He and Jeremiah were at one on one matter. "I can't understand what you *mean,* only what you say".

At kicking out time, Neville asked, "Why do I always feel uneasy, when I am with people who have divorced and married again?" "You do not condemn them?" "Of course not".

Jeremiah pondered and went to sleep. He seemed to think most clearly in his sleep. Of course he would feel uneasy. In such circumstances he would be prevented from asking his 'one question too many'. Those, who had divorced a partner and married another, often seemed eloquent about family values. Too many conversations had to be left in banal clichés. If a parent, in such a position, spoke of the need to teach children to keep promises, Neville would be sure to ask, "However do you do that?" It would not be long before he would raise the 'Ice Cream question'. Too many matters would be 'off limits'. One had to walk on eggshells. Neville was not good at this. One word and 'conversation' that would, most surely, be 'off-limits', would be that of Jesus in the gospels.

Jeremiah thought of his sons and daughter. Houses, where the sayings of Jesus were off-limits, were more amenable. Because his mother tended to lead everything back to those sayings, she needed not to say anything, for him to know what she would think. She was immune to further argument, making it clear that clever arguments did not convince her. They were unlikely to convince God either. The 'Christian' religion provided a welcome shield from such words, as did any religious, or other belief. The 'conversation' of a household is, seemingly at any rate, better without rich young men, who are told to sell all, parables like Dives and Lazarus, or sayings like "whoever among you is faultless....", and a standing order that makes forgiveness conditional on having forgiven those that are indebted to one. It is certainly easier without tasteless epithets about those who divorce and marry others.

Jesus' sayings about those who divorce partners and marry others puts every other saying of his 'off-limits', in such households, if they are churchgoers. None, living in that state, could recall anyone to his sayings, as having authority, without being open to an obvious riposte. Among those who declare belief, marrying became important. If they simply lived together, the righteous would look down their noses. It was 'living in sin'. There would be no hypocrisy. Nobody need walk on eggshells.

There is hypocrisy if, having divorced and married another, one or both attend the services of the Church. 'Thou shalt not commit adultery', whatever it may have implied originally, now, as in the days of Jesus, meant domestic infidelity. Most upright citizens tend to disapprove of adultery. It was inconsiderate of Jesus to be so ruthless in his rationality.

Life is more amenable in such households, because all know, if there is attendance at Church, that no words of Jesus can be uttered, as having final authority. Any attempt to endow them 'with authority' can, not only be rebounded; it also carries implication of hypocrisy. There can be no absolute points of reference.

While many are 'happy' to admit to hypocrisy as a general malaise, all tend react strongly when it is applied to themselves. Jesus' words about those who divorce and marry others would lead to sustained argument against their truth. If one assents to the 'ten commandments' and, on the basis of Jesus words', lives in a state of adultery, one is hardly in a position to condemn theft, killing or anything else. If one makes a virtue of one of them: why not the others? 'No man spoke like this before'.

Those of the household, if they go to Church, need 'disciples' and supporters. Their way of life constitutes a 'conversation', a standing argument against the truth of those words. Jeremiah had a vision of hell, which was not in the future. However heaven/eternal life may be seen, it must be whenever and wherever those words, and the 'Word' they articulate, are, alone, sustained, with no argument. We are forced to argue endlessly against silence, as the Inquisitor in Ivan Karamazov's parable. That is hell.

If the things, against which Jesus warns, are to be seen, in his own terms, as those which constitute the broad path that leads only to the rubbish dump, rather than as 'morally reprehensible', they take on a different significance. Jesus vehemently condemns hypocrisy. Those, indicted as hypocrites, are like shipping agents who promise to take people safely to a desired destination, take their money, but send them nowhere in an unseaworthy ship. If such things as adultery are uncleared minefields, they remove the danger signs, "Look at us: if you learn to be as we are, you can frolic in them safely".

Such a conversation may be more amenable, but can it have truth? Jeremiah's elder son might have grounds for thinking that it led him into a minefield. In England, he had fathered a daughter, whose mother was a nurse and 'fall back' friend, who had recently gone through a very painful divorce. To add to the irony, he was appearing on the local TV network, in his professional capacity, warning of the dangers of unprotected sex.

Jeremiah found those, whose words were not to be relied upon in this way, frightening. One could not know where one was. Did his elder son feel the same? It was not only that they had no words, to which they could recall him 'with authority'. There were none to which he could recall them. It was, in Jesus' words, a 'conversation', in which his words could have no 'free course'. It may be more amenable. It was one in which nobody's words could, ultimately, be trusted.

He had seen a further reason why Jesus seems to have laid such emphasis upon this matter. If one divorced a partner and *married* another, it became the foundation of a way of life into which many others were drawn, and on which much was constructed, (much as with the establishment of the kingship in Israel). If, in his words, it constituted adultery, any 'repentance' became nigh impossible.

This would not be so with an affair; yet often it is the case that churchgoers, who have divorced partners and married others, look with disapproval of those who have 'affairs'. 'Affairs' are made acceptable by divorcing a partner and marrying the other. As temporary, 'affairs' are seen as adulterous and reprehensible: no longer so, if they are made permanent.

That he put all these things behind him was not wholly true. He could not control his dreams. He had a recurring nightmare. In surreal form, it represented the telephone call he made from Liverpool Street when Hannah had assured him of undying love loyalty and affection, and then said calmly that, we had to say something...... He would dream of her being warm and affectionate, until he felt assured that she meant it. Then she would walk away with someone else, casting a scornful look over her shoulder as she went.

He was longing to go to Newfoundland for Christmas, and had bought his ticket, when he learned that, not only had Hannah been out, but taken her man with her. He could not face it. Had she gone alone, it would have been different. She went off to Church on Sunday with his son and his girl friend. His son read the lessons, but sometimes complained contemptuously of the nonsense he was asked to read. He took a long while making up his mind what to do. Joy understood. If Jimmy had stayed with one of their daughters with a new woman, she would never sleep in that bed. Linda felt sure that he would not go. He wasted his ticket.

The reason was not quite as Joy felt; but was connected with their attendance at Church. If the Minister called, he need only mention Hannah as his ex or former wife, for Jeremiah to feel, "The Lord has delivered thee into mine hand this day". He would lie in wait and ask, with acid deliberation, if he would, as the minister of the gospel, explain on what grounds he referred to her as his ex or former wife. He could have hooked him like a fish and dragged him through the marriage service and the sayings of Jesus. He would go with the intention of doing so. His son was angry at his decision. His girl friend more upset.

He felt that he had been an embarrassment to the Minister, on his last visit. Anyone divorced, who had, for whatever reason, remained single, while his or her partner had married, would be a source of unease, if the other were a member of his flock. The minister would know that an embarrassing conversation was open to him. He would have to walk on eggshells, or find himself forced to sustain an argument against the truth of the sayings of the very one, in whom he led others to believe.

Jeremiah realised that his refusal to go might, also, have caused a frisson of unease for his son's girl friend. He was fond of her. She and her family had made him welcome, but she had, herself, divorced a husband. She said that they went to Church with Hannah, when she came to England and that Hannah had spoken of him with affection. How might it be, if, when Hannah was speaking well of him, he had opened the door and walked in'? All would change. "Go away, you would have to come and spoil everything. You always did!" How might it be if

Jesus returned? This became the subject of another pamphlet. It would be, "Get back into the tomb where you belong. Why do you have to come back and spoil everything!" - more or less what Dostoevesky has the Inquisitor saying, when he imagines Jesus returning for a day.

The film of Titanic made him think of his son. He wrote to him and begged him to stop standing in church, making declarations of belief, unless he meant what he said. He sent him a copy of E.V. Rieu's translation of the Gospels. If one made such public declarations knowingly; then thought better of it, it was not enough simply to desist. One might, especially as a prominent member of a community, have influenced others.

Jeremiah was miserable. He had longed to go to Newfoundland again. His two stays there had been the happiest times he could remember for 25 years. His friends noticed how he had withdrawn into himself. Neville appeared almost every evening, when not on night shift, saying, "Fancy a quick half". Joy and Jimmy would pop in often. His former neighbours asked him up for a drink on Christmas day and suggested that he stay for lunch. He felt that he should be alone. They gave him a dinner to take home.

He learned that Hannah's man had not wanted to go, but that she had insisted. Had she done so to assert her married status, as a member of the Church? His misery became indignation.

Neville said, "My God, am I relieved to see the old aggressiveness back again!"

The episode was like Peter going fishing, but finding himself recalled to a former occasion, when he had cast on the other side of the boat. Most accounts of appearances after the resurrection were in the Fourth Gospel. Like the infancy narrative of the Third Gospel, they were all wrong as 'myths'. They were all wrong as religious tales too. What was 'wrong' with them was that they added nothing to the gospel. Jesus said nothing that he had not already said. They served to re-emphasise the completeness, 'it is finished', of Jesus' teaching.

His teaching not only omitted almost everything that any religion needed, instructions on its form of priesthood and ministry, worship, conditions for the admittance of new members, an acceptable moral code that would allow it to serve a socially valid purpose, or a coherent body of instruction on its relationship to the rulers of people; but what he did say was inconvenient. It was the most extraordinary story in the history of mankind. It took such disasters to drive Jeremiah back to it. They drove him out of the sensible 'conversation'.

There was much talk of the millennium, and the stately pleasure dome decreed by Mr Blair. Whether the date be correct or not, there would not be the millennium, but for the birth of Jesus; yet the one man ever to have lived, who was impossible of incorporation in the dome or celebrations, was Jesus as found in the gospels. The Archbishop had to scuttle off to his friends in Islamic and other communities to find something acceptable to put in the 'Faith Zone'. The one whose words were wholly unacceptable in a syllabus of Christian or religious education was Jesus.

The only one whose words no preacher could commend, unequivocally, to a congregation was Jesus, as reported in the Gospels. They could wax eloquent about the exact phrases of many prayers and their profundity; not the one given by Jesus. The only one from whom nobody, in any religion, would want to learn was Jesus. All knew much better. A kindly old Archdeacon said that he spent two hours meditating every morning, so that he could be "with my Lord". After all those hours with Jesus, he seemed not to have heard what he said about how to pray. These people were pleasant, kind and dutiful. So were Simon the Pharisee, Nicodemus, and many others.

The millennium celebration was extraordinary for its persiflage of empty words. Much was said of 2,000 years of the Christian religion. That was nonsense. There had not been 2,000 years of the Christian religion. There was talk of 2,000 years of Christian civilisation. In AD.1, Roman civilisation was at its zenith. The datum point, being the putative date of the birth of Jesus, meant that the focus must be the life of Jesus himself. That would be impossible to celebrate. If that life were the focal point, it would be all too apparent that the Christian religion and its civilisation had moved away from the teachings of that singular man, accelerating in recent years, coincidentally with his sayings being available to all.

The man, whose life and teaching made the entire celebration empty, was the very man whose birth was its foundation. That seems to summarise the influence of Jesus on the history of mankind. Jesus as described in the Gospels had gathered the ends of history into the 'middle'. It mattered little whether one was born before or after him. What was crucial was whether one moved towards or away from him and his words. "Abraham rejoiced to see my day, and when he saw it was glad". Few would do so today, especially those who prayed in public, "Thy kingdom come....", or proclaimed, "He shall come again with glory.....".

What, according to the four gospels did the teaching of Jesus amount to? In terms of their report of his public general teaching, as distinct from sayings that were occasioned by specific encounters or parables, very little. Though brief, it was complete. The teaching given to his disciples did not differ, in substance, from that which he gave in public. It is more intense and highly wrought, as in the 'farewell discourse' in the IVth Gospel.

It began to seem that the purpose of the evangelists, emphatically the fourth, (as with the opening of the epistle by that name) was to drive the new religion back from speculative doctrines about the saving death of Jesus and all that went with them, to the words and acts of Jesus himself, as redemptive. Of this, in a crude way, Jeremiah had experience, with the courts, his wife and her friends. When he stood simply on the rock of those words, his manifest inadequacies as a husband were forgotten. Instead, the argument focused on the truth of the sayings of Jesus. It was as if he hid behind Jesus and his words. When they became the matter of argument, it was Jesus who stood in the dock. He could be said to have become a 'ransom', by his life. His death gave finality to his life and words, like a full stop. As he is heard to say in the IVth Gospel, "It is completed".

Jesus' teaching does not originate or end in him. This, the miraculous events and, above all, the resurrection, reinforce. He could not have resurrected himself. He was dead. If one were to answer the question, what does the teaching of Jesus amount to? It amounts to nothing but the articulation of the word 'God' and its consequences, as a way of life. The second evangelist introduces Jesus' public life, saying, 'he came into Galilee preaching the Gospel of God'. Think of the word God, as a little child, and one arrives at the sayings of Jesus. If there be, in truth, God, that being is and must be what, logically, the word implies, unlike any other being. That is the "Holy, (separated), Spirit of God".

The hypocrisy, which the reported sayings of Jesus force on the Christian religion and, less directly, all religions, did not end with this man, but God. One needed to be very sure that there was in truth no God, to indulge in it.

How might it be if Jeremiah appeared at the Church door on Christmas Day, as Hannah and her friends emerged with the Minister of the Gospel, and said, "That 'lady' is an adulteress"

'What a disgusting thing to say, of a highly favoured lady! Anyone can see she is nothing of the kind.' The minister would agree. 'It is uncharitable, judgmental and unchristian'. It was odd that such an epithet should be seen as judgmental. If so it is judgmental to call a dog a dog. It would, in any case, not be his own judgement that he was applying. Those around Hannah, led by the Vicar, would tell Jeremiah that he should remember that it was Christmas and the time of goodwill. Whoever said such things should be cast out. They might be glad to know that he had. It was none other than Jesus himself, the very one whose birth they had celebrated, and had come to adore, as "Christ the Lord".

Attendance on services of the Christian religion assured all that, especially if one had money and position, anything said by Jesus that was inconvenient could safely be disregarded, while declaring him to be "God from God". One needed to be sure that there was no God to do this. If so, the declarations of belief were lies; lies, obviously, if there were no God; lies also, infinitely more dangerously, if there is. This raised a further question. Even if there is no God, can any society or community, based upon empty words and deceit, hope to endure?

The Archbishop made a speech, saying that those who merely cohabited, rather than marrying could not be the basis of a good society. Jesus' words about marriage and divorce, which ended, "those therefore whom God has joined together...", would seem, actually, to be fulfilled in the state which the Archbishop found reprehensible. To make use of those words in its service, the Church omitted the word 'therefore'. Its inclusion makes clear that it is the conclusion of an argument.

The argument would not just make all services or ceremonies of matrimony needless, but unwarranted intrusions between man and God. Jesus derives the divine union from the observable fact of the bisexual, created, nature of man. "Male and female created he them, wherefore shall a man leave his father and mother and cleave unto his wife, and the two shall become one flesh. Those, therefore, whom God has joined, let no man put asunder". That would lead to something like, "if you are joining this man and this woman, say so and leave God out of it. If God is joining them, leave it to God, and mind your own business".

The Archbishop implied that, until recently, almost all had been married in Church. Reading a biography of Thomas Hardy, Jeremiah found that this was not the case. Before about 1870, few, except the well-to-do, had formally married. Most cohabited, their unions being recognised by the Vicar at the 'Church Door'. It was not only that the poor could not afford formal weddings. Having little or nothing to leave, they had no need to legitimise their heirs.

The soaring rate of marital breakdown, in the wake of formalised marriage ceremonies being adopted by many, might suggest that God is not mocked, and watches over the words of his only begotten son, who also said; ".......they will be as the children of light, who neither marry nor are given in marriage". There was no provision made for the marriage of "Adam and Eve".

Chatting over a quick half with Neville led to his seeing a further aspect of this. The 'pre war' generation seems to have assumed the lifelong basis of marriage. 'Keeping to one's vows', 'Marriage is for life' or 'I believe in marriage for life', seem to have been the mores that were passed on. Divorces were difficult and expensive to obtain. Someone had to be caught committing adultery. It is not the one ground given by Jesus, which is fornication.

Few can doubt that the monogamous family is not only the basis of the most stable society, as well as being the best means by which traditional values are passed on. It is probably the most economically viable unit. It is doubtful whether actions of lawmakers, do much to maintain the family. Jeremiah thought of the 'curse' that the Lord would bring upon the faithless (adulterous) people. They would be afflicted with marital infidelity. There could be fewer afflictions more certain to undermine any society. Whereas the kingdom of England might need a stable family as its basic 'building block', the Kingdom of God did not. Were we expecting God to provide a nation, which had turned from the words of his only begotten son, led by those who say, "we see", with this 'blessing'?

Mr Blyth, in another context, had put his finger on it. He was exasperated with some, who were making much of the detailed assertions of the Creed. "I do not believe *in* any Creed", said the Vice Master, "I believe in God". In like manner, it was silly to believe *in* 'marriage for life', or even 'marriage', or 'not believe in divorce'. Could one hope for enduring marriages without belief in God, and the fear of God? Have we been led to hope for the fruits without the tree that bears them? One could not and, indeed, cannot separate one of Jesus' words from the others, all being expressions of the one word. On that matter he is himself clear. "You cannot hear my speech, because you do not perceive my word".

Alongside the apparent break up of the monogamous family has come the change in the status of women. Whether they have increased their influence is open to question. Undoubtedly it seems 'sensible'. It is hard to say what constitutes intelligence, or how it can be measured. The Rabbis recognised that, in many ways, women were wiser than men. It could be said that Eve was more clever than Adam. One consequence may be the production of a mass of under-occupied, 'intelligent', bored and possibly aggressive males. A 'submissive' role was conferred on women, by 'natural processes', as much as anything. It did not mean that they had less influence.

In the gospels they are shewn as occupying such a position. Seldom do they speak. It is forgotten that, at this time, the Jews made provision for the education of children, both boys and girls. Mothers were expected to be the early teachers of the young. Unlike the men, they don't make fools of themselves. Of Jesus' male followers, one betrayed, another denied and the remainder took to their heels. Faithful to the end were two or three women and one young man, who seems not to have been one of the 'twelve'.

In the passage in the book of the prophet Jeremiah, before his vision of the new Covenant, is "The Lord has created a new thing in the earth. A woman shall encompass a man". That would not be fulfilled by women displacing men, as 'dominant'. They would then be as men. The qualities necessary to rule and direct the lives of others are the same, whether exercised by women or men. In most cases, they are those that make for crime. One quality above all is essential. They must think, or feel, themselves to be 'as gods', in relation to those whose lives they direct. They must feel themselves to be possessed of a greater perception of good and evil, right and wrong, than others. Most women were spared this delusion. For any, having ambitions to direct the lives of others, exercising authority as 'rulers of people', the words of Jesus are 'unhearable'. Any, acting on the basis of Jesus' words, would oblige those, who presume to act as 'judges and dividers' over others, to *be* as gods. "You claim to be as gods; get on and be God!"

If the poor in spirit are heirs to the kingdom of Heaven and the meek inherit the earth, then, in their submissive role, women stand higher than the men. It would be for men to emulate them, not the reverse. This is wholly consistent with Jesus' sayings about turning back to be as little children: 'meekness' being a conferred status, rather than a 'moral' quality that can be contrived, like modesty or humility. Newly elected Presidents speak of being 'humbled'. (It does not last long.) No meek man would dream of running for office, or being a 'judge and divider' over others. Jeremiah found himself returning to something he had written, in one of his papers. In the Gospels Jesus was at one in word and act. He, himself, defined words such as meekness, poverty of spirit and the like.

Those who speak and write of 'intelligence' tend, always, to link this to educational attainment. People speak of learning to think. It is a silly phrase, as if people did not do so without schooling. It would be more appropriate to speak of learning to think in certain (approved) ways. These are, inevitably, those that appeared to uphold the accepted 'conversation' and the socio-political and economic order it sustains. Those, with less formal 'training', find it possible to think more independently and clearly. Jeremiah learned this from Jimmy,

Clifford and others. Jimmy was one of the most thoughtful men he had met.

Little children think a lot, usually very clearly. They think independently. In all but physical need, they are 'independent'. They owe nobody anything, not even their parents, as they do not ask to be born. They were not part of the surrounding adult 'conversation'. A little child tends to dominate the household.

Jesus did not promise that he and his words would bring domestic harmony, any more than he promised to bring harmony between what might now be called ethnic groups or nations.

The Archbishop's speech drew forth another pamphlet; its opening modelled on Kierkegaard's parable of the Domestic Goose. Jeremiah called it, 'The Herd of Pigs', enabling him to say that the archiepiscopal pig, at the time, was a boar, but many looked to the time when a well found sow would ascend the throne of S. Augustine. He derided the fact that the moralists in the herd, led by the Archbishop, said that children born out of wedlock could not be the basis of a good society. The great festival of the herd's religion celebrated the birth of a child out of wedlock, declaring it to have been fathered by God himself, not his mother's espoused husband.

In Hannah's case, as with most who had divorced others, it would be almost certain that she would have sworn an oath by almighty God, in order to obtain such a decree. That she and her representatives swore oaths, to asseverate false witness against a neighbour, would give welcome assurance that God had got over any hang-ups he may be thought to have had over this matter as well.

In making these public declarations of unfeigned belief, all who did so knowingly, set a lie at the heart of their life. It was not that people divorced and married others, or swore oaths, but that, having doing so, and while enjoying the fruits of these activities, they made these declarations, which is hypocritical. Jesus' words forced that on all.

Jeremiah was in no position to condemn. He looked on women to want them. Jesus was right in saying that, if one did so one had already committed adultery in one's heart. One had the will to do so, if not the nerve. One might not do so for 'base motives': the inconvenience and complications that would inevitably follow. That was to recognise it as a minefield. The concluding petition of Jesus' prayer is "lead us not into temptation, but deliver us from evil". His friend Bill, the bank manager, had spoken in such terms, when talking of 'key parties'. Bill knew that the most undesirable woman would pick up his key. "You are better, having a 'skinful' lad! At least you know that all you will end up with is a hang over!" That may not be morally noble, but there is no pretence. Bill could not face the sight of *his wife,* Jeanie, disappearing with some other man.

When anyone divorced a partner and married another, the cast off, especially if he or she remained single, while the other married again, could become the most unwelcome person on earth, even if, or, perhaps, because, they had spent years sharing every intimate detail of life together and reared children. However did this happen? Shortly after Hannah had married again, she wrote to him saying that she and her new man were taking the boys to a test match, "you know how they loved going with you". He thought, "what if I were to go too?"

If he had sat next to them and chatted, as if an old friend, all might have been well, but it would be agony. Nobody could know that he might not start recalling memories such as only husband and wife could share. Adolph Hitler would be more welcome. Sitting next to him would be something to talk about. If he had bought them all an ice cream, they could say what a very nice man he was in his private capacity.

What he could see, and had long seen, was that, if one sought to be rid of a partner and marry another, the simplest and most 'elegant' solution, for the sake of all, would be that the unwanted one should have an unfortunate accident and die. When Hannah was in her love nest and she and her lover were seeking to drive him to kill himself, it would have been a welcome solution for Jeremiah himself. Had they provided him with a massive overdose of barbiturates, he would have been grateful. One could then mourn the unwanted one suitably, speak glowingly of him for the rest of one's life, without any risk of embarrassment; but, in truth and act, be heartily glad that he had gone. It was just as when the crowd demanded the death of Jesus. Jeremiah knew, well enough, that he would bewail the need for this to have occurred, but otherwise be heartily glad that others had shouted "Crucify". He would have benefited from their doing so, just as he and almost everyone in Britain now benefited from the cruelties and rapacity of our imperial past, the deceits and cruelties of those that rule.

It was Hannah's decision to go to Newfoundland, taking her man with her that led him to think again of all these matters, driving him back to sayings in the Gospels. It was not that she went, she had been before, but that she insisted that her man went too. He would have done the same, if she had remained single, while he had married another. She would know that he had spent two months and had friends there. She would know that either openly or by implication he would have asserted the sovereignty of Jesus' words, and spoken of her as his wife. He wondered whether she had insisted on her man going with her, as if hoisting a flag.

Did it all matter? Everything went on much as before. He and the ancient Mariner came twelfth out of 130 in the 3 rivers race. They won silver in a down river race and came first in several races in the regatta. How might it have been had she not married her new husband, but simply lived with him? Then, no doubt, there might be some disapproval. How might it have been had she not been well to do, had a well appointed home in a sought after village, with a well to do husband, more than one house, and two yachts? How might it have been had she been a less well-spoken 'lady', or lived in a council flat? People might have been ready to apply the epithet adulteress. In theory, Jesus' words had to be the truth, but it was hard to think of Hannah, with her respected lifestyle, as being so. He could not gainsay the logic of Jesus' words, but they seemed harsh in their ruthless clarity, unless, one adopted the Dog's, "join the club, mate" attitude, and simply owned that it was adultery, as, in all but the act, was looking on a woman to want her. It was made doubly difficult if one assented to the "Ten Commandments".

If all who did so admitted it as such, they would not be in any position to look down on others, who might live in promiscuity, or judge any other malefactors in the name of God, thieves, murderers or bearers of false witness. If one was going to admit that a 'relationship', after divorcing a husband or wife was adultery, why bother to marry a second time? The veneer of respectability that marriage conferred made Jesus' words unbelievable. To admit that one was, in this way, committing adultery, was vastly different from implicitly assuring all that Jesus was wrong to speak thus of it. That is to impugn the truth of all that he said.

It was Joy who made him see this. She said, "Just because she went to an expensive school and talks posh and is rich, your wife would look down on us. She goes to Church: she says she believes in God and Jesus. She says that you must not commit adultery. We don't. What right has she to look down on us? I haven't never committed adultery;....and if that bugger ever did, I'd kill him", she added, referring to Jimmy.

Having been pregnant and unmarried at seventeen, marrying soon after their elder daughter was born, Joy and Jimmy had endured much abuse from the righteous. This hurt Joy; less so, it seemed, Jimmy, who was out at work. The fact that, thirty two years later, they were still enjoying each other's company, did little to affect the disdain of the righteous, many of whom wagged their heads, when they married, saying, "That wont last....". The fact that some, who had disdained them, had visited the divorce courts themselves more than once, made no difference, nor the fact that they had brought up two daughters in ways that put many to shame.

Joy spoke of the time when, early in their married life, her mother was taken ill, for a prolonged period, ever in an out of hospital. It was left to herself and Jimmy to look after her, while having two young children. Jimmy worked all hours to earn money to support himself, Joy, the children and Joy's mother. He said simply, "I had the money, she needed it, what else would you do?" Jeremiah knew, all too well, what else he would have done: kept his money in the bank! When Joy's mother died, all changed. Nieces, daughters in law, and a myriad of others appeared. She and Jimmy were left in the corner, while others arranged funerals, and many gathered like vultures. She had "let the family down". It was as if it was all they were fit for, almost like Molly clearing up after a barbecue.

She and Jimmy were wanted when anyone was in a fix, but as soon as they had done their bit, others were preferred. Jimmy had spent most of his secondary school days digging lugworms on the muds. He was amazingly quick witted. Though he said little, what he did say was always well thought, shewed keen critical awareness, had freshness and independence, and was often very funny, if he could get a word in edgeways.

He took it for granted that those of the Christian religion were hypocrites. He had learned to be a bricklayer when the lugworms declined. While almost all on the building site tended to help themselves to bits and pieces, the one who was the biggest thief, and took materials not just for his own use, but to sell to friends, was a prominent member of the Salvation army. "Its fine for such as them, they can steal and lie all week, go off to church on Sundays and get forgiveness, then do the same things next week!" It was more or less what the prophet Jeremiah said of those at the Temple.

When Joy and Jimmy lived only a few doors up the road from the Citadel, Jimmy was on his roof, removing the old straw and mortar that was under the pantiles, replacing it with roofing felt. In 'her' kitchen Joy heard the strains of a band in the distance. Rushing out into the road she stood in the street, arms outstretched, shouting, "Don't you dare", as the band marched by, underneath. There was Jimmy, eyes twinkling with innocence, broom in hand, ready to sweep three large piles of decayed mortar and straw, bird shit and other detritus onto the bonnets and caps of the worthy salvationists on their way to the citadel. "Go on, Joy. Let me".

Jimmy's sharp intelligence, and the fact of having missed much schooling, allowed him an independence of thought that few others had. Jeremiah envied him this and his integrity. He saw instantly, what it had taken his lumbering mind twenty years to see, that such services as weddings, however much religious language obfuscated the issue, implied that God was a controllable being. So did forms of absolution for sins, just as sacrificial offerings. "They are all right. They have God in their pocket".

Joy said that she wished she could be persuaded. If she could, she would be off to Church. She and Jimmy were too sharp witted not to see that such a being could not be God. It was more like the Genie in the lamp, who could be let out to do things when the lamp was polished properly. The genie did things when let out of the lamp. The God of religion was, Jeremiah thought, more akin to a garden gnome, forever fishing at the side of an infinite goldfish pond in the sky, but catching nothing, as there was no hook or line on his rod. Thus occupied, he kept a benevolent but sightless eye on the affairs of man.

Such language typifies most that passes for theology, it being obvious that an infinite pond can have no edges, sightless eyes cannot watch; any more than life *after death* can be eternal.

The wedding of their daughter duly took place. Jeremiah would not attend the service, despite the fact that the Vicar said that each case had to be judged on its merits and in the case of Joy and Jimmy's daughter, it was clearly a case for a second wedding in his Church. Those of the Church of God agreed. It was odd that Jesus did not see things thus, another example of his being theologically primitive, not to mention his making 'wild generalisations'. The new father in law explained that to adopt Jesus' attitude was unmerciful. No doubt he would think it merciful to remove danger signs at the edge of a crumbling cliff.

The father of the new husband, his wife at his side, saw fit to stand over their new daughter in law and browbeat her with the marriage service of the book of Common Prayer of 1662, of which the poor girl knew nothing, to impose her wifely duties upon her. They did not see fit so to do with regard to their son.

Despite the upset of cancelled visit to Newfoundland, and being well aware of the hurt that the seemingly inbuilt hypocrisy of the Christian religion caused to many, Jeremiah was still unable to see that, in any objective sense, it mattered.

Jesus did not think that hypocrisy did not matter. It was his one sustained indictment against the upholders of the religion of his day; but Jesus believed in God.

Chapter Twenty Nine

"When he speaks a lie he speaks of himself"

After the cancelled visit to Newfoundland, Jeremiah's elder son's girl friend parted from him. She had been a devoted companion for four years, but had discovered 'goings on', when he had brought her back to England, and was angry. His son phoned him, in very low spirits. He was drinking, smoking and taking tranquilizers, but had been doing so only for a few days. He went out again, this time, shortly after Christmas.

It was wonderful to be back in the open friendliness of the province again. The airport at St Johns was the gateway to heaven. He loved the flight on the small plane to Gander, where his son met him. They had a meal at his favourite eating house on earth, inappropriately called "Jungle Jim's", there being three feet of snow; before making their way to the coast. On his first day he walked up the road to make a surprise call on old friends. Their youngest son saw him walking up the path and rushed in to say "It's Jeremiah". It was wonderful to see them again.

After about a week, a friend of his son's arrived. He was a young man from Devon, who had met Jeremiah, fleetingly, once before. He kept a 'dog lodge' and was known as "Awesome". He called Jeremiah "Old duffer". Back in England, Jimmy and Joy moved into his house and, under Jimmy's direction, were fitting a new kitchen. E- mails went to and fro. They had finished the kitchen, fitted new units, refloored it, redecorated it and put in a new ceiling. What about a new bathroom? Having finished the bathroom; what about the hall, stairs and landing? Then they stripped all the painted doors and returned them to bare wood.

Two doors down the road from his son lived a man and his wife, who was known as the 'Boss'. They had been good friends to his son when he was in trouble, listening to him as he poured out his sorrow. Late one night, Jeremiah returned from spending the evening with his friends. There was nobody about, but a light in the basement. His son was watching a video, stopped the film and explained the story. Jeremiah went to sit down on the sofa, when a head appeared, wearing what looked like war-time gas mask glasses. Curled up on the floor was a young nurse, on vacation from Nova Scotia.

His son's difficulties were compounded by the fact that, as senior medical officer, he had a running battle with the woman who was the hospital administrator. A doctor from S Africa had been in that position. He had resigned to take his wife back to Africa, where he left her. In the emergency they had asked his son to take over. The original senior medical officer returned and wanted to resume his position. It was further complicated by the fact that, having left his wife, he had moved in with the administrator's sister or cousin. His son had, impulsively, resigned his post to seek work elsewhere, but did not find any positions to his liking, as he hated working on 'fee for service', which meant that time was spent in accounting, with consequent pressure to rush patients through. He wrote to the hospital, asking if he could resume working there.

He did not want to be senior officer, finding that the extra duties made it not worthwhile. If they let him return, he would stay there for 25 years. Jeremiah admired the way he worked. One evening, having driven back from a medical conference, four hours' drive away, he had immediately to go out. There had been an accident on the road that led down to the port. A lad in a truck had skidded and overturned, was unconscious, bleeding badly and trapped in the wreck. None of the doctors on duty thought it necessary to go, but left it to the ambulance crew and a nurse. His son got into his car and drove to the spot.

He was full of admiration for the work of the RCMP and emergency services. They had installed arc lights and warm air heaters, cut a flight of steps down the bank in the ice, and had men with cutting equipment, trying to free the victim. Eventually they got the lad free. He had broken ribs, legs and pelvis. Needing major surgery, he would have to go to one of the big hospitals at either Grand Falls, or S Johns. Someone had to decide whether to send him straight there, or take him back to the hospital and stabilise him. It was not a responsibility that could be thrown on a nurse. He decided to bring him back. Then, there was the problem of arranging transport to one of the larger hospitals. It meant that his son did not return home until about 3am. He was angry with his colleagues; "What do they train to be doctors for, to save lives or to kill?" This aspect of his work, he loved. Jeremiah felt that he was a man 'at unity with himself'. Working as he did, all was justified for him, by a simple reference to the command of Jesus to the lawyer, "Go and do thou likewise". He pointed beyond himself and medical practice to the one who said of healing the sick, "Freely have you received, freely give"; but going to an accident, when those on call had refused, could cause unease with colleagues.

There is something repugnant in medical practitioners and others in ‘professional’ positions, who attend Churches, earning a large amount of money and enjoying 'status', while condescending to their patients. They, then, suck no small advantage out of the pains and sicknesses of others. Jeremiah realised what a predicament his son was in. With the old duffer, he was free to fall back on the sayings of the gospels. He could silence him, by referring him to such words. He could not do so in Hannah's household. Hannah's man would sneer at him; might even accuse of talking like his dad. The same would be true of his professional friends, in whose company he did not seem 'at unity with himself'. While more amenable to live in a household where those words were 'off-limits', to be able to fall back on their finality saved much argument. It could be said to give rest unto one's soul; but it also tied one to them.

Was being 'at unity with oneself' to be a 'living soul'? In the Psalter and the book of Job it was 'having integrity'. To practise medicine, as he did then, was to do so, as a 'little child'. A little child, if it knew how, would rush out and save a life. That was why children wanted to be doctors. They did not think of the salaries they would earn, nor the status they might enjoy. It gave his son integrity in relation to the things he had said, when seeking to become a physician. When interviewed, he, as others, would have responded to questions about why he wanted to become a doctor in the language of the little child. He would have spoken of devoting his life to the sick and injured, not of enjoying a good salary and social position. Most would come to dismiss such ideas as 'immature', or 'unrealistic'.

He would know that, for all his mother's attendance at Church and declarations of belief, there could be little place for any, who turned back to be as little children in that household. Words of Jesus had to be 'off-limits'. If 'Go and do likewise' be given final authority, so must all else that he said. Did his elder son find such 'inconsistency' of word and words 'frightening'? The somewhat bogus position of doctors, not only enjoying large salaries, but also being seen as angels of mercy, was made clear, when Jeremiah stayed with his younger son and spoke, with admiration, of the long hours his brother worked. "I work those hours every week, and I am actually working, not 'on call' with a bleeper".

He was more highly qualified, working in telecommunications laboratories. He did not enjoy the status of a 'doctor', though he was one. Such as he, were not prayed for in churches. Those doing research, such as he had done, might contribute much to the treatments provided by medicine. It was such as they, who invented and designed lasers with which surgical procedures could be performed, scanning equipment and the like.

Awesome went to New York for a week, flying from Gander. He could drive himself there in Jeremiah's son's car, but how could the car be brought back? The nurse cheerfully agreed to go with Awesome and drive the rig back, ice or no ice. She had a sister who lived near Gander. If need be, she could stay the night. She did not, but arrived that evening, blew in and chatted for a while. When his son was feeling low, she had been on vacation, and had appeared with a meal, most evenings, sitting with him to make sure he ate it. "He thinks that nobody appreciates what he does. He needs a lot of reassurance. It's nothing that a few bear hugs won’t put right!" So powerful were they, that anyone, thus reassured, would be likely to suffer asphyxia.

Jeremiah thanked her for befriending his son in time of need. "I don't need thanks. It's what you do. I'd be there for him tomorrow if I thought he needed me. You don't ask for anything in return". With that she disappeared

They had been to Cornerbrook for a weekend’s skiing with three other women doctors. The one, with whom his son was staying in the hotel, asked why an American hockey player had "3:16", on his T-shirt. "I can tell you what that means", said Jeremiah. It's a reference to the IVth Gospel, "God so loved the world, that he gave his only begotten son......." Heard thus, it was misleading. The word 'so' could only be understood as "so greatly", whereas it meant "in this way". That chance question was like an unexpected appearance of the one who spoke those words.

Awesome came back from New York, about a week before he and his son were due to return to England. The nurse reappeared. Jeremiah came in, one afternoon, to find her sitting with him. She had brought a box of date slices, but they had eaten them all. Next afternoon she appeared with more. His son returned, saying, "I have to go to Foodland and the Liquor store." They were going out that evening, to the friends down the road. The nurse went with him.

They came back full of merriment. When his son pushed his trolley down one of the aisles, the nurse had detached herself and gone to the far side of the shop. When out of sight, she had shouted, "Have you remembered the chicken, darling? That will get them talking!"

A few days later, Awesome and his son left for England. He rushed up the steps to his house, where Jeremiah was standing, flung both arms about him, saying, "I don't want to go back, dad, I am at home here. I want to make a difference". With that he ran down, got into his rig and was gone.

A few days before their departure, there had been a telephone call from a 'lady' in England, long known to his son. When he brought the girl friend over from Newfoundland, this 'lady' had been present. When they went out in a party, she had not hesitated to monopolise his son, leaving the girl from Newfoundland on her own. She was a close friend of his sister, her mother a friend of Hannah. She offered to fetch him in her car from Heathrow and drive him to Plymouth. Jeremiah had walked in, when his son was on the phone, wandering about with the handset at his ear. It was a very long call, so he asked, "Who is it?" Awesome answered, "It's sour puss!" The 'lady' on the phone overheard and said sharply, "I heard that and I am not amused!" It was odd that she should have assumed that an overheard comment referred to her.

For the next week, Jeremiah had the time of his life. Neither the friends down the road, nor his old friends, would allow him to sit around alone. When his last morning came, his friend, Eric, said that he would drive him to a crossing place, where another doctor, a contemporary from Cambridge, would collect him. It was like returning to boarding school. He looked out for the truck to appear, counting each precious second. He recalled a remark of Molly's, when she said that she saw things, as if for the last time. It was a terrible day, with ice on the roads and snow falling. The ploughs had not been out. Eric made light of it; "I have driven along this road in far worse conditions than this". He was lying. He later said that he had never driven in such bad conditions, but that was on the telephone, when safely home and Jeremiah was back in England.

The "Boss" had said that his son needed much reassuring and would value reassurance from Jeremiah. He wanted to think that his dad felt that he was doing worthwhile work. He had complained that he seldom congratulated him. When he had qualified, Jeremiah had said, "I am very glad". If he had said, "Well done", what would he have said if he had failed?

He sat down with an exercise book and gave much thought to the matter. What value was his opinion? None at all. It had to be based on some reference point that transcended whatever he might feel. He set his son's work under the sayings of Jesus. He wrote of 'doing the truth'. He had said that, if he were given his job back, he would stay for 25 years. If circumstances beyond his control obliged him to remain there for 25 years, those words would be made true. That they were so would, then, be "wrought in God".

People, who had little in a remote township, deserved as good medical treatment as anyone else. If he set himself to provide it, he would, "make a difference". The people loved him. He told how, on his first visit, having been there only a day, at dinner and disco for the 'friends' of the hospital, Eric's wife, Ada, whom he had never before seen, introduced herself. She said, "We love your son". He had never been so proud in all his life. Relative to most others, doctors earned a lot. Working as he did, he almost justified it.

He went round the wards in the hospital most evenings, stopping to say "Good night" to each patient. He told him of Arthur in the nick at Norwich, and how that simple act lifted the spirits of inmates and how they looked forward to it. It might be of almost as great benefit as the drugs he prescribed. Such an act could make his hospital different from any other. If continued for 20 years, it might even become famous. He noted that the nurse had said that she did the same when on duty, saying "Goodnight, sleep well", to every patient on the ward.

Most of the patients in the hospital were very old. Many would go to sleep wondering if they would ever wake again. What a difference it would make, in such circumstances, to lapse into sleep with a "good night, sleep well", rather than silence. He recalled a saying of Jesus, "If you greet those that greet you, what is the good of that?"

A patient had been brought in who suffered with Parkinson's disease. The doctor at the outport clinic thought she had suffered a heart attack. The ECG indicated this. A student was there at the time. All was prepared for her to have the electric shock pads. In a moment of inspiration, his son said, "Hang on a moment, she seems too 'compos mentis' to have suffered a severe heart attack, whatever the ECG shews". He gave her drugs to control the Parkinson's spasms, then repeated the ECG; to find it normal. 'That being so, what do I do?'

He rang the consultant at St Johns. Some hours later he received a call from the chief consultant in Toronto, asking whether he would mind if he published the details of this case, which had been faxed to him. He thought that he had spotted something very significant, that a neurological condition might over-ride other indications on an ECG. The difference between noticing something like that and not doing so was almost 'chance', as were many things in life. Failure to pick up a phone or mishear something, dismissing something as trifling when it was serious, could all be matters of chance. That one heard aright; that he had spotted this phenomenon, when nobody else had, might be seen as, "wrought in God"

This he left on his son's pillow. The Boss said that it pleased him to find it.

When his son returned to Newfoundland, they spoke on the phone. He was bitter and angry. Nobody was grateful; all were very demanding. Being compassionate was a thing of the past. Jeremiah asked, "Why should people be grateful? You are well paid for what you do. You don't express gratitude to the fisherman who catches fish, the slaughter house men who kills animals, or even the people who keep the drains clear". Nobody prays for them in Church either. "Let us pray for all drain cleaners, sewage operators, pest controllers and water engineers" would not have the same ring as "all doctors and nurses, judges, teachers and those that rule the nations". Dentists don't get a mention either.

He hated the rough potholed roads, the lack of amenities, and the rough and ready manners. Jeremiah preferred the way that the Newfies approached one, baseball caps pulled own, looking as if they were going to slit your throat, but looked up, blossomed into a smile and said, "Hi, nice to see you back again", to the veneer of good manners.

On his return to England, his first call was on Joy and Jimmy, who led him to his refurbished home. It was wonderful. They wanted to know how soon he could go away again, as they had their eyes on the rest of it. "It wont cost much", said Jimmy, only a bit of paint and some plaster. His younger son and his wife had given him a lot of money to spend on the house. Jimmy also pointed out how much better the sitting room would look, with the stained floors sanded and returned to light pine.

He could not wait to return to Newfoundland. Ada came from a remote community called Rencontre. She spoke of it as if it were the Garden of Eden. If he came in summer, she and Eric would take him there.

It was February. He telephoned several times to see if his son was feeling more cheerful. He was a little more so, saying that the nurse was coming home for a weekend, and that they were going to have an evening together. They would eat one of the fish pies that Jeremiah had left in his freezer.

Awesome felt that the two were at ease with each other. Jeremiah felt that the lass was 'there', when wanted, but could leave his son to be by himself. The "Boss" telephoned and said that he seemed to be settling back again. He was ever like this after returning to the UK. Jeremiah put the matter from his mind. In mid March he had a phone call. It was Awesome. "Got news for you old duffer", said the soft, cheerful, Devon voice. "What have you gone and done now? "Nothing", said Awesome, "it's great news, I have had an E-mail. It covers two sides of A. 4".

"Its from Halifax, Nova Scotia", said Awesome. He then read two pages of ecstatic happiness, such as would make a reader of romantic fiction shed tears by the bucketful. It was from the nurse. She had such wonderful news, that she had to share it with somebody. She told the story of herself but did not identify the other person. An hour ago she had had a call from an English doctor, whom she adored. He was the man she always turned to when in any trouble. She shared all her happinesses with him. She could not dream that an educated English doctor would ever cast a second glance at a country girl from Newfoundland like herself. They had planned to hang out together when she was on holiday over Easter. He had phoned her to say that he might not be able to do so, as he had a rich lady from England, who insisted on coming over.

His son had said that he could not put the lady off. She could only come at Easter, having business commitments for the rest of the year. He hoped that the young nurse would not mind. She said that he should not consider her feelings, especially as the lady was family friend. (She had been to a college for the production of ladies.)

The doctor had replied that her feelings mattered greatly to him. He asked how she felt about him. She said that she poured out her heart. He then gave her to understand that they could be lifelong companions, and "could we make a go of it together relationshipwise?" Jeremiah did not need any training in 'form' criticism to recognise such phrases as those of his son. "Then was her mouth filled with laughter and her tongue with joy". Miracles happened; "the Lord hath done great things for us".

The E-mail's joyous happiness was the ingenuous, uncontrived expression of one who loved much. It sprang from the heart of one who was as a little child, so filled with joy that she had to share it with someone: someone at a distance, not daring to pour out her heart to anyone close by. All that this 'country girl' from Newfoundland said and did took Jeremiah straight to the Gospels. She had brought food to his son when he was hungry, comforted him when sorrowful, reassured him when he was unsure. Her E-mail shewed her to be one, 'who loved much'. Her exultant joy, that an educated English doctor had cast more than a second glance at a 'simple country girl from Newfoundland', recalled the words of Mary.

Jeremiah thought that the nurse would be an ideal companion. His son seemed wholly at ease in her company. She would be happy to make a home in his rented house, and they could build up a home for themselves, before buying one. He would not need always to be the life and soul of the party. They could go off to concerts and he would have no need to make observant comments. It would be enough just to enjoy it. She would take the fact that he had a daughter in her stride. She would not attempt to become a substitute mother, but would be as she was to her many nephews and nieces. With her as his companion he would 'make a difference'. The young nurse came of a prominent Catholic family. They could achieve unity with themselves, by abandoning their 'religious allegiances' and building their house on the rock of the sayings of Jesus.

Awesome was hesitant. "I have to tell you, old Duffer, that your son is a lying little git, and I would not want to see this lass hurt. She's too good for that". Jeremiah agreed, but said that he did not think his son would deceive one, who had been so good a friend. Awesome agreed. They both formed the opinion that jumping into bed with his son, or 'providing the joys of fornication', did not seem to be the nurse's way; at least as far as founding a lasting 'relationship' went. It seemed that friendship, love and companionship came first on her 'agenda'.

She could not bear being in the same town, fearing that the love of her life would cast her aside in favour of a rich and educated lady from England. Awesome E-mailed her to say that she need not worry on that score; he had met the 'lady'. Since she was spending $400 on her flight to Newfoundland from Nova Scotia, why not add another $300 and come over to England. She could stay with him and his dogs; then both could go up to stay with the old duffer, who was currently away from home. She would see if she could buy a ticket.

A week or so later, Awesome was uneasy, and phoned the old Duffer. He laid a cunning plan. He would telephone his son and tell him a lot of nonsense about his own 'love life'. At the last minute he would ask, "How's your own"?

He phoned Jeremiah. "All is well, old duffer!" He had done as he said. He asked, "How is your own love life then, Doc?' The reply was that the lady doctor who had provided for his son at the hotel, and another young lady from Grand Falls had both been 'kicked into touch'. The lass from Newfoundland, whom he had brought to England, agreed that it was 'all over'. The lady who was 'not amused' was being told not to come. "You are a randy little git: how will you manage without a woman in your life?" The answer was "I am making a go of it with the nurse".

The expected visit drew near. She would be in England for her birthday, and they would be with Jeremiah at the time. He spoke to his friends. "We'll give her a party to remember". Joy bakes the most delicious sponge cakes. "Find out how old she is, and I'll get the numbers". Jeremiah was busy getting his boat ready for the water. The nurse had found it impossible to get a ticket through a consolidator. "Tell her to buy one direct from Air Canada", said Jeremiah, if she cannot find the extra cash, I'll send it".

All was arranged. Jeremiah thought that it would make the party, if his son phoned to wish the lass a happy Birthday, so he rang him. "I've got Awesome coming up next week and he is bringing a friend." Without any prompting his son said, "Not-----------", and mentioned her name. It seemed extraordinary that the first name that should spring to mind was that of someone living on the other side of the Atlantic. He went on to say how kind they were all being. Jeremiah said "Could you phone her at about 9pm English time". "Why ever should I do that, dad?"

Jeremiah was aghast, but had forgotten Awesome's telephone call, only remembering the ecstatic E Mail. His son said, "in my experience, dad, it always pays to be truthful." Jeremiah resented being given the benefit of the experience of someone 25 years his junior, and was instantly suspicious. In *his* experience, phrases like "it pays to be truthful" seldom precede the truth any more than, "Yours very truly", follows it. The stream of flattery about his kindness made him wary. His son began talking like an academic, wandering about as he lectured, trying to find the right words. "I think that, if I remember rightly, what I said on the phone was that, if we had known how we felt about each other years ago, we might have made a go of it relationshipwise. I reviewed the situation historically, as it were........"

Jeremiah was thunderstruck. It might be he and Awesome who would be left to break the news. He could not sleep, but dozed off for a couple of hours. When he awoke, it was as if he were his famous namesake, hearing "Thus saith the Lord, thy son lieth, and thou knowest that he lies".

He had recalled Awesome's cunning plan and his phone call. He got up and wrote to his son, inviting him to sit in a jury and hear three witnesses. First there was the young nurse and her E mail, sent only an hour after the event. Joy and her daughter had told him that no woman would confuse a hesitant historical review with what amounted to a proposal. He imagined the evidence of Awesome being given. He had carefully planned what to say. He would be listening only for the response to his final question, and would remember those words for certain. Then there was his son's hesitant discourse. Which would he believe to be speaking the truth? His son's words, about reviewing the matter historically, wondering, 'if they had realised how they felt about each other years ago', lacked truth. Years ago they had hardly known each other. Jeremiah had met the nurse, fleetingly, on his first visit when she burst into someone else's house. He had never seen anything of her, or heard her mentioned until the last visit. To make matters worse, once Awesome had received confirmation of his intentions, Jeremiah had written to the young nurse, seeking to reassure her that his son would be true to his words.

Here was an example of words being made untrue. He felt sure that his son did speak to the nurse as she said. He confirmed as much in the phone call to Awesome. When he did so he was speaking the truth. He tended to say what he felt would make people happy, just as when he wrote to the mother of his child, saying that she and his daughter would be ever welcome, and that his only problem would be his unwillingness ever to see them depart. Then, as seemed characteristic for many, if not all, he began to have second thoughts, probably as a result of conversations with others. His rambling explanation reeked of other people's words and thoughts. "It pays always to be truthful", did not refer to an accurate recall of what he had said, but that he should be truthful with her, about his intentions. It is the right thing to do, for her sake. The Minister of the Church would no doubt say that he was right to do so, so would his mother.

He said of the nurse, "She is only a nice kid". Others had said almost the same. Some added that she had much growing up to do. 'Yes', thought Jeremiah, 'and you will have done much to assist that process!' He could imagine ministers of the gospel and 'wise' people, echoing that sentiment. They would even say that, in making her grow up, he was doing the right thing, for her sake. No doubt some might say, "It's high time she learned to live in the real world", and that he would have helped her do so. "You were right to be truthful".

Having said such things, they would go off to Church, and pray, "Our father which art in heaven. Thy kingdom come....". All would solemnly declare belief in "One Lord Jesus Christ, the only begotten son of God, God from God, Light from Light, Very God from Very God". Had he not said something about turning back to be as little children? Had he not said, "I thank thee O father Lord of heaven and earth, that thou has hid these things from the wise and prudent and revealed them to babes?" Did he not say, "Their Holy angels were ever before the face of their father in heaven"? Worse yet, he warned that any who cause offence to the least of these his little ones, "it were better for that man that a great millstone were hanged about his neck and that he be drowned in the depth of the sea?"

If publicly declared believers, in one way or another encouraged his son to discard the nurse, as "having a lot of growing up to do", were they not leading him to cause her offence?

Encouraged by all right thinking Christian men and women, he would be assuring any who might hear, that any words of Jesus, about being as little children, should be disregarded. They could forget about the possibility of holy angels before the face of their father. The very notion of supernatural beings with white wings was laughable.

Jeremiah had sought to reassure, on the basis of the sayings of Jesus in the Gospels. Had he not, on the selfsame basis, to do the opposite? Jesus had said to Peter, when he declared that he believed him to be the Christ, the son of the living God, "Blessed art thou, for flesh and blood hath not revealed it unto thee". When Peter, no doubt from 'deeply caring' motives, rebuked Jesus, for speaking of being delivered to the gentiles, Jesus said, "Get thee behind me Satan....".

He was stretched between to 'worlds' and their 'conversations'. There was no bridge over the great gulf, which separated Dives from Lazarus. By all sensible criteria, his son had done the 'right thing'. Only one 'conversation' made it otherwise, that which spoke of returning to be as little children and, "by their fruits shall ye know them". This was what he did not want. Not only would he lose his wife and home, but 'his' children also, and his happy visits to Newfoundland. It seemed that his feelings, as he awaited Eric, were being realised.

Hannah, his son and their circle were doing only that which the accredited upholders of the Christian religion taught them. They gave the same assurance as the Supreme Lord and Governor, in her Christmas broadcast. Always she recalled her subjects, in a voice simpering with hypocrisy, to the one "born this day". By repute, she is one of the richest woman on earth, a great collector of Jewellery and objets d'art: just the kind of things anyone might be forgiven for thinking were "treasure on earth". Those in high positions obviously need not hear the warning of Jesus, that their 'heart would be there also'. She assured all that, if one had had riches, position and knowledge, there existed a six lane highway that bypassed the sayings of Jesus, and led straight to the gates of heaven, without inconvenient bottlenecks like eyes of needles. Lesser folk would have to make do with the narrow way.

Over lunch at Merton, Jeremiah told John Carey of the story of the nurse. Half way through they went to the buffet to get their next course. When they sat down. Carey said "How lovely". Only then did he finish the story.

His son telephoned the nurse, explaining that she had misheard or misunderstood him. He was sorry, but it was always best to be truthful. Having thus made it 'right', he assured her that they would always be "the same good friends".

A second's thought would have told him that it had to be untrue. It would be made so, as Joy, whose thoughts, like Jimmy's, were uninhibited by any need to say the acceptable thing, saw instantly. With the elegantly educated lady in residence, could she open the door and walk in, as before? Could she, again, curl up on the floor unseen, as they watched a video, and feel so secure that she did not even feel a need to shew herself when an old duffer walked in? For his son, would he ever find another companion who would be content to be with him, leave him to be alone when he wanted, but talk merrily when he wanted to chat? Could he find another who would cheerfully accept his daughter?

The hypocrisy and lies, involved in public declarations of belief, in One Lord Jesus Christ, seemed to lead to other words being made lies, within moments of their utterance. Was that what being children of the "father of lies" amounted to? Did "our Father in Heaven", so blind and stupefy us, when we said such self-justifying things as, "we will be just the same good friends", that we could not see that they had to become lies?

Jeremiah saw that all resulted largely from of his own obduracy. Had he not spoken as he did at that talk all those years ago, he would now be at ease with a wife, and have about £30,000 a year to live on. He had obliged his sons and daughter to try and bestride an unbridgeable gulf. He would never have done so, but for what the IVth and other evangelists reported, and what those who went to Church declared. Aside from their 'reports', would it have crossed his mind that those who divorced and married others committed adultery? Now he was stuck with it.

Had his tendency to fall back to those words, caused unease about marriage to the former girl friend who had divored her husband? Jeremiah liked the lass and enjoyed her company; but there was no escaping what Jesus said. Here was an oddity. While he would have found nothing amiss in the two of them being lifelong companions, simply 'living together'; he felt that Hannah and her circle would.

The only words that, in any way, 'justified' his behaviour over the past twenty years were those spoken by Jesus. Should he now throw them aside, and join the conversation of his wife, her man, her former lover, her solicitor and the lady who was not amused? He would gain nothing if he did. He would lose everything. He had lost almost all anyway. "From him that hath not, shall be taken even that which he hath". He might as well stick with those words. "Eternal life" was about all he had left to 'go for'. Only one spoke words of eternal life. When Jesus turned to the twelve asking, "Will ye also go away?" Peter had said, "Where shall we go? Thou hast the words of eternal life".

He had constantly made matters worse, deluding himself that it would be the reverse. He had driven his wife into the arms of her lover and, probably without knowing it, provoked them into their campaign to rid themselves of him, almost by 'turning the other cheek'. Had he responded to the phone calls, without shewing himself distraught, they would not have persisted. He made matters worse not better, by recalling the treachery of Judas, by confronting the court and going to prison. He had reinforced this by acting as he did in the courts, feeling that, by being the hounded victim, Hannah would relent.

He did not 'act a part' as on stage. He acted as he did, impulsively, simply expressing what he truly thought and felt. It might seem endearing, when projected on a screen. In life it aroused contempt and made people uneasy. He would have been better advised to have heeded the poem of the later Isaiah, than films and novels. He had constantly adopted the 'wrong attitudes'. They were, however, revealing; telling him much about those with whom he dealt. He found himself cast down and often wept. Many scorned this, especially Hannah. What then of the words of the one in whom they declared belief? "Blessed those that weep, they shall be comforted".

In acting and speaking as he did, he was 'believing their report'. That may have made him a source of unease, even a threat. When Hannah had left, after telling him that he could not be otherwise than he was, given his upbringing and ancestry, he fell back on Hosea. He would not have heard of Hosea but for the report of those who went to Church and declared belief. Could or would Jesus have spoken as he did, had not those of the synagogue read and expounded the prophets?

In 'believing their report', he was ambivalent. He could not truly think that they believed what they said. He deluded himself that, because he took them at their word, they would feel bound to do so. It had the opposite effect. It provoked endless argument, defending their position and impugning the genuineness of his; so further entrenching them. They had a case, though it seemed to be becoming less true. He was coming to believe the things he found himself saying. He was achieving for himself, what he hoped to achieve in others. Instead of binding *them* to their public words of belief, he found *himself* bound by them. If it had not been so, there would have been no truth in him. It was not through any design or desire of his, that he now found himself 'doing the truth'. He had been obliged to spend the last thirty years of his life, against his wishes, making good many 'idle words'. Jesus had said that for every idle word they utter, shall the children of men be called to account, in the day of judgement. If there is God, an eternal being, that day must be ever present, not a future event.

Jesus transformed the understanding of the word 'believe'. What a nuisance that man is; or the four evangelists, reporting him as they did. In normal 'conversation', to believe is something less than to 'know'. For Jesus, if anyone declares belief and does not act thereupon, they do not believe. 'What use is it to call me, Lord, Lord, if you do not do what I say?'

Jeremiah had dug down a hole and buried himself yet again. It seemed that there was no rabbit in it, either. When he wrote to his son, it was, "whatever I command thee, thou shalt speak". He had written in the hope that he would help to bring the dream like happiness of the nurse to fulfilment, and see his son settled with a lifetime companion with whom he would be able to 'make a difference'. He achieved the opposite. By upholding the truth of the young nurse, he helped to drive his son into the arms of the one who is not amused. He had even written to him saying so. Now he had landed himself with another lot of words, which he would either have to make idle, or risk everything he enjoyed in this life.

His son had spoken about the coming visit of the 'lady', who was not amused, as his 'destiny'. Words like 'destiny' are meaninglessly neutral, when brought 'into the light'. One could say that it was the destiny of Caiaphas to speak and act as he did. It was Judas' destiny to betray with a kiss. It might be said to have been Peter's destiny to deny; but he went out and wept bitterly. Words of Jesus set all in the light. "It is necessary that the Son of Man be betrayed, but woe to that man by whom he is betrayed. It were better for him that he had never been born". Was such a comment one of condemnation? Was it not rather a sorrowful recognition of the truth?

The nurse had said; "I would be there for him tomorrow, if ever he needed me". Those words would now, surely, be made empty.

If Jeremiah had sought a life, perfectly arranged to lead him to see that the words he had read as a child, which had so impressed him with their clarity and truth, were indeed so, he had been given one. It was not well arranged for anything else. He did not arrange or want it to be thus. He had driven, not only, his elder son; but all three 'children', his wife and many others into a position, in which they had either to say 'Yes', or cast him out. Jesus had been unequivocal when sending out his disciples to represent him. Where their words were not received, they were to go forth.

Once again, if he had foreseen the outcome, he would not have written and spoken as he did. He had achieved the alienation of his elder son, along with Hannah and their daughter, younger son and his wife and so his grandsons. He had said goodbye to the event in his year that he looked forward to. It seemed 'silly'. He had hardly spoken two hundred words to the nurse. Apart from the things I have mentioned, he knew nothing of her. He had never seen the 'lady', nor spoken a word to her. He had spent hours chatting with his son's former girl friend. Why make an 'issue' of this incident?

He needed, more than ever, that there is, in reality, God, and that Jesus is his only begotten son. This seemed to summarise the crisis that the evangelists' report of Jesus, or, rather, Jesus himself, forced on the world. His wife and elder son stood in Church services, declaring belief in these things. He needed them to be true. They needed them not to be. It was the same for him, when he attended the services of the Church, though he 'half' hoped that what was declared therein was the truth. When he stood and declared belief in Jesus as God from God and Light from Light, he spoke of the one whose words and acts the evangelists reported. The more he came to know of those words and acts the more uneasy he felt. All he could hope, now, was that those words were the truth.

He was still ambivalent. He needed the sayings of Jesus to be true. They alone justified what he had found himself doing, even if he did so on what proved to be false expectations. That might be fine, 'for the past', but he was still alive. Jesus was remorseless, "He that endures to the end......"; "No man putting his hand to the plough and looking back......". However did any man speak with such ruthless clarity? How did four men come to attribute such words to anyone? It could only be that this singular man spoke as they reported.

He had done as his mother's terrier, not once, but many times. Always it seemed that, at the last gasp, a devoted owner had heard him scratching, lifted the floorboards and extricated the exhausted dog. It began to seem that others, like Hannah and her lawyers, her father and cousin, might have been left down the hole. By extraordinary chances his every childhood dream had been fulfilled. He had friends about him in such as Molly and Philip, Joy and Jimmy, Neville and Linda, and, of course, the old Dog, the Ancient Mariner, Uncle George, Alec and Tricia and others, such as he had never before known. There was ease, openness and independence of thought in their company, which made his earlier life seem like animated death. Jesus said, "I am come that ye may have life and have it more abundantly".

Even with the loss of his longed for visits to Newfoundland and all else, he could say, "I would not change a second of my life. It was perfectly designed for me". He began to see that, if anyone's life was to be perfectly designed, it had to be complete in itself. For that to be, one had to be cut off from both parents and children. Children can become a substitute for 'eternal life', a means of extending one's own life. Parents and forebears could be seen as doing the same in the 'other direction'. Both can endow one with apparent significance, as the urge to research 'family trees' shews.

Chapter Thirty

Epilogue.

"The sins of the fathers....."

The call, in which his elder son spoke of his destiny, was the last Jeremiah heard from him. He did, however, hear from his neighbours. The 'lady', who was not amused, had arrived. His son had found the right person at last. She was charming and said that his son should devote his life to working there. She would 'go to the ends of the earth for him'. Jeremiah had come to hate such extravagant words, almost sure to be made empty. He could not be sure what the words 'for him' implied; 'for his sake', or to 'get him'. Even 'for his sake' could be made to mean anything that the speaker wanted. She had been unable to build a 'relationship' with any other man for fourteen years, because of her feelings for his son.

Should he now make his words empty again? In this company, his son would be obliged to patronise and condescend to his friends, in the same way as Joy had spoken of Hannah. It could hardly be otherwise. What right had he or she to do so? In his position, Jeremiah would have done the same. Joy had said as much. When he was a lecturer, he would not have wanted to know the likes of herself and Mr Harvey. It would be his loss not theirs. It was such as they, Molly and Philip, Neville and Linda, Ernie, Sam, the 'Dog', Arthur and their like, who had led him to understand more of the sayings of Jesus in the Gospels, than any books.

In August the mother of his son's daughter phoned. She was staying with friends in Newfoundland, whose daughter was getting married. She had been invited to the wedding, and told his son that she would be coming. She had met them on a previous visit to the province, which had been something of an adventure.

On that occasion, she had flown out, not to see Jeremiah's son, who had written to welcome her. He suggested that they spent a weekend together at a place called 'Splash 'n' Putt', where there were cabins. The mother got as far as Gander and hitched to the designated meeting place with a small child and a roll of clothes. She booked into a cabin, expecting Jeremiah's son on the Friday evening. He did not appear until Sunday afternoon, with his girl friend. Until she appeared, he was quite friendly. When she walked in, he became hostile, presumably wishing to shew that he was not going to be pushed around by a woman who had borne his child. The mother set out to hitch back to Gander. A truck took her as far as a filling station near Glovertown, where there was a cafe. The woman who ran the cafe noticed that she was English and, with typical Newfie hospitality, invited her to stay with her family at Glovertown. There she spent the rest of her visit until it was time to return to Gander, thence to London. As a result she was invited to their daughter's wedding.

They did not live near Jeremiah's son. She had told him that she was coming to Newfoundland, but would not disturb him. He had written pleasantly, saying that he would like to see his daughter, almost insisting on doing so, specifying a weekend when he was free. The little girl was keen to see her daddy.

The mother phoned Jeremiah in great distress. She had phoned his son many times to make arrangements, but heard only his answerphone. On occasion, having left her name and a message, her call was answered, not by Jeremiah's son, but by a lady's cut glass accent, "How nice it was to hear an English voice. I did not realise who it was". The mother doubted the truth of this, since she had already given her name and left a message. It was August. The lady had said that if she did not come over at Easter, she had too many commitments for the rest of the year. The mother, having no idea that anyone was staying, was bewildered. She phoned back to apologise, explaining that she did not know that the 'lady' was there, but received a somewhat pompous rebuke from his son for offending his 'house guest'.

An arrangement was made, involving mother and daughter getting a lift for a journey of about three hours. The little girl would be met by an R C M P officer, who would drive her to the place where his son lived; another three hours journey. The 'lady' had too many commitments to do so herself. This was a seven-year old child in a strange land. Her daddy was not, after all, free for the weekend. She could spend the day with the 'lady' and part of the following one with her father. It upset the mother greatly. She sobbed uncontrollably. She wanted her daughter to spend time with her father, but did not want her being looked after by a grand and condescending lady, who had too many 'commitments' to collect her. For all her fine education in the 'manners of dancing mistresses', it seems not to have occurred to her to ask the mother whether she minded her doing so, had it been possible, or even minded her daughter spending the day with her.

No doubt, the mother should feel privileged that her daughter should spend time with her. God, too, should feel privileged that such people deigned to "enter his courts with praise". Jeremiah knew how easy it was to think thus. How different all might have been, had the nurse been with his son. Given the notice available, she would have made sure that she had no commitments, if it ensured that a little girl saw her daddy as she wished. Without the benefit of an expensive education in how to be a 'lady', she would have asked the mother if she minded her collecting her child. She may have exploded into rooms, and laughed with a buoyant laugh, but arrogance was not one of her qualities.

The mother was tearful. What should she do? Jeremiah could only say that, as the child wanted to go, she should allow her to do so; though he realised how hard it must be for her.

Nobody could be found to give mother and daughter a lift to the designated meeting place. She had insufficient money to pay the deposit on a hire car. This led to an acrimonious conversation between Jeremiah's son and the mother of his child. The mother confessed that, in no small part, she had provoked it, and refused to allow the little girl to go.

His son was unpleasant, accusing the mother of wanting only his money. That was unfair. She had shewn great forbearance, had never taken any legal steps to obtain support, and had only sought it when the little girl was bullied at the local school. On the occasion of a former visit, his son had been to a Canadian lawyer, who wrote to the mother threatening not only, "personal resistance but whatever legal avenues are available to him", even though he had written to welcome her. Jeremiah's son said that it had not been his wish that the lawyer had written in such a way and had done so without his authority. He had said; "Do come over whenever you feel like it. You will always be welcome. My only problem will be that I will not be able to bear seeing you both go".

Years before, he had written a card to his daughter, such as any child would treasure: "This is from your long lost father overseas. I'm sorry I can't be with you, and this is no fault of yours - I think of you a lot and you are always in my heart. If you have any problems you can call me, and I'll let you know wherever I move to, I hope that one day, when we grown-ups stop being so stupid, I'll see you again and you won't feel so sad. Until then I'm at the end of the phone and you are always in my heart". Often the little girl took him at his word. She heard her daddy's voice, on an answerphone. When she sought to speak to him, while he was staying with Hannah, it provoked such anger, that Hannah demanded court orders to prevent her doing so. Jeremiah felt that, just as with his son's words to the nurse, he was sincere, in the moment of writing, but later had second thoughts. The 'second thoughts' came from those around him.

"It's time you had another lesson from a lawyer. If you want more money, go to the CSA"! That was silly talk. He was beyond the reach of the CSA in Newfoundland. He shouted down the phone, though the mother begged him not to, as his daughter was in the room. She felt, and unwisely said, that all he and his elegant lady friend wanted, was to be seen with his daughter. She was not a doll. Understandably, this angered Jeremiah's son, who shouted, "I wish she had never been born!" No doubt, in a moment of exasperation, it was true. The little girl wept, saying, "I have not got a daddy any more".

All then went, as their custom was, to declare belief in One Lord Jesus Christ, who said much about receiving little children, whose Holy Angels were ever before the face of their father in heaven. His son may even have read those very words as the 'lesson'.

Jeremiah felt, again, that his obduracy had almost surely caused this unhappy outcome. His espousal of the truth of the young nurse's words had helped to drive his son to the 'lady'. He had driven 'his' children into the conversation of Hannah and her circle. Again, he was in two minds. If Jesus had not spoken as he did of those who divorce and marry others, would it have occurred to him that those, who did so, made adultery the foundation of their life? He was becoming less sure that this 'excuse' was true.

Again it was, "Lord thou hast deceived me and I was deceived". He had clung to the saying of Jesus, "Whoever loses wife, children home and land for my sake and the gospels, shall in this life have wives, children homes and lands, and in the coming world, life everlasting". Had he had lost these things for "my sake and the gospel's"? It seemed more truthful to say that, having lost them, he made it so, thereafter. He hated losing 'his' family, and the end of trips to Newfoundland. He hated his son's casting off of the nurse. He could hardly complain that the Lord had deceived him. Jesus made it clear that, whoever preferred his wife or family to him was not worthy of him. In the third Gospel, he spoke even more violently, "Except a man hate.......". What of those, like his own dad, who had forsaken wife and home and family to fight for 'king and country', risking incapacitating injury and death, then losing his chosen career?

Was it not best for his sons and daughter not to be encumbered with a 'dad'? It was certainly best that they 'called no man on earth their father'. It was good that he should leave them with no words of his own. His mother had been dead for forty years, yet her words, because they led back to those of Jesus, stood. Those of others did not. It was a bit late to 'change horses'. He had gone too far for that.

His mother had a 'living memory', because what she said and did pointed beyond herself to the sayings of Jesus in the Gospels. This seemed to be the case for all who did so, to whatever degree. It was true of Sam, Ernie Cole and even such as knew not the sayings of Jesus, like Socrates, or Abraham. Whatever the late Anwar Sadat may have done, he died as a peacemaker. They 'would rejoice to see his day'. It was as if Jesus stood at the head of a queue, or many queues, spreading in all directions. He 'saw the Father'. Those, at the head of each queue, might see him in that light, others could see them. In Greek the words 'see' and 'know' are closely related.

There was a threat, even in this. One could be in such a queue for fifty years of one's life, then turn and walk away. Jesus said, "He that endures to the end.....".

In Karamazov is a chapter called "An Onion". In the lake of burning oil, was a woman, who had once given a starving man a raw onion, as a gesture of contempt. An angel came to the lakeside, asking if any could recall a good deed they had done. The woman cried, "I once gave a poor man an onion". In the angel's hand appeared an onion. The woman grabbed it and was being pulled out. The stalk held. Seeing her escape, others clung to her feet. She screamed, "Let Go. It's my onion". The stalk snapped.

If Jeremiah had sought a life that was arranged to lead him to see that the words, which had so impressed him with their clarity and truth as a child, were indeed so, he had been given one. He had prayed 'Thy kingdom come'. He could be said to have got what he asked. Jesus said, "whatsoever you ask *in my name....*". What else could anyone ask in his name? It was not what Jeremiah had in mind, but was all he had left now. The ruthlessness of the sayings of Jesus struck him again, "whoever puts his hand to the plough and looks back, is not worthy......".

If he relented now, all he had said for the past 25 years would have to be retracted. He had not only spoken, but acted on that basis. He would have to own that all were silly mistakes. It was not, so much, the need to admit this to others, that dismayed him, as admitting it to himself. Had he gone to prison for nothing? If that was a mistake, he would never have met Arthur.

His son said that, while he wanted to see his little daughter, it might be better for her not to have a part time dad, though, when it suited him, he was happy to stay with them. They lived near Heathrow. That did not account for his hostility when with a lady friend. The arguments seemed cogent, as long as one forgot the sayings of Jesus. He had told the mother that he only recognised his daughter and had pleasant dealings with her, thanks to Jeremiah's influence. From the letters to his daughter; that seemed not entirely to be true.

Hannah took the view that a scheming woman had trapped her innocent son. She seemed not to realise how easily such words could be ridiculed. Had Jeremiah been standing in such a circle, he would have muttered, "She'll be claiming another virgin birth next"! One, in Hannah's circle, was also a friend of the mother and relayed these comments to her. When the mother met Hannah, she was all over them, welcoming them into her home. The only word to describe such instinctive behaviour is 'shifty'. What it meant was that neither mother nor daughter trusted her.

When Jeremiah told Linda of his son's daughter, she had laughed saying, "Join the club, my brother's done the same". Had he done as Hannah, swearing false evidence, and his friends knew, he could imagine how it would be. If, sitting with Neville and Jimmy, Awesome and the old 'Dog', he said to one of them, "You damned old liar"; before the words were out of his mouth, there would have been a chorus: "At least he did not do it under oath!" In the company that Hannah kept it could not be treated in that way. There is much to be said for being amongst the publicans and sinners, rather than 'judges and dividers'. What might have been Hannah's and the family's attitude toward mother and daughter if, like the 'lady' and her mother, they had been wealthy friends of the family, in a position to make serious trouble for her son? What, then, of the little girl's Father in heaven, in whom they declared belief? He was back to the hypocrisy of the Christian religion.

Joy and Jimmy saw the matter clearly. "The child did not ask to be born. Whatever may have been the reasons for the mother having her, she was and would, forever, be his son's daughter". That his son had said that, if she allowed the child to be born, she could expect no support from him, made no difference. What if a husband said that? She was no less his grandchild than the sons of his younger son and daughter in law. There was nothing more to be said.

He had sent a Christmas present and written a note, saying that he had stuck a ten-pound note in the parcel. The mother had phoned to say that she hoped that he did not mind that she had extracted the ten pounds and bought a few small presents for the little girl to unwrap. Her 'brother' had presents from his departed 'dad' and other relations; the little girl had none but her parents and Jeremiah. Christmas was cruel for those who were excluded.

He had nothing to lose, so wrote, not to his son, but the new lady of his life. If he dealt with the mother through a lawyer, she would be provided with the means to reply in like manner. It would take only an hour to obtain a court order in England, which could demand not only the payment of maintenance for the child, but also school fees, if the mother had her educated privately. He took it that, as she, herself, had attended a "Ladies College", she would recommend it. Such an order would be enforceable in the Canadian courts. Though the mother knew she could do so, she refused.

These events, which led to the telling of this story, forced Jeremiah to see what he had spent his life avoiding: Hypocrisy was essential to Christianity, as a religion. The words spoken by Jesus made it so. These incidents are symptoms of the disease. Hannah's adultery was as that of Gomer, a consequence and symptom of the faithlessness of Israel, as a people. As in the curses at the end of Deuteronomy, it could be seen as an affliction, visited on a faithless people. The Christian religion, in like manner, is, or has become, faithless to all that the one, whom it declares to be God from God, said. The rediscovery of the gospels has driven it to this.

Its accredited upholders, now, almost boastfully, teach men so. Carey had commented on the 'shifty accommodations' of the Christian religion in order to appear 'multi cultural' and 'politically correct'. Jesus was unequivocal. "No man comes to the Father except by me". What the accredited upholders of the Christian religion were doing was tantamount to procurement and pimping. One of the allegations made by Jesus, in his indictment of the Scribes and Pharisees as hypocrites, was that they crossed land and sea to make a convert, and, having found him, made of him and even greater child of hell than even you yourselves. Such as Hannah and her man provided welcome 'proof', that anything inconvenient, said by Jesus, could safely be discounted.

Her respected family life could be seen as a 'sign' that Jesus' words were untrue. To the sycophants, who were the ministers, they were as the mighty works, which followed Jesus. They were signs that the words, with which 'they healed the hurt of this people lightly', were the truth, not those of the one, whom they declared to be God of God and Light of Light

Jeremiah claimed that it would not have occurred to him, for example, that those, who divorced husbands/wives and married others committed adultery, had not those of the Christian religion cherished and translated those words. This was, the dilemma that faced S Paul. After a passage about the gentiles, he asked, "What *advantage,* then, has the Jew?" They had the scriptures. Was Jeremiah's claim true? He began to think not. Jesus' words seemed more to put a seal on what he knew anyway. Any little child knows that for a husband to divorce a wife, or a wife her husband, and marry another, is an act of infidelity. Given the marriage service, it makes many words idle. Little children are sensitive to this.

When grown-ups fail to do what they say, they complain, "But you said".

Jesus set it in a different light. Those having the scriptures were those who could say, "We see". It was open to them, alone, to "take the name of the Lord God in vain": more so, for those who attended the services of the Christian religion. They had the Gospels, but assured all that unwanted sayings of the only begotten son could be disregarded. As they declared, or had declared for them, that he was raised from the grave, it took the matter from Jesus to God.

In effect, they declared the resurrection and the other miraculous events, not to be of God, since those events serve to certify Jesus' words. It was those who did that, who drew from Jesus, "the blasphemy against the Holy Spirit of God shall never be forgiven". They, as it were, obliged God to choose between the words of his 'only begotten Son' and those of the sensible 'conversation'. The word 'choose' is misleading. Jesus' words articulate the unchanging word of God, as they articulate the word 'god'.

If God did not support those, who led people to set aside the words of Jesus, he would risk having no people to believe in him. Could God manage to be God, without a community of believers? That was the delusion, under which the people of Judah and Jerusalem suffered, in the days of Jeremiah the prophet. Did people need the reported sayings of Jesus, in order to believe in the true God? 'No'. If anyone believed truly in God, he or she would be led to those sayings, as giving final expression to that belief. Jesus embodied the word 'God'. The 'logic' of the prohibition to the man and woman in the garden, stood, without being articulated in that story, as did the words to Samuel. If one did as Abraham, one would not need his story. It would be one's own story. One did not need Jesus to speak of the need to fear God. If anyone truly believed in God, as the Creator of the universe, one would fear such a being. If one had such things articulated, in one's own 'scriptures', and disregarded them, it was not an 'advantage', more an indictment.

Jesus could say, with truth, that he judged no man; yet had come into the world for judgement. In word and act, he gathered up and represented the 'law and the prophets'. He embodied of the faith and 'calling' of Israel, of Abraham; that which is "our report". In casting him aside, they cast aside the embodiment of all they claimed to believe and 'reported'. Even more clearly is this so, for those of the Christian religion. The most fearful accusation, against those of religion, is made by 'believing their report'. Anyone, doing that, would oblige them to turn against him for doing so, just as in the poem, with which Isaiah answered his question.

If there is God, Jesus, as reported in the Gospels, is a truly dreadful man. If there is no God, he is the greatest deceiver ever born, unless the evangelists made it all up. That could not be. It had to be Jesus himself. He was the only truly good man ever to have lived, but said, "Why callest thou me good? Only one is good, God alone". The goodness of Jesus is that of God. If, as the infinite creator of all things, for whom all is possible, God is good; Jesus is good, derivatively. Any religion or system of belief devised by men would be bound to reject him.

One's reaction to the sayings of Jesus is one's reaction to the word and being of God. The evangelists, reporting him as they did, could never have devised such a man.

As a religion, Christianity, depends upon the sayings of Jesus being unfinished. It assumes that he had left unsaid much that needed saying. Deceitfully, in the light of Jesus' words in the upper room, it claims that the Holy Spirit makes good this omission. Jesus said that the Spirit would lead his followers to all truth, by bringing to their remembrance all the *he* said to them. The upholders of the Christian religion rely on its doing the opposite, so providing a 'new Christ'. Less directly, all religious and other beliefs need this to be so. Jeremiah had been driven to see, with his mind only, that one possibility alone gave truth to the sayings reported of Jesus, one could almost say, 'whoever may have spoken them'. It is that there is indeed God.

This Being is what the word, logically, implies: essentially unlike any other. That is the 'Holy Spirit of God'. It is that of which Jesus, alone, spoke. That being so, Christianity above all, other beliefs less obviously, need, as their very foundation, the assurance that there is, in reality, no God. He, She or It is, therefore, an 'image', whether graven or not, however beautifully carved in wood, stone, or elaborate words. That 'commandment', too, is as the sayings of Jesus, the story of the garden and that of Abraham. You did not need a commandment to know that making and revering images of 'god(s)' is a snare and delusion. You need only to think of the word 'God' and what it implies to see this. You only need think of the word 'God' and what it implies to know that the words attributed to Jesus give it complete and final expression.

One possibility, alone, could make those words untrue; that there is no God. The declarations of the Christian religion, in all its forms, had to be empty lies, "when he speaks a lie he speaks of his own", unless collectively and singly, those who made them sought, simply, to do what he said. "What use is it to call on me as Lord, Lord, if you do not do as I say?"

It is not a matter of judging or condemning individuals, in whom this infidelity and hypocrisy is manifest. That is profitless and silly, as if taking a scalpel and excising a couple of spots would cure measles. His wife, his son and the highly educated 'lady', were doing only what the Defender of the Faith, the Popes and the Archbishops, Bishops, Priests and Deacons, ministers of the Gospel, 'Captains' and 'Majors', led and taught them. By their office and ministry, they assured all that any saying of Jesus, that was inconvenient, may freely be set aside in the light of a higher wisdom, revealed to them by the Spirit, which would lead them to all truth; but not by bringing to remembrance all that he said. It could not "Take of his and glorify him"; but of anyone else but 'him'. Jeremiah had, himself, been content to say 'Amen' to this perversion, and 'thereout sucked no small advantage'. He had a large account to pay.

If one read the gospels, simply as books, "to learn of him", and asked, 'from what did Jesus redeem the world?' It would be religion, and belief in anything, or anyone, but the one true God. This is at one with the tale of the garden, in which was no temple, altar, list of laws, nor even a priest to marry 'Adam and Eve'. There are no such things in the New Jerusalem either.

The matter of divorcing partners and marrying others was not a 'moral issue', in the accepted sense. What Hannah their elder son and the highly esteemed 'lady' were doing, led by the scribes and Pharisees of the Christian religion, was assuring all that it was safe to frolic in minefields. One could hardly blame Hannah for leading her son to do so, when the accredited upholders of the religion assured all that the mines had long ago been removed; the warning notices long out of date.

Jeremiah's story is a tale told of an 'idiot', by an 'idiot'. His idiocy, for it is the appropriate term, lay in believing their report. He not only had to be an idiot to do so, but to *need* to do so. Such was his idiocy, that the sayings of Jesus provided the only basis on which he was capable of living. Trying to seek first the kingdom of heaven and its righteousness, in the hope that all that he needed would be provided, was no act of virtue. It was all he was able to do. It takes no great wisdom to give a cloak as well, if sued for a coat. It is vastly easier to do so if one does not want the cloak any more. It takes no intelligence to go two miles, when commanded to go one. It is easy, when one has nothing better to do.

One needs no cleverness to forgive those indebted to one. (There is no suggestion that one should enjoy it.) It takes a lot of cleverness to argue against so doing, while declaring belief in the one who made that demand. Not having to do that saves a lot of trouble.

The story is not only written of an 'idiot', but for the sake of other 'idiots', who may, for one reason or another, find the 'sensible' prescriptions for 'survival' (of the fittest, of course), beyond them. They might be called the 'meek'. At its simplest, to 'seek first the kingdom of heaven and its righteousness', is to live in such a way as to want and need the sayings of Jesus, which delineate that kingdom, to be the truth. The more anyone does so, the more they will feel this need. If he sold all that he had and gave to the poor, as instructed, then followed Jesus, the rich young man would need the sayings of Jesus to be true. Any who do so will find it simple to pray, "Thy kingdom Come, thy will be done". They may come to think, 'If there is God, it will be anyway'.

It is wholly good that one, alone, is given blessing and honour glory and power. It prevents anyone else from being endowed with them. It protects men and women from being led to endow any man on earth with such qualities. It might have saved many from shouting, 'Seig Heil', or 'God save the King', or assenting to such nonsense as, "May the king live forever"; however thrilling the accompanying music. It would prevent anyone believing that any political leaders or party would be 'benefactors', or that they would receive justice from any court on earth. If anyone was to receive blessing and honour glory and power, it was good that it should be 'Jesus only', if only because it enabled one to listen to the great chorus that concludes Messiah, "Blessing and Honour, Glory and Power be unto him that sits upon the throne and to the lamb", as if, Handel had written it for inept and childish idiots. That alone makes it almost worth being one. Could such exultant music be written of any other?

This was to have been the end of the story, but it is not. Another year came and went. It was Christmas again. Conscious of what of his granddaughter's mother had said, Jeremiah decided to send a collection of little things to her. Joy asked, "Would her mother mind if we sent a present to her?" Being unlike the 'lady who is not amused', she insisted that Jeremiah should ask her. The last thing she wanted to do was to 'put the mother down'. She was overjoyed.

There had been an incoming international call. It could only be from Newfoundland. It was from the 'Boss' and her husband, who phoned back later. They did not see much of his son now, who seemed moody. He had lost his students from the University, as he was not prepared to see enough patients each day. He had been to visit them on one or two evenings and spoke of 'missing the old bugger'.

A local 'group' practised in his basement and he played a guitar. They were giving their first public performance shortly before Christmas. The one person, he wanted to be there, was 'the old bugger'. They said that they would phone him. Would he come over for the concert? He jumped for joy at the thought of going there again. They gave him his son's phone number, as he was now 'ex-directory'. Jeremiah was not among those allowed to have it. His son would be happy to drive to St John's to collect him.

Jeremiah thought that his son was now alone again, hence his moodiness. He ached to go, but what of the nurse? He was taken to the scene, where Jesus dined with a Pharisee. A woman from the streets burst in. The Pharisee was affronted. Jesus rebuked him, saying that, though her 'sins were many, they would be forgiven, for she loved much'. If Jesus had popped round to Simon the Pharisee later, apologised for his words, returned to dine with him again, and the woman had seen him; she would know that his words to her were 'idle'. Even if she had not, Jesus would have known that it was so, so would his host.

He thought of his son's words, "We will be the same good friends as ever". Even if his son was on his own, but the nurse was not free to walk into his house with her laughter and bear hugs, or curl up comfortably at his son's feet, he would be complicit in the making those words idle. He thought of the concert itself. She would have loved being there as his son's companion. She would suffocate him with her bear hugs afterwards. She would have been proud of him. She would have reassured him that what he did was worthwhile. She might even have gone round the hospital to say goodnight to the patients, telling them of the performance.

Of this he wrote to the Boss and her husband, relating the story of the woman who wept at Jesus' feet. The nurse's Email led him to that story. His son had traduced her love and trust. It made it crucial that Jeremiah did not make his own words empty. They had said, somewhat disparagingly, that 'she wanted his son'.

What did they think that the elegant 'lady' from England wanted? She had more ways of getting it.

He did not care that the nurse may have, as the Boss had said, 'much growing up to do'. He hoped she would not. What she may have done mattered not. Her E-mail manifested one who loved much. That was all he wanted to know. She had brought food to his son when he was hungry, comforted him when sad, reassured him when he was unsure. For this she asked no return. When his son was in low spirits, they were on hand, so was the nurse. Where was the well-spoken 'lady', who would go to the ends of the earth for him? She could have picked up the phone and known that he was in the pit of despair. Why did his son not turn to her when in the 'vale of misery', but his neighbours and the nurse?

Jeremiah wanted to live in a world where the truth of the nurse, in that moment of her life, was that she was one who loved much. It was the words of Jesus that gave her words truth. It was the eternal world of truth, where only the words of Jesus and the 'Word', to which they gave expression, stood. Any who argue would be cast onto the dunghill, to be trodden under foot of men.

He wanted to lay-up, in 'eternity', that moment in his son's life and that of the nurse. Speaking, as he did, of the woman who wept at his feet, Jesus had done that for her. Thanks to the third evangelist, that moment, in her life, was treasured by many, 2,000 years afterwards. It would have been easy for her to adopt a way of life, in which she found herself ashamed of that moment.

Jeremiah wanted, only, to know the 'son', who had spoken as he did when he left him, who was glad to have the words of reassurance that he left behind, wanted to make a difference, and had filled one lass's heart to overflowing with joyous happiness. He did not want to know him as a son, but as a friend, for he would call no man on earth his father. The words of Jesus would have 'free course' with him. If he needed a father on earth, as he now was, Hannah's man was more fitting.

'Job' knew that one, who would vindicate him, lived, and that he will stand at the latter day upon the earth, that though worms devoured this body, yet, 'in my flesh, am I seeing God'. Jesus said, "he that has seen/known me has seen/known the Father", and "Blessed the pure in heart, (single willed); they shall see God". All this, he wrote to the Boss and her husband. What they made of it, or whether they troubled to read it, he could never know.

He phoned 'Awesome', passing on his son's phone number; he, too, being excluded from those allowed it. He had asked Hannah for it. She told him, implausibly, that she could not remember it, nor 'put her hand on it'. As it was only a four figure number, that had to be untrue. He was about to go off on holiday with his young friend Kate.

Ten days later, Jeremiah had a call from Kate. They had talked of the duffer and had decided that he should go and make peace. Kate made her views clear, forcibly and at length. When Kate had finished, she handed over to Sarah, Awesome's business partner, running a dog grooming service. Sarah was of the same opinion as Kate, more forcefully so. She reduced Jeremiah to saying little more than, 'all right'. "Will you now speak to Awesome"? Awesome said that he thought that Jeremiah should go and talk quietly to his son, explaining why he thought as he did. He was prepared to buy a ticket and fly out with him. They would tell nobody that they were coming.

Jeremiah was excited at the prospect of seeing Newfoundland and his friends again. He longed to make peace. He was excited at the prospect of another meal at Jungle Jim's. He would enquire into the availability of cheap tickets. He bought two. Awesome would provide the currency. A week before they were due to leave, Awesome phoned to say that his father had suffered a heart attack, so could not go. Jeremiah decided that he could not go alone. While feasible for two, car hire was expensive for one. Not having a credit card, it was not possible, anyway.

Sadly, he rang his friends in Newfoundland. They had different ideas and reserved a seat for him on a coach. He had spoken to them earlier, to make sure that the hotel in the town let rooms. It no longer did so. He should not think of staying there anyway, but should stay with them. He had explained that there would be two of them. Both were welcome. In order to preserve the secret they would not even tell their sons. Much was happening in England, at the time.

His younger son telephoned to ask whether he might visit them before Christmas. Jeremiah said that he could not say, as he was going away. He was no good at meeting enquiries with 'That's none of your business', so told him what he was planning to do. It was about three days before his departure. His younger son took up the matter of the way he had upheld the truth of the young nurse and her E mail. His brother had told him that the old duffer had got hold of the wrong end of the stick. "There was never anything between them". He had never met the one who is not amused, who was very nice. "What had he against her?" Jeremiah was taken aback. He mentioned Awesome's phone call.

He was known to be a liar and a 'stirrer'. Jeremiah asked, on what evidence he said such things of a good friend. He had no evidence that Awesome was either. His younger son said, "Everyone knows that he is." Jeremiah lacked Jimmy's speed of mind and was too upset by the turn of events to point out that this was certainly not true. He, for one, did not know that Awesome was either. Had he misconstrued everything? Again it was, "Lord thou hast deceived me". He rang Awesome and asked him directly, "Did you tell me the truth?"

Awesome was not angered at the allegation, "Duffer", he said, "I have never lied to you in my life. I rang you, immediately I put the phone down, and reported exactly what was said".

As a result, he became more convinced of the truth of the nurse's Email. His younger son's comments about there being 'nothing between them' recalled his brother's hesitant and rambling account of what he said to the nurse. If there was 'nothing between them', what was the talk of feelings for one another? What did 'something between them' imply? Was there nothing between a man and a woman, if fornication was not enjoyed or, as we have it, they did not 'make love'. The choice of word or phrase has the capacity to change the nature of the action. Fornication was a sharp, offensive word. It was otherwise if one spoke of making love.

From the start, Jeremiah had pointed to what his elder son said to Awesome, as the reason for his upholding the truth of the Email. His son never disputed it, though he seemed, now, to have done so with his younger brother.

He thought of the nurse, writing to one far away. She had to share her joyous happiness with somebody, not daring to do so with anyone near at hand. Did she sense that the love of her life might not do the truth of his words? She would have no reason for saying these things unless they were true, still less would she expose the fact that she loved much. If she had been misled, she would look silly.

Jeremiah could not sleep. The question, "What have you against the lady?" would not go away. He had never met her. He could have nothing against her apart from odd items of hearsay from his elder son, and that she was 'not amused'. He thought of what he had written to his son and left on his pillow. "What does my opinion matter?" His younger son was deeply religious, given to referring to the works of the 'apostle' Paul. He had told Jeremiah that he should regard the Book of Revelation as having greater authority than any saying by Jesus, it being a direct revelation from God. People did not declare belief in the author of the Apocalypse, but in One Lord Jesus Christ. Knowing his elder son, he felt sure that, neither on his visits to England, still less when the 'lady' stayed in Newfoundland, did they live together in chaste celibacy, in which case she had provided the 'joys of fornication'.

He himself had nothing against these joys. That he had not, himself, enjoyed them was not of his will, either now or in his youth. He did not have the chance and lacked the nerve. Another reason lurked at the back of his mind. Such enjoyment put one in the debt of whoever provided it. They had, as the old Dog would say, "Something on you". He mused about the Hebrew euphemism for this act. They "knew you". They took an intimate knowledge of you with them.

If the daughter of a friend of the family allowed herself to be used as, in effect, an unpaid whore, both her family and one's own expect one to 'make an honest woman' of her. Even if her family and one's own did not suggest such things, they were happy to be 'accessories after the fact'. They need say nothing. One would be well aware of their expectations.

While he himself had no 'objection' to fornication, (What did it matter if *he* did, anyway?), those, to whom his younger son referred him, certainly did. The author of the Apocalypse declared that all fornicators would be cast into the lake of fire. The 'apostle' Paul said, "Flee fornication". It was 'idolatry'. These things, his elder son would read out as lessons in Church. An upstanding doctor, therefore, had exemption, as his mother and her circle, who provided regular assurance that the Lord's words about those who divorce partners and marry others, did not apply to such as themselves, only to lesser folk, who were 'no better than they ought to be': harlots, whores and prostitutes.

Jeremiah had not given much thought to what Jesus said about such matters as fornication. He warned against it, but seems not to have adopted a condemnatory view of prostitutes. It is almost certain that the woman of whom he said, "Her sins which are many are forgiven her, for she loves much", was one herself. This was consistent with his words about the woman caught in the act of adultery. Words like adulteress, whore and fornication are offensive, *if we make them so.*

If one belonged in a 'conversation' that condemned these activities, those words would be offensive, if applied to oneself or others in that 'conversation'. Sitting with Neville in the pub, Jeremiah's elder son had given them the benefit of his views on those who contracted H I V from indulging in 'unprotected sex'. They did not deserve free treatment at the taxpayers' expense, if they were so careless. What, then, of those who fathered daughters by the same means? The awful coherence of Jesus' words struck him; "Judge not lest ye be judged, for with whatever judgment you assess others, you will yourself be assessed?"

A chance encounter focused his mind on this. He had been accosted by an attractive young woman, in her twenties, who asked him if he knew anywhere she could find a room for the night. She asked him for some money, adding, "I am quite a good looking woman". It was not until he obtained the cash, and she thanked him, adding, "I provide company too, you know", that he realised what she was. 'Poor lass', he thought, 'whatever must it be like to have to accost a shambolic old duffer to earn one's living?' When he told Joy and another of his encounter, they laughed at his naiveté. Joy said, "You should have given her our address, we could have given her a bed for the night". It would have probably been for more than one night. Joy said, cheerfully, "we'd have been the fools who had her for life, but she must be some mother's daughter". Jeremiah felt shamed. He had a house with two spare rooms. What was the girl's offence? It was probably that, as a teenager, she had been too attractive, and found that she could get what she wanted from any man. Since the encounter took place in Cromer, it was likely that the poor girl was feeding a drug addiction.

Prostitutes deal in cash. There is no pretence, no hypocrisy. They do not pretend to be anything else. They do not provide their services on extended credit. They are not like the 'rich', of whom the prophet Jeremiah said, "Their houses are filled with lies and deceit. Like fowlers, they lie in wait. They set a trap. They catch men". Prostitutes do not, in that way, seek to catch men. He was coming to see why the 'apostle' Paul, the author of the Apocalypse and Jesus himself had uttered such warnings. It took him to what he had already begun to see. These were not so much matters of what might be called 'immorality' to be condemned by the righteous, but were as minefields. Hypocrisy was serious in its consequences for others. It suggested that the warning notices could be disregarded.

Events moved too fast for Jeremiah to dwell on this. He received another phone call, this time from his daughter. Did he intend to fly out to Newfoundland any more? He lied, and said that he was not. Immediately, he felt that he should not have lied. He confessed that he was intending to go, but as a surprise. He was not staying with her brother, but with friends.

His daughter was shocked and angry. He was intent on causing ill feeling. It was only a day before he was due to set out. He was packed and ready to go; then mislaid his ticket. He felt uneasy about the entire escapade. What his daughter told him next made him gasp. The 'lady' was not only in residence, she was permanently so. They were deeply in love. Her brother was happier than he had ever been. They were soon to marry and would be having children. Unless he accepted this gladly, and put aside the business of the nurse and her E-mail, he had no business to go. They were planning to leave Newfoundland and seek work in Canada. 'So much', thought Jeremiah, 'for all the talk about devoting his life to the people of the township and going to the ends of the earth'.

He mentioned the matter of 'being just the same good friends as ever'. "Don't be silly, that is the accepted way of ending a relationship. Everyone says that, and everyone knows what it means". That may be the accepted way, in the Kingdom of England. It is not, in the Kingdom of God.

It was now impossible to go. In his hand was his ticket! Tearfully he telephoned his daughter. It was not she who replied, but her husband, who was abrupt with old duffers. All he said was, "All right. I won't go". Why did he always find himself reduced to tears? It revealed much of those with whom he dealt. On the following day his daughter phoned to apologise for her peremptory attitude.

Jeremiah spent the following days in silence. The world went on around him. He was not part of it. He was 'in it but not of it'. His granddaughter's mother phoned regularly to ask if he was all right. She told him how the recent events had made her think again about the father of her child. Hitherto she had almost put him from her mind. After Jeremiah returned from his last visit, she had written to his son. She was glad that his ways of practising medicine, rushing off to accidents when no-one else could be bothered, not being ex-directory and so on, had not changed. She was glad that he had not become just another doctor doing nicely out of his patients' misfortunes. Jeremiah had said of the little girl, that it was good that, even if her dad was absent, she might respect him for the way in which he worked. That seemed, now, to be a thing of the past.

Characteristically, saying nothing to anyone, it was Jimmy who took steps to help.

Late one evening Jeremiah had a long call from his younger son. Having invited him for Christmas, he seemed intent on pointing out the errors of his ways. It was not 'unkindly' meant. If someone is in low spirits and a mess, it seems sensible to do so. If they correct their errors, they can find a way out. He was particularly critical of his Dad's behaviour towards the 'lady who is not amused'. Did he not realise how hurtful it was for her that her future father in law treated her as if non-existent in his son's life?

Jeremiah wished that he had Jimmy's speed of mind and response. He floundered. He said, "What does the woman want; two fathers in law?" She already looked on Hannah's man as being one. She was a publicly declared believer. He felt sure that she did not think, hint, even less, say, that the union between Hannah and her preferred father in law, at whose table she sat and to whose 'conversation' she said Amen, was one of adultery. No doubt that was a wild generalisation. If it was, it was not Jeremiah who uttered it.

His younger son explained that, in his view, things were best as they were and should remain so. He and his family looked on Hannah's man as her true husband. Jeremiah referred to the dialogue between Jesus and the woman of Samaria. His son said that this assumed that the five were all her true husbands. This was getting nowhere. What was beyond dispute was what Jesus said about wives who divorced their husbands and married others.

That Jesus' death had won forgiveness for all our 'sins' seemed oddly at variance with his teachings in the gospels. If all that anyone did was automatically forgiven by attendance at Church, what was the point in his saying these things? It is different if they are warnings against walking into quagmires. He told his son that the word translated sin, at root, meant to aim at something and miss. For the first 30 years of his life, Jesus had been an accredited upholder of the very religious beliefs and traditions under which he was condemned. His younger son said that he was implying that, early in his life, Jesus had himself been a 'sinner'. "In the sense of participating in a 'conversation' that would not achieve its target, yes he was", said Jeremiah. He was told that his reference to the story of the woman, who wept at Jesus' feet, was a misunderstanding.

Jeremiah was bewildered. Devoted upholders of the Christian religion had the greater capacity to reduce him to such a state than any. They kicked away the only seemingly solid ground on which he found it possible to stand. The guiding light in his decision had been the story of the woman who loved much. Now it appeared that he had misconstrued that. When it came to understanding the gospels, all seemed to know better than he. Once again it was, 'Lord thou hast deceived me'.

He thought of the matter of the hurtful nature of his behaviour to the lady. Until a couple of days before, he had no idea that she was even staying with his son. He knew that she had been out there over a year ago. His friends had mentioned that they had met his son with a dark haired 'girl friend' some time ago. She might have paid a further visit. He knew that, though she had insisted on coming at Easter, because she was not free at any subsequent time in the year, she had been there in August. She did not seem a soul of truth. Many a time, he had sought to get his own way by such means. The only signal difference being that, whereas his attempts generally failed, leaving him looking silly and disingenuous, which he was; hers succeeded. On the occasions when he had succeeded, he ended up wishing he had not.

If he did not know that the 'lady' was in residence and had no idea that she saw him as her father in law to be, how could she be hurt at his failure to recognise her? She and his son had kept Hannah and her man informed. Since they had been content to leave him in ignorance, while informing all others, why bother about him now? If a certain addition of factors gave the result 'happiness', why add an unknown factor, which might upset the equation?

He thought of his son's parting words, "I don't want to go back to England, dad. I am at home here. I want to make a difference". He thought of the contrast, when he returned, bitter and angry. The people of the township had not changed in a fortnight. He had. How was it that, after a fortnight in England, he had changed so radically? Did he realise that this would happen, and so did not want to return to England? When he left, he, like Job, had 'integrity'. He could, knowingly or not, fall straight back upon words like "Go and do thou likewise". That was 'off-limits' in Hannah's household. It was also 'off-limits' among most of his friends in England. Recalling Carey's letter, an extraordinary thought struck Jeremiah. He said, unambiguously, that he did not believe in Jesus, because he could not believe in God. It would not have been 'off-limits', in his company, for a doctor to say, simply, that he rushed off to an accident, because Jesus said, "Go and do likewise".

Had his son discovered the truth of his youthful words to the old duffer, about his professional friends deserting him; fearing that they would do so to him, if he sought to be 'different'? He thought of the promise to his namesake, "Go not forth to them, and they will come forth to thee". His son seemed ever to feel the need to 'go forth to them', almost finding it necessary to ingratiate himself. He had no need to do so. His 'friends' soon found him, when they needed him. Jesus said, "Lend to whoever asks". He did not say that one should run about offering loans. He said, "Turn the other cheek...". He did not commend anyone to invite the first blow.

His son's words seemed to shew that he was aware of being at the parting of the ways, knowing that the one, which led to his 'making a difference', would have to be abandoned. Was his call to the young nurse a last attempt to return to the way of integrity and of forgoing the 'whole world' in order to retain his own soul? The question that followed seemed more poignant. "What shall a man give in exchange for his soul?" (In order to redeem it, as from a pawnbroker?). There may have been truth in his rambling account of what passed between him and the nurse. Did he sense, when he spoke with her, as she described, that it could never be, or that it would not be allowed? Casting her aside could be seen as being 'for her sake'. His son's professional and other friends would disdain her.

In the second Gospel, Jesus contrasts that, which enters a man's mouth, with that which comes out of a man. That which enters his mouth does not 'defile' him. It passes through him into the sewer. That which proceeds "from within, from the heart of a man" defiles him. The heart, in Hebrew 'psychology', is the seat of the will, rather than the emotions. The word 'defiled' has implications of ritual impurity, with which, in other circumstances, Jesus, as the prophets with circumcision, had little 'sympathy'. He looked it up. At root the word means to make 'ordinary'. It was almost exactly what he had written to his son. The only way, truly, to make a 'difference', was to work, so that what he did pointed beyond himself, medical science and practice, to the one who said of healing the sick, "freely have you received, freely give".

That which came out of a man's heart was, in the Revised Version's translation, "Evil thoughts, fornications, thefts, murders, adulteries, covetings, wickednesses, deceit, lasciviousness, an evil eye, railing, pride, foolishness....". It is not clear whether 'evil thoughts' are the all-embracing category, of which the rest were examples. If the word, translated 'evil', meant, at root, that which is toilsome for little or no reward, it fittingly described life on earth, unless it led to eternal life. When his younger son said that 'things were best as they were' and that he looked on Hannah, as truly the wife of the man from Oz, Jeremiah recalled him to the words of St Paul, that no adulterer would enter the Kingdom of God. It was he, not his dad, who made much of the writings of S Paul.

"I don't want to go back to England. I am at home here and want to make difference", took Jeremiah back to these words. His son seemed aware that his return to the 'conversation' of his family and friends would be the end of 'making a difference'. Did he sense that being provided with the 'joys of fornication' and 'free' taxi-rides would make an end of that dream or hope? Was he being led to pile up indebtedness, like a mortgage, a lifetime commitment to that which would make him ordinary. That was what those in England needed.

He could not make a difference without being different. Only one man and his words lead to a truly different way of life. All others are but 'variations' on a single theme. Was being 'not ordinary' the same as having, or being, a living soul, or 'retaining his integrity'? Had he already taken out too large a mortgage on the possession of the 'whole world' or, at least, the 'scrunchy drive', which his future mother in law apparently owned? Jeremiah knew how much it cost to pay off such mortgages. He had spoken of the 'lady who was not amused', as his destiny. Did he realise, even as he phoned the nurse, that he was in no position to do the truth of his words, already having too large a mortgage to pay?

The hypocrisy of the Christian religion led to a breathtaking arrogance. Here was Jesus himself, with S Paul and the author of the Apocalypse, warning of the dangers of those things that made a man ordinary, but 'we knew better', while declaring belief in him as 'God of God and Light of Light'. That is the opposite of 'meekness', as embodied and set forth by Jesus. It is hardly meek to claim that one knows better than the very man, whom one declares to be the only begotten Son of God. It was the first time that Jeremiah had given serious thought to those words of Jesus.

Fornications came first on the list of things that make a man ordinary. If those, who had influence, rejoiced at their living together, in the hope that this might lead to a 'marriage'; they might as well have encouraged both the 'lady' to provide the service and the man to enjoy it, as a way of establishing a 'relationship', having something between them, even getting a husband, or wife. It was a way of setting a trap and catching men, not just, or even primarily, in that particular, but to make them life members of their 'conversation', the 'ordinary' accepted 'conversation' of the 'prince of this world'. Marriage was spoken of in such ways. It was, for many, an assurance that one, who might otherwise be given to behaving eccentrically, would now 'settle down'. It was like domesticating animals.

If the woman in the Gospel had sought to rejoin the domesticated 'conversation' of the world, the words of Jesus would be an embarrassment. She would be shamed by their recall, obliged to make light of that moment. Those of the domesticating 'conversation' would seek to make her do so. If not, she would become an outcast, to be disdained as 'stricken of God'. Jeremiah thought again of the 'Onion'. When the woman shewed that she was going to try and get out of the lake, those therein called to her to stay with them, 'At least we know where we are'. It was as if all felt sure that, as long as they could drag everyone down the road that led only to the rubbish dump, God would have to change his 'mind', in order to remain 'most merciful'; exchanging hell and heaven as it were. It would still be hell, but with a misleading name.

Jesus speaks of eternal life as the ever-*present* reality, as it must be. That being so, the alternative must also be seen as present. If 'heaven' is 'here and now', so too must be 'hell'. Images, like lakes of burning oil, suggest that it lay in the future. The image of Gehenna did not. What is life on earth, which is nothing but a progress to the manure heap, but 'hell'? Ted Hughes wrote a fearful poem called, "At the womb door". He lists the features of a newborn babe, such as fill adoring parents with wonder, asking, "Who owns them?" In each case it is death; at least he forbore to say, 'the rubbish dump'.

Jesus' words, about that which comes out of a man 'defiling' him, cohered with Neville's musing about the breakdown of marriages. Awesome's impression of the nurse was, that 'making love', or, in sharper terms, 'fornication', was not her way of founding a lasting 'relationship'. Founded on companionship, friendship, and love, 'making love', as we like to say, would be the seal of these things.

In his youth there was much debate about the propriety of 'pre-marital sex'. Jeremiah could begin to understand why it was, following Deuteronomy, that Jesus made 'fornication' the ground, on which a man might divorce a wife and marry another without making her an adulteress. If one started from the assumption that the sayings of Jesus were finally true, responding, 'Yes, Yes', all was set in a new light. That was to be his disciple. It was what the word discipline implied, a way of learning, whereby one submitted to the instructions of a Master, to gain understanding.

In the saying, preceding that about divorce and marrying others, in the Sermon the Mount, Jesus speaks of anyone who looks on a woman to lust after her, having 'already committed adultery with her in his heart'. The saying left nobody in a position to condemn any who committed adultery. Lack of the nerve to do something is hardly a ground for adopting attitudes of moral superiority, though it might lead to one's being delivered from 'evil'. Being delivered from anything brings one no credit. All changes, if such things were seen as minefields, quagmires, or, perhaps more fittingly, as the 'broad path'. If one 'looked at a woman to want her'; one might be led to walk into them. One does not condemn people for walking into them. What would be 'condemned' would be leading others to do so, on the assurance that there was no danger.

The shiftiness of the Church, faced with the words of Jesus, is bewildering. Jeremiah had read of a report by the Church of England on marriage and divorce. It said that the 'tradition' that marriages, in which a partner had divorced another, constituted adultery, should be done away. He wrote to his own Bishop and both Archbishops, asking simply, "With whom, did this 'tradition' originate?" His own Bishop, and he of Canterbury, replied that 'it was not proper' to comment. He of York replied, that 'he took it that he referred to Mk ch.10'. Jeremiah asked him whether it originated with the author of that Gospel. He received a note saying that the correspondence was closed.

The old translations use the word 'lust'. It means to 'set one's heart on'. He knew the truth of this, from its application to any desired object. If he set his heart on a new car, he would gaze at it, repeatedly, in the showroom, in pictures, in print, or in his mind. The reasons for possessing it became overwhelming. Reasons for disposing of the old one also multiplied. He only talked of the desirability of the exchange with those who would encourage him. If one looked on a woman to set one's heart on her it would be the same. Having made the exchange, one spoke glowingly of the benefits of having done so.

This would apply to one's wife, who is, after all, a woman. One would fasten one's gaze on all manner of seemingly desirable qualities. She may appear companionable, compassionate, gentle and tender hearted. She may have a good sense of humour, intelligence, share common interests, a lovely voice; all qualities desirable in a lifelong companion. If, on that basis, one sees her as a 'God-given' companion, what if another should appear, embodying all those qualities in greater measure? Should one not trade her in for an improved model?

His younger son's remarks, about the 'lady' being hurt by the refusal of a future father in law to recognise her, seemed to signify much. She already had the recognition of the one she truly saw as her future father in law. She had, no doubt, sought it. Why should she expect the same from Jeremiah? She had done nothing to seek his recognition. Hannah did not recognise him as her husband, nor, now, did any of their children. He was the outcast. If they recognised the 'man of Oz', as Hannah's true husband, they saw him as, in reality, their adoptive father. That was how he would wish to be seen. So would Hannah. As 'Granny's' husband, he would be their children's 'rightful' grandfather. It had to be thus, if they were not to see their Granny as living in adultery. If the words of Jesus be true, it was not a choice between two 'fathers' on earth, but between one father on earth, and a Father in heaven.

Jeremiah did not seek to be seen as their father, but as a temporary foster parent. He preferred to be known as the 'duffer'. Every incident seemed to be a means of instructing him in the truth of the reported words of Jesus. If so, he did not seek it. If, since the dispute at the College, his life might be seen as being given ways in which to pay off his debts, redeeming idle words and dud cheques, while he did not seek it, he became glad to find it so, at least for much of the time. How could his elder son be forgiven his debts to the 'lady', whose mother had the coveted scrunchy drive? How could he be forgiven his debt to the nurse, his former girl friend, the doctor who provided for him, when ski-ing, the mother of his child, or the little girl herself? Being only a country girl from Newfoundland, the nurse, like his daughter and her mother, would be seen as of little consequence. What if she was, as her works seemed to shew, "one of the Lord's little ones"? According to the gospel, "her holy angels were ever before the face of her Father in Heaven". Hannah's man would scoff at such a silly idea, so would most of his son's friends. The lady who was not amused would condescend to any who thought such 'childish things'.

By her apparent readiness to settle in the remote parts of Newfoundland, abandoning home and business, his son's indebtedness was vastly increased. She had 'gone to the ends of the earth for him'. That seemed now to mean, 'collect him and take him whither she wanted to go'. No doubt the lady's mother would have expected her daughter to be taken to greener pastures. In an early flush of enthusiasm, she probably meant what she had said about devoting his life to the township. It was what those of the town wanted to hear. No doubt it began to pall, when she returned. It was almost bound to do so for a finely educated lady, accustomed to life in a cosmopolitan English town.

The former girl friend was a popular figure in the town. She was the very successful manager of the local branch of a loan company. The young nurse was from a family, at the heart of the Catholic community. This, too, might have been a reason for dropping her. Whatever her own feelings on the matter, 'Catholics' are known to take a less easy going attitude to divorce and marriage to others. She might be an embarrassment back in England. Jeremiah thought that the two might find a united 'conversation', if each let go denominational allegiance, and lived simply on the 'rock' of Jesus reported sayings. That would have been worse. What extraordinary words this man had uttered, with their capacity to embarrass, or 'wrong foot', everyone, who made public declarations of belief. Whichever way you turn they catch you.

It might be that Jeremiah's son had some hesitation in entering many houses, whose doors had, once, been open in welcome. Neville put his finger on it. He had 'said' that they were not good enough for him. The 'lady' cannot have been blind to the departure of Jeremiah from the scene. Such things may have contributed to a change of heart about his son's remaining there. He was partly to blame again.

He thought again of his son's indirect invitation. He had given his phone number and said that he would drive to S Johns to fetch him. Was this an attempt to 'get him on board'? Was he seeking 'reassurance' that he had not been made 'ordinary', another doctor doing nicely out of his patients' ailments? He would have expected his dad to phone him back to make arrangements. He could have met him at the airport, led him to his 'rig', and introduced the 'lady'. After an eight-hour drive, acceptance of hospitality en route and on arrival, Jeremiah would have another debt to discharge. He would be bound to recognise the 'lady' and the 'conversation' to which she belonged. Some had suggested the opposite motive; that his son hoped that the appearance of the old duffer might have persuaded the 'lady' that permanent attachment would be best avoided.

He wrote to his son. In the 'conversation' of the lady, her mother, Hannah and their friends, he belonged in prison. In like circumstances, he hoped that he would not act in any other way than before. He would refuse to recognise the right of any man to put asunder. Accepting him, while maintaining such attitudes, would cause unease for them, when in Hannah's household. As Jesus said, his words cause division. Thanks to his own 'inadequacy' and other factors, none to his credit, Jeremiah had come to feel ever more secure when, he could fall straight back on those words. Once he compromised, he wallowed in uncertainty. He could never 'resist evil'. All he could do was to hope to be delivered from it.

When Jesus met those, who had once followed him, he provoked them, saying, "If you abide in my words, then are you truly my disciples". They responded offensively. "We are descendants of Abraham, not children of fornication", (presumably, a reference to Jesus' birth out of wedlock). Jesus admits that they are descended from Abraham, but contrasts this with being his children. If they were his children they would do as he did. His son could not help being descended from an old duffer, but he could choose whose child he was. He had made that choice, or had it made for him by those of Hannah's 'conversation'.

In his son's position, Jeremiah would readily be led to abandon those of the township and look for greener pastures, no doubt setting up home amid a coterie of well to do professionals. If the lady's mother urged her daughter to move on from a run down port, he would be in no position to say, 'No', nor remind the lady of her earlier words. She need say nothing. He would know well what could be said. She had given up her home and her business, moved to a remote port, miles from a major town, in a remote province, 'for him'. She had accepted a man who had already a daughter.

The words of the one who spoke of 'doing the truth' would be unhearable. Established in such a 'conversation', with its banal clichés, he could speak of having 'moved on'. He would soon find it possible to look down on and condemn those, who contracted life-threatening disease by indulgence in 'unprotected sex', as burdens to the community and its finances. Sitting on portentous committees, he would find it easy to wax eloquent in his disapproval of those, who fathered unwanted children by the same means.

Jeremiah imagined a coming wedding, in England. In the chief seats in the 'synagogue', on one side, would be Hannah and her man, commending, to all, the undoubted advantages of men putting asunder; whatever was said in the service, or may have been said by some man called Jesus, in whom, of course, we all believe. To him, all gave pious recognition, even if not dropping a curtsy, as the geese in Kierkegaard's parable, at the mention of his name.

They would advertise, as clearly, that either Jesus' words about wives who divorce and marry others were best disregarded, or, if any heeded them, that a life based on adultery had a lot to be said for it; while dutifully reminding lesser folk, for their own good, of course, that God said "Thou shalt not commit adultery". 'Standards', after all, and family values had to be maintained, so that children may be brought up in the 'faith and fear of God', as the Vicar intoned. Less boldly, they advertised the undoubted benefit of swearing oaths; less openly still, that of bearing false witness. To this, those in the chief seats in the synagogue, on the other side, simpered 'Amen', as, on such a happy occasion, would the Vicar. This was no time to recall any words, spoken by some man called Jesus, for we are 'gathered in the sight of God'.

The radiant bride would enter, clad in virginal white. Some might doubt whether the lady in question had even a faint recall of the state of being, which her attire attested. She, the groom and their respective parents could not but advertise to all, the undoubted benefits of fornication. There would be merry allusions to this in speeches. It was time the groom made 'an honest woman of her'. At this, all, including the Vicar, would laugh heartily, shewing that they were men and women 'of this world'. Anything said by Jesus to the contrary counted for nothing.

The best man would make a speech saying how many other women, if not 'ladies', the groom had already 'known'. All would signal, with knowing laughter, how wise and prudent it was, to be ashamed of one man and his words. That it happens to be Jesus, adds to the merriment. Any, not so ashamed, would not be invited to 'gather in the sight of God' for the happy occasion. They might not see the fun in it all. The ordained minister of the Gospel, having duly received the Holy Ghost, for his office and ministry, from one who knew whence it came and whither it went, with such certainty that he could pass it to others, would agree that it was no time or place for anyone to recall Jesus and his words.

There is a time and place for everything. This is certainly not an occasion for anyone *not* to be ashamed of Jesus and his words, for we are gathered in "the sight of God", but, much more important, "in the presence of this congregation". God can be relied upon to be ashamed of Jesus and his words for the duration of the ceremony. Anyone should be ashamed of himself for even *thinking* of the words of Jesus in such a gathering. It would spoil the day for the happy couple and their parents, but, of course, we all believe in God and his only begotten Son. We are his disciples. We are those who abide in him and his words, standing proof that, whatever the 'Spirit' might do, it should and did not bring to remembrance anything said by Jesus.

Many of the principal guests would advertise the undoubted benefits of laying up for oneself treasure on earth, assuring all that there was not the smallest risk of anyone's heart being there also; not that it would matter if it was. Many would give wise advice on the need to have considerable care for the morrow: as many would commend the building of barns and filling them. All would concur with Hannah that it was the duty of all good men and true that they should swear oaths, on the very book, which contained the prohibition. All would agree that it was a duty for all to indicate to anyone within twenty yards, with poppies and other badges, that they had given alms. Undoubtedly all should pray in meeting-houses, to be seen by men. Of this, all are 'bearing witness'. Only fools would include in a prayer, "as we have forgiven those indebted to us"; but we all believe in One Lord Jesus Christ.

The Vicar would have adjured all that they are gathered here in the sight of God. He might, if he followed one of the older books, have warned that, those 'coupled other than the law of God permits are not joined by God, nor is their matrimony lawful'. The one man, whose words, even those (mis)quoted in the service itself, all present must disregard, is the very one whom all declare to be the only begotten son of God. One needs to be certain, beyond all doubt, that he was not raised from the dead, knowingly, to do so: even more does one need to be sure that he did not 'ascend into heaven and sit at the right hand of the Father'; more yet, that he will not 'come again with glory'.

In giving assurance to all, that nothing said by Jesus need detain anyone, those present did not sound a trumpet before them. They had a peal of bells instead. Some might think it odd that such assurance be given by those claiming to be his disciples. They might, more fittingly, be described as those, who had 'formerly been his disciples'. It would not do at all, in such resplendent company to recall what Jesus said to them. Anyone, even thinking such things, should be ashamed of himself. The IVth evangelist had no business to attribute such 'unchristian' words to Jesus.

Jesus said that any, who were ashamed of him and his words in this generation, of him will the Son of Man be ashamed when he comes in power and great glory. The condition of attendance at such a service would be absolute. Jeremiah's daughter made this clear to him in another context. "You would be welcome, dad, if you behaved yourself". None would be welcome, if he were to remind those present of the words of Jesus, even those explicitly recalled in the service. Even less welcome would be any who were not ashamed at Jesus and his words about those who divorce and marry others. Anyone making such an offensive suggestion of obviously upright and pious, caring and dutiful men and, even more, women, should be ashamed of *themselves*. The Vicar would agree. Fancy suggesting anything so tasteless!

Though greatly saddened by the collapse of his longed for visit to Newfoundland, Jeremiah could, unwillingly, see the truth of the concluding petition of the one prayer given by Jesus. He had been led into 'temptation', but delivered from 'evil'. It was a costly lesson. All he ended up with was much misery, two wasted tickets, and his car a write off.

The prospect of the forthcoming wedding saddened him most. As he pondered it, his conviction of the truth of what the four evangelists reported grew stronger, and, with it, the certainty of his vindication, as with Job, as long as he endured. The more he pondered the hypocrisy of every aspect of the wedding, the stronger it became. The words of one man, alone, made it so. It was the one, in whose name, all was done; whose words were intoned at the conclusion, 'Those whom God has joined together.....'. The irony was unbearable. As living advertisements for the opposite, Hannah and her man would be welcomed and feted by all.

Any, who, for whatever reason, manifested the sovereignty of those words, would be there under sufferance, provided they were ashamed of them, while 'gathered in the sight of God'. In the Apocalypse, those, 'gathered in the sight of God', cry, "Amen, Blessing and honour glory and power belong to him that sits upon the throne and to the Lamb". In this gathering any, who, 'by their fruits', might recall the sayings of the 'Lamb', like the nurse, his daughter, or his son's neighbours from Newfoundland, would be unwelcome. His son would have to forget the doctor, whose works recalled any words of Jesus here, in this assembly 'in the sight of God'.

Not only the words of Jesus, about divorce and marriage to others, force hypocrisy on the established Christian religion; but every word the evangelists reported. They express a single word. "The word was God". That word made the established Christian religion, all institutions that invoked it and, less directly, all religions, hypocrisy. That this should be assured Jeremiah of truth of that 'Word' and the words of the one who expressed it. It hardly mattered who spoke those words. Whoever did so, alone, spoke truly of God. It defied belief that the four evangelists devised such words. They had to have been spoken by the one, of whom it was said, "No man ever spoke like this before". Nor has any man since.

There must be God. Only an Infinite being could have devised such an indictment, in which, with supreme irony, all present accuse themselves, when making public declarations of belief. All declared, or assented to, belief in one, who said that 'whoever was ashamed of him and his words, the son of man will be ashamed, when he returns in power and glory'. In order to do so 'in peace', any, who, by word and act, might even hint that they were not ashamed of him and his words, must be excluded.

'Gathered in the sight of God', atheists, agnostics, those who might believe in Zeus, those that have familiar spirits that chirp and chatter, would be welcome. It would be just as the test match, to which Hannah said that she would take the boys. Hitler would be welcome on the adjacent seat and, with him, Adolph Eichmann, Dr Goebbels and Herr Himmler. Resplendent in full dress uniform, it would be an honour to have them. What presents they might give! They would be something for the happy couple to talk of for the rest of their lives.

Those, who might 'believe our report, to whom the arm of the Lord was revealed', would be seen as stricken of God. Would they not then be stricken for our transgressions? Was not the chastisement of our peace laid upon them? So bitter is the irony in the hypocrisy, it could only be of God. It was like the millennium celebration, which could not have been, but for the coming of Jesus, yet the one man ever born, whose words could find no place in it, was Jesus himself. No man could have devised that. Much the same would be true of any wedding in any Church. Jeremiah realised that this would be different. His words and actions would have robbed those present, who knew him, of their innocence.

It set the seal on the betrayal of the nurse's trust and love. Jeremiah thought of her and his granddaughter. She would not be welcome. His other grandchildren would. Any, who might, by their presence, manifest the truth, had to be kept away. Better sit alone with the outcasts. Better be a man of sorrows and acquainted with grief, than share in the celebration of the happy event. Better yet be seen as stricken of God.

In the Gospels, the words, of which all must be ashamed, were certified as of God, by mighty works 'such as no man can do, save God be with him'. The service itself begins with a reference to one. Anyone believing such things, in that company, would be treated with the same condescension, as those foolish enough to believe that 'holy angels were ever before the face of their father in heaven', or that 'he should come again'; 'that no man should put asunder those whom God had joined together', or that some man was born of a virgin. We have outgrown such things, but, of course, we all believe and declare that, "the third day he rose again....". What is that but a 'mighty work', which it is hard to see any but God performing?

All four gospels relate the story of the empty tomb. Two tell of Jesus being miraculously conceived. These things add nothing substantially to his teaching. Whether or not he was born of a virgin and raised from the dead, he alone speaks truly of God. The empty tomb gave him final vindication. These two stories make it impossible for the words of Jesus to be revised, whatever the upholders of the Christian religion may say of the 'work of the Spirit'. Given those events, what could 'even God' do, to certify a revision of the sayings of Jesus?

Jeremiah's debt to the nurse, though she intended no such thing, was double edged. When she spoke of having fed, comforted and reassured his son, she dismissed any need for thanks. "It's what you do. You don't ask anything in return". Knowing it or not, she almost took those words from the lips of the Lord himself, just as did Jeremiah's son, when he said, "What are they here for, to save life or kill"? In her E-mail, she had opened the door and led Jeremiah into the room, in which Jesus spoke of the woman who wept at his feet. He had never read or heard such an uncontrived expression of joy from the heart of a 'little child', who loved much, and never would again.

He hoped that she would never forget, or have cause to feel shame at that moment in her life. He hoped that, thanks to his son's betrayal of her trust and love, she would not decide 'to grow up'. He would, then, have caused one of the least of these little ones to stumble. The two of them had, in that 'moment' in their combined lives, led Jeremiah past the woman who wept at Jesus' feet, past the sheep in the parable, to the one who spoke those words. What then of the promise. "I would be there for him tomorrow, if ever he needed me"?

He would sooner live and die, upholding her truth in that moment of rapturous joy, such as evoked that of Mary; and his son, as the one who gave rise to it, and sought to 'make a difference', than find welcome in the farrago of hypocrisy, empty words and downright lies that was to be. He only felt and thought in this way, when 'cut off from the land of the living' and its 'conversation'. Then he found himself, 'ever before the face of his Father in heaven', ready to recall the words of his only begotten son, on behalf of the nurse, his granddaughter, his son's neighbours, and the rest. It did not take much to make him doubt. A replacement car was enough.

When, 'cut off from the land of the living', he returned to his reading of the IVth gospel as a child. He heard, saw and touched and smelt. Jesus said, "He that has seen me has seen the Father". Only then, did he see the significance of what he had written to the 'Boss' and her husband. Often, he saw death as an escape from the 'conversation' of lies, treachery, deceits and hypocrisy of the 'Christian world', or of the world. He had begun to ache for a return to an eternal world of truth. It would be a world in which the unfeigned love expressed in that E-mail is the reality, and, with it, the words of his son, which gave rise to it. Only one word and the words that expressed it could make that the reality of any world. They alone would, or could, be upheld in eternity.

Most significant was that he saw it as a *return* to the eternal world, whence all came, when arriving on the earth as babes. "I thank thee O father, Lord of Heaven and earth that thou hast hid these things from the wise and prudent and revealed them unto babes". Most see such a state of mind as unfortunate. Should it not be seen as a blessing? Death, after all, is the one certain fact of life. Jesus said that no man took his life; he laid it down freely. Instead of being a misfortune to be avoided, he made, of it, a 'positive' act. Socrates might be seen as doing something of the same. His refusal to seek a stay of execution, allows him to speak of the truth of eternal life.

Jesus spoke of himself as coming 'from above' and of returning thither, but included all who 'believed in him'. In the opening of the fourth gospel, the evangelist writes, "To them gave he power to be the children of God". When sending out his disciples as his representatives, he said, "whoever receives you, receives me, and whoever receives me, receives not me, but the one who sent me". The single coherence of all that Jesus is reported to have said, in all four gospels, if one perceives 'his word', is miraculous.

If there is God, there is eternal life. If there is no God there is not eternal life. Only one man speaks clearly of this. The one who spoke of the woman 'who loved much' said, "Whoever has seen me has seen the Father". Jeremiah was again recalled to Job, "I know that the one who vindicates me lives, and that he is standing at the latter day upon the earth, and that though worms devour this body, yet in my flesh am I *seeing* God".

One man and his words, *alone,* vindicate Job. In the weeks of intense misery, following the disaster of his longed for visit, cut off from the land of the living, the vale of misery was indeed a well. Only therein, did he *know*, as did Job that one who would vindicate him lived.

Jesus said that if a man hated his life in this world he had eternal life. In the 'vale of misery', Jeremiah knew this to be the truth. Is it not, then, better to be in the 'vale of misery'? When seemingly disastrous occurrences returned him thither, should they not be welcome? The accepted 'conversation' was turned on its head. It was when in a state that we would call 'depression', that he felt most assured. His debt to the nurse was inestimable. Every time he pondered her ways and, above all, her E mail, he was led back to the Magnificat, to the sayings of Jesus, and, as I have described, almost physically into his presence. When he thought of the way she was so lightly cast aside, with empty words, he was in the vale of misery. When he thought of it being sealed with the farrago of hypocrisy that would be the wedding, he wept, often with indignation.

In any other 'conversation', his family were right. He had never met the lady who was not amused. He had spoken about 200 words to the nurse. Jesus knew as little of the woman of whom he spoke. By her fruits she knew her to be one that loved much.

In the midst of all this, one little child enjoyed a happy Christmas. Thanks to Joy and Jimmy, she had a veritable bran tub of gifts. She offered some to others in her family to unwrap. Joy insisted that she was not being kind. She just felt like doing as she did. It was not only the presents that gave delight, but that two people, whom she had never met and possibly never would, had thought of her. She told all, "This came from Joy and Jimmy", as if everyone knew who they were, and she had known them all her life.

Jeremiah could write to her saying, "Don't worry over not having a 'father' at home, for we all have but one Father, even God. That is what you say every time, you say the "Lord's Prayer". It might be best that way. When she met her Daddy, she might meet him as a friend, both sharing the one Father.

His son and the elegant 'lady', as any in such a position, would look down on Joy and Jimmy, the young nurse and her like, with the same condescension as would be shewn to those, who believed in 'holy angels' being ever before the face of their Father in heaven. That is the 'conversation' of this world and of the Christian religion. It is not that of the kingdom of God. Jesus himself believed that 'their holy angels were ever before the face of their Father in heaven'. Would they patronise him? Few did so twice.

His son had railed at the mother, saying that he wished that his daughter had never been born. Though the little girl heard his words and ran out in tears, the following Easter, when the children at her school made an Easter Tree, she hung a message, 'God bless my Daddy'. His son said that it was better that he had no contact with his daughter. If she sought to know him, when she was sixteen or eighteen, she could do so. If that were to be, he would see it as vindication of his views. That disdained people might have facilitated this reunion would be overlooked. It might prove him wrong.

To allow the possibility that such as they might have gained him a daughter, as a young friend, would mean turning the accepted conversation, in which Pharaoh built the Pyramid, upside down. It would involve an admission that they had done much to repair the damage caused by the haughty ways of the one who was 'not amused'. If he admitted this, he would have to respect and look up to these people, for their truthfulness, lack of hypocrisy, and the fact that they were content to take the lowest place.

That her fruits shewed her to be one of that kingdom may have been the undoing of the nurse. It would be an embarrassment back in England. She might not be ashamed of Jesus and his words. She loved the doctor who sought to be 'different', not in affectation, but in reality and truth. She loved what seemed to her to be the 'real man', a 'living soul'. She could be cast aside without risk. She would go away and weep quietly and secretly. That would not matter, unless, by some chance, the words of the one, in whom he, his mother and her friends declared belief, were the truth.

The only possibility, which could make them so, is that there is indeed God. That, as one of 'his little ones', the nurse might have 'angels' before her Father in heaven, all would discount with a smile, as the kind of thing little children and 'nice kids' believe. It belongs with tooth fairies and Santa Claus. We have learned to put away childish things. It's high time she did. Who did she think she was, to think that an educated English doctor would cast a second glance at her? Jesus did not speak of tooth fairies.

Angels are those who bring messages, in this case from God. That makes them Holy, or 'separate', 'different' not 'ordinary'. They do not need to be celestial beings with white wings to do that.

The only words that any can bring as messages, assuredly 'of God', are those of his only begotten Son. No 'angels', who were before the face of God would be ashamed of Jesus and his words, or imply that they would ever pass away. Any who did so would be cast out onto the dung-hill. Many men and women have had visions, or heard voices from heaven. Seldom do these visions or voices recall anything that Jesus is reported to have said. For that, one would not need a vision, only read a book.

Jesus said that his words 'shall never pass away'. All, at the wedding, had such confidence that his words had long since done so, that they could pass the assurance to all around. Of this, Hannah and her man were welcome proof. Being ever 'truthful', they would declare that the one who spoke those words was:

"God of God, Light of Light, Very God of Very God, begotten not made, being of one substance with the Father, by whom all things are made, who for us men and for our salvation came down from heaven and was incarnate by the Holy

Ghost of the Virgin Mary and was made man. And was crucified also for us under Pontius Pilate, he suffered and was buried, and the third day he rose again according to the scriptures and ascended into heaven, and sitteth at the right hand of the Father and he shall come again with glory to judge both the quick and the dead, whose kingdom shall have no end".

Those, attending weddings, do not recite these hallowed and sonorous words, but pray, 'thy kingdom come', with heads resting on hands, carefully manicured for the occasion; a comforting repetition, uttered in the serene assurance that it is empty. Any, lacking that assurance, fearing that it has no end, would be an embarrassment. The young nurse who had fed him when hungry, comforted him when sorrowful, would not be there, nor would his friends nearby, who had cared for him when he was in a mess, nor his little daughter. They might recall words, spoken by Jesus himself.

Without them, he might not now be standing in this 'congregation'. That is the 'conversation' of the children of this world. Having been picked off the floor by people of no account, 'we' can aspire to better things. Any, who fed 'us' when hungry, comforted us when sad, must be cast aside; as was Jesus himself.

What if the 'Lord whom ye seek', the very one, for the coming of whose kingdom all prayed, should come 'suddenly into his Temple'? That could be discounted altogether. There were ushers and vergers on hand. He, above all, would have no invitation to 'gather in the sight of God', in the face of this congregation.

John Carey had said that it was not possible to believe in Jesus without belief in God, and found it impossible to believe in the 'supernatural'. Jeremiah found belief in, what most referred to as the 'supernatural', an impediment to belief in the true God. It usually implied apparently inexplicable phenomena, such as those, 'having familiar spirits that chirp and chatter' deal in. 'Supernatural phenomena' had a nasty habit of being found to be 'natural'. Belief in God did not to involve belief in the 'supernatural', but in that which is, by definition, infinite or eternal.

Could any sane man or woman dismiss the existence of the Infinite? It was of that, as the one, all determining, reality, of which Jesus, alone, spoke. Could those who would assemble together, assuring all that no words spoken by Jesus need be heeded, be sure of the non-existence of the Infinite? The rule of such a being can have no end.

If any, who might not be ashamed of 'him and his words', be excluded from the grand assembly, what of Jesus himself? What of God himself? Is God thought to be ashamed of his only begotten son and his words? What if he were to 'come again in glory'? To think that would be as silly and childish as believing that 'holy angels were ever before the face of their Father in Heaven'. The possibility had to be discounted, for all to pray, 'Thy kingdom come'. No 'right-minded' man or woman would want that, in the terms in which Jesus spoke. He spoke of such unthinkable things as, 'that which was whispered in the ear being shouted from the housetops'.

In the unlikely event that he might do so, he would surely have learned the error of his ways and words by now, as had the Church, 'under the guidance of the Spirit'. He should have learned by now, under the guidance of the Spirit, as had his declared disciples, that his words have long since passed away; whatever he may have said to suggest otherwise. Of this Hannah and the man from Oz, greeted by the Bride, the Groom, her mother, and all others, gave assurance. We have found a new Christ, a higher 'concept' of the anointed one of God and of God himself, than is manifested in Jesus; but, of course, we all believe in One Lord Jesus Christ, who will come again with glory to judge both the living and the dead, whose kingdom shall have no end.

There is a strange tale in the gospels. Jesus is confronted by a madman, 'possessed of many demons'. He lived in caves at Gadara, where there was a large Greco-Roman settlement. Nearby was a herd of pigs grunting happily near the cliff top, as they munched away, tails merrily curled; this being the sign of a healthy and 'gruntled' pig. Jesus cast out the demons, which infected the pigs. They went wild and ran over the cliffs, to drown in the sea. Understandably, the owners of the pigs asked Jesus to go elsewhere. They were a nice little earner, providing pork chops, gammons, bacon and sausages, for the settlers.

Anyone, believing such nonsense, needs to grow up. Not even 'nice kids' believe that kind of thing. Those who treat such tales with disdain miss their irony.

Having told Jesus to go away, their owners would 'to the synagogue repair'. There, much as those gathered in the sight of God, they would pray for the restoration of the kingdom. "Raise up thy power and come among us, Lord. Rid thy people of heathen defilement, that we may live according to thy laws, delivered unto Moses"; - "Thy kingdom come". Had they not overlooked something? The laws of God, delivered unto Moses meant *NO PORK!*

The prophet Malachi, promised, "Behold I send my messenger (angel) and he shall prepare the way before me"; - "Thy kingdom come".

The passage from Malachi, (which means, 'My messenger or angel'), does not end on that reassuring note, any more than the gospel, in which Jesus is said to have provided a vast quantity of wine for a wedding party. It continues; "The Lord whom ye seek shall suddenly come into his temple, the messenger of the covenant in which ye delight. But who may abide the day of his coming, - - for he is like a refiner's fire. - - I will come near to you in judgement, - - I will be a swift witness against the sorcerers (magi in the New Testament), the adulterers, and against the false swearers; and against those that oppress the employee in his wages, the widow and the fatherless, and that turn aside the stranger, and fear not me, saith the Lord of Hosts. For I the Lord change not; therefore, ye, O sons of Jacob, are not consumed".

Those, with ears to hear, may recall that it is with the opening words of this passage that the second Gospel begins. The 'messenger', to whom the evangelist refers, had no white wings. He was John the son of Zechariah, in the wilderness of Judea. The one, coming after him, for whom he prepared the way, the 'Lord whom ye seek, who should suddenly come into his Temple', was not 'Our saviour Christ', but Jesus himself, the very one, of whose words, all those 'gathered in the sight of God and in the face of this congregation', must be ashamed. The evangelists told a dreadful tale. Once he knew what Jesus taught, even the Baptist had doubts as to whether he was the one who should come.

Jesus spoke of the one true God as his Father. In such an assembly, 'we' would consider anyone, speaking thus of himself, presumptuous and insane; while duly and reverently praying, "Our Father which art in heaven". The Minister of the Gospel would open the service, "Brethren we are met together in the sight of God and in the face this congregation, to join this man and this woman". He would, then, waffle about Matrimony being an honourable estate, the first miracle in Cana and the apostle Paul.

Nobody would pay much attention, as the familiar words rolled from his tongue. They would be more concerned with how the Bride and Groom looked and whether they spoke their lines clearly. No doubt there would have been a rehearsal. Was not the reheasal 'in the sight of God? It was not 'in the face of this congregation', which is what matters.

The priest would link the hands of Bride and Groom, declaring, "Those whom God has joined together, let no man put asunder". All present would acknowledge that solemn adjuration, for a couple of seconds, understanding it to mean, 'let those appointed by the Defender of the Faith put asunder'. Having done that, he could 'pronounce them man and wife together'. The minister might, as is now the custom, permit the man to kiss the bride; as if he had not done so and more, many times before.

Very conveniently, and without any great effort, those 'gathered together here in the sight of God', have, in the space of twenty minutes, ascended into heaven, not to 'sit at the right hand of God', but to cast God aside and become God. Appropriately, while doing so, the one, 'who sitteth at the right hand of the Father', is cast out onto the dunghill to be trodden under foot of men. 'We' had become God. Led by the priest, '*We*' had met together to join this man and this woman. A few prayers and a hymn or two had made it, "those whom *GOD* has joined together...."; - not a bad half hour's work! Having become God, the only man ever born, whom 'we' would not have as our 'only begotten Son', would be the very one whom all declare to be, "God of God, Light of Light, Very God of very God".

Having become 'as God(s)', a 'QANGO', assembled by invitation, the one man, of whose words all should be ashamed, would be Jesus. He, in the opinion of all, could not even find the right words in the one prayer he managed to compose. That does not say a lot for the only begotten Son of God, nor his Father. The one thing, anyone might expect of the only begotten Son of God, would be that he knew how to pray to his Father. The one 'we' would *not* exalt as having honour and glory, wisdom and power would be Jesus. 'We' have no need to pray, "Lead us not into temptation, but *deliver us from evil".* 'We' have become as God(s) knowing good and evil. It is before our face that there are ever, 'angels'. They carried invitations to all thought fit to attend.

****

Post script.

Though this was drawn from imagination, a wedding took place. The consequence of the 'knot being tied' was immediate. The mother of Jeremiah's granddaughter received a sharp letter from a solicitor in Newfoundland, informing her that all support for her daughter was being terminated immediately. She had been bullied at the local primary school. With the agreement of Jeremiah's son, who would contribute to the fees, she had been sent to an independent school at which she was happy and doing well. The solicitor, now, demanded 'full and immediate clarification of the whole situation', by means of DNA tests. If they proved positive, he was prepared to enter into negotiations 'with regard to a reasonable level of support'. The little girl had to face the fact of returning to her former school immediately.

The mother assented to the tests instantly and made arrangements for them. It was very upsetting for his daughter, now aged nine. She had become accustomed to having an absentee 'Dad', who sent her cards signed "with all my love, Dad". Now she was being forced to submit to the indignity of having samples taken from her to prove it. He had demanded this, years before, saying, on that occasion, that Hannah had insisted. On that occasion, too, the mother had assented instantly. When she did so, Jeremiah's son changed his mind. He felt that his mother would find it hard to live with the certainty of having a grand-daughter, saying that it was not Hannah, who had demanded such tests, but himself. He, later, wrote to the mother saying that he had told his mother all about his daughter *and the blood tests.* She seemed happy, - 'so I've got another grandchild, Eh'- and was looking forward to welcoming her. According to the mother there had been no tests. Was this the measure of 'all my love', now that he was married to the 'lady'? What of the promise, "If you have any problems you can call me, and I'll let you know wherever I move to...until then I'm at the end of the phone and you are always in my heart?" They were of the same worth as "we'll ever be the same good friends" and, presumably, to be understood in the same way, which being translated means, "you are not wanted and never have been". It seemed a fitting epitaph for two who had married 'in the face of this congregation'. Little children's angels might ever be 'in the sight of God'. Here they had no place. That his son had been driven to this cold hearted and ruthless action, by the lady who is not amused, there is no doubt. Almost since her arrival in Newfoundland she had urged this course upon him. Now that the knot had been tied, she seemed to have become 'she who must be obeyed'.

On the previous occasion, his solicitor in Newfoundland had boasted that, though Jeremiah's son admitted and knew that she was his daughter, he could cause so many delays, that the child would be grown up before any decision was taken. His latest letter concluded, 'Failure to agree to DNA tests will result in the cessation of all support permanently'. Although the mother agreed instantly, and arranged for tests to be performed, sending the necessary forms to the solicitor, after three months they had not been signed and returned.

A month later, the mother saved enough money to pay a solicitor to write to the Botwood lawyer. The letter was not even acknowledged, making it clear that there was no intention to have DNA tests performed ethically and legitimately. It was clearly a waste of time and money, which the mother had not got, to pay a solicitor in England to write again, even though, under international agreement, the matter was subject to English not Canadian jurisdiction. Jeremiah took the matter up with the provincial government and received a helpful response, saying that the matter had been passed to the Ministry of Justice, and that a ‘rush’ had been put on the request that they should look into it; the Botwood lawyer having demanded 'full clarification of the whole situation, by means of DNA tests…'.

After a month, Jeremiah went back to the provincial government saying that he had heard nothing. The reply was that the Minsitry of Justice was being pressed for speedy action 'for the child’s sake'. No more was heard, despite the fact that, if his son had written the truth about the earlier blood tests proving his paternity, here were a doctor and a lawyer implying that 'blood tests', performed six years before were flawed. Questions as to what laboratory had performed these alleged tests also remained unanswered, not only by Botwood lawyer, the head of the Diagnostic facility at the University at St Johns, the head of the Faculty in the University, the Ministry of Justice, but even the office of the Privy Council in Ottawa.

If the doctor and his lawyer are telling the truth, it can only imply that some unidentified laboratory has been performing such analyses, using either unethical methods or faulty procedures, and may yet be doing so. The alternative is that a doctor has made a false claim that a diagnostic procedure was undertaken, when it was not, and is supported in this by his lawyer and Hannah, whom he told of these earlier tests, or so he wrote.

It would have made no difference if the mother had not agreed to the tests. The caring doctor and his new wife knew that there was almost nothing that the mother could do, though all knew that the child was his, and he had given his oath to that effect. Since they lived overseas, the costs of the mother getting any redress were beyond her ability to pay. The forms that she was required to fill in, to apply to a court, were, in these circumstances, so complex that it required a lawyer to complete them.

It seemed to carry to its conclusion the rejection of the young nurse, being no more than a 'nice kid', which in terms of her age she was not. Now it was one who was physically a little child who was being offended, in a cold and calculating manner, in order that the lady might continue to lay up for herself treasure on earth, as she advised others to do. His son and his elegant lady thus assured all that whatever Jesus may have said about those, who caused offence to the least of these little ones, could be safely disregarded, by those with wealth and position; while declaring belief in him as God of God and Light of Light, and praying with fitting reverence, "Thy kingdom come".

They must devoutly hope that there is, in truth, no God, while, assuring all, when it is seemly so to do, that that there is. That is the 'conversation' of the 'Prince of this world'; that which achieves honour among men. "When he speaks a lie, he speaks his own...."